ANTIWAR DISSENT AND
PEACE ACTIVISM IN
WORLD WAR I AMERICA

PUBLICATION OF THESE PAGES
IS ENABLED BY A GRANT FROM

Jewish Federation of Greater Hartford

ANTIWAR DISSENT AND PEACE ACTIVISM IN WORLD WAR I AMERICA

A DOCUMENTARY READER

Edited and with an introduction by
Scott H. Bennett and Charles F. Howlett

UNIVERSITY OF NEBRASKA PRESS
LINCOLN & LONDON

Library of Congress Cataloging-in-Publication Data
Antiwar dissent and peace activism in World War
I America: a documentary reader / edited and with
an introduction by Scott H. Bennett and Charles F.
Howlett.
pages   cm
Includes bibliographical references.
ISBN 978-0-8032-4011-7 (pbk.: alk. paper)
ISBN 978-0-8032-6687-2 (pdf) 1. World War,
1914–1918—Protest movements—United States.
2. Peace movements—United States—History—
20th century. 3. Dissenters—United States—
History—20th century. 4. World War, 1914–1918—
United States. I. Bennett, Scott H., editor.
II. Howlett, Charles F., editor.
D639.P77A58 2014
940.3'120973—dc23
2014015273

Set in Minion Pro by Renni Johnson.

To Larry S. Wittner. For *Rebels against War*,
which lured me to peace history—and for his
friendship ever since.—SHB

In memory of my grandmother Helen Mary
Neet. She left her native Ireland and came to
America during the Great War.—CFH

CONTENTS

List of Illustrations . . xv
Acknowledgments . . xvii

Introduction . . 1

1. Peace Organizations . . 37
    1.1. Woman's Peace Party, Preamble and Platform (1915) . . 37
    1.2. Anti-Preparedness Committee, Flyer [1915] . . 39
    1.3. Tracy D. Mygatt, "The Anti-Enlistment League" (1915) . . 41
    1.4. Fellowship of Reconciliation—USA, "The Fellowship of
          Reconciliation: Some General Considerations" [1915?] . . 44
    1.5. People's Council of America, "Resolutions" (1917) . . 47
    1.6. American Union Against Militarism, "To the People of
          New York" (1917) . . 49
    1.7. Woman's Peace Party, "Eight Alternatives to War"
          [before 1917] . . 52
    1.8. Friends National Peace Committee, "A Message from the
          Religious Society of Friends (Quakers) in America" (1917) . . 53
    1.9. American Union Against Militarism, "Peace or War? Let the
          People Say Which It Shall Be" (1917) . . 55
    1.10. Committee for Democratic Control, "Referendum" (1917) . . 56
    1.11. American Union Against Militarism, "To Men of Military Age
          Opposed to War!" [1917] . . 57

2. Socialists, Anarchists, and Wobblies . . 60
    2.1. Emma Goldman, "Preparedness: The Road to Universal
          Slaughter" (1915) . . 60
    2.2. Socialist Party of America, "Peace Program of the Socialist
          Party" (1915) . . 65
    2.3. Socialist Suffrage Committee, Antipreparedness
          Statement (1916) . . 69

2.4. Ralph H. Chaplin, "Preparedness" (1916) . . 70

2.5. No-Conscription League, Manifesto (1917) . . 71

2.6. Industrial Workers of the World, "The Deadly Parallel" (1917) . . 73

2.7. John Reed, "Whose War?" (1917) . . 75

2.8. Socialist Party of America, "The 'Majority' Report of the St. Louis Convention" (1917) . . 78

2.9. William D. Haywood and the Industrial Workers of the World, Opposition to War (1917) . . 81

2.10. "A Patriot" (1917) . . 82

2.11. "Yellow-Legs and Pugs" (1917) . . 83

2.12. Charles Schenck and the Socialist Party of America, "Assert Your Rights" (1917) . . 83

2.13. Industrial Workers of the World, Editorial, "Were You Drafted?" (1917) . . 86

2.14. Bertha H. White, "The Green Corn Rebellion in Oklahoma" (1922) . . 87

2.15. Eugene V. Debs, Canton, Ohio, Speech (1918) . . 90

3. Citizen Peace Agitators . . 95

3.1. William Jennings Bryan's Resignation as Secretary of State (1915) . . 95

3.2. Oswald Garrison Villard, "Shall We Arm for Peace?" (1915) . . 97

3.3. Frank Donnblazer, Testimony before Senate Hearing on Military Preparedness (1916) . . 100

3.4. Bob Minor, Letter from Paris (1916) . . 102

3.5. Julius F. Schlicht, "The White Feather" (1917) . . 103

3.6. John Haynes Holmes, "A Statement to My People on the Eve of War" (1917) . . 104

3.7. George W. Norris, Anti-interventionist Speech (1917) . . 107

3.8. Jane Addams, "Patriotism and Pacifists in War Time" (1917) . . 111

3.9. Randolph Bourne, "A War Diary" (1917) . . 116

3.10. Kirby Page to Howard Sweet (1918) . . 120

3.11. Firemen Resign Rather than Buy Liberty Bonds (1918) . . 122

3.12. Dorothy Day, Opposition to World War I (1952) . . 124

3.13. A. J. Muste, "What It Was Like in World War I" (1958) . . 125

3.14. Jessie Wallace Hughan, "Autobiography" (1926) . . 130

4. Female Activism and Gendered Peacework . . 133

    4.1.   Meta Lilienthal Stern, "To All Women" (1914) and "Girls, Don't Marry Pacifists!" (1917) . . 133

    4.2.   Jane Addams, "What War Is Destroying" (1915) . . 136

    4.3.   International Congress of Women (The Hague), Manifesto (1915) . . 139

    4.4.   Helen Keller, Strike against War (1916) . . 143

    4.5.   Lucia Ames Mead, "'Thinking Women' and the World Crisis" (1916) . . 145

    4.6.   Margaret Sanger, "Woman and War" (1917) . . 148

    4.7.   Mary Alden Hopkins, "Woman's Way in War" (1917) . . 150

    4.8.   Harriet Connor Brown, "America Menaced by Militarism: An Appeal to Women" (1920) . . 151

    4.9.   Jeannette Rankin, "Two Votes against War: 1917 and 1941" (1958) . . 154

5. African American and Ethnic American Antiwar Dissent . . 158

    5.1.   Patrick O'Donnell, Speech (1915) . . 158

    5.2.   W. E. B. DuBois, "The African Roots of War" (1915) . . 159

    5.3.   A. Philip Randolph and Chandler Owen, *Terms of Peace and the Darker Races* (1917) . . 163

    5.4.   Clara L. Threadgill-Dennis, "Soldiers of the Twenty-Fourth" (1917) . . 169

    5.5.   "Protest Meeting of Jugoslav Socialists" (1917) . . 170

    5.6.   Chicago Russians, "A Resolution of Protest" (1917) . . 172

    5.7.   Letter Urging Blacks Not to Join the Army (1917) . . 172

    5.8.   James P. Warbasse, "Are Not All Men My Brothers?" (1917) . . 173

    5.9.   Vincente Balbas Capo, "The Topic of the Day" (1917) . . 175

    5.10. Court-Martial of Private Sidney Wilson, 368th Infantry, USA (1918) . . 177

    5.11. The Court of Appeals Case of Captain David A. Henkes (1919) . . 179

    5.12. Chandler Owen, "What Will Be the Real Status of the Negro after the War?" (1919) . . 182

    5.13. Friends of Irish Freedom, "Women of America!" (1919) . . 184

6. Conscientious Objectors . . 186

    6.1. Ammon Hennacy, "Young Men: Don't Register for War!"
(1917) . . 186

    6.2. Noah H. Leatherman, CO Diary (1917–19) . . 187

    6.3. Roger N. Baldwin, Statement before the Court (1918) . . 188

    6.4. Erling H. Lunde, Statement to Court-Martial (1918) . . 195

    6.5. Evan Thomas, Prison Letters (1918) . . 200

    6.6. Roderick Seidenberg, "I Refuse to Serve" (1932) . . 206

    6.7. Winthrop D. Lane, "The Strike at Fort Leavenworth"
(1919) . . 214

    6.8. Carl Haessler, "The Fort Leavenworth General Strike of
Prisoners" (1927) . . 220

    6.9. Congressman Charles H. Dillon on Abuses in Military Prisons
(1919) . . 224

    6.10. COs Declare Hunger Strike to Secretary of War (1918) . . 230

    6.11. Friends of Conscientious Objectors, Amnesty Leaflet (1919) . . 231

7. Repression and Civil Liberties . . 234

    7.1. National Civil Liberties Bureau, "War-Time Prosecutions and
Mob Violence" (1919) . . 234

    7.2. William Emmett, "Mania in Los Angeles" (1918) . . 242

    7.3. Mary McDowell Case (1918) . . 247

    7.4. National Civil Liberties Bureau, "Who Are the Traitors?"
(1918) . . 253

    7.5. Lusk Committee Targets Pacifists and Radicals (1920) . . 255

    7.6. Jessie Wallace Hughan, "The Bolsheviks'll Git You" [n.d.] . . 257

    7.7. American Civil Liberties Union, *The Truth about the I.W.W.
Prisoners* (1922) . . 258

    7.8. Norman Thomas, "Amnesty!" [1919?] . . 263

8. The Cultural Front and Antiwar Protest . . 266

    8.1. Frank P. O'Hare and Kate Richards O'Hare, *World Peace*
(1915) . . 266

    8.2. Tracy D. Mygatt, *Watchfires* (1917) . . 268

    8.3. Samuel Kudish, *A Comedy in Two Short Acts* (1917) . . 270

    8.4. Fanny Bixby Spencer, *The Jazz of Patriotism (an Anti-war Play)*
(1920) . . 271

    8.5. "I Didn't Raise My Boy to Be a Soldier" (1915) . . 276

8.6. "Battle Hymn" (1915) . . 277

8.7. "Patriotism Simplified" (1917) . . 279

8.8. Elbert Lovell, "War Time Wisdom" (1917) . . 280

8.9. Witticism from the *Gaelic American* (1917) . . 283

8.10. Ditties from *Solidarity* (1917) . . 283

8.11. Ditties from the *Masses* (1915–16) . . 284

8.12. Tracy D. Mygatt and Frances Witherspoon, "An Office of Commemoration for the Dead Who Died in the Great War, and of the War Resisters' Pledge of Brotherhood to All Mankind" (1931) . . 285

9. Peace Humanitarianism Abroad . . 297

9.1. The Anglo-American Mission of the Society of Friends: American and English Friends Combine Efforts (1917) . . 297

9.2. Vincent D. Nicholson, Information for Women Volunteers [1917] . . 298

9.3. Vincent D. Nicholson, "Suggestions for Field Workers" (1917) . . 300

9.4. Location of Friends' Units and Workers in France (1918) . . 303

9.5. Katharine W. Elkinton, Letters to Parents (1917) . . 305

9.6. Joseph H. Haines, Letter to Father [William H. Haines] (1918) . . 310

9.7. Edward C. M. Richards, "Reminiscences of Wartime Relief Work in Persia" [n.d.] . . 312

9.8. Ruth Rose Hoffman, "Report to the Friends Committee of the Year[']s Work Done in Siberia under the American Red Cross" [1919] . . 314

9.9. American Friends Service Committee, "A Statement of the [Overseas] Work of the American Friends Service Committee" [1919] . . 318

9.10. American Friends Service Committee, "Appeal for German Children" [1920] . . 321

9.11. John Nevin Sayre, "The Fellowship at Work in Europe" [1921] . . 322

9.12. Vesta Zook, "Dear Sewing Circle Sisters" (1921) . . 324

9.13. Beulah A. Hurley, "Diary of a Quaker Worker among the Fifteen Million of Russia's Starving People" [1923?] . . 326

9.14. Carleton McDowell, Motives of Humanitarian Service (1918) . . 329

10. Aftermath and Legacies . . 331

    10.1. Archibald E. Stevenson, "Who's Who in Pacifism and Radicalism" (1919) . . 331

    10.2. Scott Nearing, "The League of Nations" [1919] . . 336

    10.3. People's Council, Resolution on Russia (1919) . . 337

    10.4. Louis P. Lochner, "'Stop the Next War Now!': The Present Program of the People's Council" [1919] . . 338

    10.5. Elinor Byrns, *The Women's Peace Society* (1921) . . 340

    10.6. War Resisters' International, Declaration and Principles [1921] . . 345

    10.7. Women's Peace Union, Amendment to U.S. Constitution Outlawing War (1924) . . 348

    10.8. Students at Howard University Strike for Peace (1925) . . 349

    10.9. Brown University Students' Petition against War (1933) . . 349

    10.10. Devere Allen, New War Objectors and International Pacifism (1930) . . 351

    10.11. Howard Kester, "Report of Howard Kester" (1933) . . 354

    10.12. Senate Report, "Special Committee on Investigation of the Munitions Industry" (1936) . . 357

    10.13. Smedley D. Butler, "To Hell with War!" (1935) . . 359

    10.14. Veterans of Future Wars, Manifesto (1936) . . 361

    Selected Bibliography . . 363

ILLUSTRATIONS

"Speaking of Bravery—Who's the Coward?" . . 290

"June 5th In Memoriam" . . 291

"Will Your Boy Be Forced to Follow This Leader?" . . 292

CO in striped prison uniform . . 293

Four Lights front cover . . 294

"Glory" . . 295

"War Against War Exhibit" . . 296

Following page . . 212

Anti-Enlistment League flyer

"Model Boy"

"War Against War" flyer card

"The New King in Liberty Pond"

No-Conscription League flyer

"Set Conscience Free!"

Disarmament parade flyer

ACKNOWLEDGMENTS

Numerous curators, archivists, and librarians provided immeasurable guidance and assistance in locating materials. At the Swarthmore College Peace Collection, the nation's most important archive devoted to the U.S. peace movement, Wendy E. Chmielewski, Anne Yoder, Barbara Addison, and Mary Beth Sigado were indispensable. Elsewhere, others were similarly helpful, including Jennifer Brathovde (Library of Congress), Betty Clements (Claremont School of Theology), Don Davis (American Friends Service Committee Archives), Chris Densmore and Patricia O'Donnell (Friends Historical Library, Swarthmore College), Bonnie Gordon (Tamiment Library, New York University), Bill Hurley (American Irish Historical Society), William Lefebvre (Reuther Archives, Wayne State University), Gayle D. Lynch (John Hay Library, Brown University), Tom Mooney (Nebraska State Historical Society), Tim Nenninger and Eric van Slander (National Archives), and Jeffrey Reynolds (Hope College—Joint Archives).

Our work was facilitated by outstanding interlibrary loan staffs. We are grateful to Betty McBain and Kathleen Ficuciello (Georgian Court University) and Judith Brink-Dresher, Teva Hutchinson, and Susie Bloom (Molloy College).

Several students assisted with this project. In particular, we wish to thank Christina Loxton and Nataya Culler (Georgian Court University) and Chris Siemsen (Molloy College). Theresa Howlett obtained a document from the Northwest Museum of Arts and Culture, Spokane, Washington. Anne Yoder generously shared her personal collection of documents on World War I COs; readers might wish to consult her World War I Conscientious Objectors Database, posted on the Swarthmore College Peace Collection website.

For granting permission to use documents, we thank John White-clay Chambers II (Rutgers University), Charles Chatfield (Wittenberg University, emeritus), Wendy E. Chmielewski (Swarthmore College Peace Collection), Howard Clark (War Resisters' International), Luc Cohen (the *Daily Princetonian*), Don Davis (American Friends Service Committee), Kate Donovan (Tamiment Library, New York University), Gayle D. Lynch (John Hay Library, Brown University), Peter Muste, Ethan Vesely-Flad (Fellowship of Reconciliation—USA), and Anne Yoder (Swarthmore College Peace Collection).

The then anonymous readers Cecilia M. Lynch and Doran L. Cart read the manuscript and made several valuable suggestions—and we thank them.

It's been a delight to work with the University of Nebraska Press. For their professionalism, responsiveness, and guidance, we wish to thank history editor Bridget Barry, along with Sabrina Ehmke Sergeant, Sara Springsteen, and the talented team in Editorial, Design, and Production. Copy editor Annette Wenda did an excellent job on the manuscript.

Finally, on the home front, we are enriched by and indebted to Cathy, Tricia, Julia, Sean, and Patrick.

ANTIWAR DISSENT AND PEACE ACTIVISM IN WORLD WAR I AMERICA

Introduction

For many Americans U.S. intervention in the First World War—and indeed the conflict itself—was a war of choice rather than necessity. World War I spawned the "modern" American peace movement, which represented a definite shift from the prewar peace activism in goals, methods, and membership. Unlike the pre-1914 movement, the modern peace movement, which advocated both peace and social justice, was a militant grassroots effort distinguished by liberal and radical citizen peace activists, women's peace organizations, and a progressive reformist impulse. Unlike its nineteenth-century predecessors, the modern peace movement was more secular—and secular and religious peace activists alike were more conscious of the economic causes of war, more willing to challenge social elitism within and without the peace movement, and more willing to undertake nonviolent direct action. It advocated social reform to abolish social injustice and the social causes of war. As antiwar dissent and peace activism took a secular turn, religious peace advocacy by both historic peace churches and mainline Christians expanded and became more militant—and the modern peace movement became a powerful force for world peace and social justice. According to the late historian Charles DeBenedetti, the modern American peace movement was a "movement of the left" that sought "social reformation."[1]

Historical Background

With its origins in the colonial period, the World War I peace movement had deep roots in U.S. history. The seventeenth- and eighteenth-century peace movement, religious in nature and sectarian in makeup, was based in the historic peace churches (Quakers, Brethren, and

Mennonites). In response to the Napoleonic Wars (including the War of 1812), the antebellum nonsectarian peace movement emerged. In 1815 peace advocates established the first American peace societies. The antebellum peace movement was shaped by Second Great Awakening revivalism and motivated by Christian nonviolence, religious millennialism, moral reform, and humanitarian concerns. For antebellum peace advocates, Christian enlightenment and moral education would create peace.

From the Civil War to World War I, the American peace movement adopted a "cosmopolitan" and "practical" outlook.[2] Led by male lawyers and businessmen and supported by middle-class professionals and social elites, the pre-1914 peace movement was respectable, reformist, and practical, and it relied less on religious humanitarianism. It aimed to settle disputes and maintain world order not through moral nonresistance but through international peacekeeping machinery, including international law, arbitration, conciliation, and a world court. This practical, legalistic, and internationalist approach to world peace was championed by the Lake Mohonk Conferences on International Arbitration (1895–1916, in New York) and by The Hague Peace Conferences (1899 and 1907, in the Netherlands).

The 1898 Spanish-American War and President McKinley's decision to annex Spanish colonies produced a powerful anti-imperialist movement. Led by the Anti-Imperialist League, the opponents of imperialism condemned the U.S. annexation of Puerto Rico, Guam, and, particularly, the Philippines and opposed the Treaty of Paris, which ended the war with Spain and transferred these island territories to the United States. Although anti-imperialists argued that Filipinos and other subject peoples had the political and moral right to self-determination, they were primarily concerned with the impact of imperialism on the United States. They charged that imperialism violated the U.S. Constitution, the principles of republican government, and the American anticolonial tradition. Moreover, they warned that empire would erode American democratic values and distract the nation from the more pressing needs of domestic reform. Meanwhile, Filipinos, led by Emilio Aguinaldo, launched a revolt against U.S. rule in order to win national independence. The Filipino-American War (1899–1902), a brutal guerrilla conflict marked by atrocities, scorched-earth campaigns, and torture, transformed the Anti-Imperialist League into a national movement with broad support that enrolled some thirty thousand members before its decline after the 1900 election.

Between 1901 and 1914 some forty-five new peace organizations appeared. Among them were the American Society of International Law, the World Peace Foundation, and the Carnegie Endowment for International Peace. These societies were led and influenced by educational leaders such as Stanford University's David Starr Jordan, Columbia University's Nicholas Murray Butler, philanthropists such as textbook publisher Edward Ginn and steel magnate Andrew Carnegie, legalists such as James Brown Scott and Theodore Marburg, and politicians and statesmen such as former president William Howard Taft and former secretary of war Elihu Root. Reflecting the conventional thinking of their time, these organizations were composed of persons attracted to the cause of peace as a safe, uncontroversial crusade—one that challenged secret diplomacy and balance-of-power alliances. Many of these leaders and organizations, though still supporting international peacekeeping, did not speak out against the war once the United States entered the conflict in April 1917.

Rejecting such elitism, convention, and caution, the modern peace movement that emerged in response to World War I mounted a direct challenge to the war and its causes. With its progressive leadership and rank and file that included liberals, radicals, and women, the modern peace movement would champion militant peace activism and social reform.

From the Guns of August to U.S. Military Intervention:
August 1914 to April 1917

American dissent, opposition, and resistance to World War I were broad and diverse—politically, ideologically, sociologically, and geographically. Foes of the war included liberals and radicals, men and women, elites and commoners, and U.S. citizens and alien residents. Their ranks included politicians, social gospel ministers and other religious leaders, pacifists, radicals, feminists, labor leaders and workers, publishers, intellectuals, university professors, public school teachers, social workers, isolationists, ethnic Americans, and ordinary citizens from all walks of life. Their opposition to the war was based on various grounds: religious and secular, philosophical and ethical, political and humanitarian.

Distinctly, women occupied a central role in the movement against World War I and, in many ways, helped define the modern peace movement. Pacifist and socialist suffragist women, in particular, were active in the peace movement. In addition to leading the same-sex Woman's Peace Party (WPP), women also played important roles and held leadership positions in mixed-gender groups such as the Anti-Enlistment League, the No-Conscription League, the American Union Against Militarism (AUAM), and the People's Council. In the Socialist Party (SP) a women's-led Socialist Suffragist Committee opposed the conflict, insisting that capitalism, along with its appetite for raw materials, markets, and profits, was the root cause of war.

Besides repudiating war on economic, political, religious, and humanitarian grounds, some women were motivated by notions of motherhood that viewed women as the natural nurturers of life. As the "mother half of humanity," women, the Woman's Peace Party argued, had "a peculiar moral passion . . . against both the cruelty and the waste of war." In 1915, for example, Charlotte Perkins Gilman, a feminist writer and pacifist, challenged former president Theodore Roosevelt. When Roosevelt declared that "a mother who is not willing to raise her son to be a soldier is not to be a citizen," Gilman responded with outright indignation. "Motherhood is essential to the preservation of the race, and so is fatherhood," she replied, "but being a father is by no means synonymous with being a soldier." "The business of a soldier is to kill people and to be killed," she noted, and "neither is serviceable to society." Mothers who raised their sons to be "inventors, discoverers, teachers, and world helpers," she contended, would make war an "anachronism." Some women, refusing to breed more soldiers, advocated a "birth strike" until the war ended and a peace treaty signed.[3]

Such women rejected prevailing cultural norms that equated manliness with militarism and assumed a link between the two. Challenging the male argument advocating war and preparedness to protect home and family, these female opponents of war insisted that war did the opposite. By killing and maiming fathers, husbands, brothers, and sons, war destroyed the happiness and security of families. Disappointed at the failure of the male-dominated prewar peace movement, these women were determined to have their voices heard and to take a leading part in the modern peace movement.

Almost from the beginning of the conflict in Europe, furthermore, opponents of U.S. intervention organized against the preparedness movement (1915–17). Advocates of preparedness argued that military mobilization was insurance against war. Proponents included individuals such as former president Teddy Roosevelt, former secretary of war Henry Stimson, banker J. P. Morgan, and Senator Henry Cabot Lodge; organizations such as the National Security League and the Navy League; and, eventually, President Wilson. In December 1915 Wilson presented his preparedness program to Congress, and, in 1916, Congress passed the National Defense Act and the Naval Act. The National Defense Act increased the U.S. Army from 130,000 to 223,000 men and the National Guard from 189,000 to 450,000, empowered the president to federalize the militia, and created the Reserve Officers' Training Corps (ROTC). The Naval Act funded the construction of ten battleships, six battle cruisers, ten cruisers, fifty destroyers, and sixty-seven submarines.

Notwithstanding his preparedness measures, in large part a response to the May 1915 sinking of the British passenger ship *Lusitania*, which resulted in the loss of 128 Americans, Wilson still sought to avoid war. Running for reelection in 1916 as the peace candidate, Wilson's campaign adopted the slogan "He kept us out of war."

Accompanying the preparedness movement was a public-private propaganda campaign to promote patriotism, 100 percent Americanism, and anti-German sentiment. This political, psychological, and social mobilization crusade fed war hysteria, intolerance, and suppression of civil liberties. To sell U.S. intervention and American patriotism, the government created the Committee on Public Information. Led by journalist George Creel, the committee enlisted citizen volunteers and used mass media and public relations techniques to sell the war to Americans.

In response, the antipreparedness campaign took to the streets, gave public speeches, wrote plays, created antiwar exhibits, and published pamphlets and articles that argued that preparedness made war more likely, not less, and would lead to a militarized state. In June 1915, in a direct-action demonstration organized by the Women's Committee of the Brooklyn Socialist Party, Socialist women invaded the Brooklyn Navy Yard to protest the launching of a new battleship, the USS *Arizona*. Carrying bags inscribed with "Socialist Suffrage Committee," the women shouted "anti-war" and distributed five thousand pieces of antiwar literature. Waiting nearby were the Socialist caravan and its white horse "Peace."[4]

In the spring of 1916 the American Union Against Militarism, in an innovative twist, created Jingo, a huge papier-mâché dinosaur, to rally antipreparedness sentiment. The "military lizard" carried the following inscription: "This is Jingo, the armored dinosaur: All Armor Plate and No Brains. This animal believed in Huge Armaments—He is Now Extinct." Dubbing Jingo "Dinosaurus Theodorus Rooseveltus," in a jab at the former president, a prominent advocate of preparedness, peace activists called Jingo the original militarist and noted his heavy armament. Wheeled through the streets of New York and other cities on a horse-drawn platform, Jingo became the mascot of the antipreparedness forces and was also featured in a popular 1916 "War Against War" exhibit in Brooklyn and Manhattan that attracted thousands of visitors a day.[5]

Antipreparedness advocates were emboldened by the June 1915 resignation of Secretary of State William Jennings Bryan. He advocated banning American travelers on British and French ships and forbidding U.S. firms from selling war materials to the belligerents.

Writing about the 1916 New York Preparedness Parade, journalist John Reed lamented that the nation was being "scared into 'an heroic mood.'"[6] The antipreparedness movement included elected officials such as Senator Robert La Follette (R-WI) and House majority leader Claude Kitchin (D-NC); leading publishers such as Oswald Garrison Villard; prominent citizens such as Jane Addams, Eugene V. Debs, and John Haynes Holmes; and farm leaders from state Granges and Farmers Unions. Although American Federation of Labor (AFL) president Samuel Gompers supported preparedness, other federation and union leaders opposed such measures.

Between 1915 and April 1917 peace activists formed a number of organizations to oppose the conflict in Europe and preparedness at home. Socialist pacifist feminists Jessie Wallace Hughan and Tracy D. Mygatt, along with pacifist Unitarian minister John Haynes Holmes, founded the Anti-Enlistment League (1915), which collected pledges of war resistance in an effort to persuade the government to stay out of the conflict.

Founded by Jane Addams, the Woman's Peace Party (1915) provided a link between the peace and suffrage movements. Proclaiming that women were more concerned than men with preserving human life, the WPP argued that females had a special role in the peace movement—and that the enfranchisement of women would promote peace in the political sphere. Its New York City branch, which was particularly active, published the antiwar magazine *Four Lights* "to voice the young, uncompromising woman's peace movement in America, whose aims are daring and immediate.—to stop the war in Europe, to federate the nations for organized peace at the close of the war, and meanwhile to guard democracy from the subtle dangers of militarism."[7] In 1915 the WPP, which included two future Nobel Peace Prize recipients, Jane Addams and Emily Greene Balch, also sent a delegation to visit belligerent nations in an unsuccessful attempt to mediate the conflict.

In November 1915 American pacifists established the U.S. branch of the Fellowship of Reconciliation. They were inspired by pacifist Protestants and Quakers in England who, in December 1914, had founded the Fellowship of Reconciliation. Denouncing the war and supporting conscientious objectors (cos) and civil liberties, FOR-USA soon became the major religious pacifist organization in America.

The American Union Against Militarism (1916), which claimed six thousand members and fifty thousand sympathizers nationwide, was the most important liberal antiwar group between 1914 and 1917. Led by Lillian Wald, its most active members included Paul U. Kellogg, Crystal Eastman, Roger Baldwin, John Haynes Holmes, Norman Thomas, Oswald Garrison Villard, Emily Balch, and Florence Kelly, among others. The AUAM worked to block military expansion and U.S. entry into the European war, and to remove the profit motive from the manufacture of weapons the AUAM advocated the nationalization of the munitions industry.

The Religious Society of Friends, or Quakers, formed the American Friends Service Committee (AFSC, 1917) to organize CO-led reconstruction, humanitarian, and medical projects in wartime Europe. Although many Quakers refused to bear arms, they were willing to risk their own lives on the war front to serve their Christian ideals and humanity.

The People's Council of America for Peace and Democracy (1917), dominated by antiwar progressives, pacifists, and socialists, emerged, in May 1917, from the First American Conference for Democracy and Terms of Peace. Inspired by the Bolshevik Revolution and named after the Russian workers' "soviets" (councils), the People's Council was a national pacifist federation made up of local branches. Affiliates included trade unions, farmers' cooperatives, single-tax societies, peace societies, church groups, Socialist Party locals, and individuals. Significantly, the Socialist Party championed the People's Council, whose leaders included Scott Nearing, Louis Lochner, Lella F. Secor, and Rebecca Shelly. The People's Council advocated peace without victory, rejected annexations and indemnities, and endorsed the free development of all nationalities. First proposed by the Petrograd Soviet and by the Russian republic that took power in the March 1917 Russian Revolution, these war aims were later incorporated by President Wilson into his Fourteen Points speech in January 1918.

(Wilson had initially ignored the People's Council's proposals and repressed the organization.)

Within labor circles, however, the American Federation of Labor and its leader, Samuel Gompers, challenged the People's Council. Arguing that workers had more to gain than lose by cooperating with Wilson, Gompers and the AFL supported the president's war policies. Gompers, along with prowar labor leaders in New York and Chicago, formed a counterpart to the People's Council—the American Alliance for Labor and Democracy, which enlisted workers who supported the war and the AFL's labor conservatism. By July 1917 Wilson endorsed the alliance, which received support and financing from the Creel Committee to counter the People's Council's antiwar propaganda.

America Goes to War: April 1917 to November 1918

The German U-boat campaign strengthened prowar, prointerventionist sentiment in the United States. On 3 February 1917 President Wilson broke diplomatic relations with Germany in response to Berlin's announcement that it would employ unrestricted submarine warfare. U.S. peace advocates denounced German submarine warfare but opposed war with Germany over this action. They argued that the German blockade in the North Sea did not threaten U.S. interests and that it was aimed at Britain, not the United States. They called on Americans to stay out of the German blockade zone and urged the U.S. government not to issue passports to Americans who wished to travel in the belligerent zone. They noted that the Wilson administration did not forcefully denounce Britain's North Sea blockade against Germany. (Indeed, the peace movement had long criticized the administration's inconsistent stance—its condemnation of the German blockade and submarine warfare, while acquiescing in the British blockade. In 1915 the *Masses* editorialized: "To insist upon the right of American citizens to ride into England on a British ammunition train without risk, is not neutral.") Dismissing "silly talk about honor," peace advocates argued that the United States should not wage war on the German people because of their government's policies. Socialists in East Orange, New Jersey, noted that "the sinking of privately owned steamships which are now being used to transport grain and foodstuffs abroad is no concern to the working people."[8]

Some ethnic Americans and African Americans, furthermore, opposed the war on national and racial grounds. Many Irish Americans attempted to keep the United States from entering the war on the side of Britain, while some German-speaking Americans did not want to fight against their original homeland and against kin and relatives. Among Irish Americans anti-British sentiment was strong in the aftermath of the 1916 Easter Rebellion in Ireland; the British suppressed the uprising, which sought Irish independence from Great Britain, and executed its leaders. In the United States many Irish Americans sought exemption from the draft. In August 1917 John D. Moore, national secretary of the New York–based Friends of Irish Freedom, claimed that 55 percent of men who registered had requested exemptions, making it "practically a vote against war." Accusing Wilson of making a "secret deal" with the British, attorney Jeremiah J. O'Leary noted, "The free Irish and the free Americans who fled from British tyranny are asked to go to Europe and shed their blood for Britain."[9]

Ethnic American antiwar dissent was not limited to Irish Americans and German-speaking Americans. For example, in April 1915 more than four hundred publishers of foreign-language newspapers distributed in the United States and abroad took out a full-page "appeal to the American people" in a New York socialist newspaper. Noting that U.S.-made ammunition would kill "their own blood relatives," the appeal urged American workers "not to manufacture, sell or ship powder, shrapnel or shot" to "warring nations," where "their brothers, their sisters, parents, children or relative live."[10]

After Congress declared war in April 1917, most, but not all, African Americans supported the war. W. E .B. DuBois, the leading African American intellectual, at first spoke out against the war as a white man's imperialist conspiracy to subjugate African peoples. But he retreated once the United States declared war. Other African Americans, however, maintained their antiwar dissent. Among them were socialists Chandler Owen and A. Philip Randolph, who led the Brotherhood of Sleeping Car Porters. Both edited the popular African American newspaper the *Messenger*. Neither accepted the proposition that African American wartime patriotism would lead to an end to discrimination and segregation once peace returned. There were also some African Americans who took extraordinary measures to avoid conscription; a few openly criticized the war after induction into the military and were court-martialed.

Certain religious leaders, particularly Protestant social gospel clergymen, also opposed the war. For instance, John Haynes Holmes, a prominent religious pacifist, condemned the conflict. With the outbreak of war in Europe, Holmes implored that "from this moment on every lover of civilization and servant of human kind—the social worker first among them all—must be a peace fanatic." He added, "Nor must he be content to urge this fight in the dilettante, academic, pink-tea, high-brow way too much practiced hitherto by the organized peace movement. He must join forces, . . . with Labor, and strike . . . at the things which make war—first, militarism; second, political autocracy; and third, commercialism. The axe must be laid at the roots of the tree—which are armaments, dynasties, and exploitation."[11] In addition to individual clergymen, religious denominations opposed to the war included, most notably, the historic peace churches and the Jehovah's Witnesses (then called Russellites).

The most militant and action-oriented opponents of World War I and U.S. intervention were the socialists, anarchists, and syndicalists. They argued that capitalism, imperialism, and competition for markets had caused the conflict. The Socialist Party of America and the Industrial Workers of the World (IWW) were the most important radical organizations to oppose the war, the draft, and U.S. intervention.

In 1914 the Socialist Party proclaimed its opposition to the war. Within the Socialist Party a sizable minority supported the Allied cause and would eventually endorse U.S. intervention. Prowar Socialists sought to crush German militarism and promote freedom and democracy. They pointed to the German invasion of Belgium, the German atrocities against Belgians, and the German sinking of the *Lusitania* to support their position. Nonetheless, most Socialists rejected this prowar position. For instance, Brooklyn Socialists, meeting in May 1915 after a German submarine torpedoed the *Lusitania* and killed nearly 1,200 aboard, including 128 Americans, denounced the war and calls for U.S. participation.

Three years later, in April 1917, the Socialist Party held an emergency meeting in St. Louis to debate U.S. intervention. The previous day Congress had declared war on Germany. Thus, the nearly two hundred delegates who met at the Planters Hotel were confronted with a fait accompli. The convention elected a War and Militarism Committee, chaired by Kate Richards O'Hare, to formulate the party's position. The committee submitted three reports to the convention: a majority report and two minority reports. One hundred and forty delegates voted for the majority report—subsequently known as the St. Louis Proclamation—and its militant antiwar position. Only five delegates voted for U.S. intervention. In a national referendum Socialist Party members adopted the majority report by a vote of three to one. The Socialist Party's major newspapers and periodicals also took an antiwar and anti-interventionist stance.

Similarly, the Industrial Workers of the World, a revolutionary industrial union opposed to capitalism and militarism whose members were known as Wobblies, condemned the conflict. Much of the IWW's wartime dissent focused on labor issues. Refusing to suspend its class struggle during wartime, the IWW led strikes that disrupted wartime production. This militant labor activism, along with the group's antiwar dissent, led to brutal attacks by the government, employer groups, and private organizations. Many Wobblies opposed the war, and critics denounced the IWW as pro-German. "The I.W.W. is not pro-German, nor is it pro-Ally," one Wobbly wit punned. "It is, however, pro-letarian."[12]

Because of their protests, antiwar dissidents were battered by legal and extralegal measures, mainly at the local level. Governments at all levels, private agencies, and individual "patriots" conducted repressive campaigns against radicals, pacifists, and liberals who challenged the war. Federal legislation, most notably the Espionage Act (1917) and Sedition Act (1918), restricted dissent and promoted conformity. Enacted by Congress in June 1917, the Espionage Act made it a felony during wartime to issue "false reports or statements" with "intent to interfere" with military operations, to foster "insubordination, disloyalty, mutiny" within the military, or, in addition, to intentionally "obstruct" recruitment and enlistment into the armed services. In May 1918 Congress passed the Sedition Act, which amended and broadened the Espionage Act to curtail speech and interference with the sale of government war bonds. The Sedition Act made it a felony to "utter, print, write or publish any disloyal, profane, scurrilous, or abusive language" about the U.S. form of government or the nation's Constitution, flag, or military, or to use language that brought these into "contempt, scorn, contumely or disrepute." These acts criminalized dissent and led to the arrest and imprisonment of antiwar and other dissidents.[13]

The federal government prosecuted about two thousand cases under the Espionage and Sedition Acts.[14] Among those convicted for opposing the war were Eugene V. Debs, Scott Nearing, the IWW, and radical, antiwar, and "disloyal" women.[15] Indicted in June 1918 under the Espionage Act, Eugene V. Debs, the Socialist Party's leader and former presidential candidate, was sentenced to a ten-year prison term for delivering an antiwar speech in Canton, Ohio. With this sentence Debs became, in historian Ernest Freeberg's phrase, "democracy's prisoner."[16]

In April 1918 the government indicted Scott Nearing for writing and the Rand School for publishing *The Great Madness: A Victory for the American Plutocracy* (1917), on grounds that it interfered with the ability of the U.S. government to recruit soldiers. A socialist pacifist economics professor fired by Toledo University for his antiwar stance, Nearing became executive chairman of the People's Council. From the witness stand at his February 1919 trial, Nearing explicated the pamphlet "paragraph by paragraph, page after page," along with its "anti-capitalist, pro-socialist, anti-war, pro-peace, argument before a packed court room with news going out in most daily newspapers."[17] In a bizarre twist the jury acquitted Nearing but convicted the American Socialist Society, the corporation that operated the Rand School.

Similarly, the federal government used the Espionage Act and the courts to suppress the IWW in a campaign that culminated in a nationwide September 1917 raid on the organization. The subsequent 1918 trial convicted 113 Wobbly leaders and decimated the radical union. In addition, citizen mobs attacked Wobblies—and in several cases murdered them. Although this vigilantism usually sought to crush the IWW's militant labor activism, the union's antiwar stance contributed to this repression.

Postmaster General Albert S. Burleson also suppressed radical periodicals shipped in the mail. The New York state legislature prohibited teachers from speaking against the war. New York City required teachers to sign loyalty oaths, though dozens refused. Nationwide, public school teachers and several university professors were fired, suspended, and harassed for their antiwar and radical convictions. Private groups, including the American Protective League, the National Security League, and the American Defense Society, enforced the Espionage and Sedition Acts and attacked civil liberties and free speech. The Socialist Party dubbed the assorted defense leagues "hysteria societies" and referred to their members as "Patriots of Profits."[18]

Despite these oppressive measures, peace advocates praised Wilson's January 1918 (Fourteen Points) speech that defined U.S. war aims and proposed a postwar order based on self-determination, international justice, and freedom of trade and navigation, along with the creation of an international organization—the future League of Nations—devoted to maintaining world peace. For instance, the Woman's Peace Party's executive board expressed its "admiration and gratitude." Noting the similarities between the president's Fourteen Points and the People's Council's program, Louis Lochner declared that Wilson's address was a "complete vindication of the basic principles of a lasting peace for which liberals and radicals in every country have consistently stood."[19]

One of the most important wartime developments was the creation of private agencies to protect the rights of U.S. citizens and alien residents. Peace activists and civil libertarians established several organizations to defend civil liberties in wartime. In May 1917 feminist pacifists, radicals, and socialists formed the New York Bureau of Legal First Aid (later renamed the Bureau of Legal Advice). Two months later, in July, the American Union Against Militarism, led by Roger Baldwin and Crystal Eastman, created the Civil Liberties Bureau, which, in October, became the Baldwin-led independent National Civil Liberties Board (NCLB). These groups provided free wartime counseling and legal assistance to COs and other radicals persecuted for their antiwar stance and dissent.

Conscription, conscientious objection, and draft resistance were major themes in the World War I peace movement. On 18 May 1917 Congress enacted the Selective Service Act of 1917, authorizing the federal government, in historian John W. Chambers's phrase, "to raise an army." The conscription act effectively limited the right to conscientious objection to religious pacifists in historic peace churches and other smaller religious groups whose "creed or principles forbade its members to participate in war."[20] The law did not grant CO status to secular and political objectors; it also required COs to perform noncombatant jobs in the military. In March 1918 the president designated noncombatant service as work in the Medical Corps, the Quartermaster Corps, engineering, and certain other occupations that supported the war effort. Meanwhile, ten days after the Selective Service Act became law, President Wilson issued a proclamation that required all men between twenty-one and thirty to register for the draft. Many antiwar dissenters opposed, resisted, and evaded conscription.

Conscientious objectors were the shock troops of antiwar dissent. Nearly 4,000 inductees obtained a CO exemption from active combat service. Of the 65,000 men who sought CO status, 20,000 were inducted into the army, although 16,000 of them dropped their objection during training, often after enduring persuasion, harassment, and abuse in the military camps. This left 4,000 COs who retained their convictions. Of these 4,000, 1,300 agreed to perform noncombatant jobs in the military, mainly in the Medical Corps; another 1,300 accepted civilian farmwork; and 940 remained in military training camps. Another 450 absolutists, who refused to cooperate with Selective Service officials, military officers, and procedures, were court-martialed and sent to military prisons. These prisons included Fort Leavenworth U.S. Disciplinary Barracks (Kansas), Alcatraz Island (California), Fort Jay (New York), and Fort Douglas (Utah).

Regardless of their status, COs were placed under military jurisdiction and confined to army camps. Men who refused to register were arrested, transferred to military custody, and tried in military courts. In the army camps COs were segregated and often treated poorly and abused. COs were mocked, beaten, clubbed, kicked, slapped, choked, scrubbed with stiff brushes, dunked in latrines, jabbed with bayonets, and threatened with execution. Military guards gouged their eyes, fastened ropes around their necks, dragged them by their beards, spit into their food, forced them to endure cold showers in icy weather, blasted them with fire hoses, placed them in solitary confinement, and subjected them to the "water cure" torture, which simulated drowning by forcing victims to drink excessive amounts of water. The water torture had been used in the Philippines during the Spanish-American War by Major General Leonard Wood, who commanded Camp Funston, a detention camp for COs on the grounds at Fort Riley, Kansas, during World War I. COs who resisted or defied orders were shackled by their wrists to their cell doors nine hours a day, the equivalent of a workday. At least seventeen COs died in jail. In all 504 COs were court-martialed. Seventeen men were sentenced to death, and 142 received life sentences, although these harsh sentences were later reduced or commuted.

COs were a diverse lot. They included religious and secular objectors, pacifists and nonpacifists, capitalists and anticapitalists, and U.S. citizens and resident aliens. Religious COs included members of the Friends, Mennonites, Brethren, Molokans, Doukhobors, Jehovah's Witnesses, and other denominations and sects. Political and humanitarian COs included "socialists" (Socialist Party members,

Wobblies, anarchists, syndicalists, and other radicals) who opposed World War I on grounds that it was a "capitalist" war, on class grounds that workers should not shoot other workers, and on other political grounds. Significantly, many COs were socialists, anarchists, and syndicalists. Some pacifists agreed to do noncombatant service in the military; some did not. Offered noncombatant service, one CO refused. Why? "Because I object to the whole game of war, and not to the mere business of shooting guns," he replied, in words that other like-minded COs would have endorsed. "There is no essential difference between being a soldier and patching up other men in hospitals to go out and continue the slaughter."[21]

Some religious pacifists and COs, particularly Mennonites and Brethren nonresistants, rejected all force and violence, even personal violence. During court-martial proceedings, COs were often asked if they would use force or kill to defend their wives, children, and family from rape, murder, or burglary. For instance, interrogators asked Peter P. Heppner, a California Mennonite farmer, to consider a hypothetical German invasion of the United States. Would he "fight" to save his family or prevent a German from raping his sister? "No, sir," Heppner replied. He would try to persuade the rapist to cease, Heppner explained, but would not use "violence" to stop the attacker. Similarly, the judges asked Austin Hewitt, a Wesleyan Methodist, to imagine confrontation with a German soldier in a French trench. "Would you let him kill you or [would] you kill him?" the interrogators inquired. "I would rather him kill me than me kill him," Hewitt replied. Then asked if he would "fight" a man who had murdered his mother or sister or who was "advancing" on them, Hewitt responded, "No, sir; I couldn't fight him."[22]

Some men even claimed CO status on the basis of their vegetarianism. For instance, Brooklyn vegetarian Louis Alba declared, "I am a vegetarian, and as such cannot participate in any act which leads to bloodshed and the destruction of life. The creed of vegetarianism forbids the slaughter or even the maiming of creeping things, fish, fowl, or any organic being. How much more, then, would that creed forbid the killing of man?"[23]

In June 1918 Newton Baker, the secretary of war, established a Board of Inquiry to determine the sincerity of objectors in army camps. Chaired by Major Walter Guest Kellogg, the board visited camps and interviewed COs. Kellogg later wrote, "Although I had never set eyes on a conscientious objector, I firmly believed that they were, as a class, shirkers and cowards. My first trip as a member of the Board upset most of my ideas regarding the objector. I began to see him in a new light. And an examination of over eight hundred objectors in twenty widely distributed military camps and posts has convinced me that they are, as a rule, sincere—cowards and shirkers, in the commonly accepted sense, they are not."[24]

On occasion COs waged nonviolent protests and rebellions—individual and collective—in military camps and prisons. They used work strikes, hunger strikes, and nonviolent noncooperation to resist poor conditions, the harsh treatment of COs, military regulations that violated their conscience, and conscription itself. Fort Leavenworth and Fort Riley became key sites of struggle between military authorities and COs. Absolutists such as Evan Thomas, Howard Moore, Harold Gray, Julius Eichel, and Erling Lunde openly resisted conscription and military control over their lives—and they sometimes won concessions from the government. For instance, in July 1918 officers at Fort Riley evicted COs—then on a work strike to protest military orders—from the barracks, told them to build a tent colony, issued them "raw" rations but no kitchen, and forbade them to prepare their meals collectively. In response, absolutists refused to erect the tents and went on a hunger strike. Capturing the strike's upbeat spirit, one CO announced, "Dinner time,—take in another notch in your belts."[25] The successful strike led the army to give COs a field range and permit them to prepare their meals collectively.

In November 1918 Evan Thomas waged a work strike at Fort Leavenworth to protest the treatment of Molokans, an obscure pacifist sect that emigrated from Russia to avoid conscription. Refusing to obey military orders because of their religious principles, several Molokans were court-martialed, beaten, and locked in solitary confinement with their hands manacled to the cell bars. To support the Molokans and "liberty of conscience," Thomas went on strike—and also ended up in the hole.[26] Like other prisoners in the hole, he was handcuffed, in standing position, to the crossbars of his cell door for nine hours a day.

Due to intervention by civil libertarians, in December 1918 President Wilson abolished manacling prisoners to their cell doors. On 2 December, the day before Wilson sailed to France to attend the Versailles Peace Conference, John Nevin Sayre, a FOR leader whose brother was married to one of the president's daughters, met with Wilson and presented written evidence of harsh conditions in military prisons. Wilson seemed shocked. On 6 December, at the president's instruction, the secretary of war ordered the military to cease manacling, a punishment that historian Charles Chatfield notes had become ineffective and embarrassing to the administration.

In early January 1919 the Board of Inquiry interviewed Thomas, then serving a twenty-five-year sentence (originally life) after being court-martialed in October for refusing a military command to eat, and ordered his release on 14 January. Once again, nonviolent CO protest had won concessions. Moreover, the order, issued by the secretary of war, explicitly referred to COs as "political prisoners."[27]

At Fort Leavenworth prisoners also rioted and revolted. On Christmas Eve 1918 prisoners in the mess hall rioted to protest the fraudulent distribution of food moneys and overcrowding. Then, in mid-January 1919, a race riot broke out. Later that month 2,300 prisoners, with assorted grievances, waged a several-day general strike. COs Carl Haessler, H. Austin Simmons, and Oral James led the strike, kept it nonviolent, and were spokesmen for the strikers. In a petition sent to Fort Leavenworth commandant Colonel Sedgwick Rice, the strikers demanded that men confined to solitary for taking part in the rebellion be released, that a telegram be sent to the secretary of war requesting amnesty for all men convicted by court-martial, and that the commandant recognize an elected permanent grievance committee. Rice consented. The prisoners returned to work, and conditions temporarily improved. In Washington Newton Baker ordered

113 COs, whom the Board of Inquiry had judged "sincere," to be granted an honorable discharge and released.

Six months later, in July 1919, Leavenworth prisoners, dissatisfied with poor food, defied the elected Prisoners' General Conference Committee and went on strike again. Their demands included better food and amnesty. Calling the protest "mutiny," the government broke the strike, abolished the prisoners' committee, imposed "iron rule," and levied draconian punishments.[28]

Conscientious objection was not the only form of draft resistance. To evade conscription, men often lied about their ages, jobs, health, and marital status. Erroneously believing that marriage would exempt them from the draft, thousands of draft-age men entered into sham "slacker marriages."[29] Some men took morphine or heroine, hoping to be rejected by the army as narcotic addicts. More shocking, some men mutilated themselves, by blinding themselves in one eye, by severing fingers or toes with a gun or knife, or by other means. In Florida, for instance, two black farmworkers committed self-mutilation with a shotgun. One shot four fingers off his right hand; the other blew off his right arm.

In several rural places induction sparked antidraft riots and revolts. Most notably, in the "Green Corn Rebellion," five hundred tenant farmers—white, black, and Indian—waged an insurrection against conscription in eastern Oklahoma. The armed revolt was organized by the socialist Working Class Union, which blamed U.S. intervention on corporate capitalism. "Now is the time to rebel against this war with Germany boys," the WCU proclaimed. "Boys, get together and don't go. Rich man's war, poor man's fight."[30] Planning to march to Washington DC to halt the war, the rebels sang "The Battle Hymn of the Republic" and "John Brown's Body." Three men were reportedly killed and several wounded by citizens' posses that crushed the rebellion. More than 400 rebels were arrested and 150 convicted; many were sentenced to long prison terms at Fort Leavenworth and other federal prisons. Smaller skirmishes occurred in the mountains of Arizona, Nevada, Arkansas, Georgia, and North Carolina.

Peace Humanitarianism Abroad and Postwar Developments: November 1918 to 1921

During and after the war, the American peace movement engaged in humanitarian activism overseas by providing relief, assisting reconstruction, and promoting peace. Besides highlighting the obvious humanitarian impulse, both religious and secular, these reconstruction efforts demonstrate the emergent modern peace movement's attempt to address peace, justice, and reconciliation. Through humanitarian reconstruction work abroad, peace activists sought to bind the wounds of war and sow the seeds of peace. Several U.S. peace groups, most notably the American Friends Service Committee, were involved in this humanitarian work. But the Fellowship of Reconciliation, the Mennonite Relief Committee for War Sufferers (MRCWS, and its successor, the Mennonite Central Committee), the Women's International League for Peace and Freedom (WILPF, 1919), and other groups associated with the peace movement also participated in this work. In addition, many private and public groups outside the peace movement were engaged in overseas relief, reconstruction, and humanitarian projects, including the American Red Cross, the Young Men's Christian Association (YMCA), the American Relief Administration, and the American Committee for Armenian and Syrian Relief.

Ever since its founding in 1917, the AFSC has helped victims of war and natural disasters, regardless of religious creed, political affiliation, or national origin. After World War I AFSC units and volunteers worked in nations belonging to the former Allies and Central powers. As religious pacifists many draft-eligible AFSC men refused induction into the military, but were willing to perform alternative civilian service, including dangerous humanitarian work in war zones. Similarly, AFSC women volunteers, although not subject to conscription, enlisted in overseas relief and reconstruction work.

In France the AFSC worked under the auspices of the American Red Cross and combined efforts with English Quakers in the Anglo-American Mission of the Society of Friends. The first AFSC volunteers were trained at Haverford College, a Quaker institution. Organized by physician James A. Babbitt and by Quaker philosophy professor Rufus M. Jones, the "Haverford Unit" provided relief and reconstruction in France. In 1917 the AFSC sent its first group, composed of fifty-one men and three women, to France; most of these volunteers were Quakers, although several Mennonites, Brethren, and FOR members were included. In France AFSC workers drove ambulances; reconstructed homes, roads, and villages; assisted refugees; provided funds to staff and supply the maternity hospital at Châlons-sur-Marne; and operated other humanitarian projects. Eventually, about six hundred, mostly male, volunteers served in France, often working in the shadow of aerial bombing and cannon fire. By 1920 the Anglo-America Mission had completed its projects or transferred control to the French.

In June 1917 the AFSC sent a small team of American Quaker women to Russia to work with English Friends in the district of Buzuluk. The Americans included several remarkable women, including Anna J. Haines, Nancy Babb, Lydia Lewis, and Esther White. In Buzuluk these women, along with other Friends, assisted refugees displaced by fighting between Germany and Russia and later between Reds and Whites; provided food, medical care, and training; and operated orphanages and schools. In 1921 and 1922 the Volga River–region famine, a result of drought, wars, and revolution, killed perhaps ten million Russians. Amid civil war and revolution, famine and disease, the AFSC fed much of Buzuluk with food provided by the American Relief Administration and by its own efforts. Working in "the Valley of the Shadow of Death," Anna Haines, who supervised the Buzuluk campaign, reported that Friends were feeding fifty thousand children daily.[31]

The AFSC did not limit its humanitarian and relief work to France and Russia. By December 1919 AFSC units were in Germany, Austria, Serbia, Poland, and Palestine. They operated public health and sanitation projects, fed civilians, assisted refugees, distributed clothing, worked farms, and offered other aid. In Germany and Austria the AFSC, working with the American Relief Administration, fed more than one million children. German children were given food cards inscribed with the following statement: "This food is contributed by Americans and is distributed by the Religious Society of Friends who, for 250 years, have held that love and goodwill, not war and hatred, will bring about better world conditions."[32] The Friends were not alone in their humanitarian work.

In late 1917 and early 1918 U.S. Mennonites created the Mennonite Relief Committee for War Sufferers. Working through the AFSC the MRCWS supported wartime and postwar reconstruction work in France with funds and volunteers. Many Mennonites worked in Clermont-en-Argonne, a small village in the Meuse Department, a region devastated by the battle of Verdun. By 1920 more than fifty Mennonites, most of whom had been released from Fort Leavenworth or military camps, served in the AFSC's French units. Mennonites also organized relief committees to provide assistance in southern Russia. In addition, the MRCWS supported the American Committee for Armenian and Syrian Relief, a group founded in 1915 to aid millions of Armenians, Assyrians, Greeks, and other minorities in the Middle East who were displaced, deported, and killed as the Ottoman Empire collapsed. Under the auspices of the American Committee for Armenian and Syrian Relief (later renamed the Near East Foundation), the MRCWS sent funds and a small group of volunteers to the Middle East. In 1920 the MRCWS and other Mennonite relief groups created the Mennonite Central Committee as the core Mennonite relief agency.

The American FOR also provided international humanitarian assistance and promoted reconciliation between former enemies. FOR encouraged its members to support the AFSC's "noble work of rescue and relief." For instance, in December 1919 FOR's magazine, the *World Tomorrow*, published a "Christmas Appeal," calling on readers to donate five thousand dollars to the AFSC to help starving German and Austrian children.[33]

In early 1921 prominent FOR leader John Nevin Sayre toured Germany and France with International Fellowship of Reconciliation (IFOR) members. Designed "to take some of the sting out of the [1919

Versailles] Treaty," this goodwill mission of citizen diplomacy sought to inform ordinary Germans that there were American and British pacifists who "disagreed with the harsh peace which their governments had imposed on Germany and who wanted to help Germany recover from the near-starvation and cruelties of the war." Moreover, the IFOR team promised to send aid to their German "brothers in Christ."[34] In France IFOR members worked side by side with the AFSC and Church of the Brethren—where Sayre recounted how touched he was by the sight of seven volunteers rebuilding "a spot of utter desolation north of Verdun."[35] These actions, Sayre and FOR believed, fostered reconciliation, understanding, and brotherhood— the foundation of peace.

On 11 November 1918 the Armistice was signed, and the First World War ended. Peace activism, antiwar dissent, and concern over civil liberties and social justice did not end with the Armistice, however. At the 1919 Versailles conference and elsewhere, the victorious Allies wrote postwar peace treaties. Short-lived socialist revolutions rocked Germany, Hungary, and Bavaria. Along with other Allied governments, the United States sent troops to intervene in the Russian Civil War (1918–21), in part to overthrow the Soviet regime. At home the Red Scare (1919–20) targeted dissidents and radicals—and peace activists and organizations were among those persecuted and prosecuted.

Militarist and antiradical sentiment and repression did not cease in November 1918, but rather continued and nurtured the Red Scare. In the immediate postwar period, federal, state, and local governments conducted campaigns against radicals, in particular communists, spurred by fears that radicals in the United States might try to imitate the 1917 Bolshevik Revolution. The Espionage Act remained in effect after the war, although Congress repealed the Sedition Act in late 1920. In 1919 and 1920 Attorney General A. Mitchell Palmer, a Quaker, ordered mass raids that arrested thousands of radicals and deported several hundred aliens. Louis F. Post, a former assistant secretary of labor, lamented the postwar "popular delirium," "war frenzy," and "popular hysteria" that equated radical aliens with "moral rats" and undergirded the Red Scare and "deportation crusade." Among the alien radicals deported to the Soviet Union in December 1919 aboard the *Buford*, a steamship dubbed the "Soviet Ark," were anarchists Emma Goldman and Alexander Berkman, who were arrested in June 1917 and convicted of conspiring against the Selective Service Act. As novelist John Dos Passos noted, "To be red in the summer of 1919 was worse than being a hun or a pacifist in the summer of 1917."[36] This antiradical crusade also targeted the peace movement.

In 1919, moreover, the New York state legislature established a joint committee to investigate "revolutionary radicalism" and "seditious activities." Chaired by Clayton R. Lusk, the committee included pacifism in its antiradical agenda. The committee sought, in its own words, "to show the use made by members of the Socialist Party of America and other extreme radicals and revolutionaries of pacifist sentiment among people of education and culture in the United States as a vehicle for the promotion of revolutionary Socialist propaganda." In short, the Lusk Committee concluded that "Socialists, playing upon the pacifist sentiment . . . were able to organize their energies and to capitalize their prestige for the spread of their doctrines."[37]

During the years 1919 and 1920 the Lusk Committee launched a series of raids on radical organizations and seized records, files, documents, and literature. In April 1920 the committee published its massive four-volume report titled *Revolutionary Radicalism*. The report targeted (and erroneously conflated) "pacifism," socialism, communism, and syndicalism. "The very first general fact that must be driven home to Americans," the report declared, "is that the pacifist movement in this country . . . is an absolutely integral and fundamental part of International Socialism," and the latter sought to promote internationalism in order "to supersede national patriotism . . . based upon pacifism, in the sense that it opposed all wars between nations and developed at the same time the class consciousness that was to culminate in relentless class warfare." "In other words," the report concluded, "it was not really peace that was the goal, but the abolition of the patriotic, warlike spirit of nationalities."[38]

In New York the committee's work contributed to the expulsion of five Socialist state assemblymen-elect who had been elected in 1920. It also led to the enactment of two state laws in 1921, both repealed in 1923, that sought to enforce loyalty and political conformity in education. In these and other ways the Lusk Committee contributed to the Red Scare.

Archibald E. Stevenson, the Lusk Committee's special counsel and primary author of the committee's four-volume report, was a professional antiradical. In January 1919, for instance, he testified before the Overman Committee, a subcommittee of the Senate Judiciary Committee chaired by Lee Overman (D-NC), then investigating German and Bolshevik elements in America. Stevenson named sixty-two individuals—a "Who's Who in Pacifism and Radicalism"—who had opposed the First World War. His list included wartime peace activists Jane Addams, Emily Greene Balch, Roger Baldwin, Eugene V. Debs, John Haynes Holmes, Jessie W. Hughan, William I. Hull, Rufus M. Jones, David Starr Jordan, Louis P. Lochner, Tracy Mygatt, Scott Nearing, John Sayre, Norman Thomas, and Oswald Garrison Villard.[39] In short, the postwar Red Scare, whose targets included antiwar dissidents and peace activists, continued the wartime intolerance against radicalism and dissent. The intensified Americanism, patriotism, nationalism, antiradicalism, and demand for conformity that accompanied World War I did not end with the Armistice.

After the war amnesty for imprisoned COs and political prisoners became a significant issue. The American Civil Liberties Union (ACLU), Socialist Party, IWW, AFL, and other groups advocated a general amnesty rather than individual pardons. Presidents Harding and Coolidge released most COs and "political" prisoners. Then, in the December 1933 Christmas Amnesty, fifteen years after the Armistice, President Roosevelt pardoned all World War I political prisoners and restored their full citizenship rights.

Legacies: The Significance of World War I Peace Activism and Antiwar Dissent

The World War I peace movement left several significant legacies. First, the "modern" American peace movement emerged during the First World War. This modern post-1914 peace movement transformed peace activism in America. Building on their wartime activism, peace activists built a powerful interwar peace movement that advocated peace and justice; opposed militarism, conscription, and war; and endorsed disarmament and nonviolent conflict resolution. Arguing that organized violence was rooted in social injustice, the modern peace movement championed social reform to abolish the social causes of war and conflict. For instance, the People's Council's constitution affirmed: "The peace we aim at is not mere cessation of hostilities, but a removal of the great causes of the war." Similarly, the War Resisters' International declared its intent to oppose all war and "to strive for the removal of all causes of war."[40] Among war's causes the WRI cited capitalism and intolerance rooted in differences among races, religions, classes, and nations.

After the Armistice World War I peace activists founded new antiwar, peace, and pacifist groups in the United States. Most notably, these groups included the U.S. Section of the Women's International League for Peace and Freedom, the Women's Peace Society (WPS, 1919), the Women's Peace Union (WPU, 1921), the War Resisters League (WRL, 1923), and the National Council for Limitation of Armaments (1921), soon renamed the National Council for Prevention of War (1923). Other peace groups emerged during the interwar era, creating a powerful social, political, and cultural peace movement.

In addition, U.S. and European pacifists founded three pacifist internationals. With their origins in the First World War, these transnational organizations had an immense impact on the interwar peace movement. Each of these pacifist internationals—the Women's International League for Peace and Freedom, the International Fellowship of Reconciliation, and the War Resisters' International—had a U.S. affiliate. This linked the American peace movement to a global pacifist network committed to peace *and* justice. Consistent with the modern peace movement that emerged after 1914, these pacifist organizations, contending that peace required justice, championed social reforms to abolish the causes of war. In addition, these pacifist groups, along with the broader modern U.S. peace movement, enlisted women, reformers, and radicals with a more secular impulse and progressive agenda.

The Women's International League for Peace and Freedom had roots in the U.S. women's peace movement. In April 1915 the Woman's Peace Party, along with more than a thousand delegates from neutral and belligerent nations, participated in the International Women's Congress for Peace and Freedom in The Hague. The Hague meeting created the International Committee of Women for Permanent Peace and named Woman's Peace Party leader Jane Addams president. The Woman's Peace Party became the American Section of the ICWPP. In May 1919 the ICWPP held a second international congress in Zurich. In Switzerland the ICWPP denounced the Versailles peace treaty, renamed itself the Women's International League for Peace and Freedom, established headquarters in Geneva, and elected two Americans to leadership positions: Jane Addams as president and Emily Greene Balch as secretary-treasurer. Then, in November 1919, the Woman's Peace Party reconstituted itself as the U.S. Section of the Women's International League for Peace and Freedom.

The International Fellowship of Reconciliation originated in wartime England. In December 1914 British pacifists created the Fellowship of Reconciliation, a Christian, absolute pacifist federation open to men and women. Religious pacifists in several nations established national branches, and, in November 1915, American FOR was founded by religious pacifists. Originating as a (mainly Protestant) Christian organization, in 1930 American FOR became nonsectarian. Meanwhile, in 1919 European pacifists from ten nations met in the Netherlands and founded the International Fellowship of Reconciliation.

In 1921 in the Netherlands, another group of European pacifists, including opponents of the First World War, founded an international pacifist federation named Paco (Esperanto for "peace"). This absolute pacifist federation was secular and open to men and women. In 1923 Paco renamed itself the War Resisters' International and moved its headquarters to London. In the United States the War Resisters League was founded in 1923 as the major American affiliate of the

WRI, though the Fellowship of Reconciliation, the Women's Peace Society, and the Women's Peace Union were also affiliated with the WRI. The most radical of the pacifist internationals, the WRI's left-wing secular orientation was expressed by WRI cofounder Fenner Brockway, a British socialist pacifist and World War I CO. He noted that WRI founders were "anti-capitalist as well as pacifist. We repudiated 'bourgeois' pacifism, wished to extend individual resistance to a general strike against war, and stood for 'revolution by nonviolence.' The membership was both anarchist and socialist and . . . emphasize[d] the identity of the struggle against war and the struggle against the economic system which is its cause."[41]

Coinciding with this global pacifist outreach and capturing the popular imagination were some interesting proposals to end war. During the interwar period the peace movement presented several measures to outlaw war. For instance, in 1921, Salmon O. Levinson, a Chicago attorney, founded the American Committee for the Outlawry of War, an effort that eventually led to the 1928 Pact of Paris (or Kellogg-Briand Pact), an international treaty that repudiated and outlawed offensive war. John Dewey, the noted philosopher who reevaluated his support for the First World War soon after the Armistice, was a leading intellectual spokesman for the cause. Columbia University president Nicholas Murray Butler, who chaired the Lake Mohonk Conference on International Arbitration (1907–12) and shared the 1931 Nobel Peace Prize with Jane Addams, rallied support for the Kellogg-Briand Pact. Proponents concluded that "outlawry" offered a more realistic option for peace than the League of Nations.

A few years later another interesting antiwar proposal was tendered. In February 1933 the Oxford Union Society, a debating society in Oxford, England, resolved that "this House will in no circumstances fight for its King and Country." In the United States the Oxford Pledge prompted similar antiwar pledges and spurred mass student strikes for peace. In March 1933 Brown University students led the first U.S. student strike for peace inspired by the Oxford Pledge. In April 1934, 25,000 students walked out of classes to attend rallies, where they took a similar pledge; in 1935, 175,000 students did so. Even before the Oxford Pledge, however, U.S. students had waged peace strikes. For instance, in 1925, nearly a decade earlier, four hundred students at Howard University went on strike to protest militarism, compulsory drills, and the ROTC.

During the interwar period, moreover, numerous best-selling books, pamphlets, and articles claimed that arms manufacturers had manipulated the U.S. government into entering World War I. Their publication contributed to the postwar disillusionment and the strong antiwar, anti-interventionist sentiment of the 1930s. These books included H. C. Engelbrecht and F. C. Hanighen's *Merchants of Death: A Study of the International Armament Industry* (1934), George Seldes's *Iron, Blood, and Profits: An Expose of the World-Wide Munitions Racket* (1934), and Major General Smedley D. Butler's *War Is a Racket* (1935). In response to widespread public opinion that blamed the war on arms merchants and other economic interests, in 1934 the Senate appointed the Nye Committee to investigate these charges. Although the committee did not find the munitions makers guilty of taking the United States into war, it castigated them for their excessive wartime profits. In addition, the committee's conclusions led Congress to adopt a series of neutrality acts between 1935 and 1939 that sought to prevent the United States from entering another war.

Second, the women's peace movement emerged during World War I. Moreover, women, who played a prominent role in the wartime and postwar peace movement, challenged traditional gender roles by assuming a public voice in matters of war and peace, an issue previously dominated by men. In the Woman's Peace Party and in other same-sex and mixed-gender groups, women mobilized against the First World War. The Women's International League for Peace and Freedom continued this work. After the war WILPF split, producing two other women's pacifist groups, the Women's Peace Society (which waged an educational and lobbying campaign against war) and the Women's Peace Union (which championed a constitutional amendment to end war). Led by feminist Carrie Chapman Catt, in 1925 nine national women's organizations founded the National

Committee on the Cause and Cure of War. These groups provided an organizational base for women's peace activism in the interwar peace movement. To paraphrase historian Harriet Hyman Alonso, peace and war were women's issues—no less than men's.[42]

Third, peace activists made important contributions to the wartime and postwar civil liberties movement. During the war peace activists and civil libertarians created organizations to defend COs, antiwar dissidents, and other radicals persecuted for their opposition to the war and their political views. These groups included the New York Bureau of Legal First Aid, the Bureau of Legal Advice, and the National Civil Liberties Board. During the Red Scare these agencies defended both U.S. citizens and resident aliens, who contested their deportation by the U.S. government. In 1920 the American Civil Liberties Union, the successor to the National Civil Liberties Board, took over this work and became the most prominent U.S. organization devoted to protecting civil liberties. Thus, wartime peace activists made a direct contribution to the founding of the ACLU and to the promotion of civil liberties in the United States.

Fourth, perhaps one of the most important legacies of the modern peace movement is that it contained a powerful secular impulse. This post-1914 peace movement marked an important milestone in the shift from "sacred to secular resistance" and toward a "new conscientious objection" based on nonreligious principles. Historically, peace activism was characterized by religious motives, though in the decade or so before 1914 secular middle-class peace societies emerged, including the Carnegie Endowment for International Peace and the World Peace Foundation. The war accelerated this trend toward secularization. During the war socialists, anarchists, and other political radicals based their antiwar dissent on secular principles—political, philosophical, and humanitarian. Often more antiwar than pacifist, these radicals were motivated by internationalism, worker solidarity, and a refusal to fight in capitalist wars. Similarly, COs rooted in these radical political traditions often based their objection on secular grounds. Organizations that reflected this "secularization of conscience" include the Socialist Party, the Industrial Workers of the

World, the Woman's Peace Party and Women's International League for Peace and Freedom, and, most notably, the War Resisters' International and War Resisters League. Although religious impulses represented by American FOR and the International Fellowship of Reconciliation, the Catholic Worker Movement, and mainline Protestant peace fellowships continued to influence the postwar peace movement, even religious peace activists, most notably A. J. Muste, became increasingly attuned to this secular turn. Although the legal principle of secular conscientious objection would not be established until the Vietnam War era, the World War I peace movement represents an important stage in this development.[43]

Fifth, another significant contribution was the change in government policy toward conscientious objectors. The often harsh treatment of COs in army prisons and camps during World War I, the CO protests that created headaches for army officers and conscription officials, and by 1940 the emergence of a CO lobby led the government to broaden and liberalize provisions for World War II COs. Most notably, the Selective Training and Service Act of 1940 offered COs and pacifists two major concessions. It granted CO status to any "person who by reason of religious training and belief, is conscientiously opposed to participation in war in any form." This language broadened the 1917 conscription law, which limited CO status to members of the historic peace churches and other religious sects with antiwar creeds. It also permitted COs to choose "non-combatant service" in the military or "work of national importance under civilian direction."[44] The latter option led to the creation of the Civilian Public Service (1941–47), a program that sought to honor pacifist conscience and enrolled twelve thousand COs.

Sixth, World War I—a modern, industrial, and total conflict—led postwar peace activists to promote peace as the "necessary reform."[45] With machine guns, poison gas, barbed wire, tanks, airplanes, and aerial bombing, the Great War unleashed a specter of unprecedented destruction; in the process, it demonstrated that humans had the technological means to threaten human existence. Subsequently, peace reform, though still ethical and humanitarian, would become essential to human survival. Although the peace movement did not prevent the Second World War, the Cold War, or the 9/11 wars, in a world stocked with weapons of mass destruction—nuclear, chemical, and biological—the risk of human destruction makes peace even more pressing than during the First World War.

In retrospect, World War I peace activism and antiwar dissent—mass, grassroots, innovative citizen protest against the war—transformed the American peace movement. The modern peace movement that emerged in 1914 was more committed to peace *and* justice, more grassroots, more progressive, more secular, more female-centric, and more oriented toward direct action. Moreover, World War I resistance to the draft and to the Espionage and Sedition Acts might be seen as prologue for the civil disobedience that characterized the World War II and post-1945 peace movement. Finally, peace activism and antiwar dissent were "patriotic"—and the opponents of war often couched their stance in patriotic terms. In a nation dedicated to freedom and liberty, these rebels against war,[46] no less than those who supported U.S. intervention, defended American interests and ideals, while honoring their own religious, political, and humanitarian convictions.

Notes

To keep notes to a minimum we have sourced only direct quotations. Although this synthetic introduction incorporates archival research, it relies mainly on published scholarship. The most helpful sources are listed in the selected bibliography.

1. Charles DeBenedetti, *The Peace Reform in American History* (Bloomington: Indiana University Press, 1980), 92.

2. DeBenedetti, *Peace Reform in American History*, chaps. 4–5.

3. Woman's Peace Party, "Preamble and Platform," 10 January 1915, in Woman's Peace Party Records, DG-43, reel 12.1, Swarthmore College Peace Collection, Swarthmore PA; Perkins quoted in "Roosevelt and Motherhood," *New York Call*, 30 July 1915, 5; Mrs. L. T. to Editor, "Women's Sphere," *New York Call* (Magazine and Editorial Section), 1 April 1917, 13. For a "mothers' strike" discussed by some European women, see Rose Rosner, "Alla Nazimova on a Birth Strike in Europe," *New York Call* (Magazine and Editorial Section), 4 February 1917, 10.

4. "Yell Anti-War at Launching of Battleship," *New York Call*, 20 June 1915, 2.

5. For "War Against War" quotation, see Harriet H. Alonso, *Peace as a Woman's Issue: A History of the U.S. Movement for World Peace and Women's Rights* (Syracuse NY: Syracuse University Press, 1993), 71. For other quotations in this paragraph, see "Use Sham Dinosaur to Rout Militarists," *New York Times*, 5 April 1916, 8.

6. John Reed, "At the Throat of the Republic," *Masses*, July 1916, 7.

7. *Four Lights*, 27 January 1917, 1.

8. "Editorial," *Masses*, August 1915, 11; "Stay Out of War Zone, Declares Amos Pinchot," *New York Call*, 4 February, 1917, 2; Resolution in "Socialists of East Orange Protest," *New York Call*, 6 February 1917, 2.

9. Moore and O'Leary quoted in "Irish Demand Draft Repeal," *New York Call*, 13 August 1917, 4.

10. "Publishers Appeal," *New York Call*, 5 April 1915, 4–5.

11. John Haynes Holmes, "War and the Social Movement," *Survey*, 26 September 1914, 629–30.

12. J. Stephen Dodd, "Scrambled Eggs," *Solidarity*, 11 August 1917, 7.

13. The texts of the Espionage and Sedition Acts are available online at "Digital History: Espionage Act" (1917), http://www.digitalhistory.uh.edu/disp_textbook.cfm?smtID=3&psid=3904, and "Digital History: Sedition Act" (1918), http://www.digitalhistory.uh.edu/disp_textbook.cfm?smtID=3&psid=3903.

14. The Supreme Court upheld the Espionage Act in *Debs v. United States* (1918), *Schenck v. United States* (1919), and *Frohwerk v. United States* (1919).

15. See Kathleen Kennedy, *Disloyal Mothers and Scurrilous Citizens: Women and Subversion during World War I* (Bloomington: Indiana University Press, 1999).

16. Ernest Freeberg, *Democracy's Prisoner: Eugene V. Debs, the Great War, and the Right to Dissent* (Cambridge MA: Harvard University Press, 2008).

17. Scott Nearing, *The Making of a Radical: A Political Autobiography* (New York: Harper & Row, 1972), 116.

18. See, for instance, "Many Members of Banking Firm in Jingo Trust," *New York Call*, 30 August 1915, 1–2. The SP dubbed the National Security League the "original 'Hysteria League.'"

19. The WPP quoted in "Peace Women Back Wilson," *New York Call*, 15 January 1918, 4; Lochner quoted in "Keep Up Fight for Firm Peace, Urges Nearing," *New York Call*, 15 January 1918, 4.

20. John Whiteclay Chambers II, *To Raise an Army: The Draft Comes to Modern America* (New York: Free Press, 1987); Selective Service Act of 1917 (PL 65-12, 40 Stat. 76).

21. Ernest L. Meyer, *"Hey! Yellowbacks!": The War Diary of a Conscientious Objector* (New York: John Day, 1930), 43–44.

22. See transcripts of court-martial trials of Peter Heppner (General Conference Mennonite, 28 May 1918) and Austin Hewett (5 April 1918), *Case Files of Con-*

scientious Objectors Court-Martialed during W.W.I., 1917–1919, reel 272, Mennonite Library and Archives, Bethel College, North Newton KS, taken from Anne M. Yoder, "Conscientious Objection during the Great War: A Documentary History through Personal Writings and Testimony" (unpublished manuscript, 2010). We are indebted to Anne Yoder, Swarthmore College Peace Collection, who provided the Heppner and Hewitt documents.

23. Alba quoted in "Many Draftees Refuse to Take Physical Test," *New York Call*, 13 August 1917, 2.

24. Walter Guest Kellogg, *The Conscientious Objector* (New York: Boni & Liveright, 1919), v.

25. Arthur Dunham quoted in Charles Chatfield, ed., *The Radical "No": The Writings and Correspondence of Evan Thomas on War* (New York: Garland, 1975), 164.

26. Thomas quoted in Chatfield, *Radical "No,"* 209.

27. Baker quoted in Howard W. Moore, *Plowing My Own Furrow* (Syracuse NY: Syracuse University Press, 1993), 139. Moore later recalled that this was the first time he had heard COs referred to as political prisoners.

28. For "mutiny," see [Fred Leighton], *The "Mutiny" at Fort Leavenworth Disciplinary Barracks: July 22nd, 1919* (Chicago: American Industrial, [1919]). For "iron rule," see Moore, *Plowing My Own Furrow*, 142.

29. See, for instance, "Slacker Marriages" (editorial), *New York Call*, 12 April 1917, 6.

30. The WCU quoted in *Harlow's Weekly*, 15 August 1917, as cited in Garin Burbank, *When Farmers Voted Red: The Gospel of Socialism in the Oklahoma Countryside, 1910–1924* (Westport CT: Greenwood Press, 1976), 145.

31. Anna J. Haines, *Thru the Valley of the Shadow of Death* (leaflet) (Philadelphia: AFSC, [1922?]), PG3, AFSC-Russia, Friends Historical Library, Swarthmore College, Swarthmore PA.

32. Quoted in J. William Frost, "'Our Deeds Carry Our Message': The Early History of the American Friends Service Committee," *Quaker History* 81 (Spring 1992): 37.

33. *World Tomorrow*, December 1919, 333–34.

34. For this and the previous two Sayre quotations in this paragraph, see John Nevin Sayre, "Instruments of Peace" (unpublished memoir), [92], John Nevin Sayre Papers, DG-117, series H, box 1, Swarthmore College Peace Collection, Swarthmore PA.

35. Quoted in John Nevin Sayre, "The Fellowship at Work in Europe" [1921; FOR flyer], in Fellowship of Reconciliation–U.S. Section Records, DG-13, section II, series A-5, box 1, Swarthmore College Peace Collection, Swarthmore PA.

36. Quoted in Louis F. Post, *The Deportations Delirium of Nineteen-Twenty: A Personal Narrative of an Historic Official Experience* (Chicago: Charles H. Kerr, 1923), 305, 307, 310, 312; John Dos Passos, *1919* [USA trilogy] (1932; reprint, New York: Library of America, 1996), 747.

37. Report of the Joint Legislative Committee Investigating Seditious Activities in New York State, *Revolutionary Radicalism: Its History, Purpose, and Tactics with an Exposition and Discussion of the Steps Being Taken and Required to Curb It Being the Report of the Joint Legislative Committee Investigating Seditious Activities, Part I: Revolutionary and Subversive Movements Abroad and at Home* (Albany NY: J. B. Lyon, 1920), 1:969.

38. Report of the Joint Legislative Committee Investigating Seditious Activities in New York State, *Revolutionary Radicalism*, 11.

39. "Lists Americans as Pacifists and Radicals," *New York Times*, 25 January 1919, 1, 4; U.S. Senate, *Brewing and Liquor Interests and German and Bolshevik Propaganda*, Hearings before a Subcommittee on the Committee on the Judiciary, 65th Cong., 2nd and 3rd sess. (Washington DC: Government Printing Office, 1919), 2:2782–85.

40. People's Council constitution quoted in *New York Call*, 7 September 1917, 4; WRI, "Declaration and Statement of Principles," in *International War Resistance through World War II*, edited by Charles Chatfield (New York and London: Garland, 1975), 57–68.

41. Fenner Brockway, *Inside the Left: Thirty Years of Platform, Press, Prison, and Parliament* (1942; reprint, London: George Allen & Unwin, 1947), 131.

42. Alonso, *Peace as a Women's Issue*.

43. For quotations in this paragraph, see Charles C. Moskos and John Whiteclay Chambers II, eds., *The New Conscientious Objection: From Sacred to Secular Resistance* (New York: Oxford University Press, 1993), vii, 3, 19–20, 196.

44. The 1940 draft law quoted in Mulford Q. Sibley and Philip E. Jacob, *Conscription of Conscience: The American State and the Conscientious Objector, 1940–1947* (Ithaca NY: Cornell University Press, 1952), appx. C, 487.

45. DeBenedetti, *Peace Reform in American History*, 109.

46. The phrase is borrowed from Lawrence S. Wittner, *Rebels against War: The American Peace Movement, 1933–1983*, rev. ed. (Philadelphia: Temple University Press, 1984).

CHAPTER 1

Peace Organizations

1.1. Woman's Peace Party, Preamble and Platform (10 January 1915)

[Founded in January 1915 and led by Jane Addams, the WPP was a pacifist—though not absolute pacifist—organization. Challenging separate spheres ideology, the WPP demanded a leadership role for women on war and peace issues. The WPP held that women, "the mother half of humanity," had a special concern with preserving human life. The WPP illustrates the leadership role of women in the "modern" peace movement. In 1919 the WPP would become the U.S. Section of WILPF. At its founding convention the WPP adopted the following preamble and platform.]

PREAMBLE

WE, WOMEN OF THE UNITED STATES, assembled in behalf of World Peace, grateful for the security of our own country, but sorrowing for the misery of all involved in the present struggle among warring nations, do hereby band ourselves together to demand that war be abolished.

Equally with men pacifists, we understand that planned-for, legalized, wholesale, human slaughter is today the sum of all villainies.

As women, we feel a peculiar moral passion of revolt against both the cruelty and the waste of war.

As women, we are especially the custodians of the life of the ages. We will not longer consent to its reckless destruction.

As women, we are particularly charged with the future of childhood and with the care of the helpless and the unfortunate. We will not longer endure without protest that added burden of maimed and invalid men and poverty stricken widows and orphans which war places upon us.

As women, we have builded by the patient drudgery of the past the basic foundation of the home and of peaceful industry. We will not longer accept without a protest that must be heard and heeded by men, that hoary evil which in an hour destroys the social structure that centuries of toil have reared.

As women, we are called upon to start each generation onward toward a better humanity. We will not longer tolerate without determined opposition that denial of the sovereignty of reason and justice by which war and all that makes for war today render impotent the idealism of the race.

Therefore, as human beings and the mother half of humanity, we demand that our right to be consulted in the settlement of questions concerning not alone the life of individuals but of nations be recognized and respected.

We demand that women be given a share in deciding between war and peace in all the courts of high debate—within the home, the school, the church, the industrial order, and the state.

So, protesting, and so demanding, we hereby form ourselves into a national organization to be called the Woman's Peace Party.

We hereby adopt the following as our platform of principles, some of the items of which have been accepted by a majority vote, and more of which have been the unanimous choice of those attending the conference that initiated the formation of this organization. We have sunk all differences of opinion on minor matters and given freedom of expression to a wide divergence of opinion in the details of our platform and in our statement of explanation and information, in a common desire to make our woman's protest against war and all that makes for war, vocal, commanding and effective. We welcome to our membership all who are in substantial sympathy with that fundamental purpose of our organization, whether or not they can accept in full our detailed statement of principles.

PLATFORM

THE PURPOSE of this Organization is to enlist all American women in arousing the nations to respect the sacredness of human life and to abolish war. The following is adopted as our platform:

1. The immediate calling of a convention of neutral nations in the interest of early peace.

2. Limitation of armaments and the nationalization of their manufacture.

3. Organized opposition to militarism in our own country.

4. Education of youth in the ideals of peace.

5. Democratic control of foreign policies.

6. The further humanizing of governments by the extension of the franchise to women.

7. "Concert of Nations" to supersede "Balance of Power."

8. Action toward the gradual organization of the world to substitute Law for War.

9. The substitution of an international police for rival armies and navies.

10. Removal of the economic causes of war.

11. The appointment by our Government of a commission of men and women, with an adequate appropriation, to promote international peace.

SOURCE: Woman's Peace Party Records, DG-43, reel 12.1, Swarthmore College Peace Collection, Swarthmore PA.

1.2. Anti-Preparedness Committee, Flyer [1915]

[By November 1915 social workers, religious leaders, writers, and other antiwar reformers associated with the Henry Street Settlement House, in New York City, formed the Anti-Preparedness Committee. Henry Street's founder, Lillian Wald, was chair; Crystal Eastman was secretary. In 1916 the committee evolved into the American Union Against Militarism.]

. . . We are a committee of American citizens formed to protest against the attempt to stampede this nation into a reckless program of military and naval expansion.

No danger of invasion threatens this country and there is no excuse for hasty, ill-considered action. We protest against the effort being made to divert the public mind from those **preparations for world peace** based on international agreement which it might be our country's privilege to initiate at the close of this War. And we protest against the effort being made to **divert public funds**, sorely needed in constructive programs for national health and well-being, into the manufacture of engines of death.

We are against all the various "preparedness" programs, **because they are extravagant, unnecessary, and contrary to all that is best in our national traditions.**

Believing that this statement represents the thoughtful conclusions of a large number of patriotic Americans, we urge them to support us in the following program:

GO SLOW ON PREPAREDNESS

Our immediate purpose is to prevent any unusual expenditure for armament during the present session of Congress.

STOP THE WASTE ON PREPAREDNESS

We demand public investigation of our present huge war budget so that every dollar now spent for the Army and Navy may bring 100 per cent of efficiency.

WHO WANTS PREPAREDNESS?

We stand for a Congressional investigation as to the sources of the insistent demand for a large increase in Army and Navy appropriations.

TAKING THE PROFIT OUT OF PREPAREDNESS

We stand for taking all possibility of private profit out of armament manufacture.

WHO IS TO PAY FOR PREPAREDNESS?

We hold that any increased expense for armament should be met by income and inheritance taxes, and not by taxes which place additional burdens on the poor.

We hold with the President that the time has come to develop the Monroe doctrine with its inherent dangers and difficulties, into a real Pan-American union, and therefore urge that a fifth Pan-American conference be called early in 1916, and that our delegates be instructed to recommend a federation of the twenty-one American republics in the interests of peace and democracy.

THE "YELLOW PERIL" AND PREPAREDNESS

Since the questions at issue between America and the Orient are serious and complex, we urge, as a rational approach to their solution, the appointment of a joint Government commission, representing Japan, China and the United States to study these questions and make recommendations to the various countries involved, after considering all interests concerned, local, national, and international. . . .

This is a National Crisis. If you are with us wire or write to your Congressman to Go Slow on "Preparedness."

SOURCE: American Union Against Militarism Records, DG-04, reel 10.1, Swarthmore College Peace Collection, Swarthmore PA.

1.3. Tracy D. Mygatt, "The Anti-Enlistment League" (30 May 1915)

[Jessie Wallace Hughan, Tracy D. Mygatt, and John Haynes Holmes organized the Anti-Enlistment League in 1915 to persuade young men not to enlist in the military. Operating out of Hughan's Brooklyn home, the group collected 3,500 pledges of war resistance in an effort to persuade the government not to intervene in the conflict. With U.S. entry in the war in April 1917, the league disbanded. This article explains the Anti-Enlistment League's background and includes its statement and pledge.]

. . . [W]e have been overzealous in wet-blanketing a definite peace policy for ourselves here in America. For all that it seems an excellent time to mind our own business and prepare now a means whereby to save the Socialist movement from the checkmate it has received abroad, we are more occupied in protesting we don't like war and resolving that the capitalist should be made to feed America first than in lining up our own free selves with a rigid, personal pledge that we will never enlist.

... For the unfortunate thing about our big protest meetings is this, that after the temporary uplifting that comes from any mass action, there comes the inevitable reaction: we find that we have not stopped the war; larger wheat shipments than ever are started to Belgium; Wall Street crows over a billion dollar boom. We had passed our resolution en masse, and en masse we were defeated: for, by the nature of the case, the mass action of the night before had been so general, so little specific, so loosely generated by the mass and so little upheld by the individual that when morning came and the masses had gone out, scattered to its individual workshops, there was nothing [unintelligible word] the worker but the tired consciousness of how little he counts anyway; and this feeling of futility is the last thing we Socialists want to cultivate.

Of course, we don't do it deliberately, but none the less it is there; every one of us has felt it and the insidious poison it works with our wills. To go on strike and to win a strike we have got to have mass action: to win a ballot box we have got to have mass action, and so do we have to have mass action to end war, but with a difference from the kind we have now, the difference whereby each man will have to come squarely face to face with his own responsibility, precisely as he now does when his shop strikes. . . .

The idea of anti-enlistment propaganda, as opposed to the militaristic, steadily growing under the leadership of such men as Colonel Roosevelt and Congressmen Gardner, first came to Jessie Wallace Hughan, the well-known writer of "American Socialism of the Present Day," and other socialist text-books. Early in the fall she published an article in The Call setting forth her idea and stressing the necessity of such a rigid anti-enlistment principle to offset the vicious discrimination between "offensive" and "defensive" warfare, then (and unhappily still) in vogue; and throughout the winter, with increasingly frequency, she has been addressing Socialist branches and other groups on the subject. . . .

Rev. John Haynes Holmes, . . . together with Miss Hughan and the writer, [constitute] the executive of the league. The organization is non-dues paying, hoping to carry on a wide propaganda by the voluntary financial and other assistance of those interested, like its founders, in constructive building for peace. A request for general ratification of the league's policy is at present writing before the [Socialist Party's] National Executive Committee, and it is earnestly hoped that Socialists all over the country will see in it one means the more to work for peace, and also an open sesame to propagate the Socialist position on the economic causes of war. For though the most intelligent sympathy with the league's propaganda will come from those already converted to Socialism, we believe that many non-Socialists who hate war strictly moral and religious grounds will attend a lecture of the Anti-Enlistment League, where they would not attend one on Socialism proper; and herein is the chance for plowing fresh fields, for though the Anti-Enlistment League is open to all, irrespective of political affiliation, its executive and its propaganda will be emphatically Socialist.

The preamble and pledge follows, and it seems scarcely necessary to add, on behalf of the little new league, that further information will be most gladly given and pledge blanks furnished to all those desiring them for propaganda purposes:

Statement—In view of the fact that the advocates of armament are gathering in league[s] of defense those who hold themselves ready to serve their country by killing other men, it seems that the time has come for a roll call of those of us who are prepared to serve our country by a refusal to engage in or indorse the murder called war.

The establishment of a new peace society is not contemplated, but rather the banding together in a personal policy of those whose opposition to war has become unconditional. Women, as well as men, are invited to enroll as refusing their approval to enlistment; but we ask the support of no persons who have not carefully weighed the arguments concerning war both offensive and defensive. . . .

I, being over 18 years of age, hereby pledge myself against enlistment as a volunteer for any military or naval service in international war, and against giving my approval to such enlistment on the part of others. . . .

SOURCE: *New York Call* (Magazine and Editorial Section), 30 May 1915, 7.

1.4. Fellowship of Reconciliation—USA, "The Fellowship of Reconciliation: Some General Considerations" [1915?]

[The U.S. branch of FOR was founded at a November 1915 conference in Garden City, New York. This conference appointed a Fellowship Committee to run FOR. Under the direction of FOR secretary Edward W. Evans, the committee established a temporary office at 125 East Twenty-Seventh Street, in New York City. The religious pacifist FOR sought to connect peace with social issues, a mark of the "modern" peace movement in America. Originally founded as a Protestant Christian organization, FOR had become an interfaith group by the early 1930s.]

ORIGIN

The Fellowship of Reconciliation originated in England during the closing months of 1914. It has since attained a membership of some four thousand men and women from all walks of life and with various Church affiliations, and has spread even to other nations of warring Europe. Its formation in the United States resulted from a recent visit of Dr. Henry T. Hodgkin, Chairman of the Fellowship in Great Britain, and widely known as a member of the Edinburgh Continuation Committee, the Student Christian Movement, and the Committee of the World Alliance of Churches for Promoting International Friendship. During this visit of some two months Dr. Hodgkin found an earnest response to the message of the Fellowship at various gatherings and among many personal friends. The reality and extent of the interest expressed led to a conference at Garden City, Long Island, November 11th and 12th, 1915, to consider the inauguration of the Movement in this country. This conference was attended by some eighty men and women representative of different social groups and various faiths. Although many were unknown to one another and were not united by any previous associations, they were drawn together by a common feeling that the time was ripe for a deeper expression of the Christian message. After the most serious consideration of what is involved they felt the profound need of uniting men and women of all nations in complete devotion to the principles and spirit for which the Fellowship stands. It was, therefore, determined to inaugurate the Fellowship in the United States.

CERTAIN DISTINCTIONS

The Movement thus launched differentiates itself from others occasioned by the war in certain important particulars. It is obviously not simply an addition to the already long list of peace societies. While there is no doubt that the members of the Fellowship find themselves unable to take part in war, the acceptance of the spirit of Christ as the only sufficient basis of society clearly involves for them very much more than the question of war. They view war not as an isolated phenomenon but as only one out of many unhappy consequences of the spiritual poverty of society. While it may at the present time be the most serious and most pressing problem confronting them, they conceive their task to be no less than a quest after an order of society in accordance with the mind of Christ.

The Fellowship has no program to offer as the one path toward this goal. It realizes that it is not dealing with a single problem, and that there is no one exclusive way through which the Spirit works. Its members are not committed to an organization, but are a group of persons who find the need of fellowship in devoting themselves to the expression of principles, a spirit and a message.

Nor are the members of the Fellowship under any delusion as to the extent of the gulf between the present state of society and the ideal conceived. Yet they squarely differ from those who hold that individuals are thereby excused from attempting the immediate realization of that ideal. To the members of the Fellowship the very failure of the world to accept these principles constitutes the chal-

lenge to apply them unflinchingly here and now in every relationship. Only by such daily faithfulness, they are convinced, can the
spirit of love be woven into the very fabric of personal and social life.

The ideals of the Fellowship are expressed in the statement of principles prepared for the enrollment of members. The central thought
is that Love as revealed and interpreted in the life, teachings and
death of Jesus Christ is the only sufficient basis of human society,
and that, therefore, our loyalty to our country, to humanity, to the
Church Universal and to Jesus Christ, our Lord and Master, calls
us to a life service for the enthronement of Love in personal, social,
commercial, national and international life, with all that this implies.

It is obviously impossible to make any comprehensive statement
of all the methods by which individuals may work for the attainment of this ideal. Those who are in earnest will find their own ways
of expressing themselves in word and deed. The principal spheres of
effort may be broadly indicated as follows:

1. The chief method is a life lived in complete loyalty to Christ. This
implies, as the Fellowship believes, the full acceptance and unflinching application of his revolutionary principle of Love, here and now,
in every relationship. It demands confidence in the power of Love
progressively wrought out in human society to overcome evil, and
a resolute refusal to use even for such a purpose any means which
in itself involves a violation of Love. For this reason members of the
Fellowship feel themselves unable to take part in war. This is not to
deny, however, that physical force has legitimate uses consistent with
the principle of Love.

2. Any sincere attempt to establish the Christian principle of Love
in the various group relationships of the industrial and social order,
and in political and international life is clearly comprehended by the
Fellowship ideal. Members are encouraged to consider opportunities for definite work in these fields.

3. The tremendous difficulties of living a Life truly expressive of
Christs' [sic] spirit, and of establishing his Love in the complicated

relationships of modern society call for an endeavor to discover the full implications of the principle of Love as applied not only to the questions of war and international relationships but to all the great problems of industrial and social life. This can be done by prayer and study, both individually and in groups, and there is a very real opportunity for service in the development of local groups for this purpose.*

4. While there is no desire to press for a large nominal membership, the Movement needs the co-operation of all who are in sympathy and substantial agreement with the position of the Fellowship. The responsibility for securing such co-operation must of necessity rest largely with individual members, who should, therefore, as they have opportunity, seek to express the message of the Fellowship in a personal way, by conversation, correspondence and the use of literature.* . . .

 * See "Suggestions as to Methods of Work."

SOURCE: Fellowship of Reconciliation Records, DG-13, section II, series A-1, box 1, Swarthmore College Peace Collection, Swarthmore PA.

1.5. People's Council of America, "Resolutions" (30–31 May 1917)

[In May 1917 the First American Conference for Democracy and Terms of Peace was held at Garden Theater in New York. Organized mainly by pacifists and socialists, this mass meeting attracted fifteen thousand people. The conference adopted resolutions calling for the U.S. government to announce its war aims: a democratic and nonpunitive peace with Germany along lines proposed by President Wilson and by the Russian provisional government that replaced the czar after the March 1917 revolution, an international organization to maintain world peace, and the preservation of civil liberties at home.]

[Resolutions Adopted by the First American Conference for Democracy and Terms of Peace]

PREAMBLE

United in our love for America, we are convinced that we can best serve our country by urging upon our countrymen the adoption of the following policies:

1. PEACE

The Conference favors an early, general and democratic peace, to be secured through negotiation in harmony with the principles outlined by the President of the United State[s] and by revolutionary Russia, and accepted substantially by the progressive and democratic forces of France, England, Italy, Germany, Austria and other countries, namely:

(a) No forcible annexation of territory.

(b) No punitive indemnities.

(c) Free development of all nationalities.

We favor international reorganization for the maintenance of peace. As steps leading thereto, we suggest: The adjudication of disputes among nations; simultaneous disarmament; freedom of the seas and international waterways; protection of small nations; and other similar measures.

2. STATEMENT OF TERMS

We urge the Government of the United States immediately to announce its war aims in definite and concrete terms upon the above principles and to make efforts to induce the Allied countries to make similar declarations, thus informing our public for what concrete objects they are called upon to fight, and thereby forcing a definite expression of war aims on the part of the Central Powers.

We demand that this country shall make peace the moment its announced aims shall have been achieved, and that it shall not carry on war for the territorial and imperialistic ambitions of other countries. Further, we demand that it shall make no agreement with other governments limiting its freedom of action nor any agreement or understanding looking toward an economic war after the war.

3. AMERICAN LIBERTIES

The first victims of war are the people's liberties. It was to preserve these liberties that our forefathers framed the first amendment to the constitution, forbidding Congress to abridge "the freedom of speech or of the press, or the right of the people peacefully to assemble and to petition the government for a redress of grievances."

We hereby protest to the President and Congress against the abridgement of these rights, and call upon the American people to defend them. We shall oppose with all legal means at our disposal the censorship of newspapers and of other printed matter or interference with their distribution by the postal department. . . .

We also declare that all Americans are entitled to passports to neutral countries. . . .

Secret diplomacy must be abolished. We demand democratic control of our foreign policy. We call for a referendum on questions of war and conscription. We insist on discussion in Congress, in the press and in public meetings of the terms of all alliances, agreements and treaties. . . .

4. CONSCRIPTION

We pledge ourselves to work for the repeal of all laws for compulsory military training and compulsory service and to oppose the enactment of all such laws in the future.

Inasmuch as we believe conscription laws to be unconstitutional (violating the Thirteenth Amendment, to the Constitution of the United States) we appeal to the Congress of the United States to amend the Conscription Act so as to grant exemption to all conscientious objectors, whether or not they be members of recognized religious organizations. . . .

SOURCE: Organizing Committee[:] People's Council, *Resolutions of the First American Conference for Democracy and Terms of Peace[:] New York City[:] May 30 and 31, 1917* (New York: Organizing Committee[:] People's Council, [1917]), copy in People's Council of America for Democracy and Peace Records, 1917–19, CDG-A, reel 3.1, Swarthmore College Peace Collection, Swarthmore PA.

1.6. American Union Against Militarism, "To the People of New York" (1917)

[The American Union Against Militarism, among the most influential antiwar groups, opposed preparedness and U.S. intervention. This AUAM advertisement appeared in newspapers.]

To the People of New York:

We challenge those who want war against Germany to answer this, point by point.

1. In consequence of indefensible wrongs committed against us by Germany in her attempt to starve England, President Wilson has declared and is just putting into operation a policy of "armed neutrality." This means the vigorous defense of American ships and American rights on the sea *without involving America in a European quarrel.* We ought not to abandon this policy before we have tried it.

2. Our entrance into the war would lengthen rather than shorten it. The bankruptcy of England, the starvation of Germany, together will bring a negotiated peace. But if we go into the war and back up England's credit she will renew her determination to go on until Germany is crushed. This will renew Germany's determination to wage war to the end, and the conflict will be dragged out indefinitely.

3. We cannot destroy German militarism by defeating Germany. Militarism is a condition that can be destroyed *only from within* by the democratic impulses of the people themselves. France tried to destroy German militarism *from the outside* in 1806. Under Napoleon she crushed Germany more completely than the Allies can ever hope to crush her now. That was not the end, but the beginning of modern German militarism. Fight Germany to a finish, to a "dictated peace," and you will only inflame the military passions of her people and strengthen the power of Prussian tyranny over them.

4. By going to war, we cannot vindicate those points of international law which give us a legal right to declare war on Germany. The whole body of international law has broken down among the belligerents. England and Germany have both violated international law. Nations in a death struggle always violate it. International law cannot be upheld by joining in such a struggle.

Thus without the possibility of doing honor to our country, or of shortening the agony of the world, or of destroying militarism, or of upholding international law, we should be entering into war for no intelligible gain whatever.

5. Not only should we gain nothing by going to war, but we should lose our historic opportunity to bring this war to an end by mediation, and to play the decisive part in establishing a secure organization of nations of the world. President Wilson defined the highest aim of this country in his speech to the Senate, demanding peace without victory and a league of the nations to insure peace. If we enter the war our hope of fulfilling this aim is forever lost.

6. Besides losing our opportunity to serve the world we should lose the best of our own possessions—democracy and individual liberty. True democracy and liberty cannot live in a militarized state. Conscription follows war, universal militarization of the mind follows conscription, the suppression of free speech, the enslavement of public opinion, the suspension of the writ of *Habeas Corpus* follow that, as they have in every belligerent country. War means absolute command; it means dictatorship. In the effort to conquer Prussia, England is being prussianized, and we should be prussianized even more rapidly, for the traditions of individual liberty are less anciently established among us.

We are the only great people left who are free from those habits of servile obedience to authority which are the direct result of war and militarism. At this crisis and parting of the ways let us have the courage to stand up for our liberty and independent manhood against the menace of a militarized America. We cannot bring democracy to Europe by going to war. *We can preserve Democracy in this country* by staying out.

This is your patriotic duty. Uphold the President in his policy of armed neutrality. Hold Congress to that policy. We must act only for defense. Let there be no recognition and no declaration of a state of war.

WRITE YOUR CONGRESSMAN IMMEDIATELY THAT THERE MUST BE NO DECLARATION OF WAR, TELEGRAPH THE PRESIDENT . . .

SOURCE: American Union Against Militarism Records, DG-04, reel 10.2, Swarthmore College Peace Collection, Swarthmore PA.

1.7. Woman's Peace Party, "Eight Alternatives to War" [before April 1917]

[This flyer appears to have been published by the Woman's Peace Party and other antiwar organizations. Although the w pp condemned German submarine warfare, it opposed going to war over the issue and, in this flyer, offered nonmilitary alternatives to U.S. intervention.]

Eight Alternatives to War

AVOID HASTY ACTION

1st. We can postpone until the war is over the settlement of any dispute which cannot now be settled by peaceful means.

KEEP OUT OF WAR-ZONE

2nd. We can keep American citizens off belligerent ships.

NO DEALING IN CONTRABAND

3rd. We can refuse clearance to ships of the United States and other neutral countries carrying contraband and passengers on the same ship.

PATRIOTS HAVE DUTIES AS WELL AS RIGHTS

4th. We can repudiate responsibility for American citizens who are willing to jeopardize the nation's peace by traveling as seamen with contraband on American or neutral vessels.

RUN NO RISKS FOR THE NATION

5th. We can, if necessary, keep all American vessels out of the danger zone for the present, just as the Mayor of a city keeps citizens in their homes when a mob is in possession of the street.

LET THE PEOPLE SPEAK

6th. Congress, which has exclusive power to declare war, can submit the declaration of war to a referendum vote.

A NEUTRAL CONFERENCE

7th. Even if an American ship is sunk *with loss of American lives,* we must not go to war. There is an immediate alternative. We, the greatest neutral nation, should call into conference all the neutrals whose rights are equally affected with our own and determine upon some joint method of maintaining and defending those joint rights. Acting in concert, all the neutral nations may be able to determine upon some method of enforcing their rights without recourse to war.

STOP THE WAR IN EUROPE

8th. A direct offer of mediation to the European belligerents may be made either by the United States alone or by the Conference of Neutrals. The Allies have stated terms of peace, the Germans have offered to negotiate; let the neutrals bring them together.

If You are With Us, wire your Congressmen and Senators to Further these Plans and Keep Us Out of War

SOURCE: Woman's Peace Party Records, DG-43, reel 12.3, Swarthmore College Peace Collection, Swarthmore PA.

1.8. Friends National Peace Committee, "A Message from the Religious Society of Friends (Quakers) in America" (May 1917)

[Headquartered in Philadelphia, the Friends National Peace Committee, founded in 1915 and the predecessor of the American Friends Service Committee, adopted this statement at a March 1917 meeting in Winona Lake, Indiana. Not all Quakers opposed World War I, however, and Friends who supported both the war and President Wilson issued a dissenting statement in March 1918.]

To Our Fellow Citizens:

In this time of crisis when our country's highest good is the common aim of all, we voice this deep conviction of patriotic duty.

We rejoice that even at this time, when the world is crazed by war, so many men are judging war by moral and spiritual standards, and by ideals of sacrifice. The causes for which men fight—liberty, justice and peace—are noble and Christian causes. But the method of war is unchristian and immoral. War itself violates law, justice, liberty and peace, the very ends for which alone its tragic cost might be justified.

Further, the method of war is ineffective to these ends. Might does not decide the right, ideals cannot be maintained by force, nor can evil overcome evil. True national honor is a nation's own integrity and unselfish service. Only unswerving honesty and self-control maintain it. Rights, the rights of all, are securely defended between nations as between individuals by mutual confidence, not suspicion; by universal cooperation and law, not by private armed defence.

The alternative to war is not inactivity and cowardice. It is the irresistible and constructive power of good-will. True patriotism at this time calls not for a resort to the futile methods of war, but for the invention and practice on a gigantic scale of new methods of conciliation and altruistic service. The present intolerable situation among nations demands an unprecedented expression of organized national good-will.

Unpractical though such ideas may seem, experience has taught that ideals can be realized if we have faith to practice now what all men hope for in the future. The American Nation, as a more perfect union of States, as a melting pot of races, as a repeated victor through peace, has proved practical the methods of generosity and patience. Throughout many years of an adventurous belief in the Christian principle of human brotherhood, the Society of Friends has seen the triumph of good-will in all forms of human crisis.

The peoples of every land are longing for the time when love shall conquer hate, when cooperation shall replace conflict, when war shall be no more. This time will come only when the people of some great nation dare to abandon the outworn traditions of international dealing and to stake all upon persistent good-will.

We are the nation and now is the time. This is America's supreme opportunity.

Unflinching good-will, no less than war, demands courage, patriotism, and self-sacrifice. To such a victory over itself, to such a leadership of the world, to such an embodiment of the matchless, invincible power of good-will, this otherwise tragic hour challenges our country.

SOURCE: *Masses*, May 1917, 2.

1.9. American Union Against Militarism, "Peace or War? Let the People Say Which It Shall Be" (1917)

[The AUAM argued that American citizens should decide whether the United States should go to war. Moreover, the AUAM sought to pressure Congress to oppose U.S. intervention by mobilizing anti-war public opinion. Prior to the U.S. declaration of war in April 1917, the AUAM organized a postcard referendum campaign to give U.S. citizens a democratic voice in matters of war and peace.]

Peace or War? Let The People Say Which It Shall Be

To Every American Citizen:

For two and a half years President Wilson has given the country an inspiring example of patience and thoughtful deliberation. We must now share his burden and his responsibility. It is necessary in this crisis that members of Congress—in whom is vested the right to declare war—should know what the people want them to do. We ask you to answer YES or NO to the two essential questions on the attached postal card and mail it at once to your Congressman in Washington. . . .

(Don't forget to write in the name of your Congressman on attached card before mailing your vote.)

NATIONAL REFERENDUM ON PEACE OR WAR.   YES   NO

(Note: In modifying her war zone note Germany has offered safe passage for all American passenger ships which keep to a prescribed course and which our government guarantees free from contraband.)

(1). Do you think we should enter this war in order to uphold our legal right to go into the war zone regardless of these conditions?

(Note: A national ADVISORY referendum is not unconstitutional and could be carried out by the census bureau, through the post-masters, in twenty-five days.)

(2). Do you think that the people should be consulted by referendum before Congress declares war—except in case of threatened invasion?

Sign here: Name _____

                   Address _____

SOURCE: American Union Against Militarism Records, DG-04, reel 10.1, Swarthmore College Peace Collection, Swarthmore PA.

1.10. Committee for Democratic Control, "Referendum" (1917)

[The Committee for Democratic Control was formed to counter the American Rights League and other interventionist groups. It sought to prevent U.S. intervention in World War I by publishing appeals in the *New Republic* and newspapers calling for a national referendum on a U.S. declaration of war—and often published these appeals jointly with the Woman's Peace Party of New York City.]

Referendum

A LETTER TO THE PUBLIC:—The country is in imminent peril of entering the world-war. The decision our government makes will be the most momentous in our history. It is a time for clear thought. Let us remember that the breaking of diplomatic relations does not mean inevitable war. Neither does an overt act on the part of Germany mean immediate war. For we run no danger of invasion. We have none of the urgency of sudden self-defense. We are in the most fortunate position to take a calm and critical survey of what hostilities will mean. We still have time to decide consciously and clear-sightedly whether we wish to shatter the whole structure of our position as the one powerful neutral. "Democratic control of foreign policy" is one of the new instruments with which all men of good-will hope to scotch the war-madness of the future. We have now the one chance in all history to test out this principle.

The public which elected the President as the leader of a liberal democracy should be consulted before our government takes a step which to millions will seem like the collapse of all our hopes and ideals. In his foreign policy, in Columbia, in Mexico, in Europe, the President has stood as the courageous and patient defender of democratic control. But now, inasmuch as the Constitution places the decision of war and peace in the hands of the people's congressional representatives, the people themselves must speak. Theirs, in the last analysis, is the immeasurable burden of war and the responsibility of assuming it. . . .

Prior, therefore, to a declaration of war, or to any engaging in hostilities, Congress should take measures to secure a nation-wide referendum on the question of our entrance. This should be preceded by a clear and explicit statement from the President as to the policy to which we are being committed, and the probable consequences. . . . Shall we surrender to war, when we should be working for a warless world? Shall the crisis find us numb, except for the most elementary of patriotic thrills? It is time for speaking. Do we want this war? Do we want it for any of the possible purposes that exist? Can we justify war for anything short of national self-defense? In any other cause are we ready to fling frantically away our international efficacy for good?

If you want a referendum before Congress declares war (except in case of invasion) write or wire your Congressman today. . . .

SOURCE: American Union Against Militarism Records, DG-04, reel 10.2, Swarthmore College Peace Collection, Swarthmore PA.

1.11. American Union Against Militarism, "To Men of Military Age Opposed to War!" [May 1917]

[Besides opposing U.S. intervention, the AUAM worked to protect civil liberties and the right of conscientious objection during wartime. In July 1917 the AUAM created a Civil Liberties Bureau; in October this bureau became the National Civil Liberties Board, an independent agency led by Roger Baldwin. Meanwhile, peace activists disagreed over how to respond to conscription. Some took the position that draft-eligible men should defy the law and refuse to register. Others argued that opponents should respect the law, register as COs, and rely on the courts to protect their right of conscience and dissent— and that is the position expressed in this AUAM flyer.]

To Men Of Military Age Opposed To War!

Register June 5th—and when you register, state your protest against participation in war

You can only make your protest effective by registering. See that the clerk puts down your claim to exemption from service as a "conscientious objector to war"

Read the following statement signed by men and women active in the anti-militarist movement:

The presence in this country of a considerable number of so-called conscientious objectors is generally known. In recent weeks these objectors, confronted by the Conscription Act, have been undecided as to whether they should make known their conscientious scruples against war by refusing to register, or refusing military service (as distinct from alternative civil service which may conceivably be secured hereafter) when actually drafted by the process of selection.

In realization of the necessity of concerted action in this crisis and in answer to appeals for counsel in the matter, the undersigned, after consideration which has in some cases reversed original opinion, unite in stating their belief **that all conscientious objectors should register and indicate in the way provided by the law their personal opposition to participation in war.**

Obedience to law, to the utmost limit of conscience, is the basis of good citizenship. Public understanding and sympathy, in this case, should not be alienated by misdirected action. The moral issue involved should not be confused. The opportunity provided by the act to specify one's claims to exemption from military service should not be missed by those who desire to state their objection to that service on religious or other conscientious grounds.

We therefore urge all conscientious objectors to register, stating that protest in such form as they may think best, at that time. We request that the widest possible publicity be given to this statement. . . .

A bureau of aid and advice for conscientious objectors has been established by the American Union, working in co-operation with representatives of other interested agencies. Those wishing to register [as a conscientious objector] with the bureau sign here and mail in. Contributions for the support of the bureau will be warmly appreciated. . . .

SOURCE: American Union Against Militarism Records, DG-04, reel 10.2, Swarthmore College Peace Collection, Swarthmore PA.

CHAPTER 2

Socialists, Anarchists, and Wobblies

2.1. Emma Goldman, "Preparedness: The Road to Universal Slaughter" (1915)

[Emma Goldman was a leading anarchist who attributed the conflict to capitalism and the state. She first published this essay in *Mother Earth* in December 1915 and then, with minor revisions, issued the essay as a pamphlet. In 1919 the United States deported her and other radicals to the Soviet Union. This version is from the pamphlet.]

Ever since the beginning of the European conflagration the whole human race almost has fallen into the deathly grip of the war anesthesis, overcome by the mad teaming fumes of a blood soaked chloroform. Indeed, with the exception of some savage tribes, who know nothing of Christian religion or of brotherly love, and who also know nothing of dreadnaughts, submarines, munition manufacture and war loans, the rest of the race is under this terrible narcosis. The human mind seems to be conscious of but one thing, murderous speculation. Ammunition! Ammunition! O, Lord, thou who rulest heaven and earth, thou God of love, of mercy and of justice, provide us with enough ammunition to destroy our enemy. Such is the prayer which is ascending daily to the Christian heaven.

Just like cattle, panic-stricken in the face of fire, throw themselves into the very flames, so all of the European people have fallen over each other into the devouring flames of the furies of war, and America, pushed to the very brink by unscrupulous politicians, by ranting demagogues, and by military sharks, is preparing for the same terrible feat. In the face of this approaching disaster, it behooves men and women not yet overcome by the war madness to raise their voice of protest, to call the attention of the people to the crime and outrage which are about to be perpetrated upon them.

America is essentially the melting pot. No national unit composing it, is in a position to boast of superior race purity, particular historic mission, or higher culture. Yet the jingoes and war speculators are filling the air with the sentimental slogan of hypocritical nationalism, "America for Americans," "America first, last, and all the time." This cry has caught the popular fancy from one end of the country to another. In order to maintain America, military preparedness must be engaged in at once. A billion dollars of the people's sweat and blood is to be expended for dreadnaughts and submarines for the army and the navy, all to protect this precious America.

The pathos of it all is that the America which is to be protected by a huge military force is not the America of the people, but that of the privileged class; the class which robs and exploits the masses, and controls their lives from the cradle to the grave. No less pathetic is it that so few people realize that preparedness never leads to peace, but that it is indeed the road to universal slaughter.

With the cunning methods used by the scheming diplomats and military cliques of Germany to saddle the masses with Prussian militarism, the American military ring with its Roosevelts, its Garrisons, its Daniels, and lastly its Wilsons, are moving the very heavens to place the militaristic heel upon the necks of the American people, and, if successful, will hurl America into the storm of blood and tears now devastating the countries of Europe.

Forty years ago Germany proclaimed the slogan: "Germany above everything. Germany for the Germans, first, last and always. We want peace; therefore we must prepare for war. Only a well armed and thoroughly prepared nation can maintain peace, can command respect, can be sure of its national integrity." And Germany continued to prepare, thereby forcing the other nations to do the same. The terrible European war is only the culminating fruition of the hydra-headed gospel, military preparedness.

Since the war began, miles of paper and oceans of ink have been used to prove the barbarity, the cruelty, the oppression of Prussian militarism. Conservatives and radicals alike are giving their support to the Allies for no other reason than to help crush that militarism, in the presence of which, they say, there can be no peace or progress in Europe. But though America grows fat on the manufacture of munitions and war loans to the Allies to help crush Prussianism the same cry is now being raised in America which, if carried into national action, would build up an American militarism far more terrible than German or Prussian militarism could ever be, and that because nowhere in the world has capitalism become so brazen in its greed and nowhere is the state so ready to kneel at the feet of capital.

Like a plague, the mad spirit is sweeping the country, infesting the clearest heads and staunchest hearts with the deathly germ of militarism. National security leagues, with cannon as their emblem of protection, naval leagues with women in their lead have sprung up all over the country, women who boast of representing the gentler sex, women who in pain and danger bring forth life and yet are ready to dedicate it to the Moloch War. Americanization societies with well known liberals as members, they who but yesterday decried the patriotic clap-trap of to-day, are now lending themselves to befog the minds of the people and to help build up the same destructive institutions in America which they are directly and indirectly helping to pull down in Germany—militarism, the destroyer of youth, the raper of women, the annihilator of the best in the race, the very mower of life.

Even Woodrow Wilson, . . . has now joined his worthy colleagues in the jingo movement, echoing their clamor for preparedness and their howl of "America for Americans." The difference between Wilson and Roosevelt is this: Roosevelt, the bully, uses the club; Wilson, the historian, the college professor, wears the smooth polished university mask, but underneath it he, like Roosevelt, has but one aim, to serve the big interests, to add to those who are growing phenomenally rich by the manufacture of military supplies. . . .

. . . How is a military drilled and [how are] trained people to defend freedom, peace and happiness? . . .

. . . You cannot conduct war with equals; you cannot have militarism with free born men; you must have slaves, automatons, machines, obedient disciplined creatures, who will move, act, shoot and kill at the command of their superiors. That is preparedness, and nothing else.

It has been reported that among the speakers before the Navy League was Samuel Gompers. If that is true, it signalizes the greatest outrage upon labor at the hands of its own leaders. . . .

Already militarism has been acting its bloody part in every economic conflict, with the approval and support of the state. Where was the protest of Washington when "our men, women and children" were killed in Ludlow? Where was that high sounding outraged protest contained in the note to Germany? Or is there any difference in killing "our men, women and children" in Ludlow or on the high seas? Yes, indeed. The men, women and children at Ludlow were working people, belonging to the disinherited of the earth, foreigners who had to be given a taste of the glories of Americanism, while the passengers of the Lusitania represented wealth and station—therein lies the difference. Preparedness, therefore, will only add to the power of the privileged few and help them to subdue, to enslave and crush labor. Surely Gompers must know that, and if he joins the howl of the military clique, he must stand condemned as a traitor to the cause of labor. . . .

I am no more pro-German than pro-Ally. As an Anarchist I refute both, as the "two thieves who are too cowardly to fight." . . .

It will be with preparedness as it has been with all other institutions in our confused life which were created for the good of the people and which have accomplished the very reverse. Supposedly, America is to prepare for peace; but in reality it will prepare for the cause of war.

It always has been thus—all through blood-stained history, and it will continue until nation will refuse to fight against nation, and until the people of the world will stop preparing for slaughter. . . . It is imperative that the American workers realize this before they are driven by the jingoes into the madness that is forever haunted by the spectre of danger and invasion; they must know that to prepare for peace means to invite war, means to unloose the furies of death over land and seas.

That which has driven the masses of Europe into the trenches and to the battlefields is not their inner longing for war; it must be traced to the cut-throat competition for military equipment, for more efficient armies, for larger warships, for more powerful cannon. You cannot build up a standing army and then throw it back into a box like tin soldiers. Armies equipped to the teeth with weapons, with highly developed instruments of murder and backed by their military interests, have their own dynamic functions. . . .

Militarism consumes the strongest and most productive elements of each nation. Militarism swallows the largest part of the national revenue. Almost nothing is spent on education, art, literature and science compared with the amount devoted to militarism in times of peace, while in times of war everything else is set at naught: all life stagnates, all effort is curtailed; the very sweat and blood of the masses are used to feed this insatiable monster—militarism. . . . In this civilized purpose and method, militarism is sustained by the state, protected by the laws of the land, is fostered by the home and the school, and glorified by public opinion. In other words, the function of militarism is to kill. It cannot live except through murder.

But the most dominant factor of military preparedness and the one which inevitably leads to war, is the creation of group interests, which consciously and deliberately work for the increase of armament whose purposes are furthered by creating the war hysteria. This group interest embraces all those engaged in the manufacture and sale of munitions and in military equipment for personal gain and profit. The family Krupp, for instance, which owns the largest cannon munition plant in the world; . . . had in its employ officials of the highest military position, not only in Germany, but in France and in other countries. Everywhere its emissaries have been at work, systematically inciting national hatreds and antagonisms; creating invasion hysteria.

It is not at all unlikely that the history of the present war will trace its origin to the same international murder trust. . . . Can we of today not profit by the cause which led to the European war, can we not learn that it was preparedness, thorough and efficient preparedness on the part of Germany and the other countries for military aggrandizement and material gain; above all can we not realize that preparedness in America must and will lead to the same result, the same barbarity, the same senseless sacrifice of life? Is America to follow suit, is it to be turned over to the American Krupps, the American military cliques? It almost seems so when one hears the jingo howls of the press, the blood and thunder tirades of bully Roosevelt, the sentimental twaddle of our college-bred President.

The more reason for those who still have a spark of libertarianism and humanity left to cry out against this great crime, against the outrage now being prepared and imposed upon the American people. It is not enough to claim being neutral; a neutrality which sheds crocodile tears with one eye and keeps the other riveted upon the profits from war supplies and war loans, is not neutrality. It is a hypocritical cloak to cover the countries' crimes. Nor is it enough to join the bourgeois pacifists who proclaim peace among the nations while helping to perpetuate the war among the classes, a war which in reality, is at the bottom of all other wars.

It is this war of the classes that we must concentrate upon, and in that connection the war against false values, against evil institutions, against all social atrocities. Those who appreciate the urgent need of co-operating in great struggles must oppose military preparedness imposed by the state and capitalism for the destruction of the masses. They must organize the preparedness of the masses for the overthrow of both capitalism and the state. . . . That alone leads to economic and social freedom, and does away with all wars, all crimes, and all injustice.

SOURCE: Emma Goldman, *Preparedness: The Road to Universal Slaughter* (New York: Mother Earth, [1915?]).

2.2. Socialist Party of America, "Peace Program of the Socialist Party" (May 1915)

[Meeting in Chicago on 13–18 May 1915, the SP's national committee lamented the German torpedoing of the *Lusitania* and the killing of hundreds of civilians. The sp argued that this tragedy showed the "fiendish savagery of warfare" and should inspire not revenge but the determination to "maintain peace and civilization at any cost." Blaming the war on capitalism, the committee warned "fellow citizens" to ignore militarists' attempts "to stampede" America into war, advocated the repudiation of war debts, and urged workers not to fight or manufacture weapons. The committee also issued the following peace program.]

. . . The supreme crisis in human history is upon us.

European civilization is engulfed. The world's peace is shattered. The future of the human race is imperilled.

The immediate causes of the war are obvious. Previous wars and terms of settlement which created lasting hatreds and bred thoughts of revenge; imperialism and commercial rivalries; the Triple Alliance and the Triple Entente dividing all Europe into two hostile camps; secret intrigue of diplomats and lack of democracy; vast systems of military and naval equipment; fear and suspicion bred and spread by a vicious jingo press in all nations; powerful armament interests that reap rich harvests out of havoc and death, all these have played their sinister parts. But back of these factors lie the deeper and more fundamental causes, causes rooted in the very system of capitalist production.

Every capitalist nation on earth exploits its people. The wages received by the workers are insufficient to enable them to purchase all they need for the proper sustenance of their lives. A surplus of commodities accumulates. The capitalists cannot consume all. It must be exported to foreign countries.

. . . The capitalists are constantly forced to look for new and foreign fields of investment. . . .

Hence arise the commercial struggles between the nations, the rivalries for the acquisition of foreign colonies, the efforts to defend and extend the oversea "possessions"; the policies of imperialism, the conflicts for commercial supremacy, ever growing more intense and fierce as the nations expand and the world's field of conquest narrows. Hence arise the policies of armaments every year more immense and monstrous. Hence arise the strategy, the intrigues of secret diplomacy, till all the world is involved in a deadly struggle for the capture and control of the world market.

Thus capitalism, inevitably leading to commercial rivalry and imperialism and functioning through the modern state with its vast armaments, secret diplomacies and undemocratic governments, logically leads to war. . . .

For more than half a century the Socialist movement has warned the world of this impending tragedy. With every power at their command the Socialists of all nations have worked to prevent it. But the warning has gone unheeded and the Socialist propaganda against imperialism, militarism and war has been ignored by the ruling powers and the majority of the people of all nations. . . .

To the Socialist and labor forces in all the world and to all who cherish the ideals of justice, we make our appeal, believing that out of the ashes of this mighty conflagration will yet arise the deeper internationalism and the great democracy and peace.

As measures calculated to bring about these results we urge:

I). TERMS OF PEACE AT THE CLOSE OF THE PRESENT WAR must be based on the following provisions:

1. No indemnities.

2. No transfer of territory except upon the consent and by vote of the people within the territory.

3. All countries under foreign rule be given political independence if demanded by the inhabitants of such countries.

II. INTERNATIONAL FEDERATION—THE UNITED STATES OF THE WORLD:

1. An international congress with legislative and administrative powers over international affairs and with permanent committees in place of present secret diplomacy.

2. Special Commissions to consider international disputes as they may arise. The decisions of such commissions to be enforced without resort to arms. . . .

3. International ownership and control of strategic waterways such as the Dardanelles, the Straits of Gibraltar and the Suez, Panama and Kiel Canals.

4. Neutralization of the seas.

III. DISARMAMENT.

1. Universal disarmament as speedily as possible.

2. Abolition of manufacture of arms and munitions of war for private profit, and prohibition of exportation of arms, war equipments and supplies from one country to another.

3. No increase in existing armaments under any circumstances.

4. No appropriations for military or naval purposes.

IV. EXTENSION OF DEMOCRACY.

1. Political democracy.

(a) Abolition of secret diplomacy and democratic control of foreign policies.

(b) Universal suffrage, including woman suffrage.

2. Industrial democracy.

RADICAL SOCIAL CHANGES IN ALL COUNTRIES TO ELIMINATE ECONOMIC CAUSES FOR WAR, such as will be calculated to gradually take the industrial and commercial processes of the nations out of the hands of the irresponsible capitalist class and place them in the hands of the people, to operate them collectively for the satisfaction of human wants and not for private profits, in co-operation and harmony and not through competition and war. . . .

SOURCE: Alexander Trachtenberg, ed., *The American Socialists and the War* (New York: Rand School of Social Science, 1917), 16–19.

2.3. Socialist Suffrage Committee, Antipreparedness Statement (20 May 1916)

[On 13 May 1916 New York hosted a massive Citizens Preparedness Parade that lasted twelve hours. Some 135,000 citizens participated, including several thousand women. In this statement the Socialist Suffrage Committee couched its opposition to preparedness, militarism, and war in socialist and gendered terms. The IWW newspaper *Solidarity* printed the statement.]

. . . Much has been said and written about the 20,000 women who took part in the New York "Citizens Preparedness Parade." But little has been said or written about the following leaflet distributed in large numbers during the "preparedness" week in the aforementioned city:

Women Beware! Beware lying newspapers! Beware politicians calling "Preparedness." Beware gun-making patriots! Beware fear!

Women of America, your boys are in danger! The whole American people are in danger! Of invasion? No! There is no danger whatever of invasion.

But there is danger of preparedness, and through preparedness, of war. Militarists demand "preparedness" for peace. But Europe was "prepared" and every home in Europe suffers today.

The more preparedness agitation the militarists can stir up, the more guns and armor-plate they can scare the government into buying.

Unarmed peace does not pay the munition makers.

Big business wants Mexican and South American markets. This is the biggest reason of all for armies and navies.

Fight "Preparedness"! Fight it in the public schools: Military drill leads to murder.

Fight "Preparedness." Fight it in the Boy Scouts: Target practice ends in real shooting.

Fight "Preparedness"! Refuse to consent to the enlistment of your sons in the army and navy. The soldier's life, in time of peace is full of temptation, in War it is brutal and murderous.

SOURCE: *Solidarity*, 20 May 1916, 3.

2.4. Ralph H. Chaplin, "Preparedness" (24 June 1916)

[Ralph Chaplin was a songwriter and, from March to September 1917, the editor of *Solidarity*, a major IWW newspaper. He was convicted and sentenced to twenty years in prison under the Espionage Act, at the 1917 IWW trial in Chicago. After Chaplin served time in Fort Leavenworth, the government commuted his sentence in 1923. In this poem he indicts preparedness, patriotism, capitalism, and war.]

For freedom die? but we were never free
    Save but to drudge and starve or strike and feel
    The bite of bullets and the thrust of steel.
For freedom die, while all the land can see
    How strikers writhe beneath thy crushing heel
And mothers shudder at the thought of thee!
    For freedom die . . . . ?

Defend the flag? beneath whose reeking fold
    The gun-men of our masters always came
    To burn and rape and murder in thy name!
Defend the flag whose honor has been sold
    And soiled until it is a thing of shame—
The brazen paramour of Greed and Gold—
    Defend the flag . . . . ?

Protect our land? we, who are dispossessed.
    And own not space to sleep in when we die!
    The continent is held by thieves on high—
The brood of vipers sheltered at thy breast.
    Your "liberty" is but a loathsome lie:
We have no homes nor any place to rest—.
    Defend our land . . . . ?

Resist the foe, we shall! from sea to sea
    The lewd invaders battle-line is thrown:
    Here is our enemy and here alone—
The Parasite of world-wide industry!
    His wealth is red with mangled flesh and bone.

Resist the foe, ah, crush him utterly—:

Resist the foe . . . . ?

SOURCE: *Solidarity*, 24 June 1916, 2.

2.5. No-Conscription League, Manifesto (June 1917)

[On 18 May 1917 Congress enacted and President Wilson signed the Selective Service Act of 1917. Ten days later the president issued a proclamation establishing conscription, with draft registration to occur on 5 June. In response, anarchists Emma Goldman and Alexander Berkman organized the No-Conscription League to persuade young men from registering. The group organized rallies in New York City and elsewhere. It also issued a manifesto and circulated more than one hundred thousand copies. On 15 June 1917 the U.S. government arrested Goldman and Berkman on charges of conspiracy to obstruct the draft. They were convicted, sentenced to two years in prison, and deported from the United States on the *Buford* in December 1919.]

NO CONSCRIPTION!

CONSCRIPTION has now become a fact in this country. It took England fully 18 months after she engaged in the war to impose compulsory military service on her people. It was left for "free" America to pass a conscription bill six weeks after she declared war against Germany.

What becomes of the patriotic boast of America to have entered the European war in behalf of the principle of democracy? But that is not all. Every country in Europe has recognized the right of conscientious objectors—of men who refuse to engage in war on the ground that they are opposed to taking life. Yet this democratic country makes no such provision for those who will not commit murder at the behest of the war profiteers. Thus the "land of the free and the home of the brave" is ready to coerce free men into the military yoke.

No one to whom the fundamental principle of liberty and justice is more than an idle phrase, can help realize that the patriotic claptrap now shouted by press, pulpit and the authorities, betrays a desperate effort of the ruling class in this country to throw sand in the eyes of the masses and to blind them to the real issue confronting them. That issue is the Prussianizing of America so as to destroy whatever few liberties the people have achieved through an incessant struggle of many years.

Already all labor protective laws have been abrogated, which means that while husbands, fathers and sons are butchered on the battlefield, the women and children will be exploited in our industrial bastiles to the heart's content of the American patriots for gain and power.

Freedom of speech, of press and assembly is about to be thrown upon the dungheap of political guarantees. But crime of all crimes, the flower of the country is to be forced into murder whether or not they believe in war or in the efficacy of saving democracy in Europe by the destruction of democracy at home.

Liberty of conscience is the most fundamental of all human rights, the pivot of all progress. No man may be deprived of it without losing every vestige of freedom of thought and action. In these days when every principle and conception of democracy and individual liberty is being cast overboard under the pretext of democratizing Germany, it behooves every liberty-loving man and woman to insist on his or her right of individual choice in the ordering of his life and actions.

The NO-CONSCRIPTION LEAGUE has been formed for the purpose of encouraging conscientious objectors to affirm their liberty of conscience and to make their objection to human slaughter effective by refusing to participate in the killing of their fellow men. The NO-CONSCRIPTION LEAGUE is to be the voice of protest against the coercion of conscientious objectors to participate in the war. Our platform may be summarized as follows:

We oppose conscription because we are internationalists, antimilitarists, and opposed to all wars waged by capitalistic governments.

We will fight for what we choose to fight for; we will never fight simply because we are ordered to fight.

We believe that the militarization of America is an evil that far outweighs, in its anti-social and anti-libertarian effects, any good that may come from America's participation in the war.

We will resist conscription by every means in our power, and we will sustain those who, for similar reasons, refuse to be conscripted.

... [W]e have resolved ... to make the voice of protest a moral force in the life of this country. The initial efforts of the conscientious objectors in England were fraught with many hardships and danger, but finally the government of Great Britain was forced to give heed to the ... protest against the coercion of conscientious objectors. So we, too, in America, will doubtless meet the full severity of the government and the condemnation of the war-mad jingoes, ... We feel confident in arousing thousands of people who are conscientious objectors to the murder of their fellowmen and to whom a principle represents the most vital thing in life.

Resist conscription. Organize meetings. Join our League. . . .

We consider this campaign of the utmost importance at the present time. Amid hateful, cowardly silence, a powerful voice and an all-embracing love are necessary to make the living dead shiver.

SOURCE: Henry Wadsworth Longfellow Dana Papers, DG-11, box 2, Swarthmore College Peace Collection, Swarthmore PA.

2.6. Industrial Workers of the World, "The Deadly Parallel" (24 March 1917)

[This IWW statement contrasts the IWW's antiwar position with the AFL's prowar stance. The IWW had planned to distribute the statement as a flyer once the United States declared war, but William Haywood told *Solidarity* editor Ralph Chaplin, who had published the piece, to cancel a print order for additional copies, and the IWW office never circulated the leaflet after the United States entered the war. Still, the government submitted the statement at the 1917 Chicago trial of the IWW. In 1920 the Lusk Report approvingly quoted the AFL statement, which it contrasted with the SP's St. Louis Statement.]

A DECLARATION BY THE INDUSTRIAL WORKERS OF THE WORLD

We, the Industrial Workers of the World, in convention assembled, hereby reaffirm our adherence to the principles of Industrial Union-ism, and rededicate ourselves to the unflinching prosecution of the struggle for the abolition of wage slavery, and the realization of our ideals in Industrial Democracy.

With the European war for conquest and exploitation raging and destroying the lives, class consciousness, and unity of the workers, and the ever growing agitation for military preparedness clouding the main issues, and delaying the realization of our ultimate aim with patriotic, and therefore, capitalistic aspirations, we openly declare ourselves determined opponents of all nationalistic sectionalism or patriotism, and the militarism preached and supported by our one enemy, the Capitalist Class. We condemn all wars, and, for the prevention of such, we proclaim the anti-militarist propaganda in time of peace, thus promoting class solidarity among the workers of the entire world, and, in time of war, the general strike in all industries.

We extend assurances of both moral and material support to all the workers who suffer at the hands of the Capitalist Class for their adhesion to the principles, and call on all workers to unite themselves with us, that the reign of the exploiters may cease and this earth be made fair through the establishment of the Industrial Democracy.

PLEDGE GIVEN TO NATION BY AMERICAN FEDERATION OF LABOR.

We, the officers of the national and international trades unions of America in national conference assembled, in the capital of our nation, hereby pledge ourselves in peace or in war, in stress or in storm, to stand unreservedly by the standards of liberty and the safety and preservation of the institutions and ideals of our republic.

In this solemn hour of our nation's life, it is our earnest hope that our republic may be safeguarded in its unswerving desire for peace; that our people may be spared the horrors and the burdens of war; that they may have the opportunity to cultivate and develop the arts of peace, human brotherhood and a higher civilization.

But despite all our endeavors and hopes, should our country be drawn into the maelstrom of the European conflict, we, with these ideals of liberty and justice herein declared, as the indispensable basis for national policies, offer our services to our country in every field of activity to defend, safeguard and preserve the republic of the United States of America against its enemies, whomsoever they may be, and we call upon our fellow workers and fellow citizens in the holy name of labor, justice, freedom and humanity to devotedly and patriotically give like service.

SOURCE: *Solidarity*, 24 March 1917, 1.

2.7. John Reed, "Whose War?" (April 1917)

[John Reed was a left-wing socialist, war reporter, and radical journalist who edited the *Masses*, a magazine suppressed for its radical stance and antiwar position. In 1917 Reed wrote *Ten Days That Shook the World*, an eyewitness account of the Bolshevik Revolution. In 1919 he was expelled from the Socialist Party, joined the Communist Labor Party, and returned to Soviet Russia, where he died.]

... By the time this goes to press the United States may be at war. The day the German note arrived, Wall street flung the American flag to the breeze, the brokers on the floor of the Stock Exchange sang "The Star-spangled Banner" with tears rolling down their cheeks, and the stock-market went up. In the theaters they are singing "patriotic" ballads of the George M. Cohan–Irving Berlin variety, playing the national anthem, and flashing the flag and the portrait of long-suffering Lincoln. ... Exclusive ladies whose husbands own banks are rolling bandages for the wounded, just like they do in Europe; ... The directors of the British, French and Belgian Permanent Blind Relief Fund have added "American" to the name of the organization, in gruesome anticipation. ... There is talk of "conscription," "war brides," and "on to Berlin."

I know what war means. I have been with the armies of all the belligerents except one, and I have seen men die, and go mad, and lie in hospitals suffering hell; but there is a worse thing than that. War means an ugly mob-madness, crucifying the truth-tellers, choking the artists, side-tracking reforms, revolutions, and the working of social forces. Already in America those citizens who oppose the entrance of their country into the European melée are called "traitors," and those who protest against the curtailing of our meagre rights of free speech are spoken of as "dangerous lunatics." We have had a forecast of the censorship. . . . The press is howling for war. The church is howling for war. Lawyers, politicians, stock-brokers, social leaders are all howling for war. [Theodore] Roosevelt is again recruiting his trice-thwarted family regiment.

But whether it comes to actual hostilities or not, some damage has been done. . . . I know of at least two valuable social movements that have suspended functioning because no one cares. For many years this country is going to be a worse place for free men to live in; less tolerant, less hospitable. Maybe it is too late, but I want to put down what I think about it all.

Whose war is this? Not mine. I know that hundreds of thousands of American workingmen employed by our great financial "patriots" are not paid a living wage. I have seen poor men sent to jail for long terms without trial, and even without any charge. Peaceful strikers, and their wives and children, have been shot to death, burned to death, by private detectives and militiamen. The rich has steadily become richer, and the cost of living higher, and the workers proportionally poorer. These toilers don't want war—not even civil war. But the speculators, the employers, the plutocracy—they want it, just as they did in Germany and in England; and with lies and sophistries they will whip up our blood until we are savage— and then we'll fight and die for them.

. . . [W]e want our country to keep off the necks of little nations, to refuse to back up American beasts of prey who invest abroad and get their fingers burned, and to stay out of quarrels not our own. . . .

We are simple folk. Prussian militarism seemed to us insufferable; we thought the invasion of Belgium a crime; German atrocities horrified us, and also the idea of German submarines exploding ships full of peaceful people without warning. But then we began to hear about England and France jailing, fining, exiling and even shooting men who refused to go out and kill; the Allied armies invaded and seized a part of neutral Greece, and a French admiral forced upon her an ultimatum as shameful as Austria's to Serbia; Russian atrocities were shown to be more dreadful than German; and hidden mines sown by England in the open sea exploded ships full of peaceful people without warning.

Other things disturbed us. For instance, why was it a violation of international law for the Germans to establish a "war zone" around the British Isles, and perfectly legal for England to close the North Sea? Why is it we submitted to the British order forbidding the shipment of non-contraband to Germany, and insisted upon our right to ship contraband to the Allies? If our "national honor" was smirched by Germany's refusal to allow war-materials to be shipped to the Allies, what happened to our national honor when England refused to let us ship non-contraband food and even *Red Cross hospital supplies* to Germany? Why is England allowed to attempt the avowed starvation of German civilians, in violation of international law, when the Germans cannot attempt the same thing without our horrified protest? How is it that the British can arbitrarily regulate our commerce with neutral nations, while we raise a howl whenever the Germans "threaten to restrict our merchant ships going about their business?" Why does our Government insist that Americans should not be molested while traveling on Allied ships armed against submarines?

We have shipped and are shipping vast quantities of war-materials to the Allies, we have floated the Allied loans. We have been strictly neutral toward the Teutonic powers only. Hence the inevitable desperation of the last German note. Hence this war we are on the brink of.

Those of us who voted for Woodrow Wilson did so because we felt his mind and his eyes were open, because he had kept us out of the mad-dog-fight of Europe, and because the plutocracy opposed him. We had learned enough about the war to lose some of our illusions, and we wanted to be neutral. We grant that the President, considering the position he'd got himself into, couldn't do anything else but answer the German note as he did—but if we had been neutral, that note wouldn't have been sent. The President didn't ask us; he won't ask us if we want war or not. The fault is not ours. It is not our war.

SOURCE: *Masses*, April 1917, 11–12.

2.8. Socialist Party of America, "The 'Majority' Report of the St. Louis Convention" (7–14 April 1917)

[In April 1917, the day after Congress declared war on Germany, the Socialist Party met in St. Louis to discuss U.S. intervention. The War and Militarism Committee prepared and the convention endorsed the majority report, drafted by labor lawyer Morris Hillquit. In a referendum SP members subsequently adopted the St. Louis Resolution and its militant antiwar position.]

The Socialist Party of the United States in the present grave crisis, solemnly reaffirms its allegiance to the principle of internationalism and working class solidarity the world over, and proclaims its unalterable opposition to the war just declared by the government of the United States.

Modern wars as a rule have been caused by the commercial and financial rivalry and intrigues of the capitalist interests in the different countries. Whether they have been frankly waged as wars of aggression or have been hypocritically represented as wars of "defense," they have always been made by the classes and fought by the masses. Wars bring wealth and power to the ruling classes, and suffering, death and demoralization to the workers. . . .

The forces of capitalism which have led to the war in Europe are even more hideously transparent in the war recently provoked by the ruling class of this country.

When Belgium was invaded, the government enjoined upon the people of this country the duty of remaining neutral, thus clearly demonstrating that the "dictates of humanity," and the fate of small nations and of democratic institutions were matters that did not concern it. But when our enormous war traffic was seriously threatened, our government calls upon us to rally to the "defense of democracy and civilization."

Our entrance into the European war was instigated by the predatory capitalists in the United States who boast of the enormous profit of seven billion dollars from the manufacture and sale of munitions and war supplies and from the exportation of American food stuffs and other necessaries. They are also deeply interested in the continuance of war and the success of the allied arms through their huge loans to the governments of the allied powers and through other commercial ties. It is the same interests which strive for imperialistic domination of the Western Hemisphere.

The war of the United States against Germany cannot be justified even on the plea that it is a war in defense of American rights or American "honor." Ruthless as the unrestricted submarine war policy of the German government was and is, it is not an invasion of the rights of the American people, as such, but only an interference with the opportunity of certain groups of American capitalists to coin cold profits out of the blood and sufferings of our fellow men in the warring countries of Europe.

It is not a war against the militarist regime of the Central Powers. Militarism can never be abolished by militarism.

It is not a war to advance the cause of democracy in Europe. Democracy can never be imposed upon any country by a foreign power by force of arms.

It is cant and hypocrisy to say that the war is not directed against the German people, but against the Imperial Government of Germany. If we send an armed force to the battlefields of Europe, its cannon will mow down the masses of the German people and not the Imperial German Government.

Our entrance into the European conflict at this time will serve only to multiply the horrors of the war, to increase the toll of death and destruction and to prolong the fiendish slaughter. It will bring death, suffering and destitution to the people of the United States and particularly to the working class. It will give the powers of reaction in this country, the pretext for an attempt to throttle our rights and to crush our democratic institutions, and to fasten upon this country a permanent militarism. . . .

We brand the declaration of war by our government as a crime against the people of the United States and against the nations of the world. . . .

In harmony with these principles, the Socialist Party emphatically rejects the proposal that in time of war the workers should suspend their struggle for better conditions. On the contrary, the acute situation created by war calls for an even more vigorous prosecution of the class struggle, and we recommend to the workers and pledge ourselves to the following course of action:

1. Continuous, active, and public opposition to the war through demonstrations, mass petitions, and all other means within our power.

2. Unyielding opposition to all proposed legislation for military or industrial conscription. Should such conscription be forced upon the people, we pledge ourselves to continuous efforts for the repeal of such laws and to the support of all mass movements in opposition to conscription. We pledge ourselves to oppose with all our strength any attempt to raise money for payment of war expense by taxing the necessaries of life or issuing bonds which will put the burden upon future generations. We demand that the capitalist class, which is responsible for the war, pay its cost. Let those who kindled the fire furnish the fuel.

3. Vigorous resistance to all reactionary measures, such as censorship of press and mails, restriction of the rights of free speech, assemblage, and organization, or compulsory arbitration and limitation of the right to strike.

4. Consistent propaganda against military training and militaristic teaching in the public schools.

5. Extension of the campaign of education among the workers to organize them into strong, class-conscious, and closely unified political and industrial organizations, to enable them by concerted and harmonious mass action to shorten this war and to establish lasting peace.

6. Widespread educational propaganda to enlighten the masses as to the true relation between capitalism and war, and to rouse and organize them for action, not only against present war evils, but for the prevention of future wars and for the destruction of the causes of war.

7. To protect the masses of the American people from the pressing danger of starvation which the war in Europe has brought upon them, and which the entry of the United States has already accentuated, we demand—

(a) The restriction of food exports . . . the fixing of maximum prices and whatever measures may be necessary to prevent the food speculators from holding back the supplies now in their hands;

(b) The socialization and democratic management of the great industries concerned with . . . food and other necessities of life;

(c) The socialization and democratic management of all land and other natural resources now held out of use for monopolistic or speculative profit.

These measures are presented as means of protecting the workers against the evil results of the present war. . . . The end of wars will come with the establishment of socialized industry and industrial democracy the world over. The Socialist Party calls upon all the workers to join it in its struggle to reach this goal, and thus bring into the world a new society in which peace, fraternity, and human brotherhood will be the dominant ideals.

SOURCE: Alexander Trachtenberg, ed., *The American Socialists and the War* (New York: Rand School of Social Science, 1917), 39–43.

2.9. William D. Haywood and the Industrial Workers of the World, Opposition to War (April 1917)

[William Haywood was a founding member and the general secretary of the Industrial Workers of the World. In September 1917 Haywood, along with other IWW leaders, was indicted in Chicago on charges of violating the Espionage Act. In August 1920 he was sentenced to twenty years in prison. He served time in Fort Leavenworth from September 1918 to July 1919, when he was released on bond pending the appeal of his conviction. In March 1921 he fled to the Soviet Union, where he won asylum and died in 1928.]

Since the last *Bulletin*, President Wilson has proclaimed a state of war against the Imperial Government of Germany. A volunteer army has been called for, and, possibly, conscription measures will be passed by the United States Congress. All class conscious members of the Industrial Workers of the World are conscientiously opposed to spilling the life blood of human beings, *not for religious reasons*, as are the Quakers and Friendly Societies, but because we believe that the interests and welfare of the working class in all countries are identical. While we are bitterly opposed to the Imperialist Capitalistic Government of Germany, we are against slaughtering and maiming the workers of any country. In many lands, our members are suffering imprisonment, death and abuse of all kinds in the class war which we are waging for social and industrial justice.

SOURCE: *IWW Bulletin*, April 1917, quoted in William D. Haywood, *The Autobiography of Big Bill Haywood* (1929; reprint, New York: International, 1977), 297.

2.10. "A Patriot" (14 April 1917)

[This unsigned poem appeared in the *Industrial Worker*, an IWW newspaper published first in Spokane and then in Seattle, Washington. Joyce L. Kornbluh, ed., *Rebel Voices: An IWW Anthology* (Chicago: Charles H. Kerr, 1998), 331, reprints this poem under the title "I Love My Flag"—and without the opening stanza.]

I love my country, yes, I do,
    I love my Uncle Sam.
I also love my steak and eggs
    And bread and beans and ham.
If I were dead I could not eat
    And 'tho I'd not be missed,
I'd miss my feed—Oh yes, indeed;
    I guess I won't enlist.

I love my flag, I do, I do,
    Which floats upon the breeze.
I also love my arms and legs,
    And neck, and nose, and knees.
One little shell might spoil them all
    Or give them such a twist,
They would be of no use to me;
    I guess I won't enlist.

I love my country, yes, I do,
  I hope her folks do well.
Without our arms, and legs and things,
  I think we'd look like hell.
Young men with faces half shot off
  Are unfit to be kissed,
I've read in books it spoils their looks;
  I guess I won't enlist.

SOURCE: *Industrial Worker*, 14 April 1917, 4.

2.11. "Yellow-Legs and Pugs" (5 May 1917)

[The IWW newspaper *Solidarity* published this unsigned antiwar poem.]

If soldiers all were pugilists there would not be a war,
For pugilists would want to know what they were fighting for.

FOR INSTANCE
If Tommy Atkins had been told to beat up Herman Schmitz
And Herman had been told to blow the other into bits,
  And if they had been pugilists they would have answered "No!
We will not fight unless we get a section of the dough.
We will not risk our arms and legs and shed our ruddy gore
While you who fatten on the fight make millions by the score.
Although it is a noble stunt to redden hill and dale,
We will not fight unless we get a portion of the kale."
And thus the world-wide warfare would be ended in a minute,
For bankers would not start a war if there were nothing in it.

SOURCE: *Solidarity*, 5 May 1917, 2.

2.12. Charles Schenck and the Socialist Party of America, "Assert Your Rights" (1917)

[In 1917 Charles Schenck, the general secretary of the Socialist Party, printed fifteen thousand copies of a flyer opposing conscription and

U.S. involvement in the European war. Arrested under the Espionage Act, he was convicted of attempting to obstruct the draft. The Supreme Court upheld his conviction in *Schenck v. United States* (1919). Writing for the Court, Justice Oliver Wendell Holmes established the "clear and present danger" test; this doctrine permitted the restriction of First Amendment speech in circumstances—wartime included—where language posed a "clear and present danger" to the public. The back of the flyer, not included here, was titled "Long Live the Constitution of the United States: Wake Up, America! Your Liberties Are in Danger!"]

ASSERT YOUR RIGHTS

Article 6, Section 2, of the Constitution of the United States says: "This Constitution shall be the *supreme law of the Land.*"

Article 1 (Amendment) says: "Congress shall make no law respecting an establishment of religion or *prohibiting the free exercise thereof.*"

Article 9 (Amendment) says: "The enumeration in the Constitution of certain rights, shall not be construed to deny or disparage others retained by the people."

The Socialist Party says that any individual or officers of the law entrusted with the administration of conscription regulations, violate the provisions of the United States Constitution, the Supreme Law of the Land, when they refuse to recognize your right to assert your opposition to the draft.

If you are conscientiously opposed to war, if you believe in the commandment "thou shalt not kill," then that is your religion, and you shall not be prohibited from the free exercise thereof.

In exempting clergymen and members of the Society of Friends (popularly called Quakers) from active military service, the examination boards have discriminated against you.

If you do not assert and support your rights, you are helping to "deny or disparage rights" which it is the solemn duty of all citizens and residents of the United States to retain.

Here in this city of Philadelphia was signed the immortal Declaration of Independence. As a citizen of "the cradle of American Liberty" you are doubly charged with the duty of upholding the rights of the people.

Will you let cunning politicians and a mercenary capitalist press wrongly and untruthfully mould your thoughts? Do not forget your right to elect officials who are opposed to conscription.

In lending tacit or silent consent to the conscription law, in neglecting to assert your rights, you are (whether unknowingly or not) helping to condone and support a most infamous and insidious conspiracy to abridge and destroy the sacred and cherished rights of a free people. You are a citizen, not a subject! You delegate your power to the officers of the law to be used for your good and welfare, not against you.

They are your servants. Not your masters. Their wages come from the expenses of government which you pay. Will you allow them to unjustly rule you? The fathers who fought and bled to establish a free and independent nation here in America were so opposed to the militarism of the old world from which they had escaped; so keenly alive to the dangers and hardships they had undergone in fleeing from political, religious and military oppression, that they handed down to us "certain rights which must be retained by the people."

They held the spirit of militarism in such abhorrence and hate, they were so apprehensive of the formation of a military machine that would insidiously and secretly advocate the invasion of other lands, that they limited the powers of Congress over the militia in providing only for the calling forth of "the militia to execute laws of the Union, suppress insurrection and repel invasion." (See general powers of Congress, Article 1, Section 8, Paragraph 15.)

No power was delegated to send our citizens away to foreign shores to shoot up the people of other lands, no matter what may be their internal or international disputes.

The people of this country did not vote in favor of war. At the last election they voted against war.

To draw this country into the horrors of the present war in Europe, to force the youth of our land into the shambles and bloody trenches of war-crazy nations, would be a crime the magnitude of which defies description. Words could not express the condemnation such cold-blooded ruthlessness deserves.

Will you stand idly by and see the Moloch of Militarism reach forth across the sea and fasten its tentacles upon this continent? Are you willing to submit to the degradation of having the Constitution of the United States treated as a "mere scrap of paper"?

Do you know that patriotism means a love for your country and not hate for others?

Will you be led astray by a propaganda of jingoism masquerading under the guise of patriotism?

No specious or plausible pleas about a "war for democracy" can becloud the issue. Democracy cannot be shot into a nation. It must come spontaneously and purely from within.

Democracy must come through liberal education. Upholders of military ideas are unfit teachers.

To advocate the persecution of other peoples through the prosecution of war is an insult to every good and wholesome American tradition.

"These are the times that try men's souls."

"Eternal vigilance is the price of liberty."

You are responsible. You must do your share to maintain, support and uphold the rights of the people of this country.

In this world crisis where do you stand? Are you with the forces of liberty and light or war and darkness? . . .

SOURCE: Facsimile available at "1st Amendment Online" (University of Minnesota Law School), at *Internet Archive: Wayback Machine*, http://web.archive.org/web/20020915201507/http://1stam.umn.edu/. The UMN website was developed and maintained by Professor Adam Samaha; the website was retired on 1 November 2009 but is available via *Internet Archive: Wayback Machine*.

**2.13. Industrial Workers of the World, Editorial, "Were You Drafted?"
(28 July 1917)**

[In July 1917 the IWW's General Executive Board met in Chicago to discuss the war, including U.S. intervention and the raids and violence against the organization and its members. The meeting did not produce an action plan, but participants agreed that the IWW should issue a statement, and *Solidarity* editor Ralph Chaplin published this editorial in that newspaper.]

The attitude of the Industrial Workers of the World is well known to the people of the United States and is generally recognized by the labor movement throughout the world.

Since its inception our organization has opposed all national and imperialistic wars. We have proved, beyond the shadow of a doubt, that war is a question with which we never have and never intend to compromise.

Members joining the military forces of any nation have always been expelled from the organization.

The I.W.W. has placed its self [sic] on record regarding its opposition to war, and also as being bitterly opposed to having its members forced into the bloody and needless quarrels of the ruling class of different nations.

The principle of the international solidarity of labor to which we have always adhered makes it impossible for us to participate in any and all of the plunder-squabbles of the Parasite class.

Our songs, our literature, the sentiment of the entire membership— the very spirit of our union, give evidence of our unalterable opposition to both capitalism and its wars.

All members of the I.W.W. who have been drafted should mark their claims for exemption, "I.W.W.: opposed to war."

Editor, Solidarity

SOURCE: *Solidarity*, 28 July 1917, 8.

2.14. Bertha H. White, "The Green Corn Rebellion in Oklahoma" (1922)

[Bertha H. White was among the Socialist Party's leading women members. She was assistant executive secretary of the SP from 1922 to 1924 and executive secretary from 1924 to 1925. Five years after the

1917 Green Corn Rebellion, a socialist-led anticonscription rebellion in Oklahoma, she wrote this article about the revolt.]

The story of the wartime prisoners of Oklahoma is one of the blind, desperate rebellion of a people driven to fury and despair by conditions which are incredible in this stage of our so-called civilization. . . .

As long as we can remember, we have heard of their exploitation. We are told that the tenant must mortgage his crop before he can obtain the seed to put into the ground; that when the harvesting is over out of the fruits of his labor he can pay only a part of the debt so incurred, and that a burden of old debts must be carried over and added to new loans for the season; that debt piles upon debt until life becomes only a stolid acceptance of conditions that were hopeless in the beginning. . . .

. . . And in their desperation, the tenants conceived the plan of organizing, of banding themselves together to fight the exactions of landlord and banker.

The result of these efforts was a nonpolitical organization known as the Working Class Union. It had but one object—to force downward rents and interest rates. The center of the movement seems to have been the Seminole country, where even today one meets more frequently the Indian than the white man. . . .

In 1916 the Working Class Union had attained membership throughout Eastern Oklahoma of perhaps 20,000. Although the union had disavowed any participation in politics, rumors of war had reached the officials of the organization. The issue of the campaign to them was simply a question of going to war or staying out of it.

They understood that President Wilson stood squarely upon a campaign pledge to keep America out of the European abyss, and the Working Class Union discarded its keeping-out-of-politics position and went into the campaign to re-elect Woodrow Wilson.

But they were soon wakened form the dream of security. They learned that war had come. They were told that officers would come into their pitiful homes and take from them their sons and brothers. That they would be sent across the seas to fight a people of whom they knew nothing and for reasons of which they had no faintest comprehension.

The South has a dual soul. There is the kindly South of story and tradition, with it splendid hospitality, its keen sense of honor, its rigid adherence to the pledged word. But there is also the South of the Night Riders, of the lynchings, of the Ku Klux Klan. It is this last which has written a record of desperation across the history of the war period in the state of Oklahoma. Law was not law—it was a club to beat down those already broken by oppression; it was a cloak to hide reprisals for ancient grudges and enmities.

News of conscription roused the spirit of rebellion and the Working Class Union began to hold secret meetings to discuss what they should do. They did not believe the people of the country would tamely submit to the violation of the pledges which had resulted in the re-election of President Wilson. And they decided they would not accept that violation. They agreed to hide their boys from the draft officers and to prevent troops from coming into the Seminole country.

On August 3 [1917], nearly 4 months after the declaration of war with Germany, about 150 men were camped on a hilltop near the little town of Sasakwa. They were there with the definite intention of offering resistance to any attempt to take their boys and induct them into the military service. An alarm was sent out through the community and about 50 men gathered to oppose this demonstration, which is now known throughout the section as the "Green Corn Rebellion."

The "WCUS," as they were called, had the advantage of position and numbers. They were armed—pistols and squirrel rifles and ancient shotguns in the main, it is true. But they could have annihilated the opposing forces. The men had to climb the hill. They were without protection and had to make their advance in the open. But those men were not the men who had brought war and the draft to America. The rebels knew these men—they were the postmaster, the storekeeper, the druggist—people they had known for years and against whom they had no personal grudges. They could not fire upon their friends and neighbors—so they threw down their arms and quietly submitted to arrest.

All of those who had participated in the uprising were soon under arrest, and the net swept in others who had belonged to the organization, but had no part in the rebellion. In all, nearly 300 men were involved, and when the case came to trial at Ardmore the following October *175 men received sentences ranging from 30 days in jail to 10 years at Leavenworth prison . . . .*

There are men of fine character in Oklahoma. But these are not among those who ravaged the state of Oklahoma in the name of patriotism.

SOURCE: *New Day* (Milwaukee), 4 March 1922, 68, http://www.marxists.org /history/usa/parties/spusa/1922/0304-white-greencornreb.pdf.

2.15. Eugene V. Debs, Canton, Ohio, Speech (16 June 1918)

[Eugene V. Debs, the Socialist Party leader, delivered this antiwar speech on 16 June 1918, in Canton, Ohio, before about twelve hundred people in Nimisilla Park. For this speech Debs was convicted of violating the Espionage Act and sentenced to ten years in prison. In 1920, while incarcerated, Debs ran for president on the SP ticket.]

Comrades, friends and fellow-workers, for this very cordial greeting, this very hearty reception, I thank you all with the fullest appreciation of your interest in and your devotion to the cause for which I am to speak to you this afternoon. [Applause.]

To speak for labor; to plead the cause of the men and women and children who toil; to serve the working class, has always been to me a high privilege; [Applause] a duty of love.

I have just returned from a visit over yonder [pointing to the workhouse], where three of our most loyal comrades [Charles E. Ruthenberg, Alfred Wagenknecht, and Charles Baker, who were imprisoned for opposing the war] are paying the penalty for their devotion to the cause of the working class. They have come to realize, as many of us have, that it is extremely dangerous to exercise the constitutional right of free speech in a country fighting to make democracy safe in the world. [Applause.]

I realize that, in speaking to you this afternoon, there are certain limitations placed upon the right of free speech. I must be exceedingly careful, prudent, as to what I say, and even more careful and prudent as to how I say it. [Laughter.] I may not be able to say all I think; [Laughter and applause] but I am not going to say anything that I do not think. [Applause.] I would rather a thousand times be a free soul in jail than to be a sycophant and coward in the streets. [Applause and shouts.] They may put those boys in jail—and some of the rest of us in jail—but they can not put the Socialist movement in jail. [Applause and shouts.] Those prison bars separate their bodies from ours, but their souls are here this afternoon. [Applause and cheers.] They are simply paying the penalty, that all men have paid in all the ages of history, for standing erect, and for seeking to pave the way to better conditions for mankind. [Applause.] . . .

Are we opposed to Prussian militarism? [Laughter. Shouts from the crowd of "Yes, Yes!"] Why, we have been fighting it since the day the Socialist movement was born; [Applause] and we are going to continue to fight it, day and night, until it is wiped from the face of the earth. [Thunderous applause and cheers.] Between us there is no truce—no compromise. . . .

Socialism . . . has given me my ideas and ideals; my principles and convictions, . . . It has taught me . . . to be class-conscious, and to realize that, regardless of nationality, race, creed, color or sex, every man, every women who toils, who renders useful service, every member of the working class without an exception, is my comrade, my brother and sister—and that to serve them and their cause is the highest duty of my life. [Great applause.] . . .

Yes, my comrades, my heart is attuned to yours. Aye, all our hearts now throb as one great heart responsive to the battle-cry of the social revolution. Here, in this alert and inspiring assemblage [Applause] our hearts are with the Bolsheviki of Russia. [Deafening and prolonged applause.] Those heroic men and women, those unconquerable comrades have by their incomparable valor and sacrifice added fresh lustre to the fame of the international movement. . . . The very first act of the triumphant Russian revolution was to proclaim a state of peace with all mankind, coupled with a fervent moral appeal, not to kings, not to emperors, rulers or diplomats but to *the people* of all nations. . . . When the Bolsheviki came into power and went through the archives they found and exposed the secret treaties—the treaties that were made between the Czar and the French Government, the British Government and the Italian Government, proposing, after the victory was achieved, to dismember the German Empire and destroy the Central Powers. These treaties have never been denied nor repudiated. Very little has been said about them in the American press. I have a copy of these treaties, showing that the purpose of the Allies is exactly the purpose of the Central Powers, and that is the conquest and spoliation of the weaker nations that has always been the purpose of war.

Wars throughout history have been waged for conquest and plunder. In the Middle Ages when the feudal lords, who inhabited the castles whose towers may still be seen along the Rhine concluded to enlarge their domains, to increase their power, their prestige and their wealth they declared war upon one another. But they themselves did not go to war any more than the modern feudal lords, the barons of Wall Street go to war. [Applause.] The feudal barons of the Middle Ages, the economic predecessors of the capitalists of our day, declared all wars. And their miserable serfs fought all the battles. The poor, ignorant serfs had been taught to revere their masters; to believe that when their masters declared war upon one another, it was their patriotic duty to fall upon one another and to cut one another's throats for the profit and glory of the lords and barons who held them in contempt. And that is war in a nutshell. The master class has always declared the wars; the subject class has always fought the battles. The master class has had all to gain and nothing to lose, while the subject class has had nothing to gain and all to lose—especially their lives. [Applause.] . . .

And here let me emphasize the fact—and it cannot be repeated too often—that the working class who fight all the battles, the working class who make the supreme sacrifices, the working class who freely shed their blood and furnish the corpses, have never yet had a voice in either declaring war or making peace. It is the ruling class that invariably does both. They alone declare war and they alone make peace.

"Yours not to reason why;
Yours but to do and die."

That is their motto and we object on the part of the awakening workers of this nation. . . .

It is the minorities who have made the history of this world. It is the few who have had the courage to take their places at the front; who have been true enough to themselves to speak the truth that was in them; who have dared oppose the established order of things; who have espoused the cause of the suffering, struggling poor; who have upheld without regard to personal consequences the cause of freedom and righteousness. It is they, the heroic, self-sacrificing few who have made the history of the race and who have paved the way from barbarism to civilization. The many prefer to remain upon the popular side. They lack the courage and vision to join a despised minority that stands for a principle; they have not the moral fiber that withstands, endures and finally conquers. They are to be pitied and not treated with contempt for they cannot help their cowardice. But, thank God, in every age and in every nation there have been the brave and self-reliant few, and they have been sufficient to their historic task; and we, who are here today, are under infinite obligations to them because they suffered, they sacrificed, they went to jail, they had their bones broken upon the wheel, they were burned at the stake and their ashes scattered to the winds by the hands of hate and revenge in their struggle to leave the world better for us than they found it for themselves. We are under eternal obligations to them because of what they did and what they suffered for us and the only way we can discharge that obligation is by doing the best we can for those who are to come after us. [Applause.] . . .

They [capitalists] are continually talking about your patriotic duty.

It is not *their* but *your* patriotic duty that they are concerned about. There is a decided difference. Their patriotic duty never takes them to the firing line or chucks them into the trenches. . . .

SOURCE: Eugene V. Debs, *Writings and Speeches of Eugene V. Debs* (New York: Hermitage Press, 1948), 417–18, 421, 424–26, 429–30.

CHAPTER 3

Citizen Peace Agitators

3.1. William Jennings Bryan's Resignation as Secretary of State (June 1915)

[William J. Bryan ran unsuccessfully for president three times on the Democratic-Populist and Democratic tickets. With Woodrow Wilson's election in 1912, Bryan became secretary of state and negotiated numerous peace treaties. After the outbreak of World War I, Bryan disagreed with Wilson's stern warning to Germany to cease submarine warfare and, in June 1915, resigned. Within days he explained his stance in three public statements. Excerpted here are his resignation letter and his first public statement as a private citizen.]

William J. Bryan's Letter of Resignation (8 June 1915)

June 8, 1915

My Dear Mr. President:

It is with sincere regret that I have reached the conclusion that I should return to you the commission of Secretary of State with which you honored me at the beginning of your administration.

Obedient to your sense of duty and actuated by the highest motives, you have prepared for transmission to the German government a note in which I cannot join without violating what I deem to be an obligation to my country, and the issue involved is of such moment that to remain a member of the cabinet would be as unfair to you as it would be to the cause which is nearest my heart, namely, the prevention of war.

I, therefore, respectfully tender my resignation, to take effect when the note is sent, unless you prefer an earlier hour. Alike desirous of reaching a peaceful solution of the problems arising out of the use of the submarines against merchantmen, we find ourselves differing irreconcilably as to the methods which should be employed.

It falls to your lot to speak officially for the nation; I consider it to be none the less my duty to endeavor as a private citizen to promote the end which you have in view by means which you do not feel at liberty to use. . . .

William J. Bryan's First Statement (Published 9 June 1915)

. . . Why should an American citizen be permitted to involve the country in war by traveling upon a belligerent ship when he knows that the ship will pass through a danger zone? The question is not whether an American citizen has the right under international law to travel on a belligerent ship; the question is whether he ought not, out of consideration for his country, if not for his own safety, avoid danger when avoidance is possible.

It is a very one-sided citizenship that compels a government to go to war over a citizen's rights, and yet relieves the citizen of all obligations to consider his nation's welfare. I do not know just how far the President can go legally in actually preventing Americans from traveling on belligerent ships, but I believe the Government should go as far as it can, and that in case of doubt it should give the benefit of the doubt to the Government.

But even if the Government could not legally prevent citizens from traveling on belligerent ships, it could, and my judgment should, earnestly advise American citizens not to risk themselves or the peace of their country, and I have no doubt that these warnings would be heeded.

President Taft advised Americans to leave Mexico when insurrection broke out there, and President Wilson has repeated this advice. This advice, in my judgment, was eminently wise, and I think the same course should be followed in regard to warning Americans to keep off vessels subject to attack.

I think, too, that American passenger ships should be prohibited from carrying ammunition. The lives of passengers ought not to be endangered by cargoes of ammunition, whether that danger comes from possible explosions within or from possible attacks from without. Passengers and ammunition should not travel together. The attempt to prevent American citizens from incurring these risks is entirely consistent with the effort which our Government is making to prevent attacks from submarines. . . .

SOURCE: *The Resignation of William Jennings Bryan as Secretary of State and the Documents That Present the Issue* [brochure, n.d.], 4–7, in William Jennings Bryan Papers, series 5, box 3, Nebraska State Historical Society, Lincoln.

3.2. Oswald Garrison Villard, "Shall We Arm for Peace?"
(11 December 1915)

[Oswald Villard, the grandson of abolitionist William Lloyd Garrison and owner of the *New York Evening Post*, examines the high cost of military expenditures and cautions the nation to tone down preparedness rhetoric. His views expressed the modern American peace movement's focus on social justice to remove the causes of war.]

. . . Must we arm? Is there for us nothing left but to follow in the footsteps of what we have been pleased to call the effete monarchies of Europe? Our American ideals have been of service to humanity and to liberty; to create, not to destroy; to be a refugee to the oppressed of all nations has been our chiefest aim. Millions have flocked to us from abroad to escape the evils and burdens of this very militarism we would now voluntarily embrace. . . .

But there is much in the hour to make us take note of the forces about us which would make preparation for war the chief business of our lives. Let no one think that all this sudden agitation for great armaments has come only as a result of fears born of the conflict abroad. For years there has been a military and naval propaganda at work in this country, of which only a few have been aware. There is no more dangerous and insidious force at work in Washington than the army and navy lobby. . . .

Our army and navy officers ought no more to regulate the size of our fleets and armies than our protected manufacturers should be allowed to write our tariffs, [or], . . . our trust magnates to write our anti-trust laws. . . .

. . . Selfish interests must not be allowed to write our military laws. If we must have armies and navies, let the board to control them and fix their size be constituted of real, unfettered representatives of the people, those upon whom the burdens chiefly fall. . . .

But our military and naval men none the less openly advocate upsetting one of the fundamental principles of this republic—that of the complete subordination of the military to civilian authority as the truest if not the only safeguard against militarism. The founders of this republic knew what they were about, because they had a peculiarly trying experience with British militarism; they knew what is was to be governed from afar by what were practically military governors, backed by a military force which was none the less hateful, as the Boston massacre attests, because the soldiery spoke the same language and were of the same stock. They represented not merely an alien government but military, as opposed to civilian, authority—as distasteful to the colonists as our military forces in the Philippines are to the Filipinos.

And so it is neither the duty nor the right today of any American general to instruct the people or the government as to our military policy; they belong solely to the civilian officials, the cabinet, the President and Congress. Any departure from this wise doctrine of the fathers would be fraught with gravest consequences, for it is in just such insidious ways that militarism fastens a death-grasp upon a people while they still insist that they are absolutely peaceful or anti-militaristic. . . .

. . . [I]n the last twenty years we have spent enormous sums upon army and navy together; from 1881 to 1915 our annual naval bill has increased from $13,000,000 to $147,538,981.88.

We are thus spending about seven times the endowment of Yale or Harvard Universities in a single year upon the navy alone, with nothing whatever to show for it after fifteen years at most, when the new battleships of today will be reduced to junk or shot to pieces as targets. . . .

During the first two years of the Wilson administration, we have expended for armaments more than during the entire four years of Roosevelt's rule or of Taft's government. Is it any wonder that President Wilson, a year ago—a year before he surrendered to the politicians—said to Congress: "Let there be no misconception. The country has been misinformed. We have not been negligent of national defence"? . . .

But the reader may ask whether mine has not been a negative attitude; to cling fast to our national ideals, to refuse to follow military experts in matters of policy as opposed to matters of fact, to have faith in our present forces and whether I have no concrete recommendations to make?

To this, I answer that I have such a program:

First, to insist that this nation resume its role of chief exemplar of peace and disarmament in the world—a nation devoted primarily and whole-heartedly to the arts of peace;

Second, to spend at least the price of two battleships a year, say $25,000,000, in winning the good opinion of countries with whom we might be in danger of friction, and in acquainting ourselves and our own people with them and their aims;

Third, to demand of our cabinets and Presidents that they shall recognize that war is always a failure of statesmanship and that behind war lies too often a fear of somebody else which it must be the chief duty of responsible officials not to increase by large armaments, but to allay;

Fourth, to gain for ourselves, the plain people, such control of our foreign affairs as will make Congress alone, not a handful of men the arbiters as to whether we shall or shall not go to war. . . .

I believe the time is near at hand when the masses will rise in rebellion as they ought against this whole theory of war, demanding freedom of trade and harbors throughout the world, a union of nations where there are unions of states within a nation today, and internationalism as against nationalism. . . .

This is the kind of revolution the world needs above all else at this hour—a new brand of French Revolution—a sweeping, overwhelming uniting against those who rob nations of 75 per cent of their income for war purposes, and take it away from the building of cities beautiful without slums, the reclaiming of waste lands, of our deserts and our swamps, the developing of our waterways, our water powers and our highways, the true education of our masses, the leveling of every barrier of caste and prejudice.

In short, militarism withholds vast sums from the amelioration of the lot of the poor, the ill, the suffering, the wronged, the oppressed, and I am for bitter and harsh words about it now and always; I am for turning upon those who counsel that we shall plot to murder other nations and peoples either for offense or defense as true traitors to the spirit of the nation.

SOURCE: *Survey*, 11 December 1915, 296–99.

3.3. Frank Donnblazer, Testimony before Senate Hearing on Military Preparedness (8 February 1916)

[Frank Donnblazer, a farmer and secretary of the board of directors of the National Farmers' Union (Farmers' Educational and Cooperative Union of America), testified on military preparedness before the Senate Committee on Military Affairs. Representing more than two million farmers, he presented a resolution on behalf of his organization questioning the need for an increased army and navy.]

Mr. Chairman, gentlemen, and ladies, it is something new to me to appear before a committee of this kind. I am not here from choice nor voluntarily. I was drafted into this service. . . . I am a Pennsylvania Dutchman [German] on my father's side, and Scotch-Irish on my mother's side. That is considerable of a mixture, but it is pretty good stuff. I was born in Pennsylvania in 1841. I am a farmer. . . . [and] . . . member of the grange. I have been married over 54 years. My wife is still living. We are the parents of 18 children, 9 boys and 9 girls, and I guess I have fulfilled the Scriptures. I was turned loose when I was but 13 years old. My father gave me my freedom. It is unusual for the Dutch people to do that.

I went to Texas with a drove of sheep when I was 14 years old lacking a month. I was five years with the sheep. I laid out of doors all that time. What I know I learned by experience outside of books. I went to school one winter after I quit the sheep. I studied grammar 30 minutes. . . . So what I am going to tell you is in my simple homespun way. I am not here to represent myself. I am here to represent over 2,000,000 farmers. I may have some ideas of my own, but they are my own. . . . My ancestors, my great grandfather and his brother came from Germany before the Revolutionary War. My grandfather fought seven years for the independence those folks have got. My great uncle lost his life in the Revolutionary War. My father's father, my grandfather on my father's side, was in the War of 1812. My own father was in the War with Mexico, and he joined the Union Army, was wounded at the very last of the war and died on the boat on his way home at St. Louis and now lies in a soldier's grave. I am not much of a warrior. If it were left to me, I would not let any ruler declare war. It is dangerous. But this is my idea:

I would submit it to the people who have to do the fighting and if the majority said that we should have war I would let those who vote for war go and the others stay at home. But anyhow, I believe in peace; I believe in preparedness; but first and foremost I believe in readiness, and that is why I am a member of the farmers' union. . . .

That [homes] is the best thing in the world, to have something to fight for. Should an enemy come here from any other country we are nearer ready, from what I have heard, to-day than we were when the war broke out over yonder, where if they keep on they will not have anyone left but women and children and cripples. But I am not here to talk of what I think. I am here for what the Farmers' Educational and Cooperative Union of America has declared. I am representing 22 States that are organized and 6 that are on the way, and 4 of them will be organized as State unions in March, which will make 26. . . . These questions come up which agitate the public at the locals, and they are agitated and discussed and resolutions are passed and sent with the delegates to the county union and at the county unions they are discussed again, because the delegates come from all the locals, and there may be 50 or 60 locals in the county, and even more. These resolutions are discussed and the best is taken.

It then goes to the national union. This resolution comes from the forks of the creek, and it has been discussed by hundreds of thousands of farmers. Here is what it says:

> We demand economy in all operations made by Congress, and we are especially opposed to any great increase in expenditure for the Army and Navy, but approve a reasonable outlay for coast defense by submarine or other weapons, proved by recent experience to be effective for that purpose. We are unalterably opposed to a large standing army and to any change in our military system tending to compulsory military service. . . .

Ladies and gentlemen and gentlemen of the committee, I am just here to represent the farmers' union, as I have already told you. They have their papers to read and are doing their thinking. They are patriotic, and if a war should break out and they should be called on, you would find them on hand. . . . But they see no necessity for this great preparedness. . . .

Now, Nebraska has over 44,000 male members in the farmers' union, and at their State meeting just a week or two ago they unanimously and without a single solitary objection opposed preparedness, opposed going into this expensive preparedness and telling our boys to drill and get ready to fight. A fight always looks best to me a good ways off, and the further off the better it looks to me. . . .

SOURCE: "Statement of Mr. Frank Donnblazer," in Senate Committee on Military Affairs, "Preparedness for National Defense," *Hearings*, 64th Cong., 1st sess. (Washington DC: Government Printing Office, 1916), pt. 21, 8 February 1916, 1042–44.

3.4. Bob Minor, Letter from Paris (March 1916)

[Robert Minor, a political radical, contributed articles and antiwar cartoons to the *New York Call* and the *Masses*. The *Call*'s war correspondent, he reported on the conflict in Europe, the Russian Revolution, and the postwar German Revolution and Allied invasion of Russia. In this short letter from Paris, he describes the human cost of war.]

Paris is full of one-legged, one-armed men. The streets are dotted with men, boys, cripples, and hospital aides, in a thousand nondescript uniforms.

I happened by where a train-load of wounded came in at night. My luck was unusual, as they don't want the public to see such things. They were short of "hands" and I gave a lift. French, Moroccans, Negroes from African colonies, every sort and color were there, and every "cut" of man was there. It looked as though the only part of the human body sure to be found on the stretcher was the head. Now and then a half-a-man would go by, the upper half with a piece of paper pinned to his cap to give his name in case he should become unable to tell it.

Here was a man with his eyes and nose shot off, there, one with his lower jaw gone, another with both legs and one arm off, asking me for a light, having become tired of waiting for his neighbor (a fortunate fellow with two arms and one leg) to solve the interesting problem of a patent cigar lighter.

This is just a sample. C'est la guerre! . . .

SOURCE: *Masses*, March 1916, 18.

3.5. Julius F. Schlicht, "The White Feather" (7 March 1917)

[In a letter to the *New York Call*, a socialist newspaper, Brooklyn resident Julius F. Schlicht encourages American men who oppose World War I to protest the war by wearing a white feather. In this creative cultural protest, antiwar men in America would expropriate and bestow new meaning to the symbol of the white feather. In Britain female war supporters sought to humiliate men by handing them white feathers.]

When the "munition patriots" have accomplished their object, war, which now seems inevitable, there will, no doubt, spring up a race of hysterical amazons who will decorate all able-bodied men with the "white feather" who refuse to be drawn into the present inferno.

This is the common practice in England, Canada, etc., and is looked upon with great favor by the authorities.

I would, therefore, suggest to those of us who will so signally be honored to continue to wear the white feather as a silent protest of war.

I know it will require courage of a higher sort to wear a white feather than to bedeck one's coat with patriotic colors, shout for war, but discreetly stay at home.

SOURCE: *New York Call*, 7 March 1917, 6.

3.6. John Haynes Holmes, "A Statement to My People on the Eve of War" (1 April 1917)

[A prominent Unitarian minister, pacifist, socialist, and champion of civil rights and civil liberties, John H. Holmes was an important member of the World War I and interwar peace movement. In this April 1917 sermon before his congregation at the Church of the Messiah, he defies prowar, interventionist sentiment by vowing his fight for peace.]

To-morrow morning (April 2) there will assemble in the capital city of the nation the Congress of these United States, called together in special session by proclamation of the President, to consider matters of grave moment in the life of the Republic. This assemblage of the chosen representatives of our people promises to be the most fateful in our history. Unless events now unforeseen, unexpected and in the highest degree improbable intervene, the Congress will either affirm that this country is in a state of war, or will do the more formal and decisive thing of issuing a declaration of war against the Imperial German Government. . . .

On the morning of Sunday, March 7, 1915, I declared in this church my absolute and unalterable opposition to war. "War," I said, "is never justifiable at any time or under any circumstances. No man is wise enough, no nation is important enough, no human interest is precious enough, to justify the wholesale destruction and murder which constitute the essence of war. . . . War is hate, and hate has no place within the human heart. War is death, and death has no place within the realm of life. War is hell, and hell has no more place in the human order than in the divine." I then asked what "this means in practical terms to-day?" And I answered, "It means not only that war is unjustifiable in general, but that this English war is unjustifiable for Englishmen, and this German war is unjustifiable for Germans. It means that this war which may in the folly of men, come to America to-morrow, is unjustifiable for Americans." ...

... War is in open and utter violation of Christianity. If war is right, then Christianity is wrong, false, a lie. If Christianity is right, then war is wrong, false, a lie. The God revealed by Jesus, and by every great spiritual leader of the race, is no God of battles. He lifts no sword—he asks no sacrifice of blood. He is the Father of all men, Jew and Gentile, bond and free. His spirit is love, his rule is peace, is method of persuasion is forgiveness. His law ... is "love one another," "resist not evil with evil," "forgive seventy times seven," "overcome evil with good," ...

But I must go farther—I must speak not only of war in general, but of this war in particular. Most persons are quite ready to agree, especially in the piping times of peace, that war is wrong. But let a war cloud no bigger than a man's hands, appear on the horizon of the nation's life, and they straightway begin to qualify their judgment, and if the war cloud grow until it covers all the heavens, they finally reverse it. This brings the curious situation of all war being wrong in general, and each war being right in particular. Germans denounce war, with the exception of course of the present conflict with England. Englishmen condemn war, but exclude from their indictment the present fight against the Central Empires. Americans have been vociferous in their repudiation of war as a method of settling international disputes, but are now on the verge of accepting the first chance to draw the sword which the European cataclysm has offered. Therefore do I find it necessary to state not only what I think of war, but of this war which seems to-day so near at hand! ...

In its ultimate causes, this war is the natural product and expression of our unchristian civilization. Its armed men are grown from the dragon's teeth of secret diplomacy, imperialistic ambition, dynastic pride, greedy commercialism, economic exploitation at home and abroad. In the sowing of these teeth, America has had her part; and it is therefore only proper, perhaps, that she should have her part also in the reaping of the dreadful harvest. In its more immediate causes, this war is the direct result of unwarrantable, cruel, but none the less inevitable interferences with our commercial relations with one group of the belligerents. Our participation in the war, therefore, like the war itself, is political and economic, not ethical, in its character. . . . The war itself is wrong. Its prosecution will be a crime. There is not a question raised, an issue involved, a cause at stake, which is worth the life of one blue-jacket on the sea or one khaki-coat in the trenches. . . .

. . . Once war is here, the churches will be called upon to enlist, as will every other social institution. Therefore would I make it plain that, so long as I am your minister, the Church of the Messiah will answer no military summons. Other pulpits may preach recruiting sermons; mine will not. Other parish houses may be turned into drill halls and rifle ranges; ours will not. Other clergymen may pray to God for victory for our arms; I will not. In this church, if nowhere else in all America, the Germans will still be included in the family of God's children. No word of hatred shall be spoken against them—no evil fate shall be desired upon them. War may beat upon our portals, like storm waves on the granite crags; rumors of war may thrill the atmosphere of this sanctuary as lighting the still air of a summer night. But so long as I am priest, this altar shall be consecrated to human brotherhood, and before it shall be offered worship only to that one God and Father of us all, "who hath made of one blood all nations of men for to dwell together on the face of the earth."

But if I will not, or cannot not, either as man or minister, have part in the operations of war, how can I talk of such a thing as serving the nation? . . . Let me specify at least four things which I propose to do.

First of all, I shall make it my duty to fulfill in word and deed the gracious tasks of what may be called the ministry of reconciliation. . . .

Secondly, I will serve my country in war time by serving the ideals of democracy which constitute the soul and center of her being. . . .

Thirdly, I will serve my country at this time by preparing the way, so far as I am able, for the establishment of that peace which sooner or later must follow upon war. . . .

Lastly, I will serve my country in war time, by serving the dream of international brotherhood. . . . America, for more than a hundred years, has been first among countries of the world, in recognition and service of this ideal. She has been a gathering place of all the tribes of earth—a melting-pot into which the ingredients of every race, religion and nationality have been poured. And out of it has come not so much a new nation as a new idea—the idea of brotherhood. This idea has stamped our people as a chosen people. It has set our land apart as a holy land. It has exalted our destiny as a divine destiny. And now, with the plunge into the welter of contending European nationalities, all this is gone. Gone, at least, if those of us who see not to-day's quarrel but to-morrow's prophecy, do not dedicate ourselves unfalteringly to the forgotten vision! This I am resolved to do. I will serve America by serving her ideal of humanity. I will open my heart, as she has opened her shores, to all the peoples of the earth. I will give love, as she has given hospitality, to the hated and hunted of God's children. . . .

This is my service for the days of war—the ministry of reconciliation, the defense of democracy, the preparation of the gospel of peace, the quest of brotherhood. It is the deliberate espousal of that higher spiritual loyalty which is not so much the destruction as it is the fulfillment of those lower and more carnal loyalties which stir the envy and the hate of men. . . .

SOURCE: John Haynes Holmes, *A Statement to My People on the Eve of War* (New York: Church of the Messiah, 1917), 3, 5–7, 9, 12–16, in John Haynes Holmes Papers, CDG-A, box 1, Swarthmore College Peace Collection, Swarthmore PA.

3.7. George W. Norris, Anti-interventionist Speech (4 April 1917)

[George W. Norris, a Republican senator from Nebraska, delivered this powerful antiwar speech on 4 April 1917, during the Senate debate on a resolution of war against Germany. Like many midwestern progressives, he criticized Wall Street and charged it with supporting U.S. intervention to protect profits. In the mid-1930s the Senate's Nye Committee hearings on the munitions industry bolstered the noninterventionist temper of the time.]

Mr. NORRIS. Mr. President, while I am most emphatically and sincerely opposed to taking any step that will force our country into the useless and senseless war now being waged in Europe, yet if this resolution passes, I shall not permit my feeling of opposition to its passage to interfere in any way with my duty either as a Senator or as a citizen in bringing success and victory to American arms. I am bitterly opposed to my country entering the war, but if, notwithstanding my opposition, we do enter it, all of my energy and all of my power will be behind our flag in carrying it on to victory.

The resolution now before the Senate is a declaration of war. Before taking this momentous step, and while standing on the brink of this terrible vortex, we ought to pause and calmly and judiciously consider the terrible consequences of the step we are about to take. We ought to consider likewise the route we have recently traveled and ascertain whether we have reached our present position in a way that is compatible with the neutral position which we claimed to occupy at the beginning and through the various stages of this unholy and unrighteous war.

No close student of recent history will deny that both Great Britain and Germany have, on numerous occasions since the beginning of the war, flagrantly violated in the most serious manner the rights of neutral vessels and neutral nations under existing international law . . .

The reason given by the President in asking Congress to declare war against Germany is that the German Government has declared certain war zones, within which, by the use of submarines, she sinks, without notice, American ships and destroys American lives.

Let us trace briefly the origin and history of these so-called war zones. The first war zone was declared by Great Britain. She gave us and the world notice of it on the 4th day of November, 1914. . . . This zone . . . covered the whole of the North Sea. . . .

The first German war zone was declared on the 4th day of February, 1915, . . . [and] covered the English Channel and the high sea waters around the British Isles. . . .

The only difference is that in the case of Germany we have persisted in our protest, while in the case of England we have submitted. What was our duty as a Government and what were our rights when we were confronted with these extraordinary orders declaring these military zones? First, we could have defied both of them and could have gone to war against both of these nations for this violation of international law and interference with our neutral rights. Second, we had the technical right to defy one and to acquiesce in the other. Third, we could, while denouncing them both as illegal, have acquiesced in them both and thus remained neutral with both sides, although not agreeing with either as to the righteousness of their respective orders. We could have said to American shipowners that, while these orders are both contrary to international law and are both unjust, we do not believe that the provocation is sufficient to cause us to go to war for the defense of our rights as a neutral nation, and, therefore, American ships and American citizens will go into these zones at their own peril and risk. Fourth, we might have declared an embargo against the shipping from American ports of any merchandise to either one of these Governments that persisted in maintaining its military zone. We might have refused to permit the sailing of any ship from any American port to either of these military zones. In my judgment, if we had pursued this course, the zones would have been of short duration. England would have been compelled to take her mines out of the North Sea in order to get any supplies from our country. When her mines were taken out of the North Sea then the German ports upon the North Sea would have been accessible to American shipping and Germany would have been compelled to cease her submarine warfare in order to get any supplies from our Nation into German North Sea ports.

There are a great many American citizens who feel that we owe it as a duty to humanity to take part in this war. Many instances of cruelty and inhumanity can be found on both sides. Men are often biased in their judgment on account of their sympathy and their interests. To my mind, what we ought to have maintained from the beginning was the strictest neutrality. If we had done this I do not believe we would have been on the verge of war at the present time. . . . [T]he enormous amount of money loaned to the Allies in this country has been instrumental in bringing about a public sentiment in favor of our country taking a course that would make every bond worth a hundred cents on the dollar and making the payment of every debt certain and sure. Through this instrumentality and also through the instrumentality of others who have not only made millions out of the war in the manufacture of munitions, etc., and who would expect to make millions more if our country can be drawn into the catastrophe, a large number of the great newspapers and news agencies of the country have been controlled and enlisted in the greatest propaganda that the world has ever known, to manufacture sentiment in favor of war. It is now demanded that the American citizens shall be used as insurance policies to guarantee the safe delivery of munitions of war to belligerent nations. The enormous profits of munitions of war manufacturers, stockbrokers, and bond dealers must be still further increased by our entrance into the war. This has brought us to the present moment, when Congress, urged by the President and backed by the artificial sentiment, is about to declare war and engulf our country in the greatest holocaust that the world has ever known. . . .

To whom does war bring prosperity? Not to the soldier who for the munificent compensation of $16 per month shoulders his musket and goes into the trench, there to shed his blood and to die if necessary; not to the broken-hearted widow who waits for the return of the mangled body of her husband; not to the mother who weeps at the death of her brave boy; not to the little children who shiver with cold; not to the babe who suffers from hunger; nor to the millions of mothers and daughters who carry broken hearts to their graves. War brings no prosperity to the great mass of common and patriotic citizens. It increases the cost of living of those who toil and those who already must strain every effort to keep soul and body together. War brings prosperity to the stock gambler on Wall Street . . .

Their object in having war and in preparing for war is to make money. Human suffering and the sacrifice of human life are necessary, but Wall Street considers only the dollars and the cents. The men who do the fighting, the people who make the sacrifices, are the ones who will not be counted in the measure of this great prosperity that he depicts. The stockbrokers would not, of course, go to war, because the very object they have in bringing on the war is profit, and therefore they must remain in their Wall Street offices in order to share in that great prosperity which they say war will bring. The volunteer officer, even the drafting officer, will not find them. They will be concealed in their palatial offices on Wall Street, sitting behind mahogany desks, covered up with clipped coupons— coupons soiled with the sweat of honest toil, coupons stained with mothers' tears, coupons dyed in the lifeblood of their fellow men.

We are taking a step to-day that is fraught with untold danger. We are going into war upon the command of gold. We are going to run the risk of sacrificing millions of our countrymen's lives in order that other countrymen may coin their lifeblood into money. And even if we do not cross the Atlantic and go into the trenches, we are going to pile up a debt that the toiling masses that shall come many generations after us will have to pay. Unborn millions will bend their backs in toil in order to pay for the terrible step we are now about to take. We are about to do the bidding of wealth's terrible mandate. By our act we will make millions of our countrymen suffer, and the consequences of it may well be that millions of our brethren must shed their lifeblood, millions of broken-hearted women must weep, millions of children must suffer with cold, and millions of babes must die from hunger, and all because we want to preserve the commercial right of American citizens to deliver munitions of war to belligerent nations. . . .

SOURCE: *Congressional Record—Senate*, 65th Cong., 1st sess. (Washington DC: Government Printing Office, 1917), pt. 1, 4 April 1917, 55:212–14.

3.8. Jane Addams, "Patriotism and Pacifists in War Time" (16 June 1917)

[Jane Addams devoted her life to peace and social justice. One of the pioneers in the settlement house movement, she later devoted her energies to the cause of world peace. She cofounded the Woman's Peace Party and its successor, the Women's International League for Peace and Freedom. In 1931 she was the first American woman to receive the Nobel Peace Prize. Delivered before the City Club of Chicago, this speech takes aim at those who accuse pacifists of being unpatriotic and cowardly.]

. . . In the stir of the heroic moment when a nation enters war, men's minds are driven back to the earliest obligations of patriotism, and almost without volition the emotions move along the worn grooves of blind admiration for the soldier and of unspeakable contempt for him who, in the hour of danger, declares that fighting is unnecessary. We pacifists are not surprised, therefore, when apparently striking across and reversing this popular conception of patriotism, that we should not only be considered incapable of facing reality, but that we should be called traitors and cowards. . . .

PACIFISTS AND "PASSIVISM"

First: The similarity of sound between "passive" and "pacifism" is often misleading . . . we pacifists, so far from passively wishing nothing to be done, contend on the contrary that this world crisis should be utilized for the creation of an international government able to make the necessary political and economic changes when they are due; . . .

We are not advocating a mid-Victorian idea that good men from every country meet together at The Hague or elsewhere, where they shall pass a resolution, that "wars hereby cease" and that "the world hereby be federated." What we insist upon is that the world can be organized politically by its statesmen as it has been already organized into an international fiscal system by its bankers or into an international scientific association by its scientists. We ask why the problem of building a railroad to Bagdad, of securing corridors to the sea for a landlocked nation, or warm water harbors for Russia should result in war. . . . Is it not obviously because such situations transcend national boundaries and must be approached in a spirit of world adjustment, while men's minds, still held apart by national suspicions and rivalries, are unable to approach them in a spirit of peaceful adjustment?

The very breakdown exhibited by the present war reinforces the pacifists' contention that there is need of an international charter—a

Magna Charta [*sic*] indeed—of international rights, to be issued by the nations great and small, with large provisions for economic freedom.

THE PATRIOTISM OF PACIFISTS

In reply to the old charge of lack of patriotism, we claim that we are patriotic from the historic viewpoint as well as by other standards. American pacifists believe—if I may go back to those days before the war, which already seem so far away—that the United States was especially qualified by her own particular experience to take the leadership in a peaceful organization of the world. We then ventured to remind our fellow citizens that when the founders of this republic adopted the federal constitution and established the Supreme Court, they were entering upon a great political experiment of whose outcome they were by no means certain. . . . Nevertheless, the great political experiment of the United States was so well established by the middle of the 19th century, that America had come to stand to the world for the principle of federal government and for a supreme tribunal whose decisions were binding upon sovereign states.

. . . Stirred by enthusiasm over the great historical experiment of the United States, it seemed to us that American patriotism might rise to a supreme effort. We hoped that the United States might refuse to follow the beaten paths of upholding the rights of a separate nationalism by war, because her own experience for more than a century had so thoroughly committed her to federation and to peaceful adjudication as to every-day methods of government. . . .

PACIFISTS AGAINST ISOLATION

With such a national history back of us, as pacifists we are thrown into despair over our inability to make our position clear when we are accused of wishing to isolate the United States and to keep our country out of world politics. We are, of course, urging a policy exactly the reverse, that this country should lead the nations of the world into a wider life of co-ordinated political activity; that the United States should boldly recognize the fact that the vital political problems of our time have become as intrinsically international in character as have the commercial and social problems so closely connected with them; that modern wars are not so much the result of quarrels between nations as of the rebellion against international situations inevitably developed through the changing years, which admit of adequate treatment only through an international agency not yet created. . . .

NATIONAL UNSELFISHNESS

Pacifists recognize and rejoice in the large element of national unselfishness and in the recognition of international obligation set forth by President Wilson as reasons for our participation in the great war. We feel that the exalted sense of patriotism in which each loses himself in the consciousness of a national existence, has been enlarged by an alliance with nations across the Atlantic and across the Pacific with whom we are united in a common purpose. Let the United States, by all means, send a governmental commission to Russia; plans for a better fiscal system to bewildered China; food to all nations wherever little children are starving; but let us never forget that the inspiring and overwhelming sense of a common purpose, which an alliance with fifteen or sixteen nations gives us, is but a forecast of what might be experienced if the genuine international alliance were achieved including all the nations of the earth. . . .

ARE PACIFISTS COWARDS?

When as pacifists we urge a courageous venture into international ethics, which will require a fine valor as well as a high intelligence, we experience a sense of anti-climax when we are told that because we do not want war, we are so cowardly as to care for "safety first," that we place human life, physical life, above the great ideals of national righteousness.

But surely that man is not without courage who, seeing that which is invisible to the majority of his fellow countrymen, still asserts his conviction and is ready to vindicate its spiritual value over against the world. Each advance in the zigzag line of human progress has traditionally been embodied in small groups of individuals, who have ceased to be in harmony with the *status quo* and have demanded modifications. . . .

With visions of international justice filling our minds, pacifists are always a little startled when those who insist that justice can only be established by war, accuse us of caring for peace irrespective of justice. Many of the pacifists in their individual and corporate capacity have long striven for social and political justice with a fervor perhaps equal to that employed by the advocates of force, and we realize that a sense of justice has become the keynote to the best political and social activity in this generation. Although this ruling passion for juster relations between man and man, group and group, or between nation and nation, is not without its sterner aspects, among those who dream of a wider social justice throughout the world there has developed a conviction that justice between men or between nations can be achieved only through understanding and fellowship, and that a finely tempered sense of justice, which alone is of any service in modern civilization, cannot be secured in the storm and stress of war. . . .

We believe that the ardor and self sacrifice so characteristic of youth could be enlisted for the vitally energetic role which we hope our beloved country will inaugurate in the international life of the world. We realize that it is only the ardent spirits, the lovers of mankind, who will be able to break down the suspicion and lack of understanding which has so long stood in the way of the necessary changes upon which international good order depends; who will at last create a political organization enabling nations to secure without war, those high ends which they now gallantly seek to obtain upon the battlefield.

With such a creed, can the pacifists of today be accused of selfishness when they urge upon the United States not isolation, not indifference to moral issues and to the fate of liberty and democracy, but a strenuous endeavor to lead all nations of the earth into an organized international life worthy of civilized men?

SOURCE: *City Club Bulletin* (Chicago) 10 (16 June 1917): 184–90, in Jane Addams Papers, DG-1, reel 113:47, Swarthmore College Peace Collection, Swarthmore PA.

3.9. Randolph Bourne, "A War Diary" (September 1917)

[Randolph Bourne, a social commentator and Greenwich Village bohemian, opposed World War I. His wartime essays criticized intellectuals such as John Dewey, who supported the war, terming their rationale as "technique conscious and morally blind." In "The State," an influential 1918 essay, Bourne popularized the phrase "war is the health of the state."]

Time brings a better adjustment to the war. There had been so many times when, to those who had energetically resisted its coming, it seemed the last intolerable outrage. In one's wilder moments one expected revolt against the impressment of unwilling men and the suppression of unorthodox opinion. One conceived the war as breaking down through a kind of intellectual sabotage diffused through the country. But as one talks to people outside the cities and away from ruling currents of opinion, one finds the prevailing apathy shot everywhere with acquiescence. The war is a bad business, which somehow got fastened on us. They don't want to go, but they've got to go. . . . The kind of war which we are conducting is an enterprise which the American government does not have to carry on with the hearty co-operation of the American people but only with their acquiescence. And that acquiescence seems sufficient to float an indefinitely protracted war for vague or even largely uncomprehended and unaccepted purposes. Our resources in men and materials are vast enough to organize the war-technique without enlisting more than a fraction of the people's conscious energy. Many men will not like being sucked into the actual fighting organism, but as the war goes on they will be sucked in as individuals and they will yield. There is likely to be no element in the country with the effective will to help them resist. They are not likely to resist of themselves concertedly. They will be licked grudgingly into military shape, and their lack of enthusiasm will in no way unfit them for use in the hecatombs necessary for the military decision upon which Allied political wisdom still apparently insists. It is unlikely that enough men will be taken from the potentially revolting classes seriously to embitter their spirit. Losses in the well-to-do classes will be sustained by a sense of duty and of reputable sacrifice. From the point of view of the worker, it will make little difference whether his work contributes to annihilation overseas or to construction at home. Temporarily, his condition is better if it contributes to the former. We of the middle classes will be progressively poorer than we should otherwise have been. Our lives will be slowly drained by clumsily levied taxes and the robberies of imperfectly controlled private enterprises. But this will not cause us to revolt. There are not likely to be enough hungry stomachs to make a revolution. . . .

The "liberals" who claim a realistic and pragmatic attitude in politics have disappointed us in setting up and then clinging wistfully to the belief that our war could get itself justified for an idealistic flavor, or at least for a world-renovating social purpose, that they had more or less denied to the other belligerents. If these realists had had time in the hurry and scuffle of events to turn their philosophy on themselves, they might have seen how thinly disguised a rationalization this was of their emotional undertow. They wanted a League of Nations. They had an unanalyzable feeling that this was a war in which we had to be, and be in it we would. What more natural than to join the two ideas and conceive our war as the decisive factor in the attainment of the desired end! This gave them a good conscience for willing American participation, although as good men they must have loathed war and everything connected with it. . . .

Now war is such an indefeasible and unescapable Real that the good realist must accept it rather comprehensively. To keep out of it is pure quietism, an acute moral failure to adjust. At the same time, there is an inexorability about war. It is a little unbridled for the realist's rather nice sense of purposive social control. And nothing is so disagreeable to the pragmatic mind as any kind of an absolute. The realistic pragmatist could not recognize war as inexorable—though to the common mind it would seem as near an absolute, coercive social situation, as it is possible to fall into. For the inexorable abolishes choices, and it is the essence of the realist's creed to have, in every situation, alternatives before him. . . .

But what then is there really to choose between the realist who accepts evil in order to manipulate it to a great end, but who somehow unaccountably finds events turn sour on him, and the Utopian pacifist who cannot stomach the evil and will have none of it? Both are helpless, both are coerced. The Utopian, however, knows that he is ineffective and that he is coerced, while the realist, evading disillusionment, moves, in a twilight zone of half-hearted criticism, and hoping for the best, where he does not become a tacit fatalist. The latter would be the manlier position, but then where would be his realistic philosophy of intelligence and choice? . . . War determines its own end,—victory, and government crushes out automatically all forces that deflect, or threaten to deflect, energy from the path of organization to that end. All governments will act in this way, the most democratic as well as the most autocratic. It is only "liberal" naïveté that is shocked at arbitrary coercion and suppression. Willing war means willing all the evils that are organically bound up with it. A good many people still seem to believe in a peculiar kind of democratic and antiseptic war. The pacifists opposed the war because they knew this was an illusion, and because of the myriad hurts they knew war would do the promise of democracy at home. For once the babes and sucklings seem to have been wiser than the children of light. . . .

. . . Our war presents no more extraordinary phenomenon than the number of the more creative minds of the younger generation who are still irreconcilable toward the great national enterprise which the government has undertaken. The country is still dotted with young men and women, in full possession of their minds, faculties and virtue, who feel themselves profoundly alien to the work which is going on around them. They must not be confused with the disloyal or the pro-German. They have no grudge against the country, but their patriotism has broken down in the emergency. They want to see the carnage stopped and Europe decently constructed again. They want a democratic peace. . . . They see that war has lost for us both the mediation and the leadership, and is blackening us ever deeper with the responsibility for having prolonged the dreadful tangle. They are skeptical not only of the technique of war, but also of its professed aims. . . . Their ideals outshoot the government's. To them the real arena lies in the international class-struggle, rather than in the competition of artificial national units. They are watching to see what the Russian socialists are going to do for the world, not what the timorous capitalistic American democracy may be planning. They can feel no enthusiasm for a League of Nations, which should solidify the old units and continue in disguise the old theories of international relations. . . . But why would not this League turn out to be little more than a well-oiled machine for the use of that enlightened imperialism toward which liberal American finance is already whetting its tongue? . . .

. . . The war will leave the country spiritually impoverished, because of the draining away of sentiment into the channels of war. Creative and constructive enterprises will suffer not only through the appalling waste of financial capital in the work of annihilation, but also in the loss of emotional capital in the conviction that war overshadows all other realities. This is the poison of war that disturbs even creative minds. . . .

The war—or American promise: one must choose. One cannot be interested in both. For the effect of the war will be to impoverish American promise. It cannot advance it, however, liberals may choose to identify American promise with a league of nations to enforce peace. Americans who desire to cultivate the promises of American life need not lift a finger to obstruct the war, but they cannot conscientiously accept it. However intimately a part of their country they may feel in its creative enterprises toward a better life, they cannot feel themselves a part of it in its futile and self-mutilating enterprise of war. We can be apathetic with a good conscience, for we have other values and ideals for America. Our country will not suffer for our lack of patriotism as long as it has that of our industrial masters. Meanwhile, those who have turned their thinking into war-channels have abdicated their leadership for this younger generation. They have put themselves in a limbo of interests that are not the concerns which worry us about American life and make us feverish and discontented. . . .

This search has been threatened by two classes who have wanted to deflect idealism to the war,—the patriots and the realists. The patriots have challenged us by identifying apathy with disloyalty. The reply is that war-technique in this situation is a matter of national mechanics rather than national ardor. The realists have challenged us by insisting that the war is an instrument in the working-out of beneficent national policy. Our skepticism points out to them how soon their "mastery" becomes "drift," tangled in the fatal drive toward victory as its own end, how soon they become mere agents and expositors of forces as they are. Patriots and realists disposed of, we can pursue creative skepticism with honesty, and at least hope that in the recoil from war we may find the treasures we are looking for.

SOURCE: *Seven Arts* 2 (September 1917): 535–36, 538–43, 545–47.

3.10. Kirby Page to Howard Sweet (3 February 1918)

[Kirby Page, an ordained minister of the Disciples of Christ and personal secretary for YMCA secretary Sherwood Eddy during World War I, became an influential interwar exponent of the social gospel. He coedited FOR's journal the *World Tomorrow* and wrote many books on peace and social justice. He experienced firsthand the realities of war while serving as a YMCA volunteer in France. That experience solidified his Christian pacifist views, a transformation that he explains in this letter, written from Shanghai, China, to his friend and attorney Howard Sweet.]

. . . You say that you heard that I have turned radical pacifist. Personally, I greatly dislike to use the word "pacifist" in referring to my convictions regarding the war, since this same term is used when referring to pro-Germans, anarchists, socialists and various and sundry so-called "cranks" who are opposed to the war. It is true, however, that on grounds of Christian convictions I am thoroughly opposed to all military warfare. I say "military" warfare but I am not a "non-resister" and my objection to war is not based on the theory that the use of force is always wrong.

You say that you imagine I have been turned against war because of what I have seen. My convictions are not merely a reaction or revulsion from what I have seen, they are rather the result of eighteen months of agonizing *thought* upon what I have seen and heard. It is not much of an exaggeration to say that I have thought of little else than war during these months. It has been with me night and day. In the nature of the case, no one can come in close contact with the soldiers at the front without being driven to serious thought regarding the whole question of the ethics of war. This is especially so when one is trying to present the Christian message to soldiers. . . .

Before we can decide whether or not war is justifiable we must come to a clear understanding of what war is and what it inevitably involves. . . . War is always and everywhere a *method*, and it is as a method that it must be discussed. . . .

Without attempting in this letter to give the proofs for my statements, let me merely enumerate six elements that I believe are inevitably involved in the method of war. (1) War compels the giving of supremacy to the law of *military necessity*. In the end, war compels the setting aside of moral and ethical considerations and the doing of whatever is necessary to win. Air raids, poison gas, liquid fire and boiling oil in themselves are immoral practices, but if the enemy is to be resisted they must be resorted to. The end justifies the means, is the foundation stone of all war. (2) War inevitably involves the wholesale *destruction of life* and the doing of violent and atrocious deeds. Man after man has told me that when he went over the top he "saw red" and did not really know what he was doing. In this state of mind, unspeakably [sic] crimes are committed, countless instances of which I could tell you if we were together. (3) War tends to break down the *value of human life*. This must be so, as no man can run his bayonet through man after man or live in a trench with dead and decaying bodies piled high all about him without having human life lose much of its sacredness. (4) War causes men to *hate*. (5) War involves the use of *deceit* and *falsehood* (spies and false reports). No war can be waged on a basis of absolute truth—the whole truth and nothing but the truth. (6) War compels a man to surrender his *moral freedom*. A soldier is not supposed to have a conscience or to decide for himself what is right or wrong. He simply does what is commanded, whether it be to sink the Lusitania, bomb London or Cologne or shoot down his relatives on the streets of Dublin. . . .

If you ask me what I would advocate doing under the circumstances my answer is, *Be Christian.* I mean by this that so far as I myself am concerned I cannot feel justified in doing anything that is directly opposed to the spirit and teaching of Jesus. . . . I believe in a doctrine of no compromise with evil, and that I *ought* never to do a thing that is un-Christian (although I am constantly doing such things, because of human weakness and sin in my life). My aim at least is never to do deliberately a wrong thing. . . .

You ask, "Who are you, to set your opinion against that of your own country?" . . . [A]nd the question has been the source of considerable earnest thought during these months. . . . So long as I feel this way, I should be a traitor to myself and to Him if I should go to war. Is not this so? . . . I am firmly convinced that the day will come when Christians will look upon the justification of this war much in the same way that we look upon the justification of torture or slavery. . . .

SOURCE: Kirby Page Papers, Special Collections, Library of the Claremont School of Theology, Claremont CA. Kirby Page's correspondence is organized by date.

3.11. Firemen Resign Rather than Buy Liberty Bonds (18 July 1918)

[In Spokane, Washington, two city firemen refused to purchase Liberty bonds and war stamps. The firemen, Tom W. Black and Arthur W. Remer, were members of the International Bible Students' Association (Watch Tower Society), a religious group that opposed the war, whose members were often called Russellites, after founder Charles Russell. In 1931 the group took the name Jehovah's Witnesses. Falsely attributed to Russell, who died in 1916, *The Finished Mystery* (1917) criticized the war. Rather than being fired for their refusal, Black and Remer resigned. The following news account relates their resignations and the pressure on firemen to participate in the Liberty Loan program.]

Tom W. Black, pipeman at fire station 3, yesterday agreed to resign as a member of the fire department, to take effect in 10 days, rather than buy a Liberty bond.

"I have told [City] Commissioner Tilsley that I will resign," said Black yesterday. "I have been in the department for eight years, and have a wife and four children. I am sorry that circumstances have arisen that compel me to resign to maintain my freedom of conscience, but I guess it can not be helped."

Black is the second fireman to resign during the last week for failure to buy a Liberty bond, the other being Lieutenant Arthur W. Remer of station 1, who has agreed to give his resignation tomorrow. Both Black and Remer are members of the International Bible Students' association, founded by the late Pastor Russell of Brooklyn, N.Y., whose book, "The Finished Mystery," was recently placed under the ban by the government. This sect does not believe in war, and Black and Remer, in refusing to buy bonds, said they were living up to their religious convictions.

SENDS WARNING TO 49 FIREMEN.

Letters were mailed yesterday by Commissioner Tilsley to the 49 firemen other than Black and Remer who have failed to buy Liberty bonds. Some of the men discussed the matter informally yesterday with Commissioner Tilsley, who expects to take up the active consideration of the cases tomorrow. The questionnaires returned by the men show that many of them subscribed for the first and second Liberty loans, but bought war savings stamps instead of taking any part of the third Liberty loan. . . .

MEN BOUGHT WAR STAMPS.

"I am informed that some time ago a campaign was waged among the fire stations to sign the men up for savings stamps and, that in some sections every man was enrolled as a purchaser," said Commissioner Tilsley. "Where the men show that they have bought war savings stamps to the value of a Liberty bond, I think this is good evidence that they are not slackers, and I will accept this explanation as sufficient."

"But where a fireman has bought $5 or $10 worth of war savings stamps in expectation of being relieved from the purchase of a Liberty bond, this excuse will not be accepted. I will inquire into each case separately and the facts in each case will govern. . . . and we do not propose to condemn any of them in this case without a fair presentations of the facts. . . ."

SOURCE: "Quits Job Rather than Buy Bond," *Spokesman-Review* (Spokane WA), 21 April 1918, 6.

3.12. Dorothy Day, Opposition to World War I (1952)

[In 1916 and 1917 Dorothy Day was a reporter for the *New York Call*, a daily socialist newspaper. In April 1917 she moved to the *Masses*, a lively socialist political, literary, and artistic magazine. During World War I she was a radical, but not yet a pacifist or Christian. She later converted to Catholicism and cofounded the Catholic Worker Movement.]

. . . My [reporting] assignments took me to all kinds of strike meetings, picket lines, peace meetings. Many groups were working for peace, trying to prevent our entry into the war—the Emergency Peace Federation, the I.W.W., the Socialists, the anarchists, an anti-conscription group at Columbia University. . . .

. . . I was neither a Christian nor a pacifist, and I certainly acted like neither. . . .

In April, 1917, I was given an assignment by the city editor to go to Washington with a group of Columbia students to protest the passage of the conscription act. These young radicals who made up the Anti-Conscription League chartered a bus to make the trip. . . . I was nineteen and it was an early spring. We stopped at Philadelphia, Chester, Wilmington, and Baltimore to hold meetings in the afternoon or evening at other colleges. . . . it was spring and we were all young, and a war was in the air and they were fighting a losing battle.

In Baltimore there was a sudden riot. A group of hostile students broke up the meeting and tried to beat up the Columbia students, whom they called Jew radicals. I was there in the role of reporter and stood as close to the patrol wagon as I could to get the names of those whom the police were arresting. . . . [I] had my first glimpse of mob spirit. It was not too serious, this first riot, and the police took the skirmishings good-naturedly. It was a different affair in labor struggles when I saw police ride down strikers and beat up demonstrators. . . .

I wavered between my allegiance to socialism, syndicalism (the I.W.W.'s) and anarchism. . . .

During later months there were meetings in the MacDougal Street apartment [in Greenwich Village]. I remember one especially, the night before registration day, when a group of men argued all night as to whether or not they should register for the draft, and then when morning came, registered. Their opposition to the draft seemed not so much opposition to war as to the compulsion of conscription, the denial of liberty.

After the draft law went into effect, Hugo Gellert's younger brother was inducted and put in the guardhouse in a camp on Long Island because he refused to don a uniform in the capitalist war. Hugo was the artist whose work I admired most on *The Masses*. He was a young Hungarian . . . Hugo and Mike Gold and I went to see Hugo's brother in the guardhouse and he seemed cheerful enough then, considering his tragic situation. We were shocked to hear some weeks later that he was dead. The report was that he had taken his own life, but we could not believe it. He was a happy youth, friendly with the guards who smuggled his violin to him so that he could play to them. Hugo insisted that he had been murdered. He came from a revolutionary family in Hungary and he told us gruesome tales of prisoners being tortured, their nails torn out, their bodies beaten so that forever after they were crippled, mentally and physically. . . .

SOURCE: Dorothy Day, *The Long Loneliness: An Autobiography* (New York: Harper & Row, 1952), 57–58, 60–62, 71–72.

3.13. A. J. Muste, "What It Was Like in World War I" (1958)

[A. J. Muste was an ordained minister in the Dutch Reformed Church. During World War I the Friends Meeting in Providence, Rhode Island, enrolled him as a minister in the Society of Friends. He became a leader in the Fellowship of Reconciliation, the War Resisters League, and other radical pacifist groups. Dubbed by *Time* as the "Number One U.S. pacifist," Muste was the most influential American pacifist in the twentieth century. He symbolized the modern peace movement's commitment to peace and justice through nonviolent direct action in the peace, labor, and civil rights movements. He published his autobiography serially in the magazine *Liberation*, between 1957 and 1960. Here he explains his World War I experiences.]

. . . The custom of having people rise to sing *The Star Spangled Banner* at the opening of plays, operas and many public meetings was introduced, and conformity was forced on those who disliked the practice. Military parades occurred frequently, and men were expected to doff their hats whenever a flag was carried by. Many were obviously self-conscious and uncomfortable about it. Salutes and pledges to the flag were introduced in schools. Churches put national flags near altar or pulpit. People appeased the sense of incongruity which this aroused in them by introducing a "church" flag into sanctuaries along with the Stars and Stripes. This has always struck me as rank hypocrisy. The problem is the *presence* of the symbol of nationalism and the state in a church, not the *absence* of a flag with a different color, which, in a Christian sanctuary, cannot possibly add anything to the Cross.

Those who opposed or did not readily accept the United States' entry into the War, (especially, of course, if they happened to be of German ancestry) were labeled "pro-Germans." People began to act as amateur spies and loyalty agents, reporting mysterious circles of light in the windows of neighbors living somewhere near the shore, which were assumed to be signals to prowling German submarines. Those who did not buy Liberty (sic) bonds to finance the war were suspect, and in not a few Middle Western areas where there were large German settlements, they were tarred and feathered. As one brought up to think of the Middle West as the liberal, democratic part of the land, in contrast to the aristocratic and effete East, this shocked me. A pacifist and nonconformist felt, and actually was, safer in the East during World War I. Conscription was introduced in the land to which many had fled to escape conscription. At the outset there was no provision whatsoever for conscientious objectors and many of them, after being forcibly inducted into the Army, were cruelly tortured in barracks and military prisons.

There are a number of reasons why repressive measures were so much more severe and crude during the months of which I am now writing than they were in the corresponding period of World War II. First of all, the War came in that earlier period as a first experience to a people who believed their country had passed beyond war, a people who, for this and other reasons, were imbued with optimism and a rosy view of human nature. When they became convinced that Germans were monsters and that means which they had deeply felt to be stupid and revolting had to be used against such monsters, they experienced a trauma and, in the language now familiar to nearly everybody, had to overcompensate in order to silence their inner resistance and to assuage their hurt.

WAR AS A CRUSADE

The war had to be "sold" to such people as a crusade, indeed as the last tragic war to end all war, in a much more naive and simplistic fashion than was to be the case in the later war. . . .

The sharpness and crudeness of repression in World War I was also due to the fact that much more resistance had to be overcome than in World War II. For example, the emotional nationalism served to inflame the anti-British nationalism of the Irish-Americans. Nineteen sixteen was the year of the Easter Rebellion and massacre in Ireland. The Irish were red hot anti-conscriptionists. The I.W.W. (Industrial Workers of the World) were at the height of their influence and were ardently anti-militarist. The administration arrested all the top leaders and crippled the organization.

There were strong anti-war currents in unions such as the United Mine Workers and the Machinists. The majority of the Socialist Party members maintained an anti-war stand even after United States entry. Eugene V. Debs, who was imprisoned by Woodrow Wilson's regime, is a symbol of the problem of the hour and its harsh resolution by a supposedly liberal government. The intellectuals of the pre-war period were predominantly anti-militarist, as was Wilson himself. Their abandonment of that stand was a painful experience, and not all of them did abandon it. This was true of the Socialists among them and of such a flaming and eloquent libertarian as Randolph Bourne....

EXIT FROM THE PULPIT

For the most part the people of Central Church in Newtonville, Massachusetts welcomed, or at least easily accepted, my espousal of pacifism and my pacifist activities in the first eight months or so of 1916. Towards the end of the summer, as United States entry loomed more distinctly, some warnings came of trouble ahead. The authorities of a fashionable boys' school located near the church thought it advisable not to expose the boys to pacifist corruption and decided to take them to another church on Sunday morning. Pressure from parents was probably the main factor in this decision. About the same time, a small number of the wealthier families in the church ceased attending. As these things became known in the congregation, the tradespeople, and less opulent families generally, began to go out of their way to show their sympathy. It must be said also that the large majority of Central Church families continued to stand by.

But when the United States formally entered the War in April 1917, the situation changed abruptly. I returned from the great anti-war demonstration in Washington, (where I first encountered such pacifist leaders as Judah Magnes, John Haynes Holmes, and the elder J. Howard Melish) to lead a union Lenten service in my own church. The young Swedenborgian minister refused to participate in the union service, even though it was in no sense a political or anti-war service: the fact that I had gone to Washington and had not declared my support of the War on my return made me a traitor in his eyes.

This was not true of the members of Central Church, who still wanted me to remain and to the end defended me against charges of treason and pro-Germanism. Non-pacifist church and pacifist minister somehow managed to make a go of it until the two months summer vacation intervened to give us a breathing spell.

When I returned after Labor Day, it was clear that the situation was approaching an inevitable break-up. On both sides it was the more painful because there were no personal recriminations.

It was a psychological factor having to do with the pastoral and counselling relationship which was decisive. This did not involve the young men who enlisted or were drafted, with whom I had played baseball as well as discussed Christian ethics. So far as I know, every one of them as he left said in effect that he did not know for sure whether I was right or wrong; he himself "had to go"; but he hoped I would stick to my "pacifist guns."

It was when some of these boys were wounded and one of them— brilliant, handsome and a noble character—was killed, that the parents and their friends felt that, holding the views I did, I could not adequately comfort them. To tell the truth, I did not feel that I could either. The tension in those days was too great. I resigned. Almost without exception, pacifist ministers in World War I lost their pulpits or as in Seattle, in the case of Sidney Strong (father of Anna Louise Strong) "kept his pulpit but lost his congregation," . . .

Freed from a steady job, I did considerable volunteer work for a new-born organization (which a little later took the name American Civil Liberties Union), whose director, Roger Baldwin, was a young social worker from St. Louis, himself a C.O. who served a year's prison term for his stand. After two fruitless visits, marked by the well-known run-around, I located the C.O.'s, imprisoned in their barracks at Camp Devens, near Fitchburg, Massachusetts. Not having been unfrocked, I received some belated recognition from the camp authorities and was able to set in motion activities which eventually resulted in the amelioration of the brutality toward the Camp Devens C.O.'s. We also helped secure some provisions for better treatment nationally and even some opportunity, toward the end of the war, for alternative service, which seemed an immense gain then but became a bone of contention among pacifists in World War II.

I helped also in the trials of some of the New England pacifists who fell afoul of the law, and in nearly miraculous fashion escaped being arrested and jailed myself. One thing that helped was that both the Federal Circuit Court Judge in Boston and the Federal District Attorney were true liberals and astute public servants. When they were pressed by patrioteers to get after pacifists and other non-conformists, they answered that it was much better to permit these fellows to let off steam in the open than to drive them underground. . . .

SOURCE: A. J. Muste, "Not So Long Ago," pt. 6 of autobiography, *Liberation* 2 (January 1958): 15–17.

3.14. Jessie Wallace Hughan, "Autobiography" (1926)

[Jessie W. Hughan, a socialist pacifist, taught English in New York public schools. She held a PhD in economics from Columbia University and was active in the Socialist Party. Opposing the war from the beginning, in 1915, she cofounded the Anti-Enlistment League and, in 1923, founded the War Resisters League. After the war she prepared this autobiography for school officials.]

. . . *Church*—while I was at college I joined my sister in the Unitarian Church (Unity Church, Brooklyn) and was active until about 1917. I was a Sunday School teacher for years, with a class of boys, and then superintendent of the small Sunday School. I resigned during the war because there was definite opposition to me because of my pacifist activities which was hurting the Sunday School. . . . The attitude of the Unitarian Church toward war was on the whole disappointing to me. John Haynes Holmes and a few other Unitarian ministers stood in opposition to war, but the Christian Register, as the church organ, and the majority of congregations, including our own in Brooklyn, went over to the war as vigorously as the orthodox churches. . . .

ATTITUDE DURING AND SINCE THE WORLD WAR—

. . . When the World War began my mother, sisters and myself immediately revolted against the whole thing, and antagonized some of our friends as early as the summer of 1914 by maintaining that war was always wrong, and that the U.S. ought never to enter it (at first we reserved, I think, the possibility of defense in case of actual invasion). In September, 1914, I was asked to speak on the subject at a meeting where Hamilton Holt was the chief speaker, and realized from his speech that there were upholders of Peace who yet believed that war was sometimes allowable.

During that winter I visited the heads of the various peace societies in New York trying to find out some aggressive peace action on the part of some existing group. Meeting with discouragement from all, I decided to do what I could myself, and planned an *Anti-Enlistment League,* which should line up all men and women who should promise never to enlist voluntarily or to give approval to such enlistment on the part of others. . . .

As I was a high school teacher at the time, and still am, the league, which received more publicity than its importance deserved, was the subject of much hostile comment in the Brooklyn papers. I was an active Socialist, also, and always talked against the war in speeches that I made. This activity caused me to be summoned before superintendents and boards of examiners several times, the general surveillance and excitement lasting through the war and after. They at first asked me to stop public speaking, saying that I might be brought up on charges, but I declined to do so and kept on actively with the various peace societies that began to be formed. I joined the *Fellowship of Reconciliation* at its formation—in 1916 [1915], I believe—the Women's [*sic*] Peace Party, etc., being on the executive board of each. When the U.S. entered the war, I ceased collection of signatures for the Anti-Enlistment League and tried to secure the formation of a No-Conscription Fellowship here, after the model of that in England. I was overruled by other pacifists, however.

I ran for Secretary of State on the Socialist ticket of New York in 1918 and for lieutenant-governor in 1920, and as a Socialist supported the anti-war St. Louis platform. During the war I declined to buy Liberty Bonds or work for the Red Cross, but was not dismissed from the school system, although just before the Armistice I was warned that I must go out very soon. I am still prohibited from promotion in the system because of this record . . .

After the war I continued endeavoring to push the matter of personal refusal to take part in war in the various peace groups. With the help of others I finally succeeded in organizing the *War Resisters League*, a branch of the War Resisters International, a movement in which I am now keenly interested.

During the war Mr. Archibald Stevenson began activity against the pacifists and listed me among his fifty in 1919. When the Lusk bills were in force in New York I was summoned before Mr. Stevenson's committee and refused the certificate of character and loyalty required of teachers because I would not sign the pledge of obedience without reserving matters of conscience.

SOURCE: Jessie W. Hughan, "Autobiography of Jessie Wallace Hughan," courtesy of Margaret Rockwell Finch, Hughan's niece, who prepared a typescript version of the original.

CHAPTER 4

Female Activism and Gendered Peacework

4.1. Meta Lilienthal Stern, "To All Women" (1914) and "Girls, Don't Marry Pacifists!" (1917)

[Meta Lilienthal Stern edited and contributed to the "Votes for Women" department in the socialist *New York Call.* This section highlighted news and issues of interest to women—especially socialist women. She was also active on the Socialist Suffrage Campaign Committee in New York. In these two pieces she urges women to organize for peace, while using politicized motherhood language to challenge the notion that peace and war issues should be left to men. In 1914 she urged women to mobilize to prevent U.S. entry into the war. In 1917, one month to the day that President Wilson delivered his war message to Congress, she offered a sardonic commentary on the virtues of military manhood.]

"To All Women" (2 June 1914)

This appeal is directed to every woman who may read it, be she Socialist, Socialist sympathizer, or non-Socialist; be she a suffragist, indifferent, or an anti. There is one question today that should bind all women together, irrespective of their political ideas and affiliations, and that is the question of war or peace. Let every woman who has a husband she loves or a son she has brought up with care and tenderness, or a father or brother or friend whose life is dear to her, every woman who believes in kindness and usefulness and happiness—in one word—every woman who is womanly in the best sense of the word—let her do everything within her limited power to prevent the United States of America from being dragged into this holocaust of war!

We, as women, want peace at any price; yes, at any price. The glory of human life is infinitely more important to us than the glory of the flag; the wounds and the agonized death of our loved ones something infinitely more to be dreaded than an insult to our government. We do not want the United States to interfere in Mexico. We say, let Mexico take care of itself and work out its own salvation! If the investments of American capitalists are threatened, let them take the risk! The protection of their investments is not worth the lives of our sons. We say: Let the United States settle its difficulties with Germany peaceably, by fair discussi[o]n and mutual concession! Let us not be blinded by jingoism from recognizing what justice there is in German claims and demands! We cannot resurrect the victims of the Lusitania nor appease the grief of those whose dear ones were taken by sending more young lives to a horrible death.

We, as women, must shout from the housetops that we do not want war. We must oppose and fight to the last ditch that horrible monster that threatens to bring upon us the same cataclysm of murder and destruction which we behold in Europe today. We have no vote, no direct power in the government of our country, but we have that much boasted indirect influence which some women consider all sufficient. Let us use that direct influence to our utmost! Let us not waste one day, no, not one hour, in doing something to make war on war!

What can you, the individual women do? Oh, a great deal! Here are some definite suggestions:

1. Send telegrams to President Wilson and Secr[e]tary Bryan, . . .

2. Write letters to the newspapers, . . . setting forth why you, as a wife, mother and home-maker, as a young girl or as an old lady, are opposed to war. . . .

3. Join at once either the Women's [sic] Peace party or the Anti-Enlistment League. . . .

4. Talk war all the time, to the members of your family, to your friends, to your chance acquaintances; not as war is usually discussed, as to which country is right or wrong and which stands

the best chance of winning, but the horror of war, its senseless brutality and barbarism.

5. Fight false patriotism, the patriotism unfortunately taught in our schools, which finds expression in saluting the flag, singing war songs, and glorifying militarism. Teach your children the truth about war and make them hate it.

Besides working against war as individuals, women should band together and plan monster demonstrations. There is no time to be lost. With the President's new attitude on the Mexican question, with the unsatisfactory tone of the German reply, we are facing the immediate, double possibility of becoming a nation at war. The Women's [sic] Peace party should take the lead and all other progressive women's organizations should follow. . . .

Even the question of votes for women, that big question of the hour, must be temporarily overshadowed by that burning, immediate question, of such tremendous importance to every woman's life: The question of peace or war.

Girls, Don't Marry Pacifists! (2 March 1917)

"Girls, don't marry pacifists; don't even make them your friends. A man who refuses to fight is a coward, and would fail to protect his wife, his children and his home."

This exhortation was made to the girl students of a private school in Scarsdale, N.Y., by a militaristic lady, representing the National Special Aid society.

Of course, you know, girls, that the pacifists are the men who so utterly failed to protect the women and children and homes of Europe that there are millions of widows and orphans and, wrecked and ruined homes there today, that women must perform the hardest kinds of labor, never intended for woman's strength, and that little children are neglected and homeless and threatened by starvation.

Of course, you know, also, that the pacifists are the men who are endangering the women and children and homes of this country by doing their utmost to drive the country into a useless, senseless, inexcusable war.

If you would be well protected, girls, you must marry men who have much brawn and little brain, who strut and brag and swagger, who show off brass buttons and rattle swords, who humiliate themselves before their superiors and bully their inferiors, and who regard murder as a fine art.

Coming to think of it, girls, the ideal protector was the cave man, who stole the woman he wanted from her family, carried her to his cave, and protected her by means of a club against all other cave men, incidentally also clubbing her. Yes, girls, through all history the soldier, the warrior, the conqueror, has been the noble protector of womanhood. So, marry any kind of a fighter, girls, only beware of that dangerous character, the pacifist.

SOURCE: Meta L. Stern, "To All Women," *New York Call*, 2 June 1914, 4; Meta Lilienthal, "Girls, Don't Marry Pacifists!" *New York Call*, 2 March 1917, 6.

4.2. Jane Addams, "What War Is Destroying" (March 1915)

[In this article Jane Addams, a leading peace activist and leader in the women's peace movement, presents a gendered motherhood argument against war. For Addams, gender was based on socialization, not biology.]

. . . But there are certain things now being destroyed by war in which from the beginning of time women, as women, have held a vested interest, . . .

At the present moment, however, thousands of men marching to their death are under compulsion, not of this higher type of patriotism, but of a tribal conception, because of an irrational appeal which ought to have left the world long since. They march and fight because they have been told that they must thus save their homes from destruction. . . .

I do not assert that women are better than men—even in the heat of suffrage debates I have never maintained that—but we would all admit that there are things concerning which women are more sensitive than men, and that one of these is the treasuring of life. I would ask you to consider with me five aspects concerning this sensitiveness which war is rapidly destroying:

The first is the *protection* of human life. The advanced nations know very accurately, and we have begun to know in America, how many children are needlessly lost in the first years of infancy. Measures inaugurated for the prevention of infant mortality were slowly spreading from one country to another. All that effort has been scattered to the winds by the war. No one is now pretending to count the babies who are dying throughout the villages and country-sides of the warring nations. We know only that a sudden rise in the infant mortality rate was the first casualty of the war to be reported, beginning when the troops were mobilizing.

The second aspect is the *nurture* of human life. From the time a soldier is born to the moment he marches in his uniform to be wantonly destroyed, it is largely the women of his household who have cared for him. War overthrows not only the work of the mother, the nurse, and the teacher, but at the same time ruthlessly destroys the very conception of the careful nurture of life.

The third aspect is the *fulfillment* of human life. Every woman who cares for a little child fondly throws her imagination forward to the time when he shall have become a great and heroic man. Every baby is thus made human, and is developed by the hope and expectation which surrounds him. But no one in Europe, in the face of war's destruction, can consider the fulfillment of life, and we are feeling the reaction of war's ideals in America every day.

The fourth aspect is the *conservation* of human life; that which expresses itself in the state care of dependent children, in old-age pensions; the sentiment which holds that every scrap of human life is so valuable that the human family cannot neglect a feeble child without risking its own destruction. At this moment none of the warring countries of Europe can cherish the aged and infirm. The state cannot give care to its dependents when thousands of splendid men are dying each day. Little children and aged people are dying, too, in some countries in the proportion of five to one soldier killed on the field, but the nation must remain indifferent to their suffering.

And last of all is that which we call the *ascent* of human life; that which leads a man to cherish the hope that the next generation shall advance beyond the generation in which he lives; that generous glow we all experience when we see that those coming after us are equipped better than we have been. The hope for the ascent of life is at the basis of social progress. We know that Europe at the end of this war will not begin to build where it left off; we know that it will begin generations behind the point it had reached when the war began.

If we admit that this sensitiveness for human life is stronger in women than in men because women have been responsible for the care of the young and the aged and those who need special nurture, it is certainly true that this sensitiveness developed in women carries with it an obligation. . . .

Many of us believe that throughout this round world of ours there are thousands of men and women who have become convinced that the sacrifice of life in warfare is unnecessary and wasteful. It is possible that if women in Europe—in the very countries which are now at war—receive a message from the women of America solemnly protesting against his sacrifice, they may take courage to formulate their own. At any rate, those of us assembled here will state as intelligently as we can this international revolt among thinking men and women.

We are today trying to do a difficult thing, and are doubtless doing it bunglingly; it is never easy to formulate the advanced statement. Our protest reflects our emotions as well as our convictions, but still more is the result of deep-grounded human experience. We believe that we are endeavoring to express the souls of women all over the world that when this war is over—as in time it must be, if only through the exhaustion of the contending powers—there will be many men to say, "Why didn't women call a halt before thousands, and even millions, of men had needlessly lost their lives?" Certainly, if women's consciences are stirred in regard to warfare, this is the moment to formulate a statement of their convictions.

SOURCE: *Advocate of Peace* 77 (March 1915): 64–65.

4.3. International Congress of Women (The Hague), Manifesto (15 October 1915)

[In April 1915 the U.S. Woman's Peace Party, along with more than eleven hundred delegates from neutral and belligerent nations, met at the International Women's Congress for Peace and Freedom in The Hague. That meeting created the International Committee of Women for Permanent Peace; w PP leader Jane Addams presided. In 1919 the ICWPP met again in Zurich and renamed itself the Women's International League for Peace and Freedom, and the WPP subsequently became the U.S. Section of WILPF. At the 1915 meeting the ICWPP appointed two delegations to visit belligerent and neutral nations and urge mediation. Issued in New York and based on reports filed by these delegates, the following statement shows the international role that American pacifist women played during the war.]

Here is America, on neutral soil, far removed from the stress of the conflict we, envoys to the Governments from the International Congress of Women at the Hague, have come together to convass [sic] the results of our missions. We put forth this statement as our united and deliberate conclusions.

At a time when the foreign offices of the great belligerents have been barred to each other, and the public mind of Europe has been fixed on the war offices for leadership, we have gone from capital to capital and conferred with the civil governments.

Our mission was to place before belligerent and neutral alike the resolutions of the International Congress of Women held at the Hague in April; especially to place before them the definite method of a conference of neutral nations as an agency of continuous mediation for the settlement of the war.

To carry out this mission two delegations were appointed, which included women of Great Britain, Hungary, Italy, the Netherlands, Sweden, and the United States. One or other of these delegations was received by the governments in fourteen capitals, Berlin, Berne, Budapest, Christiania, Copenhagen, Hague, Havre (Belgian Government), London, Paris, Petrograd, Rome, Stockholm, Vienna, and Washington. We were received by the Prime Ministers and Foreign Ministers of the Powers, by the King of Norway, by the Presidents of Switzerland and of the United States, by the Pope and the Cardinal Secretary of State. In many capitals more than one audience was given, not merely to present our resolutions, but for a thorough discussion. In addition to the thirty-five governmental visits we met—everywhere—members of parliaments and other leaders of public opinion.

We heard much the same words spoken in Downing Street as those spoken in Wilhelmstrasse, in Vienna as in Petrograd, in Budapest as in the Havre, where the Belgians have their temporary government.

Our visits to the war capitals convinced us that the belligerent Governments would not be opposed to a conference of neutral nations; that while the belligerents have rejected offers of mediation by single neutral nations, and while no belligerent could ask for mediation, the creation of a continuous conference of neutral nations might provide the machinery which would lead to peace. We found that the neutrals on the other hand were concerned lest calling such a conference might be considered inopportune by one or other of the belligerents. Here our information from the belligerents themselves gave assurance that such initiative would not be resented. "My country would not find anything unfriendly in such action by the neutrals," was the assurance given us by the foreign Minister of one of the great belligerents. "My Government would place no obstacle in the way of its institution," said the Minister of an opposing nation. "What are the neutrals waiting for?" said a third, whose name ranks high not only in his own country, but all over the world.

It remained to put this clarifying intelligence before the neutral countries. As a result the plan of starting mediation through the agency of a continuous conference of the neutral nations is to-day being seriously discussed alike in the Cabinets of the belligerent and neutral countries of Europe and in the press of both.

We are in a position to quote some of the expressions of men high in the councils of the great nations as to the feasibility of the plan. "You are right," said one Minister, "that it would be of the greatest importance to finish the fight by early negotiation rather than by further military efforts, which would result in more and more destruction and irreparable loss." "Yours is the sanest proposal that has been brought to this office in the last six months," said the Prime Minister of one of the larger countries.

We were also in position to canvass the objections that have been made to the proposal, testing it out severely in the judgment of those in the midst of the European conflict. It has been argued that it is not the time at present to start such a process of negotiation, and that no step should be taken until one or other party has a victory, or at least until some new military balance is struck. The answer we bring is that every delay makes more difficult the beginning of negotiations, more nations become involved, and the situation becomes more complicated; that when at times in the course of the war such a balance was struck, the neutrals were unprepared to act. The opportunity passed. For the forces of peace to be unprepared when the hour comes, is as irretrievable as for a military leader to be unready.

It has been argued that for such a conference to be called at any time when one side has met with some military advantage, would be to favor that side. The answer we bring is that the proposed conference would start mediation at a higher level than that of military advantage. As to the actual military situation, however, we quote a remark made to us by a foreign Minister of one of the belligerent Powers. "Neither side is to-day strong enough to dictate terms, and neither side is so weakened that it has to accept humiliating terms."

It has been suggested that such a conference would bind the neutral governments cooperating in it. The answer we bring is that, as proposed, such a conference should consist of the ablest persons of the neutral countries, assigned not to problems of their own governments, but to the common service of a supreme crisis. The situation calls for a conference cast in a new and larger mould than those of conventional diplomacy, the governments sending to it persons drawn from social, economic, and scientific fields who have had genuine international experience.

As women, it was possible for us, from belligerent and neutral nations alike, to meet in the midst of war and to carry forward an interchange of question and answer between capitals which were barred to each other. It is now our duty to make articulate our convictions. We have been convinced that governments of the belligerent nations would not be hostile to the institution of such a common channel for good offices; and that the governments of the European nations we visited stand ready to cooperate with others in mediation. Reviewing the situation, we believe that of the five European neutral nations visited, three are ready to join in such a conference, and that two are deliberating the calling of such a conference. Of the intention of the United Stated we have as yet no evidence.

We are but the conveyors of evidence which is a challenge to action by the neutral governments visited—by Denmark, Holland, Norway, Sweden, Switzerland, and the United States. We in turn bear evidence of a rising desire and intention of vast companies of people on the neutral countries to turn a barren disinterestedness into an active goodwill. In Sweden, for example, more than 400 meetings were held in one day in different parts of the country, calling on the government to act.

The excruciating burden of responsibility for the hopeless continuance of this war no longer rests on the will of the belligerent nations alone. It rests also on the will of those neutral governments and people who have been spared its shock but cannot, if they would, absolve themselves from their full share of responsibility for the continuance of war.

Signed by Alletta Jacobs (Holland); Chrystal Macmillan (Great Britain); Rosika Schwimmer (Austro-Hungary); Emily G. Balch (United States); Jane Addams (United States).

SOURCE: Woman's Peace Party Papers, DG-43, reel 12.3, Swarthmore College Peace Collection, Swarthmore PA.

4.4. Helen Keller, Strike against War (6 January 1916)

[Helen Keller's speech was sponsored by the Woman's Peace Party of New York City and the Labor Forum. Blind and deaf from age three, she learned to read and educated herself. A socialist, pacifist, and suffragist, Keller was a member of the Socialist Party and the Industrial Workers of the World and a cofounder of the ACLU. She read the following speech from Braille at Carnegie Hall on 5 January 1916.]

. . . I have entered the fight against preparedness and against the economic system under which we live. . . .

The future of the world rests in the hands of America. The future of America rests on the backs of 80,000,000 workingmen and women and their children. We are facing a grave crisis in our national life. The few who profit from the labor of the masses want to organize the workers into an army which will protect the interests of the capitalists. You are urged to add to the heavy burdens you already bear[,] the burden of a larger army and many additional warships. It is in your power to refuse to carry the artillery and the dreadnoughts and to shake off some of the other burdens, too, such as limousines, steam yachts and country estates. You do not need to make a great noise about it. . . . All you need to do to bring about this stupendous revolution is to straighten up and fold your arms. . . .

We are not preparing to defend our country. . . . The talk about attack from Germany and Japan is absurd. . . .

Congress is not preparing to defend the people of the United States. It is planning to protect the capital of American speculators and investors in Mexico, South America, China and the Philippine Islands. Incidentally, this preparation will benefit the manufacturers of munitions and war machines. . . .

. . . It is not a mere coincidence that six business associates of J.P. Morgan are officials of defense leagues. And chance did not dictate that [New York] Mayor [John] Mitchel should appoint to his Committee of Safety a thousand men that represent a fifth of the wealth of the United States. These men want their foreign investments protected.

Every modern war has had its root in exploitation. The Civil War was fought to decide whether the slaveholders of the South or the capitalists of the North should exploit the West. The Spanish-American War decided that the United States should exploit Cuba and the Philippines. The South African War decided that the British should exploit the diamond mines. The Russo-Japanese War decided that Japan should exploit Korea. The present war is to decide who shall exploit the Balkans, Turkey, Persia, Egypt, India, China, Africa. And we are whetting our sword to scare the victors into sharing the spoils with us. Now, the workers are not interested in the spoils; they will not get any of them anyway. . . .

"Friends," it says, "fellow workmen, patriots: your country is in danger! . . . Will you murmur about low wages when your country, your very liberties, are in jeopardy? What are the miseries you endure compared to the humiliation of having a victorious German army sail up the East River? Quit your whining, get busy and prepare to defend your firesides and your flag. Get an army, get a navy; be ready to meet the invaders like the loyal-hearted freemen you are."

Will the workers walk into this trap? Will they be fooled again? I am afraid so. The people have always been amenable to oratory of this sort. The workers know they have no enemies except their masters. They know that their citizenship papers are no warrant for the safety of themselves or their wives and children. They know that honest sweat, persistent toil and years of struggle bring them nothing worth holding on to, worth fighting for. Yet, deep down in their foolish hearts they believe they have a country. Oh blind vanity of slaves! . . .

The clever ones, up in the high places, know how childish and silly the workers are. They know that if the government dresses them up in khaki and gives them a rifle and starts them off with a brass band and waving banners, they will go forth to fight valiantly for their own enemies. They are taught that brave men die for their country's honor. What a price to pay for an abstraction—the lives of millions of young men; other millions crippled and blinded for life; existence made hideous for still more millions of human beings; the achievement and inheritance of generations swept away in a moment—and nobody better off for all the misery! This terrible sacrifice would be comprehensible if the thing you die for and call country fed, clothed, housed and warmed you, educated and cherished your children. I think the workers are the most unselfish of the children of men; they toil and live and die for other people's country, other people's sentiments, other people's liberties and other people's happiness! . . .

The kind of preparedness the workers want is reorganization and reconstruction of their whole life, such as has never been attempted by statesmen or governments. . . .

It is your duty to insist upon still more radical measures. It is your business to see that no child is employed in an industrial establishment, or mine, or store, and that no worker is needlessly exposed to accident or disease. It is your business to make them give you clean cities, free from smoke, dirt and congestion. It is your business to make them pay you a living wage. It is your business to see that this kind of preparedness is carried into every department of the nation, until every one has a chance to be well born, well nourished, rightly educated, intelligent and serviceable to the country at all times.

"**Strike against all ordinances and laws and institutions that continue the slaughter of peace and the butcheries of war. Strike against war, for without you no battles can be fought. Strike against manufacturing shrapnel and gas bombs and all other tools of murder. Strike against preparedness that means death and misery to millions of human beings. Be not dumb, obedient slaves in an army of destruction. Be heroes in an army of construction. . . ."**

SOURCE: Helen Keller, "Six Morgan Men Not in Defense Leagues through Mere Accident," *New York Call*, 6 January 1916, 1–2.

4.5. Lucia Ames Mead, "'Thinking Women' and the World Crisis" (November 1916)

[Lucia A. Mead was a pacifist, feminist, suffragist, and social reformer interested in women's rights and world peace. During World War I she promoted arbitration and the role that women could play to end the conflict. In 1919 she attended the founding conference, in Zurich, of the Women's International League for Peace and Freedom. Here, she highlights the wasteful expenditures on armaments at the expense of constructive social programs and, notably, calls for a postwar league of nations.]

Two years ago, returning from war-scourged Europe, I hoped to find American women not only working to alleviate the suffering of Belgians but deeply stirred to study the causes of war and how to ensure this being the last great war. But, while thousands were passionately knitting, even at concerts, few indeed seemed to realize that they had any responsibility to study the world problem and to help secure permanent peace. Women's clubs continued their prescribed programs and even the next year when they were free to arrange courses that would deal with the world's crying needs, they seemed deliberately to avoid putting these on their programs. The future historian could not gather from them that we were living during the prolonged enactment of the greatest tragedy in human history.

We have done the easiest thing. We have given of our abundance somewhat to palliate misery. It is said the gifts amount to what we have spent for chewing gum. . . . But for the most part, have we not all been very comfortable and are we not all becoming a little callous? It is well that we should control emotion and not let ourselves suffer when our suffering can "cut no ice." But is it well that so many thousands of privileged, cultivated women should do so little thinking on the problems which concern their own and their country's honor and future welfare and the progress of civilization? . . .

Unless a widespread public opinion demands a new order of world relationships and presents a practical program of readjustment, conditions will inevitably be vastly worse; the war settlement will breed a future world war in which our own sons may be destroyed by the still more diabolical methods which future science will develop. Whether the world is to increase suspicion, terror, and suffering will depend largely upon certain decisions to be made within a year or two at the most. The richest, freest country in the world should help in those decisions.

This war was not caused primarily by the criminal and exceptional ambition of two nations whose crushing defeat will ensure world peace. It came from false theories of economics, of force and of international relations held by people of all nations. They have spread like a plague all over America and infected the minds of the learned as much as of the humble. Many things have been hid from the wise and prudent in our colleges which might easily be revealed to mothers and home-makers. These would-be prudent ones have been frightened into sanctioning a greater expenditure of the peoples' earnings for war preparations than was ever made in time of peace by any other nation. This increase of nearly two hundred and fifty per cent, will assuredly increase suspicion, rivalry and the danger of a coalition. Our capacity to help save the world from ideas and methods which menace all progress is steadily diminishing as we imitate old-world follies. . . .

Let thinking men and women urge the President to unite with the neutrals which have so long in their distress impatiently waited for us to lead. Let them propose in the interest of all civilization to consider as a basis of settlement the allies' original claims so far as territory is concerned and leave all other matters for arbitration.

(1). That Belgium, France, Serbia, Poland and Montenegro be evacuated; that at least part of the German colonies be returned and no effort made to ruin German commerce after the war.

(2). That a league of nations be formed to which central powers as well as all others be invited, which shall pledge all members to settlement of international disputes by a world court or conciliation commission, with concerted non-intercourse and economic pressure as a penalty for broken pledges.

(3). That if general agreement for diminution of armaments can be attained, the United States will contribute generously to the rehabilitation of the little countries that have been destroyed.

To prolong this gigantic, bloody orgy to enable the allies to extort indemnities which would come chiefly from the innocent private citizens, would be treason to civilization. . . .

Here is a definite program for discussion. Something akin to this is the alternative to the prospect of many months more of hideous suffering. . . .

Will not thinking women think on these possibilities and get men to think? Will they not study the fallacies—economic, biologic and political that, unless refuted, menace the world in which their children will perhaps suffer for their father's folly as the youth of Europe today are expiating the fatal blunders of their fathers.

SOURCE: *Femina: A Magazine of Inspiration* 3 (November 1916): 393–94.

4.6. Margaret Sanger, "Woman and War" (June 1917)

[Margaret Sanger, the crusader and originator of the U.S. birth control movement, was the subject of constant surveillance by the federal government during the war. From the beginning of the conflict, she expressed her opposition to war in a periodic newsletter, the *Rebel Woman*. In 1917 she joined the American Union Against Militarism and founded the journal *Birth Control Review*. She challenges women to abandon their submissiveness and take aggressive action against war.]

Realization of the world tragedy—war—has at last been forced upon the American people. Two years ago the fiendish internecine strife of the militarists of Europe seemed remote enough. Today our women of the working class find themselves facing an outrage unparalelled [*sic*] in the history of this republic. Their husbands, sons and brothers are to be herded to the front as conscript fighters, in violation of every human instinct fostered in them by the great libertarians who founded this country.

America's participation in the war has been brought about by interested groups, not in response to the will of the majority. Not fifty per cent of the men could have been induced to vote Yes in a war referendum, not five per cent of the women. . . .

Woman hates war. Her instincts are fundamentally creative, not destructive. But her sex-bondage has made her the dumb instrument of the monster she detests. . . . She has become not the mother of a nobler race, but a mere breeding machine grinding out a humanity which fills insane asylums, almshouses and sweat shops, and provides cannon fodder that tyrants may rise to power on the sacrifice of her offspring.

Too long has she been called the gentler and weaker half of humankind, too long has she silently borne the brunt of unwilling motherhood, too long has she been the stepping-stone of oligarchies, kingdoms and so-called democracies, too long have they thrived on her enslavement. Had she not been so submissive and inarticulate, the present war could not have been imposed upon the workers, for there would not have been the big battalions of superfluous humanity to be moved about like pawns on a chessboard.

The great horde of the unwanted has proved to be a spineless mass, which did not have the courage to control its own destiny. Had woman had knowledge of birth control and brought into the world only such offspring as she desired and was physically and spiritually prepared to receive, society would have been far too individualistic to tolerate wholesale massacre for the benefit of money kings. Under such an order, the child would have been considered a priceless gift to the community. Manhood would have been too valuable to be sacrificed on battlefields. Motherhood would have been revered, and the mother's voice raised to forbid the slaughter of her offspring would have been heeded.

But unfortunately the forces of oppression have cared nothing for the poignant grief of exploited motherhood. They have turned in callous indifference from her tears, while her flesh and blood have reddened every battlefield in history. There are statues in plenty to kings, statesmen and generals who have driven her sons to the universal shambles of slaughter. But where are the statues to Motherhood?

In the present soul-trying crisis, the flower of European manhood has been sacrificed on the altar of Tyranny. The rulers of Europe are begging, imploring, crying to woman, using every subterfuge to induce her to breed again, in the old-time submission to man-made laws. Soon the war lords of America will be echoing the same plea.

To all these entreaties the working woman must answer No! She must deny the right of the State or Kingdom hereafter to make her a victim of unwilling motherhood, and the handmaiden of militarism.

Mothers of the working class, if your love for offspring, husband, sweetheart or brother stirs within you as deeply as the love that fired the mothers of France and Spain who strove to halt unjust wars by throwing their bodies across the railroad tracks to prevent troop trains from leaving, you too will rouse yourselves to action. You will make it necessary for this democracy, which has set out to conscript your men for foreign warfare, to take them over the dead bodies of the protesting womanhood of the United States.

SOURCE: *Birth Control Review* 1 (June 1917): 5.

4.7. Mary Alden Hopkins, "Woman's Way in War" (28 July 1917)

[Mary A. Hopkins, a graduate of Wellesley College and Columbia University, coedited and contributed to *Four Lights*, the magazine published by the Woman's Peace Party's New York City branch. This piece was reprinted from the periodical's 2 June 1917 issue, which postal authorities refused to transmit through the mails, nine days before the Espionage Act (15 June 1917) conferred them with such power.]

Women must not feel that they cannot help in the Great War because they are accustomed to dealing with little things. A bullet is a little thing but it is stronger than life. Women must not feel that because they work in the narrow confines of the home, they cannot help in the great work of destruction. It is a tender nursery thought that the baby in the mother's arms, properly trained, may grow up to destroy more persons and property than any man before him. And that this helpless floppy pink hand may some day write his mother's name in the blood of the enemy,—though of course it is too early to tell just yet which enemy it will then be.

Accustom your children gradually to the sight of blood. And for yourself learn to kill a little every day. One sweet woman is accustomed to ask herself searchingly each night, "Whom have I killed today?" And to fall asleep resolving to kill more on the morrow.

A woman clever with her fingers will soon be making gas masks at home. Women have often been accused of being essentially producers and conservers. Now is the time for them to lay forever that slander and prove that they are glad and eager to destroy joyfully all that the ages—and other women—have produced. Courage, sisters! It takes but a minute to destroy a boy into whose making have gone eighteen years of thoughtful care.

SOURCE: *Four Lights*, 28 July 1917, in Woman's Peace Party Papers, DG-43, reel 12.3, Swarthmore College Peace Collection, Swarthmore PA.

4.8. Harriet Connor Brown, "America Menaced by Militarism: An Appeal to Women" (15 November 1920)

[This article represents the growing militancy among women peace activists and urges them to use their newly obtained political rights in the crusade for world peace. Harriet C. Brown emphasizes the expenditures for military armaments at the expense of social and humanitarian programs.]

All women, I trust, want to use their new political power in such a way as to help humanity. We have beneficent dreams that we want to see realized, dreams of a glorified earth without sickness or poverty or ignorance or crime. We have been thinking all along that once we had the ballot we could use it to make those dreams come true. Well, we can in time, but not directly, as most of us think. Not yet! There is one thing more to do before we can settle down to the business of positive reform. We must eliminate from Congress the men who are misappropriating nearly all the wealth of the country, leaving us women next to nothing with which to do our work.

THE IRONY OF IT

See the irony of the position in which we find ourselves! We went into the World War to end war—at least the women of the country did, though I doubt if the general staff of the army and the manufacturing interests of the country which secured contracts from the War Department would have answered to that call, since in the nature of things a war to end war would put many of them out of business. . . .

But what has really happened? The men are again at home . . . but there is no promise of disarmament as the reward of all their toil and bloodshed, of all their women's tears and labor. On the contrary, a vast increase of armament has actually been authorized, which is to be paid for by a cruel levy of taxes that will take away not only from them, but from their children and their children's children, if not the very bread from their mouths and the clothes from their backs, at least the laughter from their lips, the sweetest luxuries of life, the choicest fruits of science and education and benevolence for at least a century. . . .

SACRIFICING PEACE PURSUITS

. . . We have a vast load of unpaid bills amounting for this year to over $2,838,000,000 which will make us stagger, as we try to climb upward, even without the extra burden of over $855,000,000 for enlarged military and naval establishments. Our unpaid bills are for past wars, chiefly the war with Germany. They are composed of items like pensions, war risk insurance, compensation for disability, the vocational education of mutilated soldiers, the restoration to health of diseased soldiers, the upkeep of soldiers' homes, the return to America of the soldier dead, the interest on war debts, and so on. . . .

On the average, each one of you will have to pay about $40 of that four thousand millions. If you and your husband have the average American family of three children, your contribution this year to the State will be about $200 for your family of five. That is enough to pay the fees of one child at the university this year. Instead, it will go toward the support of some stoker on an idle battleship or some orderly at a useless army post. . . .

WHAT WOMEN HAVE TO DO [TO PREVENT THE NEXT WAR]

Knowing this, what should be the program of women who want the nation's funds for constructive work, who want their sons saved for such work? What the voting women of the world decide shall be has to be. The problem is no longer to obtain the power. We have taken the first great step. Our problem now is how to use that power.

I see four things for women to do at once. . . .

i. Organize Non-Partisan Clubs

The first thing for women to do is to organize for united action against military legislation. Establish in each congressional district a non-partisan union of women for the purpose of sending to Congress representatives who will work for disarmament. Until this waste of public money on armaments is stopped, it is worse than futile for women to affiliate permanently with political parties. . . .

During the coming winter there are three definite things for women's non-partisan clubs to tell their congressmen and their congressmen's wives.

First, not a penny of increase for armaments! . . .

Second, no conscription of our youth under the heading of "universal military training," "selective draft," or any other euphemism!

Third, a reorganization of the Government Service that will strip the War and Navy Departments of their civil functions, leaving them their proper military duties and no others.

ii. Petition the President-Elect [Warren Harding]

The second thing to do is to demand of the new President-elect that, as soon as he takes office, he call a conference of representatives from every de facto government of the world for the express purpose of agreeing to disarmament, and for that purpose only. We should ask that each country be requested to name three delegates, one of whom shall be a woman, one a representative of labor, and one a representative of science or learning in the permanent employ of his or her respective government. I suggest that the conference be composed of representatives of women, labor, and learning, rather than representatives of armies and navies, of diplomacy and finance—. . . .

iii. Sign a Pledge of Passive Resistance to War

. . . By "passive resistance" I mean resistance made with tongue and pen, with brain and ballot, with moral and spiritual forces and with those weapons only. . . .

. . . The following pledge should be signed with your name and address and sent . . . to the United States Section of the Women's International League for Peace and Freedom, . . .

Believing that true peace can be secured only through reconcilia-
tion and good-will and that no cause justifies the organized destruc-
tion of human life, I urge immediate and universal disarmament and
promise never to aid in any way the prosecution of war.

IV. Join the Women's International League for Peace and Freedom
. . . If we make our demands on Congress and the incoming President sufficiently clean-cut and clear, we can get the people of the
country behind us, and, in the last analysis, the people rule. For the
time being, all other public work or charity work should take second
place with women. Let men do the relief work of the world in the next
year, even the Red Cross work. *Women alone, ordained of God to be*
noncombatants, are in position to bring peace to the world. Woe be to
them and their children's children if they shirk their plain duty now!

SOURCE: *Searchlight* 5 (15 November 1920): 8–13, reprinted in Mary Katharine Reely, ed., *Selected Articles on Disarmament* (New York: H. W. Wilson,
1921), 149–52, 159, 161–63.

4.9. Jeannette Rankin, "Two Votes against War: 1917 and 1941" (1958)

[Jeannette Rankin, a social worker and Republican from Montana,
was the first woman elected to Congress. Immortalized for her commitment to suffrage and world peace, she is the only member of Congress who voted against both world wars. Female opponents of the
Vietnam War formed the Jeannette Rankin Brigade in 1967.]

As the first woman to sit in the legislature of any sovereign nation,
I cast my first vote in April, 1917 against the entry of the United
States into World War I. As I said at the time, I wanted to stand by
my country, but I could not vote for war. I look back with satisfaction to that momentous occasion.

    I had been deeply involved in the preceding years in the struggle
for woman suffrage. That struggle and the struggle against war were
integrally related in my youthful thoughts and activities. After the
World War had broken out and it had become increasingly clear that
the United States was going to be drawn in, I was the angriest per-

son you ever saw. I was in a rage because no one had ever seriously taught us about the nature of war itself or given us any inkling of the causes of this specific war. I was not so naive as to think that war just started in a minute. Behind the scenes preparation had to be made and was made for it. But nobody in school or later had talked to us about such things. Now we seemed, in 1914, suddenly and inexplicably to be on the eve of war.

Deep down, I guess I had always felt strongly about war. I remember that in college, when I was assigned to read publicly a poem glorifying war and soldiers, I told the professor: "But this is hideous. I can't read it."

As we went about in Montana in 1914 campaigning for the vote, we would see long lines of people before the newspaper bulletin boards in every town and city. A large proportion of these people were foreign born, eagerly scanning the notices for war news that would give them some notion as to what was happening to relatives in their native countries. War was on everybody's mind. So we talked about suffrage in relation to war. I argued that women should get the vote because they would help keep the country out of war. It was a persuasive argument at that stage.

. . . I happened to suggest that, instead of sending youth into war, the old men ought to fight the wars. The papers picked up this suggestion and made a big thing of it. Then speeches began to be made and letters written to the papers on how presumptuous and shocking it was for an unmarried woman to consider herself competent to discuss such matters. . . .

In the Fall of 1916, I was elected Congresswoman-at-large from Montana. The women's vote helped. It was an additional advantage that the state was not divided into Congressional districts, because candidates who stand for something are likely to have a better chance under this set-up, especially women. Everyone could vote for both a man and a woman. It is harder to manipulate and control the voters of a whole state than those of a single district. Also people were not subjected to a radio and TV barrage and we could go from town to town, speaking on the street corners and in the homes.

Several women ran for Congress in various states that year, but I was the only one who really had a chance, and I was elected. . . . I had plans made for an extensive, and, I hoped, remunerative lecture tour on woman suffrage and peace, capitalizing on the curiosity about a "female" Representative. But Woodrow Wilson, who had been elected on the slogan that he would keep us out of war, had decided that it was the duty of all, and especially of good liberals and idealists, to support intervention. He called a special session of Congress early in April, read his famous war message, and appealed to the newly-elected Congress to declare war.

That time it took a week of tense debate to bring the matter to a vote, and in the House I was not the only one to vote "No." Forty-nine men in the House voted against entry. Among them were all the veterans of the Civil War who were in Congress. Claude Kitchin, the floor leader of the Democratic majority, voted "No" and wept unashamedly as he cried out: "It takes neither moral nor physical courage to declare a war for others to fight." It is one token of how the situation has deteriorated since that time that Kitchin was retained in the leadership in spite of this vote and the fact that he remained unenthusiastic about war measures. Champ Clark, the Speaker of the House, refrained from voting on this crucial measure. In the Senate, the elder Robert M. LaFollette made his brilliant and courageous speech and cast his negative vote, as did five other Senators.

I am sorry to have to say that the attitude of most of the leaders of the woman suffrage movement was far from sympathetic to my stand. They thought that the "cause" would have been much better off if I had taken what they considered a patriotic stand. They brought a good deal of pressure to bear on me. As a matter of fact, the war advanced the movement to give women the vote and undermined opposition to it, and there is no reason to suppose that my vote on the war declaration had any appreciable effect on this issue. . . .

. . . [In 1940 I was reelected] to Congress for a second time, after the lapse of twenty-three years. . . .

Once again, the nation was moving toward war. . . .

. . . [On 8 December Congress voted on a war resolution against Japan.] This time I stood alone. It was a good deal more difficult than it had been the time before. Yet I think the men in Congress all sensed that I would vote "No" again. If I had done otherwise, I do not think I could have faced the remaining days in Congress. Even the men who were most convinced that we had to get into the war would have lost respect for me if I had betrayed my convictions. . . .

SOURCE: *Liberation* 3 (March 1958): 4–6.

CHAPTER 5

African American and Ethnic American Antiwar Dissent

5.1. Patrick O'Donnell, Speech (8 February 1915)

[Irish Americans supported Irish independence from Great Britain. During the early months of World War I, Irish Americans rallied against U.S. support for Great Britain and the Allied cause, insisting that the United States remain neutral. In this speech at a German American rally in Chicago, translated in 1942 by the Works Progress Administration Writers' Project, Patrick O'Donnell, the president of the Allied Irish Societies, urged his audience to support efforts for an early peace.]

In behalf of all of us, who have sought refuge over here from oppression, I should like to state that we are taking an interest in this gigantic struggle as American citizens, and that we hereby issue a demand to the [belligerent] powers to make peace and unfurl the international peace banner. We 15,000 people assembled here demand it.

. . . Of course we are not belligerents, but we have to pay war taxes nevertheless, just as the people in Europe do. We have to pay, because those people are fighting over there.

There is certainly enough misery and destitution on the other side of the ocean, but over here the number of unemployed and hungry is steadily on the increase, and it is about time for the responsible circles in Washington to stop meddling in this war, which is the cause of all this misery. America is doing everything in her power right now to prolong the war, except that we have not issued a call for volunteers yet, but otherwise co-operation [with the war effort of the Allies] is evident everywhere.

American guns and American powder are doing their devilish work in the trenches, American bullets wound and kill citizens of a friendly nation.

America owes it to her citizens to close every port to the shipment abroad of war material, to recall every ship loaded with munitions or arms, and to keep all the implements of death and destruction, which could be used in war, within her borders. Only by so doing can America prove that she is the Friend of all nations and, as the song goes "The Land of the Free and the Home of the Brave."

SOURCE: *Abendpost* (German), 8 February 1915, 19–21, in U.S. Works Progress Administration, "The Chicago Foreign Language Press Survey," 1860–1930s (1942), Newspaper Division, Chicago Public Library.

5.2. W. E. B. DuBois, "The African Roots of War" (May 1915)

[In this essay DuBois considers the war an extension of imperialism, especially by the European nations, and calls upon democratically minded leaders of the white race to end racism and exploitation of "colored" peoples throughout the world. He considers Africa the real prize in the conquest for domination and the root cause of the world conflict.]

"Semper novi quid ex Africa," cried the Roman proconsul; and he voiced the verdict of forty centuries. Yet there are those who would write world-history and leave out this most marvelous of continents. Particularly to-day most men assume that Africa lies far afield from the centres of our burning social problems, and especially from our present problem of World War.

Yet in a very real sense Africa is a prime cause of this terrible overturning of civilization which we have lived to see; and these words seek to sow how in the Dark Continent are hidden the roots, not simply of war to-day but of the menace of wars to-morrow. . . .

. . . That sinister traffic, on which the British Empire and the American Republic were largely built, cost black Africa no less than 100,000,000 souls, the wreckage of its political and social life, and left the continent in precisely that state of helplessness which invites aggression and exploitation. "Color" became in the world's thought synonymous with inferiority, "Negro" lost its capitalization, and Africa was another name for bestiality and barbarism.

Thus the world began to invest in color prejudice. The "Color Line" began to pay dividends. For indeed, while the exploration of the valley of the Congo was the occasion of the scramble for Africa, the cause lay deeper. The Franco-Prussian War [1870–71] turned the eyes of those who sought power and domination away from Europe. Already England was in Africa, cleaning away the debris of the slave trade and half consciously groping toward the new Imperialism. France, humiliated and impoverished, looked toward a new northern African empire sweeping from the Atlantic to the Red Sea. More slowly Germany began to see the dawning of a new day, and, shut out from America by the Monroe Doctrine, looked to Asia and Africa for colonies. . . .

Whence comes this new wealth and on what does its accumulation depend? It comes primarily from the darker nations of the world— Asia and Africa, South and Central America, the West Indies and the islands of the South Seas. . . . Chinese, East Indians, Negroes, and South American Indians are by common consent for governance by white folk and economic subjection to them. To the furtherance of this highly profitable economic dictum has been brought every available resource of science and religion. Thus arises the astonishing doctrine of the natural inferiority of most men to the few, and the interpretation of "Christian brotherhood" as meaning anything that one of the "brothers" may at any time want it to mean. . . .

. . . We speak of the Balkans as the storm-centre of Europe and the cause of war, but this is mere habit. The Balkans are convenient for occasions, but the ownership of materials and men in the darker world is the real prize that is setting the nations of Europe at each other's throats to-day.

The present world war is, then, the result of jealousies engendered by the recent rise of armed national associations of labor and capital whose aim is the exploitation of the wealth of the world mainly outside the European circle of nations. These associations, grown jealous and suspicious at the division of the spoils of trade-empire, are fighting to enlarge their respective shares; they look for expansion, not in Europe but in Asia, and particularly in Africa. "We want no inch of French territory," said Germany to England, but Germany was "unable to give" similar assurances as to France in Africa. . . .

What, then, are we to do, who desire peace and the civilization of all men? Hitherto the peace movement has confined itself chiefly to figures about the cost of war and platitudes on humanity. What do nations care about the cost of war, if by spending a few hundred millions in steel and gunpowder they can gain a thousand millions in diamonds and cocoa? How can love of humanity appeal as a motive to nations whose love of luxury is built on the inhuman exploitation of human beings, and who, especially in recent years, have been taught to regard these human beings as inhuman? I appealed to the last meeting of peace societies in St. Louis, saying, "Should you not discuss racial prejudice as a prime cause of war?" The secretary was sorry but was unwilling to introduce controversial matters!

We, then, who want peace, must remove the real causes of war. We have extended gradually our conception of democracy beyond our social class to all social classes in our nation; we have gone further and extended our democratic ideals not simply to all classes of our own nation, but to those of other nations of our blood and lineage—to what we call "European" civilization. If we want real peace and lasting culture, however, we must go further. We must extend the democratic ideal to the yellow, brown, and black peoples. . . .

What the primitive peoples of Africa and the world need and must have if war is to be abolished is perfectly clear:—

First: land. To-day Africa is being enslaved by the theft of her land and natural resources. . . . All over Africa has gone this shameless monopolizing of land and natural resources to force poverty on the masses and reduce them to the "dumb-driven-cattle" stage of labor activity.

Secondly: we must train native races in modern civilization. This can be done. Modern methods of educating children, honestly and effectively applied, would make modern, civilized nations out of the vast majority of human beings on earth to-day. This we have seldom tried. For the most part Europe is straining every nerve to make over yellow, brown, and black men into docile beasts of burden, and only an irrepressible few are allowed to escape and seek (usually abroad) the education of modern men.

Lastly, the principle of home rule must extend to groups, nations, and races. . . . But the brute fact remains: the white man is ruling black Africa for the white man's gain, and just as far as possible he is doing the same to colored races elsewhere. Can such a situation bring peace? Will any amount of European concord or disarmament settle this injustice? . . .

We are calling for European concord to-day; but at the utmost European concord will mean satisfaction with, or acquiescence in, a given division of the spoils of world-domination. After all, European disarmament cannot go below the necessity of defending the aggressions of the whites against the blacks and browns and yellows. From this will arise three perpetual dangers of war. First, renewed jealously at any division of colonies or spheres of influence agreed upon, if at any future time the present division comes to seem unfair. . . . Secondly: war will come from the revolutionary revolt of the lowest workers. . . . Finally, the colored peoples will not always submit passively to foreign domination. . . . These [colored] nations and races, composing as they do a vast majority of humanity, are going to endure this treatment just as long as they must and not a moment longer. Then they are going to fight and the War of the Color Line will outdo in savage inhumanity any war this world has yet seen. For colored folk have much to remember and they will not forget.

But is this inevitable? Must we sit helpless before this awful prospect? While we are planning, as a result of the present holocaust, the disarmament of Europe and a European international world-police, must the rest of the world be left naked to the inevitable horror of war, especially when we know that it is directly in this outer circle of races, and not in the inner European household, that the real causes of present European fighting are to be found? . . .

SOURCE: *Atlantic Monthly*, May 1915, 707–14.

5.3. A. Philip Randolph and Chandler Owen, *Terms of Peace and the Darker Races* (1917)

[A. Philip Randolph and Chandler Owen cofounded and coedited the *Messenger*. Both were socialists; Randolph also headed the Brotherhood of Sleeping Car Porters. When the United States entered the war, Randolph and Owen published a booklet that called for a peace settlement that ended colonization and racial discrimination. Their antiwar criticism led to their arrests under the Espionage Act. Subsequently, charges were dismissed.]

. . . The object of war is usually largely economic—manufacturers seeking markets for their goods and capitalists seeking investments for their surplus capital. Munitions makers must sell guns, shot and shell. Iron and steel magnates must sell their goods. Uniform makers must dispose of their immense stores of cotton and wool. Banks must loan idle moneys. But after the war has proceeded long enough to make possible the use and sale of these goods, it is to the interest of the capitalists, manufacturers and bankers to call the soldiers off the field—to call them from their arts of destruction to begin the production anew of more goods for sale when they shall reach such a surplus. After the goods produced shall have been used, there is no gain in having the war continue, but on the contrary, the war's continuance would be a heavy debt upon the capitalist. The capitalists during the war sell immense amounts of goods. When the war ends, the government owes them huge debts. It is necessary for the soldiers to become laborers now to pay these debts. Hence the object of peace is profit—gain—just as the object of war is.

This, however, is the capitalist and ruling class point of view. This is the gain contemplated by that class. Not so with the people of the different countries. They seldom have economic gain in their minds because there is none. They are burdened with taxation during and after the war. They are compelled to pay high prices for the necessities of life. They bear the arms and give their life and limb. Their untold suffering could not be compensated by any outcome of the war. Victory on either side is defeat for the masses of the people. Loss only has been their lot. . . .

The first step then toward a durable peace is the democratization of home governments. Only private profiteers have designs on other countries. But those profiteers can afford to bribe only a few people. Monarchies and oligarchies play into their hands, for the rulers, few in number, are always easily subject to bribe. Hence the close association of the economic and the political ruling class.

The democratization of home governments means universal and secret suffrage. By universal suffrage we include women as well as men without regards to race, creed or color. . . .

Universal and compulsory education are essential to insure a wise and beneficial use of the ballot. . . . This only is intellectual democracy.

Next a referendum on war policies. Insomuch as the people have to fight the wars, to pay the taxes and to undergo the inhuman sufferings of every war, they only should have the power to declare war by a popular referendum. . . . A different policy here should be used. The nation should determine the minimum age of its soldiers, and on every such referendum, every man and woman who is subject to call should be given a right to vote on the referendum. . . . Those who offer themselves to kill and to be killed should certainly determine the entrance upon such bloody work. . . .

Another prolific source of war, another net of intrigue into which peoples have frequently been drawn, is the system of secret diplomacy. . . . All treaties and international agreements entered into should be ratified by the popular vote before such agreements take effect. . . .

In addition to the reforms just proposed, the very basic and fundamental one must be grappled with at once—economic reconstruction—fairer distribution of wealth. Exploitation is caused by the desire of the exploiter to exploit, on the one hand, and the object of exploitation—something to exploit, on the other hand. . . . With the present organization of society cupidity is inculcated, greed is fostered, voracity is stimulated, plundering is perpetuated. . . .

Herein lies the real bone of contention of the world war—darker peoples for cheap labor and darker peoples' rich lands.

The war to be sure is being fought in Europe very largely, but the thing about which the war is fought lies elsewhere. The cause rests in the grab of territory, on the one hand, and the desire to hold what has been grabbed, or to grab more, on the other hand. No single one of the big powers in this war can escape the indictment. . . .

And the present war exists because one group of whites desires to secure possessions of another group of whites, even to the extent of sacrificing millions of young white men in the bloody carnage and the horrible holocaust.

So long as there is something to fight about there will be frequently recurring wars.

The nations in making peace must search their consciences. They must recognize certain principles to secure permanent peace.

Government by the consent of the governed must be accorded to all peoples whether white or black or brown. Africa, India, China, the Islands held by Great Britain, by the United States and by other nations, must be accorded this right. This is political democracy. The first consideration of a good government belongs to the people it rules. . . .

Moreover, all of these nations hold colonies and islands in the name of civilization—not in the name of business. That, of course, is the deception practiced by civilized peoples upon those less civilized. The truth nevertheless is, that business and not civilization is the object of all these nations. The African, the Hindu, the Chinaman, and the West Indian are wanted as workers, but not as citizens. They are called upon for service, but not for friendship. . . .

Our present system of industry produces surplus capital. Capital seeks investment. When the capitalist invests in a foreign land the flag follows the investor. Back behind the flag great armies and navies are formed to enforce the ideas and opinions of those investors, upon the people in whose land the investment is made. . . . Two or more nations may invest among these undeveloped peoples. In their mad rivalry a clash comes. War ensues over the bone of contention—profits.

How can this be avoided and averted? There are many proposals, most of which we shall proceed to examine.

It would seem to be logical to provide some Permanent International Peace Commission. This Commission's function would be that of a court of law today. The court of law deals with individual breaches of the peace. The proposed court would be the judge of international breaches of the peace.

But the court of law has constituted force to execute its orders and its mandates. A league of all the nations with a force—a community of powers—greater than any individual nation's force, should be organized and established to enforce the judgments, mandates or orders of the International Peace Commission. . . .

The Pope's declaration for a reduction of armaments is sound. Economically, large armies and navies are a burden upon the citizens of every nation. Again, the possession of a large military and naval machine tends to incite the desire to use that machine, just as the possession of a gun by an individual tends to incite the desire to use it. . . .

The governments of the various nations should take out of the hands of private individuals or concerns the munitions industries, and it may be necessary to include many of the necessities of life. The ability to coin money out of war will create wars, on the one hand, and a clash of interests in a country will breed war.

Those who make goods for war use must sell them. No curb can come to that desire so long as possession of the goods remains unchanged. In order to sell such goods there must be a demand for them. In order for a demand to exist there must be a war. Those interests are usually able to bring on war when they desire. They control the government, and the government generally obeys them. Hence the necessity of government ownership and control of all munitions industries and all others which are so related as to make war highly profitable for them. . . .

So long as African territory is the object of unstinted avarice, greed and robbery, while its people with dark skins are considered as just subjects of exploitation—now here and now there in slavery, enforced labor, peonage and wage slavery—just so long will the conditions smolder and brew which needs must inevitably be prolific in the production of future war. . . .

The United States, too, has no unsullied escutcheon in her dealing with her island subjects.

The sugar, tobacco, fruit, rice, coffee and rubber trusts have been given a free hand in Cuba, the Philippines, Hawaii, Porto Rico, Hayti and San Domingo.

The methods of government employed by the United States have been democratic on their face, but autocratic in substance. It is true that periodical elections are held, but the heavy hand of the government, combined with the big trusts, has always been able to elect its candidate through sheer coercion. Yet the world is given a fiasco for the appearance of democracy. . . .

We propose an International Council on the Conditions of Darker Races.

The International Peace Commission would be the bigger body and the Council on the Conditions of Darker Races would be the associate body to deal with that special phase of dark races.

The work of the Council on the Conditions of Darker Races should be, first, to set minimum wages for labor in different countries where these darker, undeveloped peoples live; to set the maximum hours of work and the conditions of employment. . . .

Second, the education of the natives must be put under the Commission's charge. . . .

But, in so much as all of these nations are making immense profits from their hold on these colonies, a tax might be exacted on all the business they do, for the education of the natives. . . .

The Council on the Conditions of Darker Races must set up certain reasonable standards for suffrage. . . . Whatever those standards are, the Council must adopt immediately methods for their rapid attainment by all the natives. . . .

Peace is the object of those who have so assiduously addressed themselves to the preparation of this message. . . .

So long as these darker races are economic footballs for the great capitalists, just so long will wars continue to come. When the wars come, millions of young white men in the very flower of their youth, will be sent on their journey of life, armless, legless, maimed and mutilated.

Dark-skinned soldiers may not be wanted in the beginning of the wars, but when the great white nations are hard pressed, they will always call for dark-skinned soldiers to pull their chestnuts out of the fire. The consequence, then, is that a war between whites means war in which the blacks must also give their lives.

To maintain peace we must remove the conditions which create war. Democracy must be enthroned. White and black workingmen must recognize their common interest in industry, in politics, in society, in peace. Secret diplomacy must go. Universal suffrage must prevail. Universal education must be established everywhere. Wage slavery must be abolished. The means and resources of wealth must be socially owned for the common welfare. This will remove the incentive for war.

The people must always vote on whether they want war and conscription.

Free speech, free press, liberty of thought must be maintained in time of war as in time of peace. . . .

And now America—the United States of America—to twelve million black souls, always loyal and true, grant that freedom from lynching, Jimcrowism, segregation and discrimination. Stop the disfranchisement in the South which makes your cry of "making the world safe for democracy" a sham, a mockery, a rape on decency and a travesty on common sense.

Finally, in the words of the Petrograd Council of Workers and Soldiers' Deputies:

Workers of all countries—black and white! "In extending to you our fraternal hand over mountains of corpses of our brothers, across rivers of innocent blood and tears, over smoldering ruins of cities and villages, over destroyed treasures of civilization, we beseech you to re-establish and strengthen international unity without regard to race or color."

Herein lies the only security for peace—permanent, durable and democratic peace—a peace in which the black and white world will be made safe for democracy.

SOURCE: A. Philip Randolph and Chandler Owen, *Terms of Peace and the Darker Races* (New York: Poole Press Association, 1917), 2–3, 9–10, 12–20, 25–28, 30–32.

5.4. Clara L. Threadgill-Dennis, "Soldiers of the Twenty-Fourth" (27 November 1917)

[Clara Threadgill-Dennis, an African American teacher, was a graduate of Tillotson College in Austin, Texas, and the wife of a school principal. In August 1917 members of the all-black Twenty-Fourth United States Infantry were involved in a Houston race riot that took the lives of four black soldiers and sixteen civilians. After courts-martial nineteen soldiers were executed and sixty-three sentenced to life imprisonment. Writing in the *San Antonio Inquirer*, a black newspaper, Threadgill-Dennis defended the soldiers and raised a disquieting question: why should African Americans, denied civil rights at home, fight in a war for democracy in Europe? In response the government charged her and the paper's editor with violating the Espionage Act by inciting insubordination among the troops. Although the case against Threadgill-Dennis was dropped, the editor was convicted and sentenced to prison.]

Be brave, don't feel discouraged, rest assured that every woman in all this land of ours, who dares feel proud of the Negro blood that courses through her veins, reveres you, she honors you.

We would rather see you shot by the highest tribunal of the United States Army because you dared protect a Negro woman from the insult of a southern brute in the form of a policeman, than to have you forced to go to Europe to fight for a liberty you can not enjoy.

Negro women regret that you mutinied, and we are sorry you spilt innocent blood, but we are not sorry that five southern policemen's bones now bleech [bleach] in the graves of Houston, Tex.

It is far better that you be shot for having tried to protect a Negro woman, than to have you die a natural death in the trenches of Europe, fighting to make the world safe for a democracy that you can't enjoy. On your way to the Training Camps you are jim-crowed. Every insult that can be heaped upon you, you have to take, or be tried by court-martial if you resent it.

I needed you in Austin this week. If some of that sixty-three members of the immortal 24th; [sic] had been in Austin, I would not have been insulted by a street car conductor when I asked for a transfer that was due me, my business manager of Scarborough's Store, my husband would not have been insulted by a street car conductor, when he had paid his fare and had dared sit in a vacant seat in front of a white woman. The teachers of this city would not have been insulted in the Capitol of the Lone Star State when they were told by the Superintendent to go there to listen to the Governor of Texas tell them why they should take our Liberty Bonds.

Oh, no, colored soldiers, you will have died for what white men die every day, you will have died for the most sacred thing on the earth to any race[,] even the southern white man, his daughter's, his wife's, his mother's[,] his sister's[,] his neighbor's sister's protection from insult.

Be brave and face death fearlessly.

SOURCE: *San Antonio Inquirer*, 24 November 1917, as cited in Report by Department of Justice Agent Willard Utley, "Re: *San Antonio Inquirer*," 27 November 1917, Records of the Military Intelligence Division, General Correspondence Relating to Negro Subversion, RG 165, M-1440, roll 2, file 10218, National Archives, College Park MD.

5.5. "Protest Meeting of Jugoslav Socialists" (February 1917)

[The Socialist Party had a large immigrant membership and many foreign-language members. In Chicago, home to a large Slavic community, Socialist Slavic workers adopted the following antiwar resolution.]

"The meeting of Jugoslav workers in Chicago, held February 18, 1917, expresses in principle its standpoint against wars of the capitalistic order, acknowledges the conclusions of the Internationale, which order each Socialist Party to work against war. Vigorously we protest against the work of those who are fanning up war, and their newspapers which misuse the critical situation to push the United States of America into war.

To the workers of America, the adventures undertaken by some capitalistic circles in the interests of huge profits, do not promise any benefits or gains, on the contrary great burdens will fall on the shoulders of the workers. All the sacrifices in lives and health the workers must bear. Economic crises, unemployment and high prices will oppress the workers. The accumulated debts of war, the workers will have to pay.

The United States cannot profit by participating in a European war. A small circle of international capitalists would acquire great gains, which will throw the whole country back and hinder any progress.

Keeping peace is in the interest of the working class, the democracy of the United States; for that reason it is not only a Socialist but also a civic duty to do all possible to avert war.

The Jugoslav workers do not want to be traitors of their class. They assert that their work for keeping peace has nothing in common with treason against the country in which they live, but that the true interests of the United States of America are damaged and treason is committed by those who, from pure and great egotism, drive the States to war, misery, financial and cultural catastrophe."

At the meeting the fact was accentuated that the causes which make military crises a chronic disease must not be forgotten.

As long as society rests on capitalistic foundations the world's peace is in danger day and night.

The only security is the collapse of the capitalistic system. Protesting against the attempts to enter war the meeting calls the Jugoslav workers to enter into the Socialist Party, to create a mighty resistance against capitalism; by destroying capitalism, the cause of war will be destroyed.

SOURCE: *Radnicka Straza* (Croatian), 28 February 1917, 1–3, in U.S. Works Progress Administration, "The Chicago Foreign Language Press Survey," 1860–1930s (1942), Newspaper Division, Chicago Public Library.

5.6. Chicago Russians, "A Resolution of Protest" (7 September 1917)

[Many Russian immigrants opposed the Conscription Act. In Chicago ethnic Russians adopted a resolution condemning conscription and the threat to deport Russian aliens who did not enlist in the U.S. Army.]

We, Russian citizens, who are gathered at a massmeeting [*sic*] on August 28, 1917, at the West Side Auditorium,—protest against the persecution of Russian citizens in forcing them to renounce their citizenship rights in Free Russia to take first citizenship papers under the threat of deportation in case of refusal. We protest against the mobilization of Russian citizens who did not take the first papers of their own free will for service in the United States Army. During the war they are forced to join the army, whereas in peace time they are deprived of citizenship rights.

Neither the kaiser nor the tsar forced citizens of foreign countries to join their armies; still less should the United States, which professes itself to be a fighter for freedom and democracy, do so.

SOURCE: *Russkaya Pochta* (*Russian Post*), 7 September 1917, in U.S. Works Progress Administration, "The Chicago Foreign Language Press Survey," 1860–1930s (1942), Newspaper Division, Chicago Public Library.

5.7. Letter Urging Blacks Not to Join the Army (30 April 1917)

[After the United States entered the war, some southern blacks expressed strong reservations about joining the armed services. Members of the Bureau of Investigation, subsequently the Federal Bureau of Investigation, monitored African American dissent. The following field report was filed from Memphis.]

. . . Assistant U.S. Attorney Roberson[,] Clarksdale, Miss., has forwarded to me the following anonymous letter or circular which was found in the neighborhood of Friars Point, Miss. Mr. Roberson states that he is keeping up a watch through the local authorities and will advise me of any developments. The letter follows:

"Young negro men and boys what have we to fight for in this country? Nothing. Some of our well educated negroes are touring the country urging our young race to be killed up like sheep, for nothing. If we fight in this war time we fight for nothing. Rather than fight I would rather commit self death—

Signed by a Negro Educator.

[P.S.] Stick to your bush and fight not for we will only be a breastwork or shield for the white race. After war we get nothing." . . .

SOURCE: Report of Agent W. E. McElveen, 30 April 1917, in Records of Military Intelligence Division, General Correspondence Relating to Negro Subversion, RG 165, M-1440, roll 2, file 3057, National Archives, College Park MD.

5.8. James P. Warbasse, "Are Not All Men My Brothers?"
(7 August 1917)

[Born to German immigrant parents, James Warbasse was a graduate of Columbia University College of Physicians and Surgeons and served as an army surgeon during the Spanish-American War. In 1918 he and his wife founded the Cooperative League of the USA. In 1918 he was expelled from the Kings County, New York, Medical Society for writing an article condemning compulsory military training. Below is a statement that he gave to *Viereck's Magazine* on optional military service for drafted German Americans; it was reprinted in the *New York Call*.]

. . . When one casts about for the greatest atrocities which governments inflict upon their subjects, it is difficult to find one that is more revolting than compelling a man to shoot those of this own flesh and blood. This atrocity is so utterly inhuman that I can think of it only as being quite as revolting as compelling a man to shoot the father or brother or son of some other man.

. . . Unfortunately, this movement on the part of German-Americans fails to take any step to save their fathers and brothers. It offers help from neither one angle nor another. It does not deter Germans from shooting Americans, nor Americans from shooting Germans. In the end the German fathers and brothers will be shot, just the same. It simply compromises with the provision that the young German-Americans should be occupied killing the fathers and brothers of other men while the other men would thus be relieved and made available for employment in killing the fathers and brothers and the German-Americans. They say, in fact, to the other soldier, ["]I have not the heart to kill my father; you kill him and I will kill yours." . . .

It is my own feeling and, of course, I am aware that this is extremely unpatriotic, that I have no more right to kill another man's father than I have to kill my own. . . .

. . . Are not all men my brothers? Are not governments the atrocious organizations which compel men to act contrary to their most humane instincts? . . .

If the German-American desires exemption as a conscientious objector, why does he wish to be a half-hearted one? If he desires to display his bravery, why not be wholly brave? Why not demand the same consideration for other men's fathers as he does for his own? Why not display the ethical culture of which he is so capable? . . .

Perhaps we have depreciated the significance of the suicides of the German-Americans in this country. It is possible that they destroyed themselves because they were not willing to be parties to the destruction of your brother and my brother. Perhaps their humanity transcended the bounds of their own narrow families. I do not know; but one of them, Peter Markeit frankly said, "I kill myself because I do not want to kill another mother's son." He was willing to write himself down a slacker and give to the word a new and hallowed significance.

What is the meaning of alternative service in industry? It means some industry accessory to the military program which aims to kill Germans. How much is a man relieved of responsibility when, instead of pulling the trigger of the gun which kills his brother he forges the bullet? . . .

. . . Does not our industrial profit-making system compel kin to destroy kin? Are not the suffering and deaths of the slums and the mines expressions of the industrial warfare, of which the great European war is but another? When the mother drives her daughter to prostitution, is this any less of an expression of the destruction of one's own blood and flesh than straightforward shooting. So far as killing and compulsion go, no man can be compelled to kill his own brother, any more than he can be compelled to prostitute his own daughter. . . .

Let us be honest, if we cannot be humane. There is no compromise with war. One is either for or against the policy of settling international disputes by means of force. All honor to the German-Americans who beg the government to excuse them from killing those of their own flesh and blood! More honor to those who recognize the brotherhood of man, and who are neither too humble nor too proud to own that all men are flesh of their flesh and blood of their blood—brothers in a common human family!

SOURCE: *New York Call*, 7 August 1917, 8.

5.9. Vincente Balbas Capo, "The Topic of the Day" (10 November 1917)

[Signed into law by President Wilson on 2 March 1917, the Jones Act established civilian government in Puerto Rico and conferred U.S. citizenship on its people, though a provision did allow Puerto Ricans to decline this status. Puerto Rican journalist and nationalist Vincente Balbas Capo, who rejected U.S. citizenship, edited the anti-American newspaper *Heraldo de las Antillas*. In an editorial titled "The Topic of the Day," he criticized the conscription of Puerto Ricans into the U.S. Army, arguing that those who had declined U.S. citizenship should not be drafted. Convicted by a jury of violating the Espionage Act, he was sentenced to eight years in a federal penitentiary. In 1919 the U.S. Court of Appeals reversed his conviction. Between 1898 and 1932, U.S. officials referred to the island as "Porto Rico," and that spelling appears in the document below.]

"The Prevost [Provost] Marshall of the United States has decided that the Porto Ricans who have declined American citizenship are obliged to serve in the Army."

—La Democracia.

Just as it sounds, the above statement is exactly this: "The Prevost [Provost] Marshall has decided." So that had the Provost Marshall decided, contrarily, those who have not sworn American citizenship would not have been called to the "colors"—or what has the same effect but in different words—that what one man decided is to be law for 288 men. . . .

With due deference to La Democracia, the Prevost [Provost] Marshall has not the power to decide which affects man's conscience. . . .

The law reads that all citizens of the United States are obliged to active service, to take up arms; but it does not refer to those who are not American citizens. And should that law enact such a step, it would be nothing less than a law without foundation because may La Democracia know, that Porto Ricans those who have not sworn allegiance to the American flag, we constitute a people of Porto Rico, as an entity about to disappear, may be, but not as yet extinguished. . . .

The people of Porto Rico has not declared war on any nation whatsoever and is therefore neutral. The above may sound awkward, but let it be known as a fact to all Porto Ricans, those who are now citizens of the United States, that Congress provided you with that citizenship in order that you be obliged to take up arms in defense of the American flag, without which privilege human conscience would have been violated had you been enlisted.

It is logical, therefore, that in order that Porto Ricans be called to shed their blood for the American flag, they were given American citizenship, it is reasonable that those who have not sworn flag are not compelled to defend another but the flag of Porto Rico; that flag, that flies yet as the moral representation and symbol of the people of Porto Rico, who yet exists as a political body. . . . The flag does not wave lawfully over the castles of Porto Rico; but lives there—in the hearts of every Porto Rican, . . . those who have not sworn American citizenship. . . . No matter how powerful the foe may be, only for that dear flag would the sacrifice be offered. . . .

[Compelling men] as slaves to defend a cause for which they have no ideal [is dangerous;] it sounds impossible that the Prevost [Provost] Marshall could decide to engross the American army with men whose ideals are not the same as those of Americans [and that renders Porto Ricans] weak and powerless, driven by force!!! That all has been decided by the Prevost [Provost] Marshall, but he who thus decided, who thus presses on the defenseless and the weak, he who compels, based on might, that man be driven by force to fight for a flag that is not his own, he who thus drives man has no right to claim that man be a true, loyal soldier. . . .

As soon as the statement of La Democracia was known, although, no explanation of the decision of the Prevost [Provost] Marshall was given, we, who have been so interested in the affair, have been the object of numerous inquiries on the matter from Pariahs [the term used by the provost marshal for Puerto Ricans who opposed serving in the U.S. Army] all over the island and to one and all the same answer and information has been given:

> "Resistance against the mighty is of no avail—when—ever called to the front—we have to go—but never before solemnly expressing to the Military Commission *that we are not citizens of the United States*; that we are not ready and willing to swear loyalty to the American flag—but if nevertheless we are compelled to defend a flag, to which respect is due, but with which we have no moral ties nor progeny—let the Prevost Marshall's will be done! His and only his will the responsibilities be of human error. And then may be that that decision find a place in the pages of history more due to its effects than to the motives of its existence. . . .
>
> "Oh! Washington, be thou witness of this struggle; behold man's conscience trampled upon by Might; . . . behold the Statue of Liberty and the Right of Man cast to the winds in fragments. . . ."

SOURCE: Cited in *Balbas v. United States et al.*, 257 Fed. 17 (1st Cir. 1919).

5.10. Court-Martial of Private Sidney Wilson, 368th Infantry, USA (2 July 1918)

[The Military Intelligence Division uncovered examples of African American opposition and resistance to the war. Sidney Wilson, a black army private, wrote the following letter to his draft board in Tennessee and to a newspaper in Memphis. Fictitiously signing the letter Captain G. H. Hill, Wilson condemned the conscription of black men. Court-martialed on 2 July 1918 at Camp Meade, Maryland, he was sentenced to ten years' hard labor and then dishonorably discharged.]

... CHARGE: Violation of the 96th Article of War.

Specification 1: In that Private Sidney Wilson, company "K," 368th Infantry, did, at Camp Meade, Maryland, on or about the 27th day of April, 1918, willfully attempt to hinder and obstruct the work of drafting citizens into the service of the United States by threatening and attempting to intimidate one H. D. Everett, Chairman, Local Board, Division No. 2, Shelby Country, Tenn., in a letter of the following tenor, to wit:

Binghampton[,] Tenn
April 27, 1918
Dr. H. B. [*sic?*] Everett

Dear Sir

[I]t afoads [affords] to the Soldiers Boys w[h]ich you have Sint [sent] So Far away from home a great Deal of Pledger [pleasure] to write you a few lines to let you know That You Low Down Mother Fuckers Can put a Gun in our Hands but who is able to take it out[?] We may go to France but I want to let you know that it will not be over with untill we Straiten up This State[.] We feel like we have nothing to Do with this war. So if you all Thinks it Just wait until uncle Sam puts a Gun in the niggers Hands and you all will be Sorry of it because we is Show goin [going] to Come Back and fight and whip out the united States, because we have Colored luetinan [lieutenants] up here, and they is Plan[n]ing against this country ever[y] day. So all we wants now is the amanation [ammunition][.] Then you all can look out[.] For we is coming.

Wrote By
Captain G. H. Hill ...

5.11. The Court of Appeals Case of Captain David A. Henkes (28 November 1919)

[In 1917 David A. Henkes, a German American officer, petitioned to resign his commission in the U.S. Army because of his parents' ethnic and family ties to Germany and Austria. Although he had served honorably with the American Expeditionary Force in France during the war, his petition was denied and he was court-martialed. Convicted of "aiding the enemy," he was sentenced to twenty-five years' hard labor at Fort Leavenworth. In 1919 his conviction was overturned on technical grounds. Although Henkes's antiwar sentiments were conditional, his case demonstrates the role of ethnicity in dissent toward World War I.]

Ex parte HENKES.

(District Court, D. Kansas, First Division. November 28, 1919.) . . .

. . . Habeas Corpus. Petition by David A. Henkes for writ to secure his discharge from the United States Disciplinary Barracks at Ft. Leavenworth. On demurrer of petitioner to the response of the commandant of the United States Disciplinary Barracks. Demurrer sustained. . . .

POLLOCK, District Judge. This is an application for writ of habeas corpus. The facts, briefly stated, are, as follows:

Petitioner, for many years prior to our entrance into the late war, was a captain in the regular army. His father was born in Germany; his mother in this country. On account of his lineage petitioner had an aversion to engaging actively in a war against a nation of his kindred. Hence, on May 26, 1917, he tendered his resignation, not stating therein his actual motive for so doing. Acceptance of this resignation was recommended by his superior officer, to whom it was tendered. On the same day petitioner wrote to the Honorable Secretary of War a letter, giving his true reasons for tendering his resignation, as follows:

San Antonio, Texas, May 26, 1917.
From: Capt. D. A. Henkes, 16th Inf.
To: The Secretary of War, Wash., D.C.
Subject: Resignation.

1. In the event that the reasons stated in my letter of resignation are not deemed sufficient, I feel it my solemn duty to further state the following:

2. Further service as a commissioned officer must sooner or later take me to Europe, and there bring me in conflict with those who are my relatives and friends, although for the time being legal enemies. My father came from Germany. My mother was born here shortly after the arrival of her parents. We have many other relatives and friends there. I cannot force myself to the conviction that I am capable of making war on my kindred upon their soil in a manner that would become my duty and station. I earnestly request that I may not be required to undergo this ordeal. I seriously doubt my ability to withstand it, and would avoid in the interest of my country, family, and friends what at least appears the probable consequences.

3. As an only alternative, if my services will not be dispensed with, I would suggest duty in another field. However, I most earnestly believe that it is to the manifest interest of the government that my services as a commissioned officer of the army be terminated by the acceptance of said resignation.

4. I sincerely regret to feel called upon to avoid the usual methods of communication. The subject and emergency appears to admit of no alternative, and I trust my efforts may be pardoned.

D. A. Henkes.

Later, on June 29, 1917, when en route overseas with his command, petitioner wrote another letter, addressed to the Adjutant General of the Army, as follows:

United States Expeditionary Force, France, June 29, 1917.
From: Captain D. A. Henkes, 16th Infantry.
To: The Adjutant General, War Department, Washington, D.C.
    (Through Military Channels.)
Subject: Resignation.

1. On May 26th I forwarded a letter tendering my resignation as an officer of the army. . . .

2. [Nearly identical to number 2 above.]

3. If my services will not now be dispensed with, I request duty in another field, or such duty as will not require me to actively participate against my own blood or personally direct others in doing so. I trust that my bequest may not be construed as disloyalty to my own country, or that same is inspired by a consideration of personal safety. I am willing to take transport duty in the submarine zone, or other duty of a similar nature, all of which I will perform to the best of my ability. However, I believe it but just that one so situated and whose services may be judged by a question of loyalty should not be placed in a position of trust or authority. I therefore beg that my services as a commissioned officer be now terminated by the acceptance of my resignation.

D. A. Henkes.

On October 10th, after having served with credit and distinction in the field, and after having been importuned to recall what he had expressed in the former communications, he wrote a further letter to the Adjutant General, as follows:

American Expeditionary Force, October 10, 1917.
From: Capt. D. A. Henkes, 16th Infantry.
To: The Adjutant General, War Dept. (Through Military Channels.)
Subject: Resignation.

1) Pursuant to the provisions of Par. 79 A. R. [Army Regulations], I hereby tender my resignation as officer of the army, to take effect at earliest date.

2) My reasons have heretofore been stated, particularly in letter dated June 28 last, and are a matter of record.... I trust that those in position of authority and greater responsibility may see fit to recommend acceptance.

D. A. Henkes....

SOURCE: Captain David A. Henkes Case, 28 November 1919, 267 *Federal Reporter*, 1919, 276–78.

5.12. Chandler Owen, "What Will Be the Real Status of the Negro after the War?" (March 1919)

[Chandler Owen, an African American socialist, had little optimism that the "war for democracy" abroad would result in a better life for blacks returning from the battlefield or for those who supported the conflict.]

Much has been said pro and con concerning the status of the Negro after the war. Some Negroes maintain that the war has been helpful to them on the ground that the demand for labor in the North and West enabled thousands of Negro workers to leave the prejudiced Southland and go where they might receive better treatment on the one hand, and better wages on the other. His condition after the war has received but scant and superficial consideration, which was usually by ignorant and venal Negro leaders who were trying to bully him into some false optimism about after the war conditions in order to secure his unquestioning services during the war....

What, anyhow, have been the usual results of all people's participation in wars?

1. Loss of life—especially the flower of youth.

2. Loss of rights and privileges. Free speech, free press and freedom of assemblage have, as a rule, been denied in war time. Other rights are taken away also.

3. Loss of limb. Tens of thousands of invalids without arms, legs,

etc., are usually returned as charges on society and wretches to themselves.

4. Loss of source of production and the consequent loss of goods for consumption. When the young manhood is killed or maimed, it is not possible for it to act as a means of economic production, which also means that the things which may be consumed are lessened.

5. Tax burdens increased. Tax burdens are increased to pay for the war, and to provide pensions for soldiers or their families. These taxes, like most taxes, are paid by the people.

6. Misery of participants. Soldiers become public charges in old soldiers' homes and other places of detention.

7. Increase in prostitution. This follows the decrease of males due to death in battle, with the consequent excess of females.

8. National and race hate. These usually are left and it takes a half century or a century to cool that passionate ardor.

Such have been the gains of people after wars from time immemorial. . . .

Optimism as to the status of the Negro after the war is ill-timed. Like all other peoples who have fought battles for their country, the Negro will have to return to engage in a political and industrial fight with his own country to secure his just rights. Not an inch or ell will be yielded except through compulsion and necessity. No one will say to the Negro, "you have fought so gallantly and vigorously, your loyalty was so unadulterated and true, you were so patriotic that we are going to give you the vote in the South; we are going to cut out Jim-Crow cars; segregation in places of public accommodation will be made unlawful; lynching will be stopped by the stern arm of the Government; you shall no longer be subject to peonage and vagrancy laws." This indeed will not happen. . . .

What the Negro gets after the war may be very different from what he intended to fight for! Such, however, has been the course of history.

SOURCE: *Messenger*, March 1919, 13–15, 17.

5.13. Friends of Irish Freedom, "Women of America!" (1919)

[The Friends of Irish Freedom, an American Irish group, expressed alarm that Article 10 of the League of Nations would require the United States to send troops to help imperial powers maintain their empires and crush revolts by subjugated peoples. In particular, the Friends feared that Article 10 would oblige the United States to defend British control of Ireland. In this circular the Friends appealed to U.S. women, who had recently won the franchise, to organize against the League of Nations.]

Do you wish your Sons and Brothers, Husbands and Sweethearts, sent to War, not to fight for Liberty, but to uphold Tyranny?—sent to suffer and die in the waterless deserts of Africa, in the feverish jungles of Asia, in the icy fields of Russia, not for America's sake, but for England and Japan and the International Money Power?

WOMEN OF AMERICA!

This will happen if America enters the League of Nations! For instance, Article Ten says:

"The members of the League undertake to respect and preserve as against external aggression the territorial integrity and existing political independence of all members of the League. In case of any such aggression or in case of any threat or danger of such aggression, the Council shall advise upon the means by which this obligation shall be fulfilled."

This means that America would be bound to help the British and Japanese Empires to keep their bloody grip on the peoples they have enslaved. Some day Korea, India, Ireland, Egypt, South Africa, will strike for freedom. True Americans would wish to help them. But instead, if any nation even sympathized with them, thus creating a "threat or danger of aggression," the Council of the League could Order America to send soldiers—YOUR BOYS, YOUR MEN—TO SHOOT DOWN THE PEOPLE OF IRELAND, INDIA, KOREA, EGYPT AND SOUTH AFRICA, AND TO BE SHOT DOWN IN THESE DISTANT LANDS.

There is no doubt about this: We must do it when the Council "advises" us to, because we "UNDERTAKE" to do it as an "OBLIGATION."

WOMEN OF AMERICA!

How do you like the prospect?

But Article Ten is only one of twenty-six articles, everyone of which would ENTANGLE AMERICA IN EVERY WAR THAT STARTS ANYWHERE ON EARTH . . . .

And this Council, meeting in Geneva, Switzerland, will consist of nine men, including six Europeans, all but one appointed by Kings, one Japanese appointed by the Mikado, one Brazilian and only one American. And everyone knows how American diplomats, when they are surrounded and flattered by "Lords" and "Nobles," lose their Americanism.

And if the Council fails to agree on a question, it goes to the Assembly, where the BRITISH EMPIRE HAS SIX VOTES, BUT THE UNITED STATES HAS ONLY ONE!

This League means ENDLESS WAR, the cost of which will MAKE THE COST OF LIVING HIGHER AND HIGHER, while permanent CONSCRIPTION will BREAK UP YOUR HOMES and send your boys to die and rot in distant lands!

Furthermore this League would destroy the Independence of our Great Republic by making it a mere province in the super-empire miscalled a "League of Nations."

The lie is being spread that American women support this League. Women's clubs endorsed it before they read it, because they thought it meant Peace. But now that you can read it and see that it "breeds, sanctions and commands war," you, possessing the vote, can kill it!

WOMEN OF AMERICA!

Crush this monstrous thing! ACT—ACT NOW—ORGANIZE—let the Senators in Washington know that you demand the defeat of this un-American League for War. . . .

SOURCE: Office of the National Secretary, Friends of Irish Freedom Papers, box 3, American Irish Historical Society, New York.

CHAPTER 6

Conscientious Objectors

6.1. Ammon Hennacy, "Young Men: Don't Register for War!" (1917)

[In 1917 Ammon Hennacy, a socialist, atheist, and nonpacifist CO, was sentenced to two years in prison for refusing to register for the Selective Service. He served time in Atlanta Federal Penitentiary with anarchist Alexander Berkman and socialist Eugene V. Debs, who both had been convicted for antiwar activities. Reading the Bible and Leo Tolstoy in prison, Hennacy became a Christian pacifist and later a notable Catholic Worker. In 1917 Hennacy wrote and distributed the following antiwar sticker and poster in Cleveland.]

YOUNG MEN
DON'T REGISTER FOR WAR!
It is better to go to jail than
to rot on a foreign battlefield

The poster said:

YOUNG MEN
Are you going to
REFUSE TO REGISTER
for military service in a foreign country
While the rich men
who have brought on this war
stay at home
and get richer by gambling in food stuffs?

WE WOULD RATHER DIE OR BE IMPRISONED
FOR THE SAKE OF JUSTICE, THAN KILL
OUR FELLOW MEN IN THIS UNJUST WAR.

Signed _____ Young Men's Anti-Militarist League

SOURCE: Ammon Hennacy, *The Book of Ammon: The Autobiography of a Unique American Rebel* ([1953?]; reprint, Salt Lake City: [Ammon Hennacy Publications], 1970), 10.

6.2. Noah H. Leatherman, CO Diary (1917–19)

[Noah Leatherman, a religious nonresistant, was denied CO status. Between registering for the draft and reporting for induction, he joined the Church of Christ, Mennonite (Holdeman), an offshoot of the Old Order Mennonite Church. He spent time at Camp Funston (Kansas), Camp Dodge (Iowa), Fort Riley (Kansas), and Fort Leavenworth (Kansas). Court-martialed for refusing to work, he was sentenced to twenty-five years, but released in January 1919. In the military camps he suffered physical abuse because of his religious-based refusal to cooperate with the military or obey military orders. In a diary, later self-published, he recorded his wartime experiences, along with the following statement that explains his religious motives.]

THE BASIS FOR MY BELIEF IN NONRESISTANCE

Since I have accepted Christ Jesus as my personal Savior, who is the Son of God, The Prince of Peace, whose kingdom is not of this world, and through the shedding of His Blood I have been redeemed and saved, to Him I owe all hope of eternal life, having been born again according to His Word, and have become a member and subject of His kingdom. I, therefore, owe my first allegiance to Him, to live, not only in time of war, but in my everyday life in accord with His teaching and commandments as He taught in Matthew 22:37: Thou shalt love the Lord thy God with all thy heart, and with all thy soul, and with all thy mind, and thy neighbor as thy neighbor as thyself. In Matthew 5, His Sermon on the Mount, He said: Blessed are the merciful; for they shall obtain mercy. Blessed are the pure in heart; for they shall see God. Blessed are the peacemakers; for they shall be called the children of God. Blessed are they which are persecuted for righteousness' sake; for their's is the kingdom of Heaven. Blessed are ye, when men shall revile you, and persecute you, and shall say all manner of evil against you falsely, for my sake.

Agree with thine adversary quickly, whiles thou are in the way with him. And, Ye have heard that it hath been said, An eye for an eye, and a tooth for a tooth. But I say unto you, That ye resist not evil; but whosoever shall smite thee on the right cheek, turn to him the other also. Luke 6:27, 28: But I say unto you which hear, Love your enemies, do good to them which hate you. Bless them that curse you, and pray for them which despitefully use you. And as ye would that men should do to you, do ye also them likewise. Luke 6:35, 36: But love your enemies, and do good, and lend, hoping for nothing again; and your reward shall be great, and ye shall be the children of the Highest, for He is kind unto the unthankful, and to the evil. Be ye therefore merciful, as your Father also is merciful. Luke 10:3: Go your ways: behold I send you forth as lambs among wolves. Matthew 6:24: No man can serve two masters, for either he will hate the one, and love the other; or else he will hold to the one, and despise the other. Ye cannot serve God and mammon. Since good alone can overcome evil, the use of violence must be abandoned. Be not overcome of evil, but overcome evil with good. (Romans 12:21) Follow peace with all men, and holiness, without which no man shall see the Lord. (Hebrews 12:14) And the fruit of righteousness is sown in peace of them that make peace. (James 3:18)

SOURCE: Noah H. Leatherman, *Diary Kept by Noah H. Leatherman While in Camp during World War I* (Linden, Alberta: Aaron L. Toews, 1951), [1].

6.3. Roger N. Baldwin, Statement before the Court (30 October 1918)

[Roger N. Baldwin was a prominent social worker and civil libertarian. From his upper-middle-class suburban Boston background, he became a philosophical anarchist and pacifist. When the United States entered the war, Baldwin moved from St. Louis to New York City to direct the Civil Liberties Bureau of the American Union Against Militarism. (He also led the CLB's successors, the National Civil Liberties Bureau and the American Civil Liberties Union.) Declaring himself a CO and refusing to cooperate, he was convicted of violating the Selective Service Act and sentenced to a one-year prison term.

After the war he led the ACLU for many years. On 30 October 1918, prior to sentencing, he made the following statement to the court.]

... I am before you as a deliberate violator of the draft act. On October 9, when ordered to take a physical examination, I notified my local board that I declined to do so, and instead presented myself to the United States Attorney for prosecution. I submit herewith for the record the letter of explanation which I addressed to him at the time.

I refused to take bail, believing that I was not morally justified in procuring it, and being further opposed to the institution of bail on principle. I have therefore been lodged in the Tombs Prison since my arraignment on October 10. During that period I have been engaged daily at the Department of Justice offices in systematizing the files of the National Civil Liberties Bureau, of which I have been the director. These files had been voluntarily turned over to the Department for examination, and had, through much handling, become seriously disarranged. That work being completed, I am before you for sentence.

And, by the way, may I take this occasion, your honor—this is quite aside from the proceedings—to express my thanks for the courtesy of every officer of this court, and of the Department of Justice, through these trying weeks. It has been exceptional.

The compelling motive for refusing to comply with the draft act is my uncompromising opposition to the principle of conscription of life by the State for any purpose whatever, in time of war or peace. I not only refuse to obey the present conscription law, but I would in future refuse to obey any similar statute which attempts to direct my choice of service and ideals. I regard the principle of conscription of life as a flat contradiction of all our cherished ideals of individual freedom, democratic liberty, and Christian teaching.

I am the more opposed to the present act, because it is for the purpose of conducting war. I am opposed to this and all other wars. I do not believe in the use of physical force as a method of achieving any end, however good.

The District Attorney calls your attention your Honor, to the inconsistency in my statement to him that I would, under extreme emergencies, as a matter of protecting the life of any person, use physical force. I don't think that is an argument that can be used in support of the wholesale organization of men to achieve political purposes in nationalistic or domestic wars. I see no relationship at all between the two.

My opposition is not only to direct military service, but to any service whatever designed to help prosecute the war. I could accept no service, therefore, under the present act, regardless of its character.

Holding such profound convictions, I determined, while the new act was pending, that it would be more honest to make my stand clear at the start and therefore concluded not even to register, but to present myself for prosecution. I therefore resigned my position as director of the National Civil Liberties Bureau so as to be free to follow that personal course of action. But on the day my resignation took effect (August 31) agents of the Department of Justice began an examination of the affairs of that organization, and I was constrained to withdraw my resignation and to register in order to stand by the work at a critical moment. With that obligation discharged, I resigned, and took the next occasion, the physical examination, to make my stand clear.

I realize that to some this refusal may seem a piece of wilful defiance. It might well be argued that any man holding my views might have avoided the issue by obeying the law, either on the chance of being rejected on physical grounds, or on the chance of the war stopping before a call to service. I answer that I am not seeking to evade the draft; that I scorn evasion, compromise and gambling with moral issues. It may further be argued that the War Department's liberal provision for agricultural service on furlough for conscientious objectors would be open to me if I obey the law and go to camp, and that there can be no moral objection to farming, even in time of war. I answer first, that I am opposed to any service under conscription, regardless of whether that service is in itself morally objectionable; and second, that, even if that were not the case, and I were opposed only to war, I can make no moral distinction between the various services which assist in prosecuting the war—whether rendered in the trenches, in the purchase of bonds or thrift stamps at home, or in raising farm products under the lash of the draft act. All serve the same end—war. Of course all of us render involuntary assistance to the war in the processes of our daily living. I refer only to those direct services undertaken by choice.

I am fully aware that my position is extreme, that it is shared by comparatively few, and that in the present temper it is regarded either as unwarranted egotism or as a species of feeble-mindedness. I cannot, therefore, let this occasion pass without attempting to explain the foundations on which so extreme a view rests.

I have had an essentially American upbringing and background. Born in a suburban town of Boston, Massachusetts, of the stock of the first settlers, I was reared in the public schools and at Harvard College. Early my mind was caught by the age-old struggle for freedom; America meant to me a vital new experiment in free political institutions; personal freedom to choose one's way of life and service seemed the essence of the liberties brought by those who fled the medieval and modern tyrannies of the old world. But I rebelled at our whole autocratic industrial system—with its wreckage of poverty, disease, and crime, and childhood robbed of its right to free growth. So I took up social work upon leaving college, going to St. Louis as director of a settlement and instructor in sociology at Washington University. For ten years I have been professionally engaged in social work and political reform, local and national. That program of studied, directed social progress, step by step, by public agitation and legislation, seemed to me the practical way of effective service to gradually freeing the mass of folks from industrial and political bondage. At the same time I was attracted to the solutions of our social problems put forth by the radicals. I studied the programs of socialism, the I.W.W. European syndicalism and anarchism. I attended their meetings, knew their leaders. Some of them became my close personal friends. Sympathizing with their general ideals of a free society, with much of their program, I yet could see no effective way of practical daily service. Some six years ago, however, I was so discouraged with social work and reform, so challenged by the sacrifices and idealism of some of my I.W.W. friends, that I was on the point of getting out altogether, throwing respectability overboard and joining the I.W.W. as a manual worker.

I thought better of it. My traditions were against it. It was more an emotional reaction than a practical form of service. But ever since, I have felt myself heart and soul with the world-wide radical movements for industrial and political freedom,—wherever and however expressed—and more and more impatient with reform.

Personally, I share the extreme radical philosophy of the future society. I look forward to a social order without any external restraints upon the individual, save through public opinion and the opinion of friends and neighbors. I am not a member of any radical organization, nor do I wear any tag by which my views may be classified. I believe that all parts of the radical movement serve the common end—freedom of the individual from arbitrary external controls.

When the war came to America, it was an immediate challenge to me to help protect those ideals of liberty which seemed to me not only the basis of the radical economic view, but of the radical political view of the founders of this Republic, and of the whole medieval struggle for religious freedom. Before the war was declared I severed all my connections in St. Louis, and offered my services to the American Union Against Militarism to help fight conscription. Later that work developed into the National Civil Liberties Bureau, organized to help maintain the rights of free speech and free press, and the Anglo-Saxon tradition of liberty of conscience, through liberal provisions for conscientious objectors. This work has been backed both by pro-war liberals and so-called pacifists. It is not anti-war in any sense. It seemed to me the one avenue of service open to me, consistent with my views, with the country's best interest, and with the preservation of the radical minority for the struggle after the war. Even if I were not a believer in radical theories and movements, I would justify the work I have done on the ground of American ideals and traditions alone—as do many of those who have been associated with me. They have stood for those enduring principles which the revolutionary demands of war have temporarily set aside. We have stood against hysteria, mob-violence, unwarranted prosecution, the sinister use of patriotism to cover attacks on radical and labor movements, and for the unabridged right of a fair trial under war statutes. We have tried to keep open those channels of expression which stand for the kind of world order for which the President is battling today against the tories and militarists.

Now comes the Government to take me from that service and to demand of me a service I cannot in conscience undertake. I refuse it simply for my own peace of mind and spirit, for the satisfaction of that inner demand more compelling than any considerations of punishment or the sacrifice of friendships and reputation. I seek no martyrdom, no publicity. I merely meet as squarely as I can the moral issue before me, regardless of consequences.

I realize that your Honor may virtually commit me at once to the military authorities, and that I may have merely taken a quicker and more inconvenient method of arriving at a military camp. I am prepared for that—for the inevitable pressure to take an easy way out by non-combatant service—with guard-house confinement—perhaps brutalities, which hundreds of others objectors have already suffered and are suffering today in camps. I am prepared for court martial and sentence to military prison, to follow the 200–300 objectors already sentenced to terms of 10–30 years for their loyalty to their ideals. I know that the way is easy for those who accept what to me is compromise, hard for those who refuse, as I must, any service whatever. And I know further, in military prison I shall refuse to conform to the rules for military salutes and the like, and will suffer solitary confinement on bread and water, shackled to the bars of a cell eight hours a day—as are men of like convictions at this moment.

I am not complaining for myself or others. I am merely advising the court that I understand full well the penalty of my heresy, and am prepared to pay it. The conflict with conscription is irreconcilable. Even the liberalism of the President and Secretary of War in dealing with objectors leads those of us who are "absolutists" to a punishment longer and severer than that of desperate criminals.

But I believe most of us are prepared even to die for our faith, just as our brothers in France are dying for theirs. To them we are comrades in spirit—we understand one another[']s motives, though our methods are wide apart. We both share deeply the common experience of living up to the truth as we see it, whatever the price.

Though at the moment I am of a tiny minority, I feel myself just one protest in a great revolt surging up from among the people— the struggle of the masses against the rule of the world by the few— profoundly intensified by the war. It is a struggle against the political state itself, against exploitation, militarism, imperialism, authority in all forms. It is a struggle to break in full force only after the war. Russia already stands in the vanguard, beset by her enemies in the camps of both belligerents—the Central Empires break asunder from within—the labor movement gathers revolutionary force in Britain— and in our own country the Nonpartisan League, radical labor, and the Socialist Party hold the germs of a new social order. Their protest is my protest. Mine is a personal protest at a particular law, but it is backed by all the aspirations and ideals of the struggle for a world freed of our manifold slaveries and tyrannies.

I ask the Court for no favor. I could do no other than what I have done, whatever the court's decree. I have no bitterness or hate in my heart for any man. Whatever the penalty I shall endure it, firm in the faith, that whatever befalls me, the principles in which I believe will bring forth out of this misery and chaos, a world of brotherhood, harmony and freedom for each to live the truth as he sees it.

I hope your Honor will not think that I have taken this occasion to make a speech for the sake of making a speech. I have read you what I have written in order that the future record for myself and for my friends may be perfectly clear, and in order or [to] clear up some of the matters to which the District Attorney called your attention. I know that it is pretty nigh hopeless in times of war and hysteria to get across to any substantial body of people, the view of an out and out heretic like myself. I know that as far as my principles are concerned, they seem to be utterly impractical—mere moon-shine. They are not the views that work in the world today. I fully realize that. But I fully believe that they are the views which are going to guide in the future.

Having arrived at the state of mind in which those views mean the dearest things in life to me, I cannot consistently, with self-respect, do other than I have, namely, to deliberately violate an act which seems to me to be a denial of everything which ideally and in practice I hold sacred.

SOURCE: Roger N. Baldwin, *The Individual and the State: The Problem as Presented by the Sentencing of Roger N. Baldwin* (New York: Graphic Press, 1918), 6–11.

6.4. Erling H. Lunde, Statement to Court-Martial (15 October 1918)

[Erling H. Lund, a CO and graduate of the University of Chicago, protested the harsh treatment of fellow COs at Fort Riley. Court-martialed at Camp Funston, Kansas, for refusing to obey military orders, he was sentenced to life imprisonment, later commuted to twenty-five years. Erling's statement to the court was published by his father, Theodore Lunde, president of the Chicago-based American Industrial Company. Theodore also published several pamphlets that exposed the army's mistreatment of the Hofer brothers and other COs. During World War I Theodore refused to make war materials and lost his factory.]

Gentlemen of the court martial: I am before you today not because I have committed any crime against the military establishment as such nor against organized society, but because I am a conscientious objector to war; I am here because I have dared to live my ideal of universal brotherhood and love, and my convictions against war,— convictions which have been declared sincere by the Board of Inquiry consisting of Major Stoddard, Judge Mack and Dean Stone. Furthermore, I am before you gentlemen, because of the deliberate action of the military authorities in sending Colonel J. C. Waterman on September 17th to command me to perform non-combatant military work, which I could not conscientiously do, and which they knew I could not, as a matter of principle, do. . . .

With my ballot and by means of written communications to my servants in Washington, I have tried to make my stand on war and conscription effective, but without success.

Again, when I registered and stated that I was a conscientious objector to war, I voted against war, although it was a late and limited referendum on such a momentous question.

I claimed exemption on conscientious grounds in my questionnaire, but that was not recognized, as I belonged to no established creed.

My only remaining weapon is to refuse to be a soldier, by refusing to do a soldier's work, as long as I am held under the Selective Service Act. No other choice is left me, since my responsibility to God, in living Christ's teachings, cannot be altered by political action of any kind. Political sanction of war by a government does not alter the immorality of war or compulsion.

I could have avoided danger or punishment, if cowardice had been my motive in making this stand, by accepting a safe job drafting in the Ordnance Department, by entering the Quartermaster's Department, by entering the Quartermaster's Training Corp at the University of Chicago, under my former dean, or by joining the Scoutmasters Sanitary Detachment. All these were definitely offered to me, because I had the necessary fundamental training. . . .

After my induction into the army, since President Wilson had promised recognition of conscientious objectors, I complied with the law as far as possible, and lived up in every detail to the Executive Order of March 20th, 1918, at Jefferson Barracks, where I was quartered for several weeks with a miscellaneous company.

Next I was transferred, without guard, along with three other conscientious objectors, to Fort Leavenworth, where the Board of Inquiry was to interview us. Here I still continued to co-operate with the military authorities in what, I was given to understand, was a temporary situation pending final disposition of my case. We had excellent quarters and considerate officers, no attempt being made to make soldiers of us. Consequently I volunteered my services as "kitchen police" and "room orderly." I also worked helping the civilian carpenters put the finishing touches on the "C.O." camp up on the hill under the trees. Finally, feeling sure that my desire to help out would not be taken advantage of, I worked for several weeks as third cook, making food for the "C.O." company. I took no pay, so this was all gratis.

After being examined by the Board of Inquiry, consisting of Major Stoddard, Judge Mack and Dean Stone, and my objections to both combatant and non-combatant service being adjudged sincere, and being placed in Class I A, I was transferred, together with about a hundred conscientious objectors, to Fort Riley, to do non-combatant work. We were assigned to Major Platte of the Quartermaster's Department. His first request was that we build our own detention camp. Apparently my conscientious objections to non-combatant service were to be disregarded entirely. I, along with some fifty others, refused, and I stated my objections.

Then, as a punishment for refusing to do this non-combatant service and "kitchen police" for ourselves and a group of hay-makers, and in order to force us by physical necessity to build our own place of detention, we were sent out into an open field on which some tents were erected, but not trenched, and a tap of running water. The latter had to serve fifty men for drinking, cooking, washing and bathing. Our only latrine was a couple of shovels, and a spot assigned, whereon we could dig a hole and build a shelter. With no mess hall or kitchen we were exposed to the sun, rain, flying dust and flies. Furthermore, we were expected to walk five blocks with our mess kits, three times a day, to receive our individual rations, until, after starving two days and making a protest to Washington, we were issued rations in bulk, a field stove, pots, etc., so that we could cook collectively.

I refused, however, to accept this punishment, it being a direct violation of Secretary Baker's Executive Order of June 1st, 1918, to the effect that, pending the determination of our final status, we should not receive any punitive treatment for refusing to perform any service, which we stated was contrary to our conscientious principles. . . .

. . . I refused to be forced to do this non-combatant service, or to submit to the punishment of preparing our own meals under the intolerable unsanitary conditions; in other words, to keep myself in the status of a soldier. The only reason I received food meanwhile (and that was badly prepared and very poorly balanced in essential food values), was because the other boys were willing to cook for me.

As a protest against my scruples being disregarded and my being kept a soldier under the conscription act after my sincerity had been definitely established by the Board, I went on a hunger strike for twelve days, and forced feeding for one day, only retracting from this strike when I saw the possibility of unethical interpretation of my motives in voluntarily starving myself.

Finally, to bring the issue to a head as to whether we would consent to be soldiers or not, the military authorities in the person of Colonel J. C. Waterman, offered me and the other conscientious objectors in the tent colony, a chance to apply for service in the Quartermaster's, Medical, or Engineering Corps, and upon my refusal to apply, ordered me to do "camp police" work—distinctly non-combatant service. I told Colonel Waterman, who gave the order, that I could not consciously do the work, but that I was willing to keep myself and quarters clean without military orders; whereupon I was sent to the Post Guard House. Here I was again punished for not doing "camp police," namely cutting grass on the post, by being put in solitary confinement on bread and water for three days.

That the purpose of the authorities, in commanding me to clean up that pile of rubbish in the tent colony, was not to test my willingness to keep my own quarters clean, (as stated in Secretary Baker's order of June 1st, 1918,) but to see whether or not I would take commands to the extent of doing general "camp police," i.e., non-combatant service pure and simple, was shown by the Colonel's subsequent actions in ordering those who obeyed his first command, (to shovel the rubbish in the tent colony,) to next rake the parade ground, and then putting those who refused on conscientious grounds, into the guard house. . . .

Gentlemen, these are the facts in my case since I have been in the army; and if President Wilson's provisions for conscientious objectors have not been carried out, the blame must rest upon Colonel Kirkpatrick and Lieutenant W. E. Donaldson, who are responsible for punishing me, and the other fifty conscientious objectors, for refusing to do what we had stated we could not conscientiously do.

Gentlemen, during all my stay in the army, and now, my actions, in refusing to become a soldier, have been prompted by deep religious and moral convictions against war, which includes militarism and conscription, without which modern warfare is impossible. . . . What good is democracy, freedom, or human liberty, if in the process the weapon resorted to bring it about and maintain it, destroys the people seeking and giving it, and also denies the fundamental principles on which it is based? If a democracy has to be transformed, temporarily, into an autocracy, every time armed forces have to be employed to settle international disputes, you can never have real individual liberty. . . .

In view of these facts, and many others too numerous to mention, (and here I might give you a few facts regarding the machinations of the International Armament Ring and the International Money Trust, but there is no time for that), I believe that we must purge our present day society of the autocratic weapon of force which reaches its zenith in our modern militarism and meets each individual conscience in the form of conscription, or compulsion. I believe our only real defense against possible invasion lies in Tolstoian non-resistance, exemplified by the Quaker's experience with the Indians in Pennsylvania, and in the action of the Finns in 1905, when they won their constitution in the face of the worst militarism in the world, by making their demands and then simply refusing to work, sitting quietly unarmed, and so overwhelming the cossacks that the latter refused to fire at the command of their officers.

We, as a free nation, must definitely and permanently abandon the "direct action" of the militarists, anarchists, and I.W.W.'s—for exactly the same philosophy directs each one—and instead employ the "political action" or "non-direct action" of the real socialists and pacifists. Hitherto, there has been a deliberate, if not ignorant, confusion of these philosophies and agencies. The former rely on "force" both for defense and offense in maintaining and spreading their culture among their fellow men and sister nations; the latter rely entirely on "political action,"—in other words, for defense, on non-resistance and the living example of the brotherhood of man and love, and for offense, on the courageous declaration of the truth, exemplified by living that truth. . . .

The cry that this is a war to end wars we will dismiss as utter folly. That was the battle cry of the allied forces which defeated Napoleon and French militarism. . . .

Gentlemen, I believe that there is nothing to fear from any mistakes we may make in abandoning "force" and adopting brotherly love between nations. No mistake can be more costly than the present mistake of a world war. It is high time we throw away the organized force—militarism and conscription—which make this horror possible, and try something else as a guarantee of world peace, and human liberty and justice. . . .

Underlying the sum total of human effort, however, must be that unswerving faith in Christ's teachings of universal brotherhood and truth, and in his counsel against force when he said, "Thou shalt not kill." Without this faith your cause is lost before you start; with it, success is assured.

This is my religion, gentlemen, simple in its statement, but fraught in its practical applications with so many difficulties, including the maximum penalty which you can give. However, I have no just claim to this faith unless I live it. . . . All I expect and demand of you gentlemen sitting in the court martial is that you judge me as a Conscientious Objector to War and not as a soldier . . .

SOURCE: Erling H. Lunde, *Defense of Erling H. Lunde: Conscientious Objector to War Made before a Court Martial at Camp Funston, Kansas, October 15, 1918* (Chicago: American Industrial, 1918).

6.5. Evan Thomas, Prison Letters (1918)

[Evan Thomas was a secular absolutist CO who refused to cooperate with military authorities and waged work and hunger strikes to protest conscription and the harsh treatment of Molokans and other COs at Fort Leavenworth and Fort Riley. His determined stance and insistence that pacifism must be active and militant inspired radical COs during World War II, during which he chaired the War Resisters League. In these letters to his mother and brother, he discusses his CO experiences and the reasons for his resistance.]

[Evan Thomas] to [Norman Thomas], 8 June 1918

. . . Frankly, I am a C.O. because of freedom, first, last, and all the time. I knew I would never join the army after my first long visit to a British training camp, and I knew this for one reason—that to enter the army was to become a slave so far as I was concerned. Then it became absolutely necessary for me to work out the relation of the individual to society. It was then I found that freedom and love and truth were always dependent on each other. You see, I am an individualist through and through, so far as my philosophy is concerned. I am a C.O. not because I believe fighting is wrong but [rather] because no free man can be conscripted or submit to the army machine. I would resist labor conscription as well as army conscription. I think disarmament and leagues of nations, etc., the most futile sort of talk apart from individualism. War will end when the people refuse to be conscripted. . . . Disarm every nation and you could have war in ten years provided States could still conscript individuals.

If there is any conscription in this new C.O. order I go to Leavenworth. I am a C.O. because I honestly believe in Freedom—not a compromise, but Freedom. . . .

[Evan Thomas] to [Mother], 23 July 1918

What can I do or say to get you to understand what I am after in going through all this mess, which is nothing like as bad as the trenches physically but is perhaps worse otherwise? I left [Camp] Upton happy because I thought you understood that however mistaken I might be from the point of view of others, yet I was doing the only thing I could conscientiously do. I also thought that you were coming to see that I consider that I am in an active positive fight for a new freedom just as much as Ralph and Arthur [his brothers who joined the army]. Our methods differ. They think war is the best method, or perhaps they would put it, organized, armed resistance is the best method. . . . I believe if the idea of conscription can be given a death blow there may be some real chance for permanent peace. I see little hope in leagues of nations or such utopian ideas as total disarmament. If America is big enough—and by America I mean the bulk of the people, for the government can't be too far ahead of them—if America is big enough to establish now in this colossal war the precedent that conscription should not be applied to individuals who are ready to work but are conscientiously opposed to war and to being "Prussianized," then I believe this country will have taken one of the biggest steps towards accomplishing the very things President Wilson is so eloquent about, and war in the future will have been given a body blow. If this nation is not ready for this, then I consider it my task to try to help . . . get that idea before the public. Otherwise I would be in the trenches. How often have I not told you that I am a C.O. not merely because I believe war wrong but because I think the very biggest fight for people who believe as I do lies in trying to end military conscription. . . .

Now, as I say, it may be absolutely impossible for this government to release us because the people aren't ready for it. But in that case my place is in prison, just as otherwise I would consider my place in the trenches. I am ready to go to prison, and for the hundredth time I tell you it is with no spirit of bitterness. I don't think that I am being persecuted. I appreciate the government's real effort to be liberal. I am sorry for Secretary [of War Newton] Baker. But, at the same time, he has accepted the method of militarism to overcome militarism. I believe in a different method. We can't get together. Therefore you will say I am defiant. In a sense I am. That is, I refuse to obey a law I don't believe in. I will refuse to work in prison but with no antagonism towards President Wilson or Secretary Baker or the prison authorities. You say I look defiant and talk defiant at times. You mean I am determined to see this business through, and so I am. Where people are on opposite sides in a great struggle, it is impossible not to get emphatic and seem defiant at times.

I am not sure that I know a correct definition for conscience, but what I call conscience certainly is not merely a check, always inhibiting and suppressing, giving warnings: you must *not* do this and you must *not* do that. With me it tells me equally strongly what I must do. I will tell you frankly that some of the religious objectors I have met get terribly on my nerves. They think only in terms of what they must *not* do. They think in terms of "goodness," which is all right; but a man ought to be something more than "good" in this world. Frankly, this makes religious people think too much about themselves and, while it may keep them good, I am inclined to think that it takes a lot of energy and moral and mental worry that might a lot better be spent in creative ways or in great active fights for human betterment and human happiness. . . . I am much more concerned with what I can do. I am out to fight for freedom, not for myself alone but for generations to come. My contribution is little at best, but what there is of it I want to have it count. At present I believe it will count most in prison if the government insists. . . . I am ready to work, but freedom is vastly dearer to the human race than the poverty stricken relief work we try to do for people who are crushed and made wretched by industrial and national wars.

[Evan Thomas] to [Norman Thomas], 28 July 1918

We all moved to Ft. Riley last Thursday. From what they tell us, I judge the present intention is to keep the C.O.'s here rather than at Ft. Leavenworth.

. . . On arriving here at Ft. Riley we were put into barracks too small for us, but otherwise very comfortable. Then began the effort to get men to work on farms or driving trucks, etc. This is only a military post, and the farms are part of the military reservation. Most of the men refused to work, but quite a few consented. Then we were told that we were to move into a tent colony and that we must build the camp.

In the meantime I had been trying to manage the kitchen police and room orderlies and so keep it out of the hands of the military. This worked splendidly at Leavenworth, but here more of the men balked. I saw that any cooperation on our part was impossible. We got together and had a meeting, and it was plain that every man was ready to draw different lines on this working proposition. Then the problem arose: are those who won't farm to do kitchen work and cleaning of latrines and rooms for those who do, etc., etc? Of course the government's game is to get every man to work as much as possible, and if they could get twenty or thirty men to do barrack duty almost every day for men who were doing the work elsewhere they would be the gainers. Then we found [that] building a tent colony for ourselves meant moving two big wooden shacks—kitchen and mess hall, digging trenches for water pipes, constructing our own latrine, and doing our own plumbing.

Some men were ready to do this. Others were not. Again I saw the impossibility of cooperating on this for very good reasons. To cooperate here means we must become in fact part of the military machine. We must work under army orders—when we are ordered and as we are ordered.

More and more we were being treated as a bunch of soldiers and ordered around as such, although this was stopped when we balked. [Howard] Moore, [Harold] Gray, and I shifted and declared our intention of doing absolutely no more work of any sort except keeping ourselves clean. We refused to put up tents, do kitchen duty, or help in cleaning except around our own bunks. This stand seems silly, but if you were here you would understand the necessity of it. Some of the most laughably ridiculous situations have arisen that most humorous writers of comedies could ever have conceived of. The question on both sides was where to draw the line, and I can assure you that no men ever spent more time splitting hairs than we. It had to stop. To do any work of a cooperative nature here came to mean that we were actually part of the military. . . . The officers would try to get me to work by leading [us] from one act to another, and then fail to see why we should draw the line where we did; the thing had to stop. Their game of course is to get some work out of us and keep us here for the remainder of the war. The major as much as told us that he hoped there would be no court martial if we did as we were required and were human about it. The answer to that is, "Why not go to the trenches?"

Last evening [27 July] things came to a head. All men who refused to work were told to move over to the tent colony. The number at first was comparatively small, but lots of these fellows do nothing but watch certain other men and do as they do—especially the religious men are apt to follow the leader in this game. The result was [that] about fifty men finally handed in their names as refusing to do any work at all—not even kitchen work.

So after supper we absolutists were moved over to the tent grounds, furnished with tents and stakes, told that rations would be issued to each man individually and that no two men could cooperate in preparing their food. Each man could build his own fire and cook his own food. No latrine was furnished us and we were forbidden the use of any latrine in the place. Then the men began on that poor lieutenant, and on no stage have I heard anything so funny. First some of the men refused to help put up even their own tent, and then the question was: should they be allowed to sleep under a tent if they were invited to do so by men who were willing to put one up? Each tent holds eight men. At first the lieutenant said no. Then the men heckled him until he gave his consent. . . .

Gray, Moore, and I and a number of the [Camp] Upton socialists stuck by our statement and put up no tent. We slept in the open and then were too warm. Probably some of these other C.O.'s will put up tents for everybody, but as far as I am concerned I do no more work. If the government insists on holding me here they must construct my shelter and feed me. I intend to take the same stand in prison. Either they let me go where I can do the work I feel I ought to do (and they can investigate it all they like for all I care) . . . or take absolute care of me. . . .

Tell Roger Baldwin about this and tell him we are laughing and ready to be laughed at, but we are serious enough in our stand. The military either takes care of us or we will rot on the ground. You need not think that I intend to spend the remainder of the war in comfort doing nothing but taking care of myself. . . . If the military insists on holding me then they must do everything for me. They can wash my dishes and the pots and pans, clean my rooms and let me live in real comfort and luxury or else I'll rot on the ground. The other two alternatives are prison or freedom. Either one I am perfectly ready for. . . . I am not blaming the military in any way. They have not ordered us to work, nor have they tried to double-cross us. They have been on the level, but necessarily for them they have forced me to the logic of my own anti-conscription position.

SOURCE: Charles Chatfield, ed., *The Radical "No": The Correspondence and Writings of Evan Thomas on War* (New York: Garland, 1975), 146–47, 153–55, 158–61.

6.6. Roderick Seidenberg, "I Refuse to Serve" (1932)

[Born in Germany, Roderick Seidenberg immigrated to the United States as a young boy. At Columbia University he studied architecture and became friends with Randolph Bourne. A political and absolutist CO, Seidenberg was court-martialed at Fort Riley in November 1918 for refusing an order to clean the parade ground. He was sentenced to life imprisonment but was pardoned in 1920. He published this account of his CO experience at Fort Leavenworth and the 1919 CO strike in the *American Mercury*.]

I

. . . To steal, rape or murder, to slap an officer's face and call him a son of a bitch—these are the standard peace-time entrance requirements to the Disciplinary Barracks. But in time of war too firm a belief in the words of Christ, too ardent a faith in the brotherhood of man, is even more acceptable. But prisons are democratic institutions, and no matter how one entered, one's number was stenciled on one's trousers and the back of one's shirt in white to mark a new beginning. One might rise and receive a white star as a trusty, but it was just as likely that one would sink, first into the red-numbered lock-step gang, and finally into solitary, where the digits in yellow marked the lowest depths of the vast military hierarchy. We sank to the yellow bottom, for our offense was the gravest one can commit—in prison. Even the murder gang, who had trampled to death an unfortunate "rat," enjoyed the comparative freedom of wandering about in a basement cell-block when they were not exercising in the sunlight of the yard. Our case was different; we had offended military pride. We must be broken.

The first to arrive at Leavenworth who refused to work were six stalwart Molokans, true Christians if ever there were any. They went cheerfully into the "hole," each one in a pitch-dark cell on bread and water, manacled standing to the bars of their cells for nine hours every day—to sleep, exhausted, on the bare cement floor. Others followed. Evan Thomas, who had at first accepted work, hearing their fate, joined them in heroic protest. That is like him—a fiery spirit beneath his unflinching calm.

Leavenworth was taken by surprise. There were not enough dark cells. The officers had never before encountered a like demonstration. Each morning the executive officer inquired of our health and smilingly offered us the rock pile. Each morning we declined. Two weeks passed, and the executive officer no longer smiled. We had broken not only the rules of the institution, but its traditions as well. No one had ever stood this treatment for more than a few days. The commandant, Colonel Sedgewig [sic] Rice, paid us a visit. What were these men like? Who were they? What did they want?

One day, Prisoner 15122 was unshackled and led to the executive office. In the morning's mail the prison censor had found a bronze medal with appropriate testimonials from the Carnegie Hero Commission, inscribed to Howard Moore for bravery in risking his life to rescue a drowning girl. A hero medal for a yellow slacker! . . .

Two weeks and a new trial! Reeling like drunkards, we returned from the executive office to our solitary cells. This time we were to have food, then another trial and two more weeks without food. But manacled we must be, nine hours every day. It was the end of December 1919 [1918]; the war had been over since the eleventh of November. The Molokans, refusing, because of their strange religious scruples, everything but a little milk, even when permitted food on the alternative fortnights, had stood the treatment for fifty-five days without a sign of weakening.

I was in the middle of my third term when word came from the Secretary of War that henceforth prisoners of the Army were no longer to be manacled. The Secretary, his feet planted on his desk, had listened coldly to the venerable Mrs. Fanny Villard, standing before him pleading. He would do nothing. Yet later he reversed his decision. We were placed in a stockade outside the prison walls—all but the two Hofer brothers, who had died. . . .

III

In the stockade, beyond the prison wall we played, we read books, we received and wrote letters once more, and we ate, with relish, the indescribable food of Leavenworth. Half our numbers were religious objectors: Hutterites, Dunkards, Seventh Day Adventists, an orthodox Jew, and the six Molokans. The rest of us were so-called political objectors: Socialists, humanitarians, individualists. We talked. It was good to talk again. Acquaintances grew into friendship; we were held together by a common experience, whatever our individual points of view.

But the diversion of the day was the visit of Major Adler—chief psychiatrist of the Disciplinary Barracks . . .

We were now subjected to the delicate mental probings of this kindly Harvard professor. He was not a man who believed in brute force—except perhaps on a national scale. . . .

. . . Our lapses from rectitude, it was apparent, were of a subtler order; they arose from defections that only psychiatry could reveal.

We had refused to participate in organized slaughter; we were considered insensitive and unfeeling toward the higher causes of humanity. We had thought to stand aloof from the madness of war; we were anti-social and doctrinaire. We had taken what appeared to us the one direct and positive and unarguable position for peace; we were negative obstructionists. We had refrained from any propaganda, we believed in freedom of conscience; we were ego-centric heretics. We thought ourselves tolerably sane; we were psychopathic.

"All these things might be passed over," Major Adler announced with pontifical finality, "if only you people had the faith of your convictions." He looked about the barracks. "But I don't see any Christs or Savonarolas. You fellows are rationalizing; other people are acting. You're negative." . . .

Life in a barracks is dreary at best. Twenty-four hours of the same company would be trying if that company were of one's own choosing. But here we were, thrown together through no will of our own, a strange lot—half of us praying, the other half arguing, all of us suffering from the sheer inanity of our position.

I tried to write. With meagre spirit I made some sketches. A drawing, poorly done, picturing a prisoner in solitary, reached New York, via underground channels, where it was printed as a marker. A copy of it found its way back to Leavenworth. The censor pasted it over his desk, little knowing that it had made such a long trip home. Sending a kite over the wall was one of the prison entertainments. A kite is an underground letter. Smuggled from prisoner to prisoner, our mail would at last be added to that of the executive office. From here it went forth uncensored and unnoticed. At other times our letters were intrusted to a friendly guard or a sympathetic sergeant. Even in solitary we managed to remain in contact with the outside world. But that was not so simple.

The scheme by which it was accomplished was the work of Clark Getts, an objector who had access to every part of the prison. . . . Thus he would happen to be in the basement at the moment when we were having our fortnightly scrub. . . . The shower-baths were at one end. . . . Getts, standing in the shadow of a column, would snatch off his clothes and join us. . . . We let the water run like a deluge while we splashed. And Getts circled about, getting the address of a relative, bringing us the latest rumors, the news of the prison, the outlook of Washington, and the happenings at Versailles. It was all done in a cloud of steam and Getts was gone before we knew it. . . .

We had been at the stockade a month now. Some more objectors stopped working and after a few days in solitary they were sent to our barracks. The effect of seeing us at play beyond the prison walls was not lost upon those who remained to toil and labor under harsh discipline. Friendly as the general prisoners were to the objectors, this could not fail to arouse a sense of injustice, and to add to the unrest of the prison. That unrest flared into a strike.

V

On Christmas Eve there had been a riot in the dining-hall. Fifteen hundred men went on a rampage. We were still in solitary, and I ventured to predict that we would be held responsible. We were. On Christmas Day we were lined up in front of our cells and lectured. It was our example that had caused the unrest among the men.

Actually the whole prison smoldered with a sense of injustice. The food was beyond description, a steamed and slimy flow of garbage. . . .

. . . The men were bullied when they were not being spied upon by "rats," mostly depraved room-orderlies. But worst of all they smarted under the terrific sentences which were the common fate. Fifteen, twenty, forty years—it was all one to the poor wretches who were to spend the rest of their lives in that hell. Every day the huge lock-step gang wound its way like a great serpent to the rock quarries, full of resentment at the brutalities of the guards and the merciless work they were forced to do. One or two guards were killed. A race riot broke out. Rival gangs, for even prison has its gang life, its intrigues and its politics, were stealthily revenging themselves upon one another. The place was overcrowded and demoralized.

By the end of January things had come to such a pass that one day the first gang suddenly refused to work. That night the quartermaster's warehouse burned to the ground. The following morning, after having been called to work, the men were sent back to their cells. At noon, they were all assembled once more in the prison yard, and called to their gangs. "First gang, second gang, third gang . . ." No one moved. It must have been a terrifying moment.

Outside the walls the 49th Infantry awaited orders. Colonel Rice expostulated; again he asked the men to work. A few went; the rest stood with arms folded, which is the prescribed posture before prison officials. They were led back to their cells.

Now the men acted with quiet deliberation. . . . At the beginning of the strike they had organized themselves. Under the leadership of H. Austin Simons, the son of a judge, Carl Haes[s]ler, a Rhodes scholar from Oxford and instructor in philosophy at the University of Wisconsin, and others, the entire prison had been mobilized to stand firm with arms folded. There must be no violence! From the rail of the second tier, Simons made an impassioned speech to the men in his cell-block. His words carried the day. In each wing a committee drew up resolutions.

Colonel Rice was equally brave. He acknowledged that the prisoners had grievances, and wisely he consented to arbitrate. It was a momentous decision and a triumph for the prisoners. Colonel Rice listened to their demands: that men in solitary for complicity in the disturbance be immediately restored to regular status, that a telegram be sent to the Secretary of War petitioning for amnesty, that the commandant recognize a permanent grievance committee. Colonel Rice proposed to go to Washington himself to present the resolutions. The men were accorded a grant of time in order that the prison might vote upon the proposal. Unanimously they voted to resume work in the morning.

A general reduction of sentences followed the colonel's return; men were released, and a grievance committee became an established institution. But not for long. . . . Six months later the conscientious objectors who still remained were suddenly transferred to Fort Douglas in Utah, and six days later a second strike broke out.

It was crushed with bullets, and Leavenworth returned once more to the peaceful days of iron discipline.

VI

One morning, not long after the first strike, we were ordered to pack our belongings. Rumors flew about. . . .

A new executive officer of the Disciplinary Barracks paid us a visit. He was exceptionally short—a little fellow with the rank of major. Gruffly he ordered the guardhouse sergeant to open our cell. He marched in, accompanied by two captains and two lieutenants. It was very impressive. He asked us to gather around him. Silence. Raising his head slightly, he announced that he was not afraid of any of us. There was an involuntary titter, followed by an embarrassing silence. "I'm not afraid of any of you or all of you!" he repeated sharply. "Well, Major," Howard Moore spoke up in that charming soft manner of his, "we're not afraid of you either." The major was thrown completely off his stride; the ice was broken. He smiled. "You fellows aren't so hardboiled as I thought. We'll get along all right. There're some damn regulations against it, or I'd have you shot, of course. Meantime, what are you going to do with yourselves? I could have some knitting sent down." Everybody laughed. We were friends.

The younger officers were more apt to be hostile. Few lieutenants could resist the temptation to distinguish themselves at our expense. One night we were treated to a drenching with a high pressure fire-hose. We had been talking after the lights were out. For this we spent the night barely above water, with our clothes, our shoes and all our belongings floating about us. An investigation followed. The lieutenant was duly exonerated, and the Third Assistant Secretary of War, himself, the Hon. Frederick D. Keppel, explained that the officer's somewhat unusual measures had been justified, since he was faced with a mutiny. But we received no further punishment.

These little episodes served to break up the long monotony of our days and remind us, if ever we should forget it, that we were in the hands of the military. But was not the whole world in the hands of the military? We, at least, had a measure of consolation in feeling that we had made a choice agreeable to ourselves, whatever the consequences. . . . We were obdurate with an ease that surprised us as much as it did the military, and if our resistance was calm, aloof, even indifference, it was not without an explosive effect upon those whose business it was to break it down. "If those damn bastards only had a change of heart, I wouldn't mind having them in my outfit!" said a major. We had learned to become fighters, and to fight hard.

VII

New men were constantly added to our group, men who had stopped working. Our cells were badly overcrowded and once more we were shifted back to the Disciplinary Barracks. The first tier of cells in the sixth wing was to be our home, we were informed, until released. When would that be—in ten, in twenty years? Many of us still had life sentences. We did not take them seriously.

ANTI-ENLISTMENT LEAGUE

Working Men and Women of the United States:

Your brothers in Europe are destroying each other; the militarists in this country may soon try to send you to the trenches. They will do so in the name of "Defense of Home" or "National Honor," the reasons given to the people of every one of the twelve nations now at war.

But **DO NOT ENLIST.** Think for yourselves. The Workers of the World are YOUR BROTHERS; their wrongs are your wrongs; their good is your good. War stops Trade, and makes vast Armies of Unemployed.

DO NOT ENLIST. The time for Defense by Armies is over. Belgium, Germany and Great Britain have defended themselves with the mightiest of fortresses, armies or navies; and today each country suffers untold misery. War can avenge, punish and destroy; but war can NO LONGER defend.

DO NOT ENLIST. Your country needs you for PEACE; to do good and USEFUL work; to destroy POVERTY and bring in INDUSTRIAL JUSTICE.

WOMEN, REFUSE your consent to the enlistment of your men; the TRUE COURAGE is to STAND FOR THE RIGHT and REFUSE TO KILL.

PEACE IS THE DUTY—NOT WAR
MIGHT IS NOT RIGHT
USE YOUR LIGHT
DO NOT FIGHT

Join the ANTI-ENLISTMENT LEAGUE, 61 QUINCY ST., Brooklyn, N. Y.

- -

I, being over eighteen years of age, hereby pledge myself against enlistment as a volunteer for any military or naval service in international war, either offensive or defensive, and against giving my approval to such enlistment on the part of others.

Name...

Address..

Committee, JESSIE WALLACE HUGHAN, Secretary,
TRACY D. MYGATT.

Forward to the Anti-Enlistment League,
61 Quincy Street, Brooklyn, New York.

Anti-Enlistment League [1915–April 1917] flyer. Founded in 1915 by Jessie W. Hughan, Tracy D. Mygatt, and John H. Holmes, the league urged men not to enlist in the military. After the United States entered the war, the founders disbanded the group. In Anti-Enlistment League Collected Records, CDG-A, Swarthmore College Peace Collection, Swarthmore PA.

"Model Boy," American Union Against Militarism. Opposed Senate bills to create a large standing army and require compulsory military training for men. Composed by Art Young, the drawing condemns Prussian militarism and implores Congress not to adopt such ideas. In American Union Against Militarism Records, DG-04, box 2, Swarthmore College Peace Collection, Swarthmore PA.

"War Against War" flyer card, February 1917. Mass meeting in New York City on 8 February, organized by Socialists and trade unionists, with speeches in several languages. "War Against War" was the Socialist antiwar slogan. In Henry Wadsworth Longfellow Dana Papers, DG-11, box 2, Swarthmore College Peace Collection, Swarthmore PA.

"The New King in Liberty Pond," *New York Call*, 25 March 1917, sec. 2, p. 1.
Composed by Ryan Walker, this graphic depicts an armed man (militarism)
bayoneting opponents of compulsory military service. Courtesy of Tamiment
Library, New York University.

No-Conscription League flyer, May 1917. Mass meeting at Harlem River Casino on 18 May. The league was organized by anarchists Emma Goldman and Alexander Berkman. In Henry Wadsworth Longfellow Dana Papers, DG-11, box 2, Swarthmore College Peace Collection, Swarthmore PA.

Set Conscience Free!

For 143 years America has stood a haven of refuge to the people of every land. AMER-
ICA has meant LIBERTY to the oppressed of all the earth, and those whom persecution forced
to leave their native countries have gladly sought the protection of this "land of the free." But
of late we have begun to change this.

DO YOU KNOW

That AMERICA WHICH STANDS TO THE WHOLE WORLD FOR LIBERTY OF
CONSCIENCE, though the war has been over four months, is still holding in a military prison
at Leavenworth, Kansas, 500 men who could not take part in a war which their CONSCIENCES
told them was wrong?

That AMERICA WHICH STANDS FOR JUSTICE has released some conscientious objectors on various technical grounds but has failed to recognize the sincerity of many men who
have deliberately chosen every hardship and abuse in military camp and at last prison terms of
25 and 30 years in place of the bomb-proof jobs which were offered them in the medical corps
or on civilian farms, for the sole reason that their consciences would not permit them to compromise their principles?

"Set Conscience Free!" Friends of Conscientious Objectors [1919]. Some COS
remained in prison after the November 1918 Armistice; others, though released,
remained convicted felons. Peace and civil liberties groups organized a postwar
campaign to obtain amnesty for COS who served prison time to uphold antiwar
and pacifist convictions. In Subject File: Conscientious Objection/Objectors
Material, 1919, Swarthmore College Peace Collection, Swarthmore PA.

That AMERICA WHICH BOASTS OF HUMANITY has permitted her conscientious objectors to be treated as shamefully as Russia would have handled them in her darkest days! Did you know that these men whose sincere idealism you cannot doubt whatever you think of their views, in some cases have been held under ice-cold showers until they collapsed; strung up in cells until their eyes bulged and their tongues hung from their mouths; dragged on the ground by cruel guards and bayonetted into unconsciousness, fed bread and water for long periods of time, and chained day after day by their wrists to the bars of prison cells?*

That AMERICA WHICH HAS ALWAYS BEEN PROUD TO LEAD THE NATIONS IN GENEROSITY, has stood indifferently by while Germany, Austria, Bulgaria, Russia and Italy have been opening their jails and allowing their political prisoners to walk out free men and women? Did you know that England's foremost citizens, including 83 Members of Parliament, 16 Bishops, writers, professors and scientists, have already petitioned the English government to free the English conscientious objectors?

Why are not O U R public men, Senators, Congressmen, college presidents, asking for the freedom of American Conscientious Objectors, like these men abroad?

Why are not ordinary American citizens petitioning our government to perform this simple act of justice?

Lest America be shamed before the nations with which she is now striving for a peace which shall last.

LET US FREE THE CONSCIENTIOUS OBJECTORS AND ALL OTHER POLITICAL PRISONERS BEFORE ANY MORE DIE OR LOSE THEIR SANITY.

As soon as this falls into your hands do these things without delay.

1. Write a letter to your newspaper telling it what you think of Americans imprisoning other Americans because they happen to think differently.

2. Ask your labor union, your lodge, your church, to pass a resolution about this matter and forward one copy to Secretary of War Baker and cable the other to President Wilson at the Peace Conference.

3. Write a letter to your representatives in the state legislature and to your Congressman and your Senator.

4. PASS THIS ON and write Jules Wortsman, 302 Grand Street, Brooklyn, N. Y., for more of these leaflets. He will send you as many as you can handle.

5. Send a contribution to him so we may reach many thousands like yourself.

Printed by

Friends of Conscientious Objectors

302 GRAND STREET, BROOKLYN, N. Y.

*See Congressional Record, March 4, 1919, page 5280. Send ten cents for booklet giving complete information.

DISARMAMENT PARADE

NOVEMBER 12th, 1921   NEW YORK CITY

**DEMANDS OF THE CONFERENCE FOR LIMITATION OF ARMAMENT
IMMEDIATE ACTION FOR COMPLETE and UNIVERSAL DISARMAMENT.**

This demonstration is organized by the Women's Peace Society, Box 494, General Post Office, New York,
and the Women's Peace Union, 2 Spadina Road, Toronto, Ont., Canada.

SLOGANS CARRIED IN THE PARADE:

"Forward out of error,
Leave behind the night,
Forward through the darkness,
Forward into Light."

"Immediate, Universal, Complete Disarmament."

"Thou Shalt Not Kill."

"The World War Cost
10 Million Men (killed)
and
186 Billion Dollars.
Was It Worth It?"

"War Cannot be Civilized—It Must be Abolished."

"The Pope says: 'Abolish Conscription.'"

"War is not inevitable. Human Nature does change."

"Chemists, help World Peace, refuse to make Poison Gas."

"Disarmament Means DISARMAMENT—Not Limitation."

"Not One Soldier
Not One Sailor,
Not One Dollar
FOR WAR."

"Let Us Be Reasonable. Disarm. Limitation Is A Snare."

"How the U. S. Spends Money:
68% for Past Wars—3,855 Million Dollars.
25% for Future Wars—1,424 Million Dollars.
7% for all Pursuits of Peace—57 Million Dollars."

"End War Before War Ends the Race."

"Write President Harding that You Want Disarmament. Do it TO-DAY."

"Women of the World Unite to Save Life."

"Stop the Next War NOW. Disarm the World."

"Mothers Pay the Heaviest War Tax."

"Scientists, Use your Genius for Peace—Not War."

"On Earth Peace, Goodwill toward Men."

"If All Disarm No Nation Need Fear."

"Causes of War:
Preparedness
Greed
Fear."

"Scrap the Battleships and the Pacific Problems will settle themselves."

"Trade Barriers Lead to War—abolish them."

"Build Schools, not Battleships."

"War means Death, Famine, Pestilence."

"The only way to abolish War is to abolish Preparations for War."

"Exploitation Leads to War—Abolish it."

"Fear is our worst Enemy."

"Cooperation pays better than Competition. Let's try it between Nations."

"Cannon follows Concessions—Abolish Concessions."

"93 Cents of every dollar the U. S. spends goes for War—Past or Future."

"We will not give our Children for another war."

"WAR—NEVERMORE!"

"The Way to stop killing is to stop preparing to kill."

"The Way to Disarm is to Disarm."

"If You want Peace, don't prepare for War."

"Preparedness prepares for War, not Peace."

"Mothers, Do You Teach Your Sons to Save Life or to Kill?"

"War is never a Solution; It is an Aggravation."

"93% of your Income Tax goes for War, past or future. Are You Willing?"

"What is a reasonable amount of Disarmament? Complete and Universal Disarmament."

"For Once the Ideal and the Practical are the same."

"Complete disarmament is the desire of thinking people."

"The Idealism of today becomes the Common sense of tomorrow."

"It Must Not Happen Again."

"The Golden Rule."

"It is easier to enforce Peace than any Limitation of War."

Disarmament parade flyer, November 1921. Slogans carried in the parade, organized by the Women's Peace Society and Women's Peace Union. In Women's Peace Society Records, DG-106, series I-IV, box 1, Swarthmore College Peace Collection, Swarthmore PA.

In time they were all reduced, now one, then another. They were reduced to three years, to five years or perhaps to one year. I received a sentence of a year and a half. . . . Meanwhile the gates were open to us. Like the Christians in Shaw's "Androcles and the Lion," we had only to throw a pinch of incense on the altar of militarism to gain our freedom. Colonel Rice was surprised to find us adamant against accepting our "good time." Actually we had long ago lost this allowance, which he now offered to us under military parole. We might, moreover, have received immediate release, if only we had consented to do some work. The major in charge of construction asked me if I would assist in designing an officer's club-house. I declined—with regrets.

We now numbered close to a hundred men. We enjoyed such freedom as the cell-block permitted, but it was a dreary freedom at best. We were never permitted outside, even for exercise, and the months passed without our ever seeing the sunshine except through the barred windows. . . .

I began to lose something of my New York provincialism and to learn of this America. Here were men from all quarters and from all walks of life: religious farmers from the Middle West who alone seemed capable of community living; I.W.W.'s from the Far West; Socialists from the East Side of New York; men from Chicago, from the South; men who had been sailors, carpenters, college students, tailors. One was a statistician, one a prize-fighter from Philadelphia, one a music teacher . . . I missed a few of the older friends who were no longer with us—Evan Thomas, with whom I could talk of philosophy and a *Weltanschauung*; Maurice Hess, a Dunkard, now a college professor, a man of exceptional erudition and amazing courage behind the mildest exterior.

But most of all, in a way, I missed my friend Sam Solnitski. His racy, ironic humor helped many an hour along. In the guardhouse at Fort Riley, while we awaited trail, he would pace up and down with me, telling of his life in Poland, of his escape to America to avoid military service, of his days in this country as a skilled worker on the uppers of women's shoes—the very finest—for prostitutes! Best of all, however, he had read, it seemed to me, all of literature—in Yiddish. Now he told the grand stories of Maupassant, of Balzac, of Anatole France, in a mixture half-English, half-Yiddish, which made these tales of elegant ladies and Parisian life more real than ever. Solnitski had distinguished himself at his court-martial. In his own way he had attempted to explain to the twelve precise majors of the court the reasons for his opposition to military service—but in vain. He broke off in despair: "Ow, shucks, what's the use!" The court stenographer immortalized the words.

There were other men no longer with us—Harold Gray, son of the Detroit multimillionaire; Harry Lee, the witty organizer of waiters, who had served "pimps and prostitutes, priests and politicians, but never a captain!"; [Arthur] Dunham, a Philadelphia Quaker, and a number of others I had come to know well. . . .

Six months passed in this fashion. At four o'clock one sharp, cold morning we were ordered to pack our belongings; once more we were to be moved. . . . At the great outer gate we were shackled in pairs, then, under heavy guard, we left Leavenworth. Two by two, in a long column, we were marched to the railroad station.

Two days later, weary, exhausted, anxious, we arrived at Fort Douglas above Salt Lake City.

SOURCE: *American Mercury*, January 1932, 91–99.

6.7. Winthrop D. Lane, "The Strike at Fort Leavenworth" (15 February 1919)

[A civil liberties reporter and activist, Winthrop Lane witnessed the January 1919 Fort Leavenworth strike. Arriving at Leavenworth several days before the strike began, he was authorized to move freely around the prison and among the inmates. Intending to see Leavenworth under "normal conditions," he had an insider's view of the strike, which he called "one of the most dramatic events in penal history."]

The strike of prisoners at the United States Disciplinary Barracks at Fort Leavenworth, Kansas, week before last, was no ordinary prison mutiny. It presented many of the characteristics of a typical labor disturbance in the world outside. . . . The 2,300 men who took part in it were still units in the military machine; with the exception of 400 conscientious objectors they had once been soldiers. They were subject to military discipline. Their officers were lieutenants, captains, majors and colonels. . . . Yet they organized themselves in the approved labor union way and presented their demands just as if they had the full power of collective bargaining. In spite of walls separating one group from another, in spite of barred doors and double guards, they held mass meetings and discussed their grievances. . . . and planned a course of action. They elected representatives to meet with their superior officers and voted on whether they would return to work. And they did this while one thousand armed soldiers of the 49th Infantry regiment waited outside the prison walls, ready to enter and shoot at command . . . .

. . . On April 1, 1918, the population of the barracks was 1,508. By November it was 3,005—exactly double. Today it is 3,600. . . . every discomfort of overcrowding has to be borne as well as the human mind can bear it. All of this created an unprecedented atmosphere of tension, rebellion and protest.

From the point of view of administration, the situation was still further complicated by the sending to the barracks of a large number of conscientious objectors. These men obstinately refused for the most part to regard themselves as criminals, even in the military sense. For the first time in the history of the barracks, large numbers of men refused to work. This brought about increased use of the solitary cells and increased tension between the objectors and the guards. Individuals were beaten up for following what they believed to be the dictates of their conscience. . . .

Then, on January 25, [1919] came the order for the release of 113 conscientious objectors. . . .

Before the discharge of these objectors nothing had happened to reveal the full strength and nature of the men's sullenness. The embers of discontent were there; the officers felt them, the prisoners felt them. Only a spark was needed to set them off. That spark came on the afternoon of Saturday, January 25, when a Negro, who was playing cards with a white man in the yard, assaulted his opponent. Others mixed in the fray and although guards and officers quickly broke up the fight, two Negroes were taken to the hospital with injuries. . . . [This led to further race riots and punishment, which increased prison discontent and tension.]

On Wednesday afternoon, January 29, the "first gang," composed of about 150 prisoners working outside the walls, quit on their jobs. . . .

This was the first overt act of the strike. . . .

One of the members of the "first gang" was a conscientious objector. In civilian life he had had been a newspaper reporter and a poet; he was known as a "radical." That night he had a conference with friends in his wing. He told them that he no desire to participate in a strike for such petty objects as the men of the first gang were considering [more tobacco, better food, and mail, along with their resentment over the equal treatment of blacks]. . . .

. . . Forty-eight hours later this man, H. Austin Simons, was the acknowledged spokesman of the strikers. . . .

That noon [30 January] the men were lined up in yard as usual, to be marched out to work. This was to be the final test. Would the prisoners acknowledge their obligations, or would—one shuddered as he filled in the alternative, with the infantrymen waiting outside.

An officer called out the gangs. "First gang," he shouted, and waited for it to form in line. No one stirred.

"There ain't no first gang," came a voice from the ranks.

"Second gang," shouted the officer.

"There ain't no second gang," came another voice.

"To hell with work. We want to go home," shouted a prisoner.

"Third gang," called the officer.

"There ain't no third gang," came from another quarter. The officer folded his sheet and turning to Colonel Rice remarked that the prisoners of the United States Disciplinary Barracks seemed to be on strike.

Colonel Rice stepped forward. He raised his voice and asked the men to tell him why they refused to work. . . .

No one moved. Two thousand prisoners stood with their arms folded, motionless except for the occasional shouting of individuals. . . .

"We want to go home," shouted some. "We want better food," shouted others. One man brought a laugh by bawling at the top of his lungs, "Give us liberty or give us death."

. . . Yet no one wanted to reveal himself as a leader in the presence of half a dozen prison officers. Few smiled, for though they were suddenly realizing the proportions of their own mass movement, they did not know how to control it or give it direction.

Suddenly the ranks opened and a small prisoner with closely shaven head and wearing a long ugly raincoat pushed forward. With his intent expression he had somewhat the appearance of a Franciscan monk. I had seen him in the Atlantic branch of the Disciplinary Barracks at Fort Jay and knew him to be the close friend and legal ward of a man long prominent in social work. An officer called, "Here is a speaker, sir." There was a quick hush. Beginning in a low voice, the prisoner said:

Sir, I have been here only a few days. I was transferred four days ago from the Disciplinary Barracks at Fort Jay. I am in no sense a leader of these men. I can speak for myself, however, and [here he raised his voice so that he could be heard throughout the yard] I think I speak for many others in these silent ranks, when I say that our object in thus seeming to oppose authority is that this is the only way in which we can make articulate our demand to know what is to become of us. What, sir, is the government going to do with us?

I am a conscientious objector. I realize that in thus separating myself from this mass I make myself a marked man among your officers. I am willing to do this, sir, if I can enlighten you, and through you others, in regard to the meaning of this protest. My own sentence happens to be twenty years, but my case is only one. There are hundreds of men in this prison bearing sentences of fifteen, twenty and twenty-five years (I am not now speaking of objectors only) who were new to military method and requirements, and who committeed [sic] offenses for which the peace-time judgments would be only a few months or at most two or three years. Are these men to remain here for the rest of their lives?

Sir, the armistice was signed nearly three months ago. The war is over. The government has already released 113 of our fellows. Has it not had time to investigate the justice of other claims? You ask, sir, what are our grievances. I answer that this is our grievance. These men, as I read them, intend no violence. You see them here with their arms folded, refusing it work. That is the method of their protest. We ask, and we ask of you because you are the one immediately in authority over us, what is our future? In the remarks that you have just made you have cleared the air more than in your talks yesterday in the wings. At least we may now guess where you stand. But we recognize that your authority is limited. And we wish our protest and our inquiry to be carried over these walls and to reach the seat of authority in Washington. We ask this question and we adopt this method because we are prisoners and because this is the only method known to us. . . .

The prisoner, W. Oral James, stepped back into his place. It was evident that his remarks had made a deep impression upon one part of his audience at least—his fellow prisoners. . . . There were smiles on their faces now. One felt that indecision had vanished and that at least they knew what they were striking for. . . .

The next morning [31 January] no attempt was made to take the men out to work. . . .

The committee met with the commandant and several other officers at 2:30 that afternoon. When the seventeen prisoners marched into the room, Colonel Rice asked them if they had a spokesman. Simons stepped forward. He said:

Sir, on behalf of the general prisoners confined in this barracks, I am authorized to present to you the following statement of demands which I shall read:

"We, the men now confined to the U.S.D.B., Fort Leavenworth, Kansas, having been convicted by courts-martial, present the following as essential for the restoration of normal conditions:

"1. That, the commandant immediately release from solitary confinement all men now there for having participated in this movement from its beginning, and that he promise that no man involved in this movement shall be punished or discriminated against in the future for his part in it.

"2. That the following telegram be sent to the secretary of war at once: 'General prisoners confined to the U.S.D.B., Fort Leavenworth, petition, with approval of commandant, for amnesty to all convicted of courts-martial. Senators [George] Chamberlain and [William] Borah, American Bar Association and public opinion generally declare sentences unjust and amnesty the proper redress. Our release is just as urgent as that of the 113 conscientious objectors recently discharged. Democratic military justice requires amnesty. (Signed) Prisoners' General Committee elected at request of officers.'

"3. That the commandant recognize a permanent grievance committee to be elected by the men; and that this committee shall have the right to discuss with the authorities such improvements of conditions as seem in the committee's judgment to be desirable."

Colonel Rice took up the points one by one. . . .

. . . [Rather than sending a telegram] Colonel Rice offered instead to deliver the message, in person, and explained that he was making an official trip to Washington in two days. To this the committee finally agreed . . . .

The third point caused no difficulty, whatever, for Colonel Rice immediately said that he would be entirely willing to discuss matters with a general prisoners' committee, so long as such a committee displayed a proper sense of leadership and remained representative of the men.

The men returned to their wings. They were given an hour—all they asked for—in which to report the decision of the other prisoners. . . .

At last the committee returned, four hours after its appointment. A new spokesman stepped to the front.

"Sir, I am spokesman this evening, general prisoner 17,380 [H. Austin Simons], who acted as spokesman this afternoon being somewhat tired."

Thus spoke Carl Haessler, graduate of the University of Wisconsin, Rhodes scholar at Oxford, editorial writer, Socialist, conscientious objector. He continued:

"Sir, I have to report that the general prisoners confined in this barracks have voted unanimously—unanimously sir—to return to work tomorrow morning and to restore a normal state of affairs upon the conditions agreed upon this afternoon." . . .

SOURCE: *Survey* 41 (15 February 1919): 687–88, 691–93.

6.8. Carl Haessler, "The Fort Leavenworth General Strike of Prisoners" (1927)

[Carl Haessler, an ethnic German, was a socialist, pacifist, and CO. A Rhodes scholar, he taught philosophy at the University of Illinois–Urbana. Fired in 1917 for his radical views, he went to the *Milwaukee Leader*, a socialist newspaper. Drafted in 1918, he refused to don a military uniform and was court-martialed. He received a twelve-year prison sentence and served time at Fort Leavenworth and Alcatraz before being pardoned in 1920. He later headed Federated Press, a left-wing news service (1922–56); did public relations work for the Congress of Industrial Organizations and its 1937 Flint sit-down strike; and counseled COs during the Vietnam War. He was a leader in the January 1919 Fort Leavenworth strike.]

The 3,700 men constituting the prison population of Ft. Leavenworth in January 1918 [1919] will probably remember that month as one of the most profoundly stirring of their lives. Far more than Woodrow Wilson's hollow call to youth to save a democracy owned body and soul by the Morgan bankers, more even than the spectacle of the world at war, did the almost unanimous mass rising in America's largest military prison make clear to its participants the meaning of unified joint action. Not every convict took part in the general strike that brought the war department of the strongest nation on eart[h] to its knees. But those who scabbed will also remember the surging of overwhelming cooperative action that all but engulfed them too.

Perhaps 500 men, mostly white-collar jobholders and short timers, continued at their desks and flunkey tasks or volunteered to man the engine room, the ice machine and some of the essential services. These men feared to return at night to their cells where the strikers were awaiting them. They were housed in the prison auditorium on emergency beds or on the floor with a couple of blankets apiece in the dead of the Kansas winter. One was so cold that he slept in the sacramental robes which the Roman Catholic priest stored in a closet between his Sunday visits from town. The sacriledge [sic] was discovered but forgiven. Even the church did its bit toward strikebreaking.

The 3,200 men on strike remained in the cell houses except those elected to the strike committee that conferred with the commandant at his request. The strikers entertained themselves for the three or four days of the strike by chess and checker games, wrestling matches, swapping stories, listening to the reports of their committeemen and debating them, improvising lecture courses and in sleep. Meals were served regularly by the prison administration. The food was of better quality than before the outbreak of the strike and there was more of it. High spirits were the rule. The prisoners felt that they were on the way to victory just as the administration knew it had been beaten.

How was this feeling brought about?

It is an interesting experiment in the solidarity of mobilizing and directing mass discontent. A small but highly organized and highly conscious body of prisoners led the great majority almost without the knowledge of anybody but the leaders and their opponents, the military command of the prison. This small body of leaders were the political objectors to the Wilson war, the few score men of draft age who had gone through all the stages of the conscription process without being either bullied, bribed or bamboozled into becoming some part of the war machine. They had comparative freedom for their purpose after they arrived in Ft. Leavenworth from 1917 on to serve sentences of three years to 99 years or life. Their purpose was general revolutionary propaganda and, if the occasion proved favorable, revolutionary action. They had a taste of both but on so small a scale, viewed from the national perspective, that their accomplishment was only a tiny experimental one.

The political objectors found after armistice of November 1918 that they had as comrades a somewhat larger group of religious and pacifist objectors, commonly known as conscientious objectors. The politicals as a rule had no conscience so far as means of furthering their main purpose was concerned. They deemed socialism, or Communism as many of them began to call it after the Russian revolution, as more important than any specially ordained way of achieving it. So they were prepared to fight the conscienceless authorities with their own weapons. Where the commandant used spies and propaganda, the politicals did likewise and with better effect. In a few months they had the roughneck ordinary military convict tattooing red flags instead of the national emblem on their arms and chests. In some weeks more they had them rejecting every chance to shorten their terms by applying for reinstatement with the colors.

This could not have been done, the politicals clearly recognized, without the help of favoring circumstances. The war had ended, yet the ferocious sentences imposed by stupid and brutal court martials went on unrevised. The prison kitchen, designed for feeding 1,200 inmates, creaked and strained to care for 3,700. Food became a universal grouch. Cells were packed with two to 16 men. Guards were in considerable part the unconvicted dregs of the army. They had not been wanted in the combat or training units of the war machine. Officers practically likewise—arbitrary, cruel, dishonest, callous. The growing symptoms of revolt cried for leadership and the radical agitators, the political objectors, were there to supply it.

Trouble began Christmas eve, 1918. The supply of bread from the overtaxed prison bakery ran out at supper time. Prisoners who complained were hectored by a brainless captain. Soon the entire room was a chaos of yells, songs, anger and laughter. The laughter rose when officers who tried to bully the mob into silence were hit by flying raw onions and baked potatoes. The prisoners were finally led out of the mess hall two at a time and locked safely into their cell wings while soldiers with shotguns and machine guns stood guard from the gallery above.

A gorgeous Christmas dinner surprised the mob the next day. But it was interpreted as a sign of weakness in the prison regime. And disorder continued to increase.

Race riots broke out with the several hundred Negroes the victims of the terrible assaults by the white "hard guys" who broke arms, knocked out teeth and bruised their helpless prey into jelly. The objectors realized that they, as the next most conspicuous minority in jail would be the next target for the spontaneous and misdirected mutinous energy of the prison roughs.

In a council of war the politicians therefore determined to supply the mutineers with a better policy and program. The general strike, with its three demands of amnesty, better jail conditions and release from solitary cells of some of the gangsters, resulted. The new policy was accepted by the gangsters, who were glad to have the help of the politicals' intelligence and, as they believed, social and political pull outside the walls. They were glad also to find in the authorities a more worthy object of their rage.

The politicals and the gangsters working unitedly constituted practically the entire articulate and conscious elements in the prison. What they agreed on was certain to be followed by almost every one else. As a result, the military was surprised, one Friday toward the end of January, to have the prisoners stand at a unit in refusing to turn out for work. They remained in the prison yard with folded arms until they were ordered back to their cells. No attempt was made to call them to work in the afternoon. That night committees were hastily elected and secret communication established from wing to wing. Saturday morning the mutineers met the commandant. They were fully organized and conscious of their aims. There was no work that morning and the afternoon was a holiday as the prison worked on a 44-hour week.

That night the commandant surrendered. He agreed to go to Washington to present the amnesty demands, he agreed to improve the food, to reduce the number of men per cell, to increase the letter-writing privileges, to enlarge the visiting hours and rights to play or walk in the prison yard, to exterminate the bedbugs and to meet any other reasonable requests. The gangsters in the hole were brought back to daylight. He left for Washington that night.

Sunday passed quietly. On Monday the officers tried to get the men back to work but they refused to budge until a wire was received from Washington stating that all cases would be reviewed and that material reductions in sentence would be made except in cases of civil felonies, of which there were less than a dozen in the prison population. Many would be freed as soon as the papers could be put through, the commandant telegraphed.

The men then returned to work. Their strike had been successful beyond their dreams. A mere headless destructive mob had been turned into an organized, disciplined and completely unified body of men whose insistence on a single comprehensive program had been carried to victory. The political prisoners had not produced the mob but they had supplied the direction for it. The two factors cooperated in a neat little revolutionary experiment behind the walls and under the guns of Ft. Leavenworth. When the tide of events produces similar conditions on a national scale, it may be that men of national caliber will be ready to carry out a similar experiment on national, and international lines.

SOURCE: Carl Haessler, "The Fort Leavenworth General Strike of Prisoners: An Experiment in the Radical Guidance of Mass Discontent," *Labor Defender,* January 1927, 10–11, copy in Subject File: Conscientious Objection/Objectors Material, 1919, box 1, Swarthmore College Peace Collection, Swarthmore PA.

6.9. Congressman Charles H. Dillon on Abuses in Military Prisons (January 1919)

[Congressmen Charles H. Dillon (R-SD, 1913–19) and Stanley H. Dent (D-AL, 1909–21), the chairman of the House Committee on Military Affairs, publicized the mistreatment of COs in this statement. The information was provided by Theodore H. Lunde, whose son, Erling, a CO, witnessed some of these incidents.]

Mr. DILLION. Mr. Chairman, a number of letters have reached me relative to the treatment accorded our soldiers in court-martial proceedings and in the military prisons. I have not made any personal investigation of these alleged abuses, but information comes from so many sources that there must be some foundation for the charges. I append a statement just received through the mail entitled "Example of brutalities, tortures, and deaths to political prisoners under military regime":

TO CONGRESSMAN [STANLEY H.] DENT [JR.] [D-AL], CHAIRMAN, HOUSE COMMITTEE ON MILITARY AFFAIRS, WASHINGTON.

HONORABLE SIR: At your request I beg to submit a resume of inhuman treatment of military and political prisoners, which I respectfully recommend for your kind and immediate consideration and action, as some are already dead, others dying by inches, while all are more or less in constant jeopardy of life or health:

1. Jacob Wipf and the three Hofer brothers, religious objectors, with families, served one year in Arizona prison for failure to register. Transferred to Spanish dungeon of Alcatraz, San Francisco Bay. Stripped to underwear. "Strung up" for 36 hours. Five days without food; 1 glass of water every 24 hours. Slept on cold, damp floor in the stench of their own excrements, beaten, and otherwise manhandled. Contracted scurvy. Sent to Fort Leavenworth, from a temperate climate to a cold climate; put in solitary on bread and water; "strung up" nine hours per day seven days per week; slept on the bare floor with cold drafts passing over their emaciated bodies; two contracted pneumonia and died; one was sent home with the bodies. Jacob Wipf is on a hospital cot when telling this story. These men were all married and have one or more children, therefore should not have been drafted at all. (Report carried to Theo. H. Lunde, president American Industrial Co., of Chicago, by an Army officer.)

2. Clark Getts, Chicago attorney, graduate of Wisconsin University, conscientious objector, was given two periods, two weeks each, in solitary confinement on bread and water at Fort Leavenworth for smuggling to the outside world information of the cruel-

ties practiced upon him and his confreres, after which he was put in the ward for the violently insane by Capt. Chambers; in constant jeopardy of life and mind, as the inmates are not confined in cells but mingle promiscuously. Writer's son, who with others (including officer who carried the information) vouch for Getts's mental condition, in defiance of Capt. Chambers, implores me to do something for this unfortunate man. Writer in person brought the case under the personal notice of Secretary Baker, who promised to investigate it, but whose general attitude did not impart any hope of results. The chains of the solitary are humane as compared with the physical danger and torture of a sound mind in such environments.

3. Howard Moore, conscientious objector, an efficiency expert, winner of the Carnegie medal for bravery and $500 for saving a girl from drowning; in solitary at Fort Leavenworth after much suffering at Fort Riley.

4. David Eichel, conscientious objector, statistician, formerly with prominent life-insurance company, in solitary at Fort Leavenworth. Went through 10 days' reign of terror at Camp Funston.

5. Francis X. Hennessy, Hyman Block, Stein, Haugan, all conscientious objectors, put in the insane ward at Fort Leavenworth, which can only be interpreted as camouflage for the benefit of inspector from Washington, being that none are insane, and that if Hennessy is possibly a little affected it is the result of the brutalities accorded him and the others at Fort Riley, where he was "strung up" and given the "water cure," and at Camp Funston, where he went through the "10-day reign of terror," under Capt. Gustave Taussig.

6. Seventh Day Adventists have been put in solitary for refusing to work on Saturday, their Sabbath.

7. Mennonites have been put in solitary because their religion forbade them to put on uniforms or prison clothes.

8. Fischer was beaten so severely that he became a raving maniac. . . .

10. Peters, No. 14589, Mennonite, from Fort Oglethorpe, Ga. Lieut. Massey, when reading sentence, told him he was no longer a citizen, and therefore not entitled to hold his religious belief. Ordered

to work at the point and prodding of the bayonet. Put in solitary under roof in barn, with only a small, square window for air, under a blazing August sun, on bread and water. Refusing to eat for five days, he fainted, was revived, and put back. Later taken to hospital totally demented and a wreck of a former splendid physique. Pneumonia, influenza, heart trouble, and a general breakdown. Finally discharged as mentally deficient. . . .

11. Detention camp, Fort Ogelthorpe. Captain ordered soldiers to put C.O. waist deep in feces of latrine pit, splash him all over with the filth, sergeant in charge leaving him to be pulled out by his fellow C.O[.]'s.

12. Same captain, same time, ordered C.O. Schwargengraben taken by the heels and dipped to his eyes in the feces of latrine pit. Sergeant proceeded to put him "away in." Peters warned him of danger of killing by suffocation before filth could be removed from mouth and nostrils.

13. Polish drafted deserter brought to Fort Ogelthorpe during August. Had yellow jaundice. No food or medical attention for two days. Provost sergeant ordered him out to work under curses and oaths. Too sick to work. Sergeant ordered him to stand up; tried, but fell back on bunk. Sergeant grabbed and beat him; too exhausted. Sergeant called prison officer, Lieut. Masey, who grabbed and shook him viciously and ordered guard with fixed bayonet to force him out. Pole, leaning against wall for support, was jabbed four times in back with bayonet, until exhausted, he fainted away. Taken to guardhouse and left on bunk for two days, until chaplain, Father Shear, came to call the mail. Duncan called the reverend father's attention to Pole's condition; he was horrified; said Lieut. Masey should be court-martialed, and threatened to prefer charges. He only "bawled him out," preferring no charges.

The Pole later died in the hospital as a direct result of cruel treatment. Duncan saw most of this, as did Davis.

14. Case of supposed spinal meningitis in this hospital. Doctor took too large culture from spine; patient now a raving maniac in barred room across hall from me, probably mentally unfit for life.

Attendant who saw operation and has medical knowledge said it should have been taken in two portions.

15. Erling H. Lund, Chicago, graduate with honors from the University of Chicago; three years engineering at Armour Institute of Technology; was refused deferred classification on accusation of having married to evade draft. Was appointed inspector of materials on the Santa Fe, but was refused furlough and sent to camp. Application withdrawn when motive questioned. Did voluntary work at Fort Leavenworth; earned good will of Capt. Laird for establishing harmony between officers and conscientious objectors. Resented coercive measures and intolerable conditions at Fort Riley, put in solitary, court-martialed at Camp Funston, sent to Fort Leavenworth for life, commuted to 25 years in disciplinary barracks, conditions of which are so dangerous and intolerable as to cause a yearning for solitary again. Now in hospital convalescing from scarlet fever. Was declared a sincere conscientious objector by Judge Mack's commission. Author of Defense of Conscientious Objectors to war.

16. Harold Gray, son of President Gray, of the Detroit Red Cross. Took Red Cross post in England, but soon found he belonged among the conscientious objectors; returned to America and joined the others in suffering and solitary.

17. Evan Thomas, a minister, and brother of Dr. Norman Thomas, of New York, cosufferer with the above, whose sufferings in solitary were much accentuated due to his height, which compelled a stooping position when chained to the bars of the double-decked solitary cell.

18. Charles P. Larsen, artist, at Fort Leavenworth. Suffered with others the intolerable conditions at Fort Riley. Underrationed, food attacked by flies from near-by latrine used by venereally diseased soldiers. Protest punished by imprisonment in guardhouse cell in basement, dark, air foul, deprived of toilet articles, breathing sweepings, etc. Protest brought solitary confinement. Later taken to Camp Funston and was a cosufferer during 10-day reign of terror.

19. Abraham Gelerter, vegetable dealer, orthodox Jew, Camp Upton to Fort Jay, April 11. Is greatly surprised and thanks his God for having survived the terrible punishments received for merely

objecting to murder. The brutal sentries beat him until he was unable to recognize himself and encouraged the other prisoners to do the same. Commandant declared that all conscientious objectors deserved to be killed. ["]September 15 I arrived at Fort Leavenworth, and, being a vegetarian, had to go twice on hunger strike to get proper food, though far from adequate. Two periods of two weeks in solitary, handcuffed to cell nine hours per day. Compelled to bathe and shave on Saturday, my Sabbath. Dragged to the bath, knocked down, forcib[l]y undressed, held under shower, and scrubbed with coarse soap. The brutalities of the soldiers made me scream with pain. I was taken out of the hole to the hospital November 22 for observation.["]

20. J. E. Haugen, sheet-metal worker, Lutheran, conscientious objector, shared the intolerable conditions at Fort Riley. Guardhouse, court-martial, transfer to Fort Leavenworth, with solitary and accompanying cruelties.

21. The so-called "mutiny" at Fort Leavenworth: The "crusher gang," composed of physically unfit, were ordered to do twice as much work as formerly. Refusing, the "punishment gang" was sent over; but, seeing how matters stood, they also refused.

All were ordered into solitary, and Acting Warden Fletcher started after them with a bat. A prisoner, Stratton, shouted, "Don't do that," for which he was beaten into unconsciousness lasting 50 hours. When Stratton spoke, the warden drew a pistol, tried to fire at him, but cartridge failed to explode. Stratton raised a stool to protect himself, and, in fear of his life, threw it at the warden.

Floyd Ramp received a double compound fracture of the skull.

After being locked in solitary, two big brutes—Wingfield and "Mack," the former with a bat and the latter with a piece of pipe— were set to task of beating them. Ray and Axuara were beaten unmercifully, and two besides Stratton were unconscious for a long time. Many were handcuffed to doors, feet barely touching the floor. Hodges, Baskett, and Plahn were sick, and prison doctor ordered mattresses, which warden later removed. On the third day they were taken down so the prison inspector should not see them. . . .

SOURCE: "Speech of Hon. Charles H. Dillon[:] Introducing Examples of Brutalities, Tortures, and Deaths to Political Prisoners under Military Regime" (Washington DC: Washington Printing Office, 1919), copy in Subject File: Conscientious Objection/Objectors Material, 1919, box 1, Swarthmore College Peace Collection, Swarthmore PA.

6.10. COS Declare Hunger Strike to Secretary of War
(21 August 1918)

[In a letter to his brother written on the same day, 21 August 1918, Evan Thomas informed Norman that he and the other three COs on hunger strike were aware of the seriousness of their actions and were willing to die for their convictions. "Give me liberty or death," Evan proclaimed. "We mean to starve until we are released." Six days into the strike, however, officials force-fed Thomas through a tube inserted down his throat—and after fourteen days he resumed eating. For refusing to eat, Thomas was court-martialed in October and sentenced to life imprisonment, subsequently reduced to twenty-five years. From Fort Riley, Kansas, these COs, Evan W. Thomas, Erling H. Lunde, Harold S. Gray, and Howard W. Moore, sent the following letter to Secretary of War Newton Baker, with a copy to Roger Baldwin, leader of the National Civil Liberties Bureau. Once made public, this letter embarrassed the government.]

We, the undersigned, have refused to obey the Selective Service Act under which we have been conscripted into the United States Army. Realizing the difficulties facing the Government in the question of conscientious objectors, we have heretofore endeavored to comply, so far as we were able, with the provisions made by the President for conscientious objectors.

After having met the Board of Inquiry appointed to decide as to our sincerity, and over a month having elapsed, we have now decided, as we are unalterably opposed to the principle of conscription and believe it to be un-American as well as the very backbone of militarism and war, hereafter to resist any restrictions on our liberty under the Selective Service Act.

We are ready and eager to work for society as private citizens, nor do we desire to engage in propaganda work against the State, but to live useful, constructive lives in society.

We have read the President's Order of July 30, 1918 regarding [alternative civilian service for] conscientious objectors, and we understand that the Government is not prepared to exempt conscientious objectors from compulsory service. We have therefore determined to refuse to eat as long as we are kept from following the pursuits we feel called upon to follow in life. We fully realize the gravity of this stand, but we are determined to starve rather than passively submit to an Act which we believe to be opposed to the principles which we hold dearest in life.

SOURCE: Charles Chatfield, ed., *The Radical "No": The Correspondence and Writings of Evan Thomas on War* (New York: Garland, 1975), 173–74.

6.11. Friends of Conscientious Objectors, Amnesty Leaflet (1919)

[This leaflet was printed by the Friends of Conscientious Objectors, based in Brooklyn, New York. To obtain additional copies or to make contributions, readers were instructed to contact Jules Wortsman, whose brother Gustus was a CO serving twenty years at Fort Leavenworth. In December 1918 Jules was part of a delegation that met with Secretary of War Newton Baker to request the release of imprisoned COs. Along with other peace and civil liberties groups, the Friends of Conscientious Objectors aided COs and campaigned for amnesty.]

SET CONSCIENCE FREE!

For 143 years America has stood a haven of refuge to the people of every land. AMERICA has meant LIBERTY to the oppressed all of the earth and those whom persecution forced to leave their native countries have gladly sought the protection of this "land of the free." But of late we have begun to change this.

DO YOU KNOW

That AMERICA WHICH STANDS TO THE WHOLE WORLD FOR LIBERTY OF CONSCIENCE, though the war has been over four months, is still holding in a military prison at Leavenworth, Kansas, 500 men who could not take part in a war which their CONSCIENCES told them was wrong?

That AMERICA WHICH STANDS FOR JUSTICE has released some conscientious objectors on various technical grounds but has failed to recognize the sincerity of many men who have deliberately chosen every hardship and abuse in military camp and at last prison terms of 20 and 30 years in place of the bomb-proof jobs which were offered them in the medical corps or on civilian farms, for the sole reason that their consciences would not permit them to compromise their principals?

That AMERICA WHICH BOASTS OF HUMANITY has permitted her conscientious objectors to be treated as shamefully as Russia would have handled them in her darkest days! Did you know that these men whose sincere idealism you cannot doubt whatever you think of their views, in some cases have been held under ice-cold showers until they collapsed; strung up in cells until their eyes bulged and their tongues hung from their mouths; dragged on the ground by cruel guards and bayoneted into unconsciousness, fed bread and water for long periods of time, and chained day after day by their wrists to the bars of prison cells?*

That AMERICA WHICH HAS ALWAYS BEEN PROUD TO LEAD THE NATIONS IN GENEROSITY, has stood indifferently by while Germany, Austria, Bulgaria, Russia and Italy have been opening up their jails and allowing their political prisoners to walk out free men and women? Did you know that England's foremost citizens, including 83 Members of Parliament, 16 Bishops, writers, professors and scientists, have already petitioned the English government to free the English conscientious objectors?

Why are not OUR public men, Senators, Congressmen, college presidents, asking for the freedom of American Conscientious Objectors, like these men abroad?

Why are not ordinary American citizens petitioning our government to perform this simple act of justice?

Lest America be shamed before the nations with which she is now striving for a peace which shall last.

LET US FREE THE CONSCIENTIOUS OBJECTORS AND ALL OTHER POLITICAL PRISONERS BEFORE ANY MORE DIE OR LOSE THEIR SANITY . . . .

* See Congressional Record, 4 March 1919, page 5280.

SOURCE: Subject File: Conscientious Objection/Objectors Material, 1919, box 1, Swarthmore College Peace Collection, Swarthmore PA.

CHAPTER 7

Repression and Civil Liberties

7.1. National Civil Liberties Bureau, "War-Time Prosecutions and Mob Violence" (March 1919)

[In March 1919 the National Civil Liberties Bureau, forerunner of the American Civil Liberties Union, published this fifty-six-page pamphlet. It contains an annotated list of prosecutions and mob violence resulting from wartime hysteria, antiradicalism, and intolerance—sentiments that continued beyond the Armistice. Including incidents that occurred from 1 April 1917 to 1 March 1919, this pamphlet updated a 1918 edition listing cases to May 1918. The excerpts here focus on opposition to the war and conscription.]

. . . This list of cases is compiled from the correspondence and press clippings of the National Civil Liberties Bureau. It is by no means a complete record. . . .

. . . It will be noted that by far the largest proportion of all the cases throughout involve members of the I. W. W., Socialist Party and Non-Partisan League. Of those cases which do not, all but a comparative few involve citizens of German descent.

That hundreds of cases have not come to our attention through press clippings is evident from the published statements of the Attorney General setting forth the number of prosecutions instituted and convictions obtained. . . .

II. CRIMINAL PROSECUTIONS.

1. Espionage Act and Treason Cases.
(Including also cases under act in relation to threats against the President.)

a. Convictions.

(1) For Statements in Private Conversation or Correspondence

12/13/17. **Seattle, Wash.**—**Louise Olivereau,** Socialist and I. W. W. sympathizer, sentenced to 10 years on several indictments, chargnig [*sic*] interference with the draft. . . .

2/24/18. **Van Meter, Ia.**—**Abe Moore** fined $1,500 on condition that he buy $1,000 worth of Liberty Bonds for alleged attack on Red Cross and recommending resistance to the draft.

3/6/18. **Fargo, N. D.**—**Henry von Bank** convicted for alleged statement "I would rather see a pair of old trousers flying from the school house flag pole than an American flag." Conviction reversed on appeal. . . .

4/18/18. **Lincoln, Neb.**—**Rev. H. M. Hendricksen,** convicted of obstructing recruiting and enlistment. . . .

5/4/18. **Sioux Falls, S. D.**—**Conrad Kornmann,** 10 years and $1,000 fine for opposing the Liberty Loan in a letter to a friend. . . .

5/6/18. **San Juan, P. R.**—**Gerard Liebisch,** 4 years on a charge of advising drafted men to surrender to the enemy. . . .

5/9/18. **Rock Island, Ill.**—**Lee Lang,** Socialist, 2 years for violation of the Espionage Act. . . .

5/16/18. **Aberdeen, S. D.**—**Walter Heynacher,** 5 years for alleged draft obstruction. . . .

5/28/18. **New Britain, Conn.**—**John Kunz,** convicted for the alleged remarks, "Young men are fools to enlist and go across to be blown up" and "Germany had a perfect right to sink the Lusitania." . . .

6/4/18. **Denver, Colo.**—**J. A. Miller,** 2 years on a charge of telling a young man that he was a fool to fight in this rich man's war and that there was graft in the Red Cross. . . .

7/20/18. **Los Angeles, Cal.**—**L. N. Legendre,** 2 years for saying, "This is a war fostered by Morgan and the rich."

7/18/18. **New York, N. Y.**—**Arthur Roth,** 5 years for alleged seditious statements in an intercepted letter to a friend.

7/24/18. **Detroit, Mich.**—**Wm. Powell,** 20 years and $10,000 for alleged remarks to the effect that the government was a lie throughout, that German barbarities were only fiction, that the Germans were right in sinking the Lusitania, that Germany would wipe the Allies off the earth in three years. . . .

11/1/18. **Chicago, Ill.—August Weissenfels**, 10 years for opposing his son's enlistment in the Army. . . .

12/14/18. **Omaha, Neb.—Tom Kerl**, fined $2,000 and costs for alleged seditious remarks. . . .

(2) Convictions for Statements in Public Addresses or Public Print.

10/—/17. **St. Louis, Mo.—Frank A. Feldman**, 3 months for alleged remarks tending to obstruct the draft.

10/4/17. **Davenport, Iowa.—Daniel H. Wallace**, ex-British soldier and radical, 20 years for a speech on conscription and the war. Went insane and died in jail.

10/22/17. **Trenton, N. J.—Frederick Krafft**, former Socialist candidate for Governor, 5 years and $1,000 for criticism of conscription in a street corner speech.

10/26/17. **Mankato, Minn.—A. L. Sugarman**, State Secretary Socialist Party, 3 years for a speech about conscription. . . .

12/1/17. **San Juan, P. R.—Vincente Balbas Capo**, 8 years and $4,000 fine for an editorial in his paper as to drafting of Porto Ricans who had declined United States citizenship.

12/18/17. **Fargo, N. D.—Kate Richards O'Hare**, 5 years for "discouraging enlistments." . . .

4/19/18. **Minneapolis, Minn.—J. O. Bentall**, Socialist candidate for Governor, and J. A. Peterson, candidate for Republican nomination for United States Senate, sentenced to 5 and 4 years, respectively, for speeches and articles during their campaign activities.

4/30/18. **Los Angeles, Cal.—Robert Goldstein**, 10 years and $5,000 for producing film "Spirit of '76" disparaging the British Government. . . .

5/4/18. **Minneapolis, Minn.—E. A. Engelin**, 5 years for alleged attempt to incite mutiny and obstruct enlistments in a speech.

5/9/18. **Peoria, Ill.—C. H. Kamann**, 3 years and $5,000 for making alleged seditious remarks to children in his history class. . . .

6/1/18. Kansas City, Mo.—Mrs. Rose Pastor Stokes, Socialist, 10 years for writing a signed communication to the Kansas City Star about a speech delivered by her on the government and profiteering. . . .

6/10/18. Boston, Mass.—John J. Ballam, Socialist, 1 year for saying in effect that working men should not go to war because they would be required to kill other workingmen in different uniforms.

6/21/18. Brooklyn, N. Y.—Joseph F. Rutherford, Wm. E. Van Armburgh, R. J. Martin, Fred H. Robison, A. H. McMillan, G. H. Fisher, C. H. Woodworth, each 20 years for publication and distribution of "The Finished Mystery" and for the activities of the International Bible Students Association. . . .

6/29/18. Kansas City, Mo.—Jacob Frohwerk, 10 years for writing alleged seditious articles for the Missouri Staats Zeitung.

7/6/18. Providence, R. I.—Joseph M. Coldwell, state organizer of the Socialist Party, 3 years for alleged seditious statements in a speech.

7/19/18. Los Angeles, Cal.—Ricardo Magon and Librado Rivera, 20 and 15 years, respectively, for alleged seditious statements in a Mexican anarchist newspaper.

8/6/18. Cleveland, O.—Rev. Manasses C. Bontrager, Amish Mennonite bishop, fined $500 for an article deploring the buying of Liberty Bonds.

8/11/18. Cleveland, O.—Rev. W. A. Werth, two years for alleged statement made at a soldier's funeral that the army was rotten with foul disease. . . .

9/11/18. Cleveland, O.—Eugene V. Debs, former Socialist candidate for president, 10 years for alleged seditious remarks in a speech at Canton, O[hio]. . . .

11/21/18. Chicago, Ill.—Rev. David Gerdes, a Dunkard, 10 years for alleged seditious sermon. . . .

12/6/18. Philadelphia, Pa.—Joseph V. Stilson, secretary, 3 years and Joseph Sukys, business manager of Lithuanian Socialpaper Kova, 3 months for publishing alleged seditious matter.

12/30/18. Philadelphia, Pa.—Martin Darkon and **Louis Werner**, editors of the Philadelphia Tageblatt, each 5 years; **Herman Lemke**, business manager, 2 years; and **Peter Schaefer**, president, and **Paul Vogel**, treasurer, each 1 year; for alleged pro-German editorials.

12/31/18. **Portland, Oregon—Dr. Mary Equi**, Socialist and I.W.W. sympathizer, 3 years and $500 fine on a charge of violating the Espionage Act.

1/9/19. **Chicago, Ill.—Victor L. Berger, Adolph Germer, J. Louis Engdahl, Irwin St. John Tucker** and **Wm. F. Kruse**, heads of Socialist Party, convicted under Espionage Act and sentenced to 20 years each for their activities as speakers and writers for the Socialist Party. . . .

[1/9/19]. **Madison, Wis.—Louis B. Nagler** convicted for alleged statements against the Red Cross, Y.M.C.A., etc.

(3) Convictions for Distributing Literature.

6/16/17. **Topeka, Kan.—I. T. Boutell**, Socialist, 6 months for distributing leaflets "A Good Soldier," by Jack London, to drafted men.

11/2/17. **Sioux Falls, S. D.—Emanuel Baltzer and 26 Socialists** sentenced from 1 to 2 years for circulating a petition charging unfair administration of the draft. Conviction set aside by U. S. Supreme Court upon filing of a confession of error by the attorney general and cases remanded to lower court. . . .

11/17/17. **Albany, N. Y.—Clinton Pierce, et al**, 4 Socialists, convicted for distributing leaflet, "The Price We Pay."

12/21/17. **Philadelphia, Pa.—Charles T. Schenck and Dr. Eliz. Baer**, Socialists, convicted of conspiracy for distributing pamphlet relative to the Draft Act.

1/11/18. **Denver, Colo.—Perley Doe**, Socialist, 18 months for circulating chain letter criticising the accuracy of statement that the war was brought on by Germany's breaking her pledges.

1/—/18. **Des Moines, Iowa.—D. T. Blodgett**, 20 years for circulating leaflet opposing the re-election of Congressmen who voted for conscription.

2/12/18. **Parkersburg, W. Va.—Floyd Teter, Alman J. Stainaker and Fred E. Thompson**, each fined $10,000 and costs for conspiracy to obstruct recruiting arid enlistment in publishing and distributing an alleged seditious article. . . .

5/6/18. **San Juan, P. R.**—**Florencio Romero,** 4 years for circulating anti-draft literature and attempting to form an antimilitarist league....

6/6/18. **Seattle, Wash.**—**Emil Herman,** State Secretary, Socialist party, 10 years for alleged obstruction of recruiting in having printed and distributed circulars entitled, "Don't Be a Soldier, Be a Man."...

7/11/18. **Providence, R. I.**—**Emil Yanyar,** Socialist, convicted of conveying false information tending to obstruct recruiting and enlistment in distributing circulars stating that 10,000 men in the state and 4,000 men in Providence had refused to register.

10/26/18. **New York, N. Y.**—**Hyman Rozansky** (turned State's evidence), 3 years; **Jacob Abrahms, Samuel Lippman** and **Hyman Lachowsky,** each 20 years and $1000; and **Mollie Steimer,** 15 years and $500 for publishing and circulating a revolutionary pamphlet denouncing intervention in Russia....

2/19/19. **New York, N. Y.**—**American Socialist Society** convicted under the Espionage Act for publishing Scott Nearing's pamphlet, "The Great Madness." The same jury acquitted Nearing, although it was admitted that he wrote the pamphlet....

(b) Indictments Found, Trial Pending or Result Unknown.

11/—/17. **Sioux Falls, S. D.**—**Former U. S. Senator R. F. Pettigrew,** indicted under the Espionage Act for writing in opposition to war....

11/24/17. **New York, N. Y.**—**Jeremiah A. O'Leary,** advocate of Irish freedom, and others, indicted for conspiracy to violate the Espionage Act....

4/1/18. **Lincoln, Neb.**—**Rev. Hiltner,** indicted for alleged remark "the German emperor is right. Might makes right. America had no business entering the war."...

4/12/18. **Syracuse, N. Y.**—**Oscar Oschner,** Russellite, indicted under Espionage Act for selling "The Finished Mystery."...

5/15/18. **Los Angeles, Cal.**—**Mrs. Clara Gutormse,** indicted under Espionage Act for alleged hostile reception to Red Cross solicitor....

7/10/18. **Cleveland, O.**—**J. S. Switensky, Wasil Sawczyn** and **Paul Ladan,** I.W.W.'s, editors of a Ukrainian paper, Robytnik, indicted for publishing an article tending to interfere with the prosecution of the war....

9/24/18. **New York, N. Y.—A. I. Shiplacoff** and **John Reed**, Socialists, indicted for alleged disloyal language about the Army and Navy in opposition to intervention in Russia at a Socialist meeting on September 13, 1918.

10/10/18. **Fargo, N. D.—Walter T. Mills**, indicted for alleged seditious utterances in a Non-Partisan League speech. . . .

10/29/18. **Milwaukee, Wis.—Victor Berger, E. T. Melms, Oscar Ameringer, Louis Arnold and Eliz. Thomas**, all prominent Socialists, indicted under the Espionage Act. . . .

(c) Acquittals and Disagreements in Espionage Act, Draft Act and Treason Cases.

. . . 2/21/18. **Tacoma, Wash.—Frank Bostrom**, acquitted of violation of Espionage Act, in selling Wallace's book "Shanghaied in the European War."

3/14/18. **Indianapolis, Ind.—13 Montenegrins** acquitted by direction of judge, of conspiracy to violate draft.

3/19/18. **Indianapolis, Ind.—-Joseph Zimmerman**, Socialist, acquitted of charge of violation of Espionage Act by seditious utterances in a public speech advocating the withdrawal of the United States from the war. . . .

3/26/18. **Philadelphia, Pa.—Adolph Werner** and **Martin Darkow**, editors of Philadelphia "Tageblatt," acquitted on charge of treason based on alleged pro-German editorials.

4/—/18. **Shreveport, La.—State Senator S. J. Harper**, acquitted of wilfully interfering with military forces in distributing pamphlet. . . .

7/26/18. **Los Angeles, Cal.—E. K. Brooks**, acquitted on charge of calling the flag "a dirty rag." . . .

10/5/18. **New York, N. Y.—Max Eastman, Floyd Dell, C. Merrill Rogers, Arthur Young and John Reed**, Socialists, tried for the second time for publishing articles and cartoons in "The Masses" interfering with' enlistments. Jury disagreed again. Indictments later dismissed. . . .

2/19/19. **New York, N. Y.—Scott Nearing** acquitted of alleged violation of the Espionage Act by writing "The Great Madness."

(2) Obstructing the Draft Act.

... 6/—/17. **Columbus, Ohio.**—A. A. Hennacy and H. E. Townsley, 2 years for advising refusal to register. ...

7/21/17. **Cleveland, O.**—C. E. Ruthenberg, C. Baker and A. Wagenknecht, 1 year for inducing men not to register. Supreme Court affirmed sentence 1/15/18.

10/23/17. **New York, N. Y.**—C. R. Cheyney and L. C. Fraina, 30 days each for conspiracy to violate Draft Act, by remarks made in public meeting on conscientious objectors. Appealed. ...

1/15/18. **New York, N. Y.** Emma Goldman and Alexander Berkman, sentenced to 2 years and $10,000 fine for conspiracy to violate conscription act, upheld by U. S. Supreme Court. ...

3/27/18. **Springfield, Ill.**—Mr. and Mrs. Fadoo Meyers, 90 days each for advising their sons not to register. ...

(3) Convictions Under State and Local Laws.

... 11/10/17. **Atlantic, Ia.**—W. Theo. Woodward, 6 months and $600 for belonging to the People's Council, a violation of a state law. Prison sentence suspended. ...

11/17/17. **New York, N. Y.**—Nathan Levine, Socialist, 1 year and 20 days for the alleged remark that he would rather go to prison than be drafted for the army.

11/30/17. **Faribault, Minn.**—E. B. Ford, Eliz. Ford, Socialist Labor Party members, and **Ed Bosky**, $500 and 1 year for "discouraging enlistment" by editorial in their paper. ...

12/8/[1]7. **Los Angeles, Cal.**—Robert Whitaker, Floyd Hardin and **Harold Story**, sentenced to 6 months and an aggregate fine of $1,200 for unlawful assembly in connection with Christian Pacifist Conference. ...

1/11/18. **Nome, Alaska.**—Bruce Rogers, Socialist, convicted of violation of territorial sedition act for printing "We must make the world safe for democracy if we have to 'bean' the Goddess of Liberty to do it." ...

1/26/18. **Philadelphia, Pa.**—Casper Oberstadt, 30 days and $150 fine, Louis Abrahamson, Isadora Axelrod, Walter A. Ebbits and

Solomon Bold, Socialists, each 15 days and $150 fine for distribution of anti-conscription leaflets. . . .

2/26/18. **St. Paul, Minn.—A. C. Townley** and **Jos. Gilbert,** president and secretary of Non-Partisan League, indicted for circulating pamphlets "tending to discourage enlistments." Gilbert sentenced to one year. Reversed on appeal. . . .

3/12/18. **Chicago, Ill.—J. W. Beckstrom,** fined $50 for refusing to stand when "Star Spangled Banner" was played in the theatre. . . .

7/31/18. **Mt. Vernon, N. Y.—Father E. W. Heinlein,** $200 and 2 months (suspended) for refusing to ring his church bells to celebrate an American victory. . . .

V. CONSCIENTIOUS OBJECTORS IN PRISON, MARCH 1, 1919

The following list of 179 conscientious objectors so far as the Bureau has been able to ascertain were still confined in Federal Prisons, civil or military, on March 1, 1919. Almost all of them are in the Disciplinary Barracks at Fort Leavenworth, Kansas. It is probable that the following list does not include more than half the conscientious objectors still in confinement at that date [serving sentences ranging from one to thirty-five years, as well as unknown sentences]. . . .

SOURCE: National Civil Liberties Bureau, *War-Time Prosecutions and Mob Violence: Involving the Rights of Free Speech, Free Press, and Peaceful Assemblage (from April 1, 1917, to March 1, 1919)* (New York: National Civil Liberties Bureau, 1919), in American Civil Liberties Union Records, CDG-A, box 1, Swarthmore College Peace Collection, Swarthmore PA.

7.2. William Emmett, "Mania in Los Angeles" (17 January 1918)

[In 1918 three Christian ministers in Los Angeles were convicted for opposing the war. This account captures the intolerance, supported by LA officials, toward antiwar dissent and all things German in the city. It also illustrates how prowar and antiwar ministers, and others, invoked Christianity to support or oppose the war.]

The student of social pathology cannot fail to take notice these days of the unheard-of human reversions to brute panic and excesses.

The East St. Louis massacre is a blot upon the pages of our history. But from the point of view of intellectual progress, mental epidemics, such as are now sweeping over Los Angeles, are fraught with even greater danger. War hysteria has reached a height at which sane men must stand aghast. Press, pulpit, people, and courts, even, seem equally mad with war-frenzy.

The thing began to come to a head during the recent visit of Billy Sunday, who daily offered to God the most ferocious prayers for the destruction of Germany and the extermination of every German. The Rev. Chas Edward Locke, pastor of the First M.E. Church, preached that pacifists were worse than pro-Germans, and that all of them should be exported to Berlin. The city authorities fell in line with the popular mania. A so-called Loyal League was formed under the leadership of Major Judson, to go gunning for any one that should pronounce the word "peace" in any manner.

A handful of Christian ministers, mostly from the northern part of the State, being grieved at the continuous preaching of the gospel of hate, decided to hold at Long Beach a conference to emphasize a broader view of humanity and to attract other Christian ministers to a saner view of things. The programme, one of the most innocuous conceivable, bore the title: "Conference of Christian Pacifists: a Religious Meeting, Non-Political and Non-Obstructive." It was announced to discuss such books as "Why Men Fight," by Bertrand Russell, and "Newer Ideals of Peace," by Jane Addams.

The Long Beach Council of Defence, together with the Mayor and police, decided that they would not allow pacifist meetings of any kind. They refused to look at the programme or the names of the speakers; and yet by intimidation prevented every owner of a hall from allowing its use for the meetings. The original organizer of the conference, Rev. Floyd Hardin, pastor of a Methodist church, thought that there would be less prejudice in Los Angeles, and so obtained a hall there. The Los Angeles police, however, decided to break up any peace meetings before they should get started at all. So they placed officers at the hall and, without giving reason for their action, refused entrance to any one. But the Christian Pacifists meantime obtained a small room in the Douglas building for a meeting chiefly of the out-of-town delegates.

The action of the police seems a bit ridiculous in view of the fact that at no time was there any prospect of the conference being attended by more than a few dozen people. Even with the free advertising the police action brought the conference, at no time were more than twenty-five or thirty people present besides the police officers and secret service men. The meetings lasted three days and were finally held in private homes, but no arrests were made except at the first meeting in the Douglas building. Here Rev. Floyd Hardin, Rev. Robert Whitaker, pastor of a Baptist church, and Harold Storey, a Quaker theological student, were arrested and were later released on bail. Otherwise the meetings were not interfered with by the police or the Federal officers, who were present throughout. A Federal officer placed on the stand during the trial stated that he had been delegated to arrest any speaker making seditious remarks, but found nothing that would warrant his making an arrest.

The trial of the three men arrested, which has just been concluded in the Los Angeles police court, Judge Thomas P. White presiding, is probably the climax of perversity in American jurisprudence. The men were found guilty of "holding an unlawful meeting," "refusing to disperse when so ordered by the officer," and "disturbing the peace." The judge sentenced each defendant to six months in the county jail and $1,200 fine.

The prosecution made use of statements like the following, alleged to have been made by the prisoners, some time or other at some place or other, for it was not pretended that they had said these things at the meeting where the arrest was made. First, Mr. Harold Storey, in a sermon on the text, "Thou shalt love they neighbor as thyself," was accused of saying that it was difficult for many Christians to conceive of the carpenter of Nazareth thrusting a bayonet into the breast of a brother. Secondly, the Rev. Floyd Hardin was alleged to have said at another meeting that he would prefer to go into eternity with his own blood on his hands rather than with that of a brother. Thirdly, the Rev. Robert Whitaker was accused of having said somewhere that under certain circumstances he would prefer the ideals of the Bolsheviki or the I.W.W. to those of the Merchants' and Manufacturers' Association. These were the traitorous utterances which were alleged against the defendants themselves.

Much extraneous evidence was brought before the jury, as, for instance, this: At the meeting in the Douglas building the Christian Pacifists had borrowed from an adjoining office a typewriter desk in the drawer of which a copy of *The Masses* was found; though it was established that none of the defendants nor any one in the audience knew of its presence, or even knew the magazine itself, yet this magazine was the first piece of evidence handed to the jurors and intently studied. . . . Bishop Paul Jones, of Salt Lake, had prayed somewhere, "God forgive them, for they know not what they do"—in supposed reference to the war. The Rev. Sidney Strong, of Seattle, had distributed copies of the Sermon on the Mount and quoted the words, "If thine enemy smite thee upon one cheek, turn to him the other also." The attorneys for the defence objected to the introduction of this kind of evidence, but Judge White apparently ruled that all peace propaganda was in effect the same kind, and that therefore anything said anywhere at any time against war or for peace would establish the nature of the conference.

The jury consisted of three men and nine women. All of them stated it as their conviction that the right of free speech did not extend to the discussion of peace while the country was at war, but declared their belief that they could give the defendants a fair trial, and stated that they would clear them in case the Court should instruct the jury that the defendants had not transgressed the law. Both jury and judge, apparently, were entirely under the influence of the ideas now predominant in the community, viz., that it is traitorous to talk, or pray to God, for peace. One clergyman, by the way, wrote to the Los Angeles *Times* thus: "The reply of the Christian clergyman to the weakling of to-day is that Jesus Christ was the man who first put the fist into pacifist. Yours for Christian service"!

. . . The prosecuting attorney, Mr. Richards, admonished the jury that Jesus had said, "Bring hither mine enemies and slay them before me." "Some spunk to that," he added, and then continued: "Members of the jury, look upon these defendants. You know that if they were living in Germany and attempted to hold peace meeting there, some fat Government official would put them into a meat-grinder and grind them into sausage to feed to their dachshunds. But we cannot do that here; we can only put them into jail."

. . . In his arraignment of the prisoners he [Judge White] said in substance that any one who teaches that Jesus of Nazareth would not fight is using religion as a cloak for seditious and traitorous propaganda, for this war is the Holy War of God, and since the state derives its authority from God, the United States had gone into this war at the command of God, and he that resisteth the state resisteth God. In sentencing the prisoners, Judge White declared that "now the people of Los Angeles were giving notice through the courts to all the world that they would tolerate no peace meetings within their city, and that he would make a public example of these men to deter others from preaching their pernicious doctrines there."

The temper of the community is clearly seen in the many letters to the press, which appear almost daily. Not only do the people oppose German music, language, and literature, but some are insistently demanding that there shall be no observance of Christmas, since the Germans keep Christmas; any one who has a Christmas tree or sings "peace and good will on earth," this year shall be considered a pro-German and a pacifist and shall be adequately punished. Major Judson has pledged his organization to oppose any kind of "pacifist noise" in Los Angeles. The authorities are openly abetting violence in the name of patriotism. A certain Colonel Blake was put on the stand during the trial as a hero because had had broken up a prayer-meeting in a private home in Pasadena, though he declared he did not know who or what pacifists were, but he did not want that kind around in his city.

. . . Probably the city of the Angels will thus have the historic distinction of having sent three inoffensive Christian ministers to jail for three years for having prayed to the God of heaven that the blessing of peace might again come back to earth.

The serious aspect of such mania as that of Los Angeles is that it is known in Germany and Russia. President Wilson has certainly tried to appeal to the German people against their rulers, but these appeals will come to naught if the German people only see us in our unreasoning fury as a mad bull, against whom they must fight to the uttermost.

SOURCE: *Nation*, 17 January 1918, 58–59.

7.3. Mary McDowell Case (1918)

[In 1918 Mary S. McDowell, a Latin teacher at Manual Training High School in Brooklyn, was fired by the New York City Board of Education for her pacifist convictions. Motivated by her Quaker-based religious principles, she refused to engage in school-assigned war activities and refused to sign an unqualified loyalty oath. She appealed her dismissal in state court and lost. In 1923 the Board of Education, acknowledging that her punishment had been "too severe," reinstated her.]

... Brief for Mary S. McDOWELL, Respondent....

The charges in this case are *conduct unbecoming a teacher*. The specifications of the charges are:

That heretofore and on or about January 10, 1918, she made substantially the following statements to the Board of Superintendents:

1. That she did not consider it right to resist by force the invasion of our country, that she would not do her part in upholding the national policy of resistance to invasion, that she would not uphold our country in resisting invasion and that, if our country were resisting invasion, she *believed* it to be *her conscientious* duty to *refuse to bear arms in order to repel the invaders.*

2. That she did not want to help the United States government in carrying on the present war, and that she was unwilling to assist the government by every means in her power in carrying on the present war.

3. That she would not *urge* her pupils to support the war.

4. That she would not *urge* her pupils to perform those Red Cross services which either promote the war of the United States against the German Government or better the condition of the soldiers in the field.

5. That she would not *urge* her pupils to buy Thrift Stamps, the sale of which supports the United States Government in carrying on the war against the German Government.

6. That she does not believe that a *teacher* is under a *special* obligation to train his or her pupils to support the United States Government in its measures for carrying on the war.

7. That she is opposed to the war of the United States against the German government.

The statements to the Board of Superintendents on January 10, 1918, which constitute the sole basis of the foregoing specifications, were made in response to questions put to her by members of the Board on that date. The questions and answers respecting her beliefs on the subject of war, referred to as Exhibit No. 2, are as follows: . . .

Mr. Tildsley:
Q. Miss McDowell, do you *believe* this country should resist by force of arms an invasion by a hostile army? A. I cannot speak for the country all together. I can speak for myself only. Personally, I would not resist by arms invasion, at least if I live up to what I think. Can't always tell what we might do in an emergency.

Q. Do you *believe* that the country should, the country? A. The country as a whole does not believe as I do. . . .

Mr. Shallow: . . .
Q. You are one of the people? A. Yes. But I don't care to force my opinion on another person. I think it well if one believes in things to let them be known but I have no desire to force my opinion on anyone else.

Mr. Ettinger:
Q. Do you *believe* that the country would be justified in resisting invasion by a hostile army? A. Well, again it refers to the situation, it depends upon what the country believes, . . .

Q. That means if you believe it is right to resist they should do what they think is right? A. I imagine the majority of the people now think it is right to resist an invasion.

Mr. Tildsley:

Q. But you don't? A. I think I should not by force of arms; there are many ways of resisting.

Q. If one was threatening, would you resort to a sword or fighting arms? A. It would depend upon the circumstances, I don't think I would have a sword or gun to kill one with, I would have to trust to some different kind of method, which one I cannot tell. . . .

Mr. Shallow:

Q. Would you uphold your country in resisting invasion? A. I could uphold it as being a proper act for the country but not as being a proper act for me.

Dr. Ettinger:

Q. Would you do your part in upholding the country? A. What is my part?

Q. The obligation of every citizen of this country to carry out the instructions of the country even to the extent of bearing arms, even to performing any service required by the Government, and to assist by every means in your power. A. It if were the law that I should have to bear arms, I should believe it my conscientious duty to refuse.

Q. Would you do other duties to aid this country in carrying on the war? A. That would depend upon what it was.

Q. In preparing food, clothing for the soldiers, etc. A. I think that a very detailed question, it is rather—to make in a theoretical way. . . .

Mr. Tildsley:

Q. Or do anything else that the Government might require? A. I might do something else.

Q. To help the war? A. I should not want to help the war.

Q. Are you willing to assist the Government at the present time by every means in your power in carrying out the present war? A. No.

Q. Are you willing to impress upon your pupils their duty of supporting the Government in its measures for carrying on the present war? A. I would not urge the pupils to support the war. A great many in my class have promised to, almost all of them, I think; I don't object to reminding them of their promises.

Q. Do you feel that with your *beliefs* you can do the full duty required of teachers at this time by the Board of Education? A. It seems to me that I can do all that is necessary. . . .

Q. Are you able with your *view* to perform the duties that are imposed upon the teachers of the Manual Training High School by the principal? A. I have spoken to the principal about the matter and I have told him that I could do the routine work of the Clubs that he is planning but I cannot urge them.

Q. To do what? A. To do the different patriotic services. I could remind them of their promises.

Q. Can you urge your pupils to join the Red Cross? A. Why, I think I might.

Q. Answer more directly. A. That is, of course, those services, those that I object to are those that are toward helping the war. That is the way it seems to me that it is better to draw the line since I am against war not to help it and to try to help those other powers that lead toward peace. Such as the President, for instance, has designated.

Q. Are you willing to urge the girls in that school to do definite Red Cross work that looks toward the help of the wounded, such as making bandages? A. As I said the object that seems most [to] appeals to me is the non-combatant part of the Red Cross. Of course I have no objection to encouraging, yes.

Mr. Ettinger:
Q. Would you urge your pupils to do Red Cross service for the bettering of the condition of the soldiers in the field? A. I would not make a point of doing that.

Mr. Tildsley:

Q. The Manual Training High School is at present engaged in several distinct kinds of service in the support of the Government in carrying on the war and the teachers in this school are expected to take part in the oversight of those services. Question one. Are you, Miss McDowell, taking part in the sale of Thrift Stamps? A. I have laid the matter before the girls in my class and that sort of thing is included in the pledges. Thrift Stamps in saving the class has started and organized with a member to report on such things. I think the class will do most of the work. I don't doubt they will do as they promise.

Q. Are you willing to urge the pupils in your class to buy Thrift Stamps? A. Why, I think I would say just as I said before. I am willing to state the case and I [am] thinking of suggesting that the different pupils state the case more specifically to this little group that has formed in the class, and I am willing to remind them of their promises. . . .

Mr. Straubenmuller:

Q. Is your statement then that "I would not urge"? A. Yes. . . . I think the pupils have their personal liberty and personal reasons.

Mr. Tildsley:

Q. Do you *believe* that a teacher in the public high schools is under a special obligation to train her pupils to support the Government in its measures for carrying on the war? . . . [Mr. Edson urges her to answer] A. I don't feel that it is necessary.

Mr. Tildsley:

Q. You don't feel what is necessary? A. For the teachers to encourage the support of this war in high schools. In school our time is full. . . . [Students] sometimes get it [prowar measures] to the detriment of their school work. I have heard it said by the teachers in school and the *principal said something that indicated* the same thing, *that the war activities were detrimental to their school work.* It seemed to me that he regretted it very sincerely and as *he said that the most patriotic service that a pupil could render was to do his work thoroughly. The most important thing for them was to aid in the process of being well-trained citizens, and the most important thing in that line was to do the work before them, the need of thoroughly well-trained disciplines . . . .*

. . . She has therefore been a teacher in the City High Schools since February, 1905, a period of thirteen years . . . She is regarded as a capable and efficient teacher and her record is flawless.

The fact of her membership in the Society of Friends has been well known to the officials of the Board of Education. In the report of the Principal of the Manual Training High School, dated March 30, 1914, the question as to her influence on the students in the "development of habits of honor, orderliness, self-reliance, self-control, courtesy and good physical posture" was answered as follows:

> "*In every way for the best. Reared a Quaker, graduated from Swarthmore, she is a fine example for girls. I am impressed with her conscientiousness, her earnest desire to give the best. She is not of the 2.30 type*" (Exhibit H).

And in the report of the same Principal on April 22, 1915, in answer to the same question, he said:

> "*All are excellent. She is a Quaker, and her example could not be better*" (Exhibit H).

Miss McDowell has always been an earnest and devoted member of the Society of Friends. Since the beginning of the war she has been interested in various forms of war relief and particularly in the work of American Friends Service Committee. The latter is an organic part of the American Red Cross, with the title "Bureau of Friends Unit of the Department of Civil Affairs," and is engaged in civilian relief and reconstruction work in the devastated area in France. Her brother Carlton is now engaged in France as a member of this unit. From her salary she has been contributing for the past eight months the sum of $35 per month to this work. . . .

SOURCE: "Brief for Mary S. McDowell, Respondent," [5 December 1919], 1–9, in Mary McDowell Papers, CDG-A, Swarthmore College Peace Collection, Swarthmore PA.

7.4. National Civil Liberties Bureau, "Who Are the Traitors?" (1918)

[The NCLB insisted that dissent, even in wartime, was patriotic. In this leaflet the board argues that prowar citizens who advocate violence against antiwar dissenters are not "patriots" but "traitors" to U.S. constitutional law and the tradition of American liberty.]

WHO ARE THE TRAITORS?

"I want to utter my earnest protest against any manifestation of the spirit of lawlessness anywhere or in any cause . . . A man who takes the law into his hands is not the right man to co-operate in any form or development of law and institutions."

—Woodrow Wilson, Nov. 12, 1917. . . .

. . . "If the people all understood why it is that we are going into this war, they would rise and crush these traitors down to earth.

"There are men walking about the streets of this city tonight, who ought to be taken out at sunrise and shot for treason . . ."

—Elihu Root, Aug. 15, 1917.

We are witnessing in America today the spectacle of deliberate incitement to mob violence on the part of leading men in public life, hysterical with the spirit of war. In the name of a united country behind a war for democratic ideals, one or another of them counsels us to mob, whip, shoot and kill all those who by word or deed dissent from their notions of patriotic conduct.

But these men are not patriots. They are false to every tradition of American liberty, constitutional rights and orderly legal processes. They do not find American courts sufficient to deal with "sedition and treason." Violence better suits their passion. They are not even meeting the popular test of "standing behind the President."

These "leading citizens" are our real traitors. They are the destroyers of democratic government and constitutional rights.

Hear what the President of the United States has to say about them—

"I have been very much distressed, my fellow citizens, by some of the things that have happened recently. The mob spirit is displaying itself here and there in this country. I have no sympathy with the men that take their punishment into their own hands, and I want to say to every man who does join such a mob that I do not recognize him as worthy of the free institutions of the United States. . . ."

—From the speech before the Buffalo Convention of the American Federation of Labor, November 12th, 1917.

Secretary of War Baker on the occasion of the mob outrage on Rev. Herbert S. Bigelow, of Cincinnati, said:

"The cause of the United States is not aided, but is hurt, by that kind of thing. No night riders are needed, and when the country is at war for liberty and justice they make a humiliating contrast to our national ideals and aims."

In the light of these words, note what some of these distinguished "patriots" have to say.

Elihu Root before the Union League Club, New York City, August 15th, 1917, (*N.Y. Times*):

"I feel that there are still some Americans who do not quite understand why we are fighting. If they did, these pro-German traitors who are selling our country, who are endeavoring by opposition and obstruction, in Congress and out of Congress, to make what America does in preparation for the war so ineffective that when our young men go to the firing line, they will meet defeat, if the people all understood why it is that we are going into this war, they would rise and crush these traitors down to earth.

"There are men walking about the streets of this city tonight, who ought to be taken out at sunrise and shot for treason, and if we are competent and fit for our liberty, we will find them out and get at them.

There are some newspapers published in this city every day, the editors of which deserve conviction and execution for treason."

James W. Gerard, ex-Embassador [*sic*] to Germany, at Pittsburgh, November 13th, 1917, (*N.Y. Times*):

"We should 'hog-tie' every disloyal German-American, feed every pacifist raw meat and hang every traitor to a lamp-post, to insure success in this war. And our traitors are not all German-American, . . ."

Rev. Henry VanDyke, of New York, November 1st, 1917, (*N.Y. Times*):

"I would hang any candidate for mayor who said that the United States was not justified in entering the war. I'd hang every one whether or not he be a candidate for mayor who lifts his voice against America entering the war."

Ex-Governor Warfield of Maryland at Baltimore, November 4th, (*N.Y. Times*):

"Karl Muck shall not lead an orchestra in Baltimore. I told the police board members that this man would not be allowed to insult the people of the birthplace of the Star Spangled Banner. I told them that mob violence would prevent it if necessary, and that I would gladly lead the mob to prevent this insult to my country and my flag."

That this hysterical spirit of lawlessness may not overthrow established constitutional processes, it has been necessary to organize for the maintenance of our liberties. The National Civil Liberties Bureau, which publishes the leaflet, stands for no "ism." It makes no distinction as to whose liberties it aids in defending. With lawyers and correspondents all over the country the Bureau is helping to uphold those institutions of orderly society which the war so seriously threatens. . . .

SOURCE: American Civil Liberties Union Records, CDG-A, box 1, Swarthmore College Peace Collection, Swarthmore PA.

7.5. Lusk Committee Targets Pacifists and Radicals (1920)

[In 1919 the New York state legislature authorized a joint committee chaired by Senator Clayton R. Lusk to investigate "revolutionary radicalism" and "seditious activities." The Lusk Committee spearheaded the postwar Red Scare in New York. The committee's report targeted "pacifism," in addition to socialism, communism, and syndicalism—and, further, conflated these revolutionary movements. These excerpts come from the committee's four-volume report.]

. . . The very first general fact that must be driven home to Americans is that the pacifist movement in this country, the growth and connections of which are an important part of this report, is an absolutely integral and fundamental part of International Socialism. It is not an accretion. It is not a side issue. European Socialism concentrated its efforts in three directions:

The first was to organize labor as a step-daughter, an acolyte, a coadjutor of the great Socialist policy, in order to obtain a great mass of supporters for the revolution.

The second was the use of political action as a means and not an end; as a means for obtaining gradual control, or for obtaining paramount influence until the complete triumph of Socialism would make parliamentary government a thing of the past.

The third purpose was the creation of an International sentiment to supersede national patriotism and effort, and this internationalism was based upon pacifism, in the sense that it opposed all wars between nations and developed at the same time the class consciousness that was to culminate in relentless class warfare. In other words, it was not really peace that was the goal, but the abolition of the patriotic, warlike spirit of nationalities.

The entire program, in all its three sections, was based upon the ideas of one man and largely on the ideas expressed in one of his writings. The founder of Socialism and its present dominating force is Karl Marx. Its Ten Commandments are the Communist Manifesto of Marx, issued in 1848. This is true of the American, as it is true of the European movement. To understand every present campaign, every present alliance, we must read the Communist Manifesto. . . .

It is the purpose of the Committee in the succeeding chapters of this section to show the use made by members of the Socialist Party of America and other extreme radicals and revolutionaries of pacifist sentiment among people of education and culture in the United States as a vehicle for the promotion of revolutionary Socialist propaganda. The facts here related are important because they show that these Socialists, playing upon the pacifist sentiment in a large body of sincere persons, were able to organize their energies and to capitalize their prestige for the spread of their doctrines. . . .

SOURCE: *Revolutionary Radicalism[:] Its History, Purpose, and Tactics with an Exposition and Discussion of the Steps Being Taken and Required to Curb It[:] Being the Report of the Joint Legislative Committee Investigating Seditious Activities, Filed April 24, 1920, in the Senate of the State of New York, Part I: Revolutionary and Subversive Movements Abroad and at Home* (Albany NY: J. B. Lyon, 1920), 1:11, 969.

7.6. Jessie Wallace Hughan, "The Bolsheviks'll Git You" [n.d.]

[Jessie W. Hughan was a socialist pacifist. A New York City high school teacher, she suffered harassment and persecution as a result of her pacifist activism and radical politics. In January 1919 the Senate Judiciary Committee included Hughan on a list of radicals who had opposed World War I. The names were provided by Archibald Stevenson, special counsel for the Lusk Committee. Hughan, a poet, parodies Stevenson in this poem.]

Little Archie Stevenson has come here to stay,
To sweep the agitators out and keep the Reds away,
To shoo-oo the revolutions off and put the folks to sleep,
And chase the I.W.W. and earn his board and keep.
But when we hear the soap-box a-shrieking in the dusk,
And the bombs begin to rattle in the brain of Papa Lusk,
And the headlines flare and flicker and we dream about
    The Hun,—
We huddle in committees and have the mostest fun,
A'listenin' to the witch-tales that Archie tells about—
For the Bolsheviks'll git you ef you don't—watch—out!

Once there was a working-class that wouldn't say its
    prayers;

It mocked at all its masters and it shocked its millionaires,
But when it waved the red flag and the neighbors ran
    to hide,
There was two-big-black-things a-standing by its side;
The one it was a Trotzky and the other a Lenine,—
And when the neighbors peeped again, no master could be
    seen,
And you couldn't find a millionaire in all that land about,—
For the Bolsheviks'll git you ef you don't—watch—out!

So you'd better mind your manners and your masters kind
    and true,
And vote for all the millionaires who make the jobs for
    you;
And don't you wear a red tie, and don't you go on strike,
And don't you join a union that the old man doesn't like,—
But when the boss comes riding by, throw up your hats
    and shout,—
Or the Bolsheviks'll git YOU, TOO, ef you DON'T—
WATCH—OUT!

SOURCE: Jessie Wallace Hughan, *The Challenge of Mars and Other Verses* (New York: Correlated Graphic Industries, 1932), 43–44.

7.7. American Civil Liberties Union, *The Truth about the I.W.W. Prisoners* (1922)

[Founded in 1920, the ACLU became the most important civil liberties organization in the United States. In the immediate postwar era, the ACLU continued the work of its predecessor, the NCLB, and provided legal assistance to dissidents prosecuted for their radical views and opposition to World War I. In this pamphlet the ACLU defends the Industrial Workers of the World and challenges the wartime legal assault on the organization and its members.]

Whatever you think about the I.W.W., the imprisonment of 96 of them now in Leavenworth is a challenge to every believer in free speech.

They are in prison solely for expressions of opinion. Every charge of violence or sabotage has been thrown out by the courts. They are on the same footing before the law as Debs and others.

This pamphlet gives all the facts from the records. Read it and if you are convinced of its justice, help secure their release.

THE I.W.W. AND THE WAR

The three conspiracy prosecutions against the 151 members of the I.W.W. convicted during the war were based on the theory that the regular industrial program and activities of that organization obstructed the war. The I.W.W. was singled out among the labor organizations of the United States because of its historical anti-war position and its general revolutionary teachings. The evidence in all three cases failed to show any program of obstruction or any acts intended to obstruct the war. Lawyers who have examined the record with care state that the theory on which the prosecutions were based was not borne out by the evidence. One of the government's prosecutors in the Chicago case himself volunteered the statement that "the I.W.W. were convicted *on general principles.*"

Individual members of the I.W.W. made speeches or wrote articles or letters opposing the war just as did hundreds of other persons who were never prosecuted, but there is no evidence of any conspiracy to obstruct it. As a matter of fact, all the defendants of military age, except one in the three cases, complied with the Selective Service Act. Further and more important, the I.W.W. organization was in complete control of the loading of munitions and war supplies on the docks at Philadelphia and Wilmington. Yet there was not a single instance of obstruction, violence or sabotage. These longshoremen performed their work to the entire satisfaction of officials and employers and maintained a general spirit of cooperation and wartime patriotism.

In view of these facts it must seem extraordinary to many that the courts could have convicted in all three of these cases, and that the convictions could have been sustained by the courts of appeal. This result is to be explained by considerations outside the law. . . .

... Then there is Clyde Hough, local Secretary of the I.W.W. in Rockford, Illinois, who, like many others outside the I.W.W., did not believe in the war or in the draft. As he was of military age he had to face the issue on registration day, June 5, 1917, when he went down to the jail with fifteen others and gave himself up rather than register. He was sentenced to a year, was in jail when the Espionage Act was passed, and was still in jail during the period covered in the Chicago indictment, under which he was convicted and sentenced to five years for "conspiracy." He was not even put on the stand. There was no evidence whatever against him except that he personally refused to obey the draft act....

Then there was Ralph Chaplin, a young man who made his living as an artist and writer, and who was editing "Solidarity," the official I.W.W. weekly during the early months of the war. Chaplin was opposed to the war and the draft, and said so plainly. He expressed his opinions over his own signature in the columns of "Solidarity." It was on these expressions of opinion alone that he was sentenced to twenty years, for "conspiracy." ...

COMMENT ON THE CONVICTIONS

The one lawyer in the United States outside those involved in the case, who read the 40,000 page record of the Chicago trial and analysed it, is Major Alexander Sidney Lanier, formerly of the Bureau of Military Intelligence, War Department, at Washington, who did that work as part of his official duties. His conclusions therefore carry great weight. In a public letter to President Wilson, he condemned the whole proceeding. The following are extracts from it.

My dear Mr. President:

A very earnest passion for justice to all men of whatever race, color or condition of life, constrains me, after mature reflection, to write you in regard to the case of the United States vs. W. D. Haywood, et als,—Industrial Workers of the World—with a view to giving you an unbiased opinion of the case, should you be appealed to for executive clemency in behalf of the defendants . . .

2. While evidence in the record discloses that several of those defendants said and did things for which they could have been successfully prosecuted under the Espionage law, and for which they should have been prosecuted, convicted and punished, the evidence is, in my opinion, insufficient on the whole, to show and establish beyond a reasonable doubt a conspiracy as charged in the indictment. Congress never conscripted labor, as it might have done, and there is no law of which I am aware that prohibits working people from striking and co-operating in formulating plans for a strike and methods to make their strike a success. . . .

(Signed) ALEXANDER SIDNEY LANIER
—*The New Republic*, April 19, 1919 . . .

THE CAMPAIGN FOR AMNESTY

Efforts for amnesty are widespread and persistent. There are and have been a number of independent campaigns, notably on the part of the American Federation of Labor, the Socialist Party, the General Defense Committee of the I.W.W., the American Civil Liberties Union, special amnesty committees and local groups, and by several periodicals in the liberal, labor and radical movement. . . .

FOR LAWYERS[:] A STATEMENT OF THE PRESENT STATUS OF THE I.W.W. CASES, PREPARED BY OTTO CHRISTENSEN, ATTORNEY FOR THE ORGANIZATION

The following statement of the present legal status of the three cases was prepared by Otto Christensen of Chicago who as attorney for the I.W.W., knows them intimately. This statement carries an analysis of the charges and the findings of the courts. It was written to show that the I.W.W. prisoners are now on precisely the same legal basis as other political prisoners convicted under the Espionage act.

The Government secured convictions against members of the I.W.W. in three cases, namely, its cases prosecuted at Chicago, Illinois; Wichita, Kansas; and Sacramento, California. In each of these cases the defendants prosecuted an appeal . . .

We propose, in this brief, to consider the action of the Courts of Appeals and their effect upon the cases of the defendants. . . .

Chicago Case

The indictment in this case contained five counts. The first, second and fifth counts may be designated as the *industrial counts*, and the third and fourth counts may be designated as the *war counts* . . . .

The District Court withdrew the fifth count from the consideration of the jury and the Circuit Court of Appeals acquitted the defendants of the industrial offenses charged in counts one and two . . . .

The third count of the indictment charged a conspiracy under Section 37 of the Penal Code to procure certain persons to refuse to register for military service under the provisions of Section 5 of the Selective Service Act, and the proclamation of the President of May 18, 1917, made pursuant thereto; also to procure certain other persons to desert the service of the United States in violation of the provisions of Article 58 of the Articles of War.

The conviction of the defendants on this count was affirmed by the Court of Appeals. The defendants now confined in the penitentiary at Leavenworth were on the 30th day of August, 1918, respectively sentenced to a two-year term of imprisonment on the third count. Within a week after the Court imposed sentence all commenced serving the same in the United States penitentiary at Leavenworth, Kansas. Each of these defendants has served his sentence on this count. Therefore, the conviction of the defendants on Count three is no longer pertinent to a consideration of the subject of amnesty, pardon or commutation of sentence.

Each of the defendants is now serving a sentence on count four only. (Espionage Act.) Therefore, the character of the offense charged in count four is alone the subject of inquiry in determining whether amnesty should be extended to these defendants, a pardon granted or their sentences commuted.

Briefly, the fourth count charges a conspiracy to cause insubordination in the military and naval forces and to obstruct the recruiting and enlistment service

"By means of personal solicitation, of public speeches, of articles printed in certain newspapers (here twelve newspapers are designated by name, of which eight are printed in various foreign languages), circulating throughout the United States, and of the public distribution of certain pamphlets entitled, 'War and the Workers,' 'Patriotism and the Workers' and 'Preamble and Constitution of the Industrial Workers of the World,' the same being solicitations, speeches, articles and pamphlets persistently urging insubordination, disloyalty and refusal of duty in said military and naval forces and failure and refusal on the part of available persons to enlist therein."

The charge here does not embrace any industrial activities. It is limited to the expression of opinions publicly, the circulation of literature and newspapers which the pleder concludes, were of such character as would cause insubordination and disloyalty and refusal of duty in the military and naval forces.

. . . In fact, up to the time this indictment was returned there was no statute in the United States, even in war time, restricting the right to strike. . . .

SOURCE: American Civil Liberties Union, *The Truth about the I.W.W. Prisoners* (New York: American Civil Liberties Union, 1922), [1], 5, 16, 28–29, 38, 40–43.

7.8. Norman Thomas, "Amnesty!" [1919?]

[After the war peace and civil liberties advocates waged a campaign to win amnesty for those imprisoned for their antiwar stance. Norman Thomas, who wrote this flyer, was a socialist pacifist, ordained Presbyterian minister, Fellowship of Reconciliation leader, and prominent civil liberties activist who cofounded the National Civil Liberties Bureau and its successor, the ACLU. The flyer was published by People's Print, an imprint operated by the People's Freedom Union, the organizational successor of the People's Council.]

There are in the United States some hundreds of Political Prisoners under the Federal laws along; no one knows how many more there are under the various State laws. By Political Prisoners we mean men and women whose offense primarily involves not a crime against the common law but their loyalty of expression of conscientious convictions. In the United States this term includes somewhere between 100 and 200 conscientious objectors still in jail, as well as the men and women convicted under the Espionage Law, under which law not one German spy, so far as can be learned, was ever sentenced.

In practice, the Espionage Law was a weapon of attack not only against the Socialist Party and the I.W.W., which were opposed to the war, but also against the Non-Partisan League which supported it. It was a weapon in the struggle against radicals rather than against Germans. That its victims still remain in jail and that the law itself is still on the statute books proves this fact. America, unlike France and England, was never in immediate or imminent danger from the external foe or internal heretic. Yet to-day neither England, nor France, nor Italy has in her jails any considerable number of these prisoners of conscience. That shame is reserved for the United States. Not only are these men and women denied their liberties, but they are confined with criminals in jails utterly unfit for the imprisonment of the worst offenders against society. Eugene V. Debs was deliberately transferred from the comparatively easy routine of life in a West Virginia penitentiary to the iron discipline of Atlanta. This, with the full knowledge of the fact that he is a man well on in years, not robust in health, who finds the heat of the Atlanta climate peculiarly hard to bear. His offense was simply this, that during the war he declared that it was an economic struggle, which the President of the United States now says ought to be a matter of common knowledge to every child. Supposing Mr. Debs was unwise in saying what he did when he did, is that any reason, simply from the standpoint of expediency, why he should be confined now that the war is won? What is true of one conspicuous man is true in a greater or less degree of many inconspicuous folk who have shared the same fate. That fate in case after case has included positive torture. This is particularly true, for instance, of those conscientious objectors who have been confined in solitary cells under conditions deliberately intended to break men. One such prisoner has spent 107 days in solitary out of little more than a year. Others have been for as much as eleven consecutive weeks in solitary, half the time on a diet of bread and water.

The continuance of these conditions is a prime cause of violent unrest. It makes mock of our professions not only of democracy, but of humanity. It proves that as a people we are afraid of thought; that we who were willing to fight a great war in behalf of the word "democracy" will not tolerate that dissent of opinion and open discussion of problems upon which all true democracy rests. These political Prisoners are for the most part heroes and martyrs in the struggle for industrial freedom. It is, therefore, peculiarly the duty of Organized Labor to secure a General Amnesty. Labor's attitude in this matter is an acid test of its own wisdom and idealism. But not only Organized Labor but all loyal Americans are challenged by the very existence of a class of Political Prisoners.

Heretics, whether religious, scientific, political or economic are often obnoxious to a complacent majority. Over and over again the heretic has been wrong. Yet all progress begins with a heretical minority. In confining her political heretics in jail, America is denying her own hope of peaceful progress. Immediate Amnesty is not a matter of mercy but of right, a partial atonement for a great wrong. We demand it not merely or chiefly in justice to some of the bravest of our fellow citizens, but for the sake of the life and honor of the American Democracy. While these Political Prisoners are confined in jails, penitentiaries, or internment camps, we are not free. . . .

SOURCE: Norman Thomas, "Amnesty!" (New York: People's Print, [1919?]).

CHAPTER 8

The Cultural Front and Antiwar Protest

ANTIWAR PLAYS

8.1. Frank P. O'Hare and Kate Richards O'Hare, *World Peace* (1915)

[Frank O'Hare and his wife, Kate, were midwestern socialists. Kate ran for U.S. Congress on the SP ticket in 1910, edited the St. Louis–based socialist periodical the *National Rip-Saw*, and in 1917 was imprisoned for an antiwar speech. The O'Hares dedicated their 1915 play, *World Peace*, "to the world peace and human brotherhood that can be realized when co-operation and justice have replaced competition and militarism in world commerce." In the final act the "Drummer," who references baseball, calls upon peace mediators to end this tragic conflagration as soon as possible.]

. . . ACT III

The stage is set to represent a great council chamber. About the walls are hung the flags of all nations and on the back wall hangs a great map of Europe all splashed with blood.

(LEFT) Seated in ornate chairs are the King of England, the King of Belgium, the King of Servia, the King of Italy, the Czar of Russia and the President of France; the Kaiser, the Emperor of Austria-Hungary and the Sultan. The European statesmen, bankers, business men and the armament maker are standing just behind the rulers.

(CENTER) Seated about a long table are the Mediators—America, Columbia, Peace, History and Democracy. Standing just behind them are Medical Science, Red Cross, Charity, Religion and Messenger, American banker, business man and speculator, and the "drummer."

(RIGHT) The common people of all nations. . . .

[As each makes a plea for peace] The "Drummer" springs forward to speak to the mediators.

DRUMMER. Here is the place for "Buttinski" to get busy. I've listened to your highbrow talk until my ear aches. For God's sake! Let's drop the "bull" and get down to "brass tacks." We all know what we have always fought for has been this (draws a handful of bills and silver from his pocket and throws it on the table) the "long green," the "iron men," the "mazuma." We've togged War out in all sorts of "glad rags" and tried to give him "highfalutin" principles but it was the "jitneys" we were after. But we had just as well get next to this— the game is played out boys—we got to start a new deal. "I'll fight as long as I got a fighting chance, but I am no hog for punishment and I know when I got enough. God knows you all got enough now, but you don't know how to yell "quit," so I got to do it for you.

Fighting don't make any money, it just lets a few buzzards hog it all and leaves every one else dog poor. If you want to see the wheels begin to hum and the working class get into the collar to make coin for you, drop your guns like sensible men, shake hands and don't pout and snivel like white livered kids—be game. You can never pile up any bank accounts blowing each other's heads off—war is a damned costly game to play at.

Over in little old U.S.A. we got forty-eight countries as big and just as important as many of yours. We don't spill any good money fighting each other, neither do we let any state hog the seaports. We extend the glad hand over the state line, every state uses our harbors and then we come over here and clean out your piles because you are always fighting among yourselves. That ain't all either—there are twenty republics on that Western Continent and we don't blow any money on forts or make gouging each other's eyes out our national pastimes. Your twaddle about racial differences is all bunk, there is no more difference in men or business interests between Spain and Sweden than between a Texas cowman and a Connecticut Yankee. We business men used to fight over in U.S.A. just like you kings do until we found out it was a fool thing to do. We learned that there was no money to make cutting each other's throats, so we organized to help each other instead of slitting gullets—now we got things coming our way. Use your forts for granaries, melt your cannons down for carwheels, set your soldiers to work building railroads and planting crops and then watch the coin come rolling in.

What's the fun in being a king anyway when you got to fight all the time for a chance to pose like a cigar store Indian with a crown tipped over one eye? Gee! I wouldn't trade a seat in the bleachers with another good, live shoeman for a pal watching the Browns pound the stuffin' out of the White Sox for any worm-eaten throne in Europe. Forget it boys! Get down and be real, live human beings and you will lose your appetite for war. . . .

SOURCE: Frank P. O'Hare and Kate Richards O'Hare, *World Peace: A Spectacle Drama in Three Acts* (St. Louis MO: National Rip-Saw, 1915), 45, 55–57.

8.2. Tracy D. Mygatt, *Watchfires* (1917)

[Tracy Mygatt was a leading figure in the women's peace movement. Set from June to December 1916, the play highlights the importance of internationalism and brotherhood through characters from different nations. Act 1 is set in New York City, act 2 in Berlin, and act 3 in London. Returning to New York, act 4 brings the main characters together in the United States to signal the importance of peace. The play was completed shortly before America's entrance into the war.]

... ACT IV

[Main characters in the final scene in act 4: the Chairman, a passive pacifist; Sidney Stevenson, an active female pacifist; the Reactionary; Mary Greer, daughter of an English munition maker; and Frieda, a German socialist arrested and imprisoned for peace agitation in Germany, who later sails to America, only to die in the final act, pleading for Americans to bring peace.]

TIME: *Before Christmas 1916.*

SCENE: *A large living room in a private house in New York. Portraits and books lines the walls. A score of men and women, several of whom look fagged, are seated at a long table, writing and discussing in low tones. The meeting has been going on for some time. . . .*

THE CHAIRMAN: I think a motion to adjourn—

SIDNEY: (*Crossing to the table, with strange calm.*) Mr. Chairman, forgive me, but I think first I should like to lay before the Committee a plan I proposed to you yesterday,—the plan for the great symbolic demonstration, which should at last adequately voice America's desire for Peace. May I go on?

ALL: Yes, yes, this is the time.

THE REACTIONARY: Wouldn't it be more respectful to—to the young lady to defer action? (*Waves a hand towards Frieda's body*)

MARY: (*Who is standing above it, head bent*) I think—I'm sure— Frieda would be glad to have you to go on *now*.

SIDNEY: One moment, then, I've been dreaming big this time (*she smiles*). I want our demand voiced in something more than letters to congressmen and senators, though letters there must be, and something more than meetings, though meetings too, in every city of the land,—Watchfires, as it were, Watchfires, burning from coast to coast, that our people may see them far away, and that as, in Europe, the watchfires signalled mobilization for war, so here they may be Watchfires of Peace. But there's another thing to do here in New York, at the world's gateway. We have a great harbor—the ships of the world ride up and down it, and in that harbor is the symbol of the pure and free America, the America that shall be, the figure of Liberty. I want boats, boats flying the colors of the world, to gather in the Harbor, in our safe haven, and one by one, each to bring its nation's offering, there to our Statue, where a living woman to symbolize America shall receive them into her safe and loving keeping; and the people of New York, the men and women of the Melting Pot, shall see it as America's pledge to the future. And perhaps (*her voice grows lower*) perhaps the boats of the warring nations will come forward in couples, England and—(*she falters for a moment, her eyes resting on Frieda's body*) England and Germany together, the vanguard, the vanguard of the new day, of the people's will to peace. (*All look at her, fired at last by her vision*)

THE CHAIRMAN: Is it the sense of the meeting that we undertake this?

ALL: Yes, yes.

THE REACTIONARY: . . . I think the Harbor Demonstration is a good idea. A little novel, perhaps, but, with time to develop it—

MARY: Not too much time, gentlemen! The soldiers in the trenches urge us to speed.

SIDNEY: (*As they all rise*) To light our Watchfires upon the waters that sweep around the world! . . .

CURTAIN

SOURCE: Tracy D. Mygatt, *Watchfires: A Play in Four Acts*, 2nd ed. (New York: Tracy D. Mygatt, 1917), 40, 48–49.

8.3. Samuel Kudish, *A Comedy in Two Short Acts* (21 June 1917)

[Antiwar periodicals published short plays and songs that criticized and satirized the war, conscription, repression, and assault on civil liberties. This short play argues that the Thirteenth Amendment prohibits conscription and satirizes the government's attack on free speech to enforce conformity. It appeared in "*FACTS*," the People's Council publication.]

[Act 1 occurs at a February 1917 naturalization proceeding. An applicant is awarded U.S. citizenship after affirming to "uphold" and "fight" for the U.S. Constitution.]

. . . ACT II

Time—June 1917.

Place—Police court.

Persons—Police magistrate; the applicant already a citizen.

Magistrate—You are charged with speaking against the law. Do you plead guilty.[?]

Citizen—No, sir.

Magistrate—The officer that arrested you says you read the Constitution at an open-air meeting. Is that true?

Citizen—Yes, sir.

Magistrate—The officer said the section you read is against the draft law?

Citizen—It was the 13th amendment of the Constitution, sir.

Magistrate—Was it against conscription?

Citizen—Yes, sir.

Magistrate—Is that all you read?

Citizen—Yes, sir.

Magistrate—Six months' hard work for you. And, remember, when you get out, obey the law.

(*Curtain*)

SOURCE: *"FACTS,"* 21 June 1917, 15.

8.4. Fanny Bixby Spencer, *The Jazz of Patriotism (an Anti-war Play)* (1920)

[One of California's richest women, Fanny B. Spencer was a social and political activist. Her attitudes toward militarism and war are expressed in her four-act play *The Jazz of Patriotism*. Excerpts from act 4 highlight her conviction that capitalism and patriotism are among the causes of war and that women should be involved in matters of war and peace—a view that captures the modern peace movement's progressive reform idealism.]

[It is the fall of 1918, in Mrs. Holden's living room. Earlier, Mrs. Holden, a pacifist, had criticized her minister, Mr. Thorp, for his timidity in refusing to call out war profiteers and those from the Defense League. At the beginning of this act, an exchange takes place between Mrs. Holden; Mrs. McConnell, a Wilsonian whose one son was killed in action and who now questions the war; and Helen, the daughter of Mrs. Holden and a teacher, whose husband, Joseph, is an imprisoned CO and the son of Mrs. McConnell.]

    ... HELEN. Suppose one has no moral consciousness. Suppose one is conscious of nothing but blank duration of time, varied only by flashes of acute suffering. That's my state of mind, and all because the one with whom, my life is bound up has chosen to deny that he is subject to human laws.

    Mrs. HOLDEN. I don't believe that Joseph makes any such denial. He recognizes and follows human laws so long as they are just and pure, but when they conflict with the higher laws he cannot compromise. The laws of God are supreme.

HELEN. And so he must hang by his hands to the dungeon doors of Fort Leavenworth. I tell you there are no laws of God. There is no God, or such things would not be allowed to be.

Mrs. MCCONNELL. God is not personality. God is Consummate Nature. That is why the laws of God permit of evil, pain and death, real and undeniable. . . .

Mrs. HOLDEN. But what is the Source of human inspiration?

Mrs. MCCONNELL. Life is the Source of human inspiration. The Conscientious Objectors in prison prove this. They belong to various schools of religious thought and many claim to have no religion at all, but whatever their creeds or negations they are all impervious to the sophistry of war heroics. This is not from any extraordinary, divine guidance being given them, but because they have the living instinct to see that the moral standards of the time are artificial and unnatural. In other words, they are possessed of a rational ideal. Such knowledge innate and unwarped in the human soul is the Light of the Spirit.

HELEN. Conscientious Objectors aren't human. I know they're not. If Joseph were human he would have followed Dick Calkins [a family acquaintance whose wife is a "featherweight patriot" and critic of Mrs. Holden] to a sheltered place inside the war machine, from which he could come back to me sound and sane. But no, he must throw himself under the wheels of the machine and be ground to dust. Oh, it is not right for him to follow the Light of the Spirit, as you call it, to the inevitable destruction of his body and mind. Even the trenches would have been better than where he is, locked in darkness and filth, starved and beaten and tortured. If he has renounced all personal ends in life, I haven't. I want my husband.

Mrs. MCCONNELL. You still have your husband.

HELEN. I want him here beside me. I care for nothing but to get him out of prison.

Mrs. HOLDEN. We're doing all we can to obtain his release.

HELEN. But nothing can be done because he won't obey any military orders, not even in prison.

Mrs. HOLDEN. He will come out transfigured.

HELEN (*excitedly*). He will come out insane or dead. Only last week they sent a dead man home dressed in the uniform. In life he had refused to put on the uniform and had sat in the dungeon in his underclothes until he got pneumonia and died. But in death they had him. His body had to submit to their discipline at last. Militarism will have its way. What's the use of bucking against the force of iron and steel? What is the Conscientious Objector's ideal anyway but one single, consuming idea?

Mrs. HOLDEN. One single, clear vision in a world gone blind.

HELEN. A filmy dream. I hate it. I would lie, I would steal, I would kill to get my husband out of prison, but I can't get him out by any means at all, because he is bound hand and foot by his merciless principles. . . .

Mrs. MCCONNELL. Think, Helen, we're all suffering. I have a son dead on the battlefields of France. I, his mother, in ignorance and stupidity encouraged him to follow after a stupendous mirage, and in its horrible reality he lost his life. I have another son who is being tortured in the dungeon of a military prison—your husband, dear, but still my son—who, in spite of opposition from you and me, followed the course of the wiser brave. Without a murmur he is making his sacrifice that the counterfeit by which his brother was deceived may be exposed. It is for you and me to give him our moral backing without flinching and to bear his sufferings as bravely as he does himself. . . .

Mrs. MCCONNELL. Some day the prostrate world will know that blood does not buy freedom. Some day humanity will rise in moral resurrection from this tomb of tradition. Then it will look back over history and see that only false or transitory ends have ever been gained by war. In America we boast of our freedom paid for by the blood of our forefathers in the revolution, but now in 1918 what is left of that freedom but shattered fragments? And look at poor France. Where is that virile spirit flown that once caused her to rise against the wrongs of the Bourbon monarchy? It could not transcend the blood streams of the guillotine. As a natural consequence of the violence of her revolution, France accepted the perfect imperialism of Napoleon from which she has never recovered physically or morally. . . .

HELEN. The only angle of the war that I have any sympathy with is the Bolsheviki defense. If I were a Russian I wouldn't hesitate to make use of a machine gun.

Mrs. MCCONNELL. Bullets can't defend ideas, for ideas and lead have nothing in common. The only valid aggression or defense in the whole scheme of struggling nature is positive non-resistance. . . . The solidarity of a group which has the will and intelligence to remain inert till the moment arrives for concerted constructive action is more powerful than the biggest and best equipped army that ever went out to fight. Without the spilling of any blood the industries necessary to society could be taken over and controlled by the workers if the desire to do so were strong enough. The capitalist system is rotten to the core, and all that is needed to topple it over is a non-resistant and irresistible will on the part of those who are exploited by it. . . .

Mrs. HOLDEN. Oh, these terrible years! Can the world ever forget them?

Mrs. MCCONNELL. The world mustn't forget them. The horror of them must be buried into the consciousness of the race till war becomes repulsive even in historic perspective. I would be willing to spend the rest of my life in prison if I could by so doing help to lay the foundation stones for a universal strike against war and its advance agent, preparedness for war.

HELEN. You can't, and you're throwing your life away trying to. People will always reverence war. Wait till the next "war to end war" comes along. You'll see the crowd running after its tinsel on parade with the same bleer-eyed lust as now. . . . Yes, your noble humanity can't be happy without its occasional war spree . . .

Mrs. HOLDEN. Humanity is essentially spiritual. If it were not so it would not be able to produce one Conscientious Objector, but every war has had its isolated dissenters and this war has summoned thousands to punishment for ideals. The power is latent in the breast of humanity to overcome the degeneracy of war.

HELEN. The superstition that war is sublime sacrifice is bred in the bone of the race. The old traditions of war heroism will always be stronger than the impulse to real heroism can ever become. Take the women in this war for example, thousands of them, millions of them, all over the world sitting knitting—knitting their brains out. Why? Not because they are supplying anything needed by the soldiers (the factories can manufacture knitted goods much more easily and satisfactorily), but because it is a war tradition that women shall knit while men fight.

Mrs. HOLDEN. I believe that women will be the first to see war in its true light, though they are the most deceived by it now.

HELEN. I doubt it when I see some of your famous pre-war pacifist women occupying themselves with the milder forms of war work such as food conservation with its corollary of enemy starvation. Oh, yes, war is very wrong and unnecessary in time of peace, but when the big horn begins to blow then our peace societies and our antiwar periodicals suddenly discover that "This war is different; this is a war for humanity, a righteous war, a war for world peace.["] So it is now and so it ever shall be.

Mrs. MCCONNELL. We who know the truth about war can do but one thing—pledge our lives to the overthrowing of the evils that cause it. Capitalism and patriotism are the body and soul of war.

Mrs. HOLDEN. In the universal commune war will be an extinct phenomenon. . . .

SOURCE: Fanny Bixby Spencer, *The Jazz of Patriotism (An Anti-war Play)* (Long Beach CA: George W. Moyle, 1920), 104–7, 110–14.

8.5. "I Didn't Raise My Boy to Be a Soldier" (1915)

[This song was written by Alfred Bryan, and the music was composed by Al Piantadosi. This popular antiwar song inspired harsh criticism from Teddy Roosevelt and a number of hostile parodies, including "I Did Not Raise My Boy to Be a Coward."]

Respectfully dedicated to Every Mother—Everywhere

First Verse:
Ten million soldiers to the war have gone,
Who may never return again.
Ten million mother's hearts must break
For the ones who died in vain.
Head bowed down in sorrow
In her lonely years,
I heard a mother murmur thro' her tears:

Chorus
I didn't raise my boy to be a soldier,
I brought him up to be my pride and joy.
Who dares to place a musket on his shoulder
To shoot some other mother's darling boy?
Let nations arbitrate their future troubles,
It's time to lay the sword and gun away.
There'd be no war today,
If mothers all would say,
"I didn't raise my boy to be a soldier."

Second Verse
What victory can cheer a mother's heart,
When she looks at her blighted home?
What victory can bring her back
All she cared to call her own.
Let each mother answer
In the years to be,
Remember that my boy belongs to me!

SOURCE: Library of Congress, http://www.loc.gov/item/ihas.100008457.

8.6. "Battle Hymn" (8 January 1915)

[This popular anarchist and socialist labor song has had many renditions. This version appeared not long after World War I broke out in Europe. Evoking the popular Protestant hymn, it mocks those who kill in the name of Jesus Christ.]

Onward, Christian Soldiers,
    Marching now to war;
In the name of Jesus,
    Wallowing in gore.
Hoch der Royal Masters!
    Tell us when to shoot;
Forward, then, to murder,
    See us Christians scoot.

CHORUS
Onward, Christian Soldiers,
    Marching now to war;
Give 'em hell and blazes,
    Never known before.

Onward, then, ye people.
    Join our happy show;
Shoot the bloody heads off
    Th' likewise Christian foe.
We are not blind heathen;
    Godly nations we;
One in faith and duty,
    And artillery.

CHORUS
Onward Christian Soldiers,
    Singing in our joy;
In the name of Jesus,
    Kill some mother's boy.

Onward, Christian Soldiers,
    Lift your hearts to God—

See the mangled bodies,
    Quiv'ring in the sod.
Younder is the village,
    Which they've sacrificed;
Rape their wives and loved ones.
    In the name of Christ.

CHORUS

Onward, Christian Soldiers,
    Raise the cry again;
Let us all be patriots,
    For Jesus sake, Amen!

SOURCE: *New York Call*, 8 January 1915, 6.

8.7. "Patriotism Simplified" (21 June 1917)

[The socialist press often published satirical antiwar barbs. This piece, printed in the column "The Guillotine," invoked the Roman Empire and those Romans who sought to profit financially from war.]

Patriotism Simplified

Patrioticus—Hail, Simplicissimus! Didst thou purchase a "Liberty Bond"?

Simplicissimus—Nay, Patrioticus; hath Liberty been placed in bondage?

P.—No one but Simplicissimus would put the question so; but, since thou asketh it, the bond hath been oversubscribed. No thanks to thee, we now have two billion ducats with which to carry on the war.

S.—And will those who have preferred the ducats receive thanks in return? Fain would I rather have two billion ducats than two billion thanks.

P.—They will likewise receive the ducats, with interest at 3 ½ per cent.

S.—Then thou wilt not carry on the war? Methought thou didst plan to spend the ducats, not to give them back.

P.—We have invested them, Simplicissimus.

S.—Invested them in war? Doth war pay 3 ½ per cent?

P.—Indeed, thou art Simplicissimus. We will consume the ducats in carrying on the war—to pay for the ammunition which killeth the enemy.

S.—From whence cometh the ammunition?

P.—From my ammunition factory.

S.—And dost thou sell ammunition and also provide the ducats with which to pay for it? When I desire ammunition, Patrioticus, truly I shall deal with thee.

P.—I but lend the ducats, Simp. Did I not tell thee that I shall receive them again with usury? The government hath promised me 3 ½ per cent.

S.—Then it is the government that investeth in war? And will the government's profits exceed 3 ½ per cent?

P.—Again thou talkest like a Simplicissimus. The government doth not wage war for profit.

S.—How, then, will the government return thy money with usury?

P.—It will raise the money by taxation. If thou were not Simplicissimus thou wouldst not ask such questions. When thou art drafted for service mayhap thou wilt understand. For this is a world war, Simplicissimus. The people of all nations are shooting each other, and all the governments must . . . raise sufficient money to pay for the guns and powder.

S.—Didst thou say all the people are fighting?

P.—Yes, all. Thou wilt know it when thou, too, art drafted. And it follows, Simp, that all the people must be taxed.

S.—It dawneth upon me, Patrioticus. You say I shall be drafted?

P.—Yes, verily. The people of all nations are being drafted, and thou canst not hope to escape.

S.—And I shall be rent in twain in the performance of my duty?

P.—Very likely. One cannot hope for much else until the dawn of peace.

S.—And when peace cometh, Patrioticus, I shall be taxed forever more?

P.—Even so.

S.—To pay for the ammunition that blew me up?

P.—It must be so, Simplicissimus. Otherwise there would be repudiation, and the honor of the nations would be besmirched.

S.—And is that why thou callest it a "Liberty Bond"?

P.—More. It is why, we call thee Simplicissimus.

SOURCE: *New York Call*, 21 June 1917, 6, transcribed by C.W.W.

8.8. Elbert Lovell, "War Time Wisdom" (June and July 1917)

[Elbert Lovell had a column titled "War Time Wisdom" in *"FACTS,"* the newsletter published by the People's Council. In the June and July 1917 issues, he printed the following and other observations.]

Editor, War time Wisdom:

Don't you realize the majority rule in everything—that is, their representatives do? Why shouldn't these representatives be permitted to rewrite the Bible? What sort of Democracy would this be if they couldn't dictate individual conscience? How dare a man dream that his conscience forbids him to fight when we have decided that his conscience urges him to fight?

I think, Mr. Editor, that every conscientious objector should be put on the battlefield at once. He wouldn't keep his conscience much longer or his life, either.

Scornfully,

A. MERRY CUSS.

The spirit of our offer of Democracy to the German people seems to be well summed up in the proverb: "Death levels all ranks."

Judging from what's happening to Democracy at home, it looks as if the aim of this war will be to make the world safe *from* Democracy.

THE LIBERTY LOAN

seems to be quite as "popular" as conscription. That reminds me, F.P.A. [fellow peace activist?] said, "there's a difference between being a patriot and not wishing to go to jail."

... "I thank God we have at last got rid of those male and female creatures who sang, 'I didn't raise my boy to be a soldier.'"—*Col. Roosevelt.* We presume you raised your boys solely for that purpose. Mere useful productivity is disgraceful.

THE REVOLUTIONARY, MOTHER GOOSE

Mary had a little lamb,
One of the human brood.
The kind that plutocratic gents
Conscript for cannon food.
The lamb went out to vote last fall

"To keep us out of war,"
But the poor boob was doublecrossed,
See what he voted for.

———————————

Little Jack Horner
Stood on a corner
With an anti-draft petition.
He was grabbed by a bull,
Through political pull
Locked up—and charged with sedition.

FACT-ORS

200,000 coffins ordered by War Department.
Let Uncle Sam take care of you, my boy!
DOUBLE-EXTRY.

12 July 1917 Issue

A good many people have assured me that when the authorities attempt to enforce the conscription law, riots will result. Then why not prosecute the authorities for inciting to riot?

Roosevelt's spectacular African hunt has been outclassed by our trip. Three Thousand Miles in Search of an Enemy.

Patriotism pays. Never mind the 3 and ½ per cent, never mind the income tax exemption, just think of the spiritual satisfaction of knowing that you have paid for 1,007 bullets, 1,007 safeguards for Democracy, 1,007 convincing arguments against Prussianism, 1,007 friendly messages to the German people against whom we have no quarrel.

HOW TO END THE WAR—Disarm the German people: 1,007 arms removed by each $50 bond.

A patriotic financier is one who offers your life to his country.

"A number of wealthy New York women have pledged themselves to serve only three-course dinners during the war. 'Three-course patriotism' may prove a popular slogan, especially among people who customarily have only two."—*Masses*.

"Raise something for the war" was the battle cry; and immediately several thousand patriots began raising prices.

BIRTH CONTROL INFORMATION.
War is a method of preventing overpopulation. Who said: "I Didn't Raise My Boy to be a Soldier?"

SOURCE: *"FACTS,"* 21 June 1917, 13, 15; 12 July 1917, 12.

8.9. Witticism from the *Gaelic American* (24 March 1917)

[The *Gaelic American* was a weekly Irish (Catholic) American newspaper published in New York City. Owned and published by John Devoy, it endorsed Sinn Fein and Irish independence and republicanism. Like much nationalist Irish American sentiment during the war, the paper opposed U.S. military support for the British.]

If they're ordered to do so, inmates of insane asylums in the State of New York may work on hospital supplies for the Allies, but they're not crazy enough to think of fighting for them.

SOURCE: *Gaelic American*, 24 March 1917, 5.

8.10. Ditties from *Solidarity* (June and August 1917)

[Pithy statements condemning capitalist wars were a benchmark of radical working-class newspapers. *Solidarity* was a newspaper published by the syndicalist Industrial Workers of the World. It included one- to two-liners on patriotism from the blue-collar Wobbly side of the fence.]

23 June 1917 Issue

Every worker in the harvest fields this summer is going to carry a little red book—to show that he is not a "slacker" in the class war. There are no exemptions. Have YOU registered?

When they make a rebel kneel to kiss the stars and stripes, it isn't the flag they want him to kiss—but Capitalism.

Wouldn't it be better to stay in this country and defend what little you've got than to go all the way to France to defend something you haven't got at all?

11 August 1917 Issue

The I.W.W. is not pro-German, nor is it pro-Ally. It is, however, proletarian.

SOURCE: *Solidarity*, 23 June 1917, 2; 11 August 1917, 7.

8.11. Ditties from the *Masses* (1915–16)

[Published monthly from 1911 to 1917, the *Masses* was an innovative radical, political and cultural magazine known for its artwork and cartoons. The magazine opposed World War I. After its editor Max Eastman, along with several staffers and contributors, was tried under the Espionage Act for obstructing recruitment by the U.S. military, the magazine folded.]

October–November 1915 Issue

Italy finds a solution of the over-population problem

There was an old women who lived in a shoe,
She had so many children she didn't know what to do,
She didn't see how they all could be fed,
So she sent them to battle and now they're quite dead.

February 1916 Issue

It is proposed in the Reichstag to raise soldiers' pay to 11 ¼ cents a day. It is too bad to see commercialism creeping into outdoor sports.

SOURCE: *Masses*, October–November 1915, 9; February 1916, 7.

8.12. Tracy D. Mygatt and Frances Witherspoon, "An Office of Commemoration for the Dead Who Died in the Great War, and of the War Resisters' Pledge of Brotherhood to All Mankind" (1931)

[Tracy D. Mygatt and Frances Witherspoon were writers, pacifists, and civil liberties activists who opposed World War I and were involved in many peace, justice, and civil liberties organizations. In this commemoration ceremony performed on Armistice Day, peace activists remembered those who died in World War I. Dedicated to world peace, the ceremony honored cos, war resisters, disarmament, and the 1928 Kellogg-Briand Pact, an international treaty that renounced war. "True patriotism," the authors argue, is the renunciation and outlawry of war.]

(The people being gathered about him beside International House, the Minister, standing on the steps, shall raise his hand and say:)

In the Name of God, Amen.

Citizens, of these United States, and men and women of the lands beyond the seas, we gather beside International House, on the Eve of the anniversary of Armistice Day, to take part in a two-fold service,—a service of commemoration for the dead who died in the Great War, and of high consecration to the peace of the world. This house by which we stand is dedicated to peace and amity. Graven upon its portals are words signalizing the hope and faith that this house may truly stand as a meeting-place for true and honest hearts, regardless of barriers of race and nation,—"That Brotherhood May Prevail."

Wherefore here most fittingly, in the course of our service, we shall call upon the War Resisters to take again upon their lips the solemn pledge of brotherhood to all mankind.

And that we may the better realize the high solemnity of this hour, on Armistice Eve, I ask you to cast aside your several differences, and join with me in your hearts in prayer to the Father of all.

(Then the Minister, standing, shall pray:)

Oh, God, who last made of one blood all nations of men, we beseech thee to have pity upon all mankind. Forgive us, oh God, our great forgetfulness. Forgive us for the long, vast sin,—the sin of War. Strike, in this solemn hour, the scales from all eyes, that they may see war as it is, the very desecration of thy faith in us thy children, the very desecration of our faith in thee, our strength. In the name of thine ancient prophets, in the name of him who lived to preach peace to them that are far off and to them that are nigh. Amen.

(Then the Minister shall say:)

Twelve years ago this very night, millions were engaged in the deadliness of conflict. They fought at the behest of governments. Governments told them it was the last war. Then came the Armistice. And maimed and broken men, thousands of whom had believed they were fighting the war to end war, at last saw peace. But never truly peace. Never to this day. For at the best it is but a precarious peace, armed to the very hilt. Everywhere men are asking themselves for what have they struggled.

Yet even in the midst of the Great War—and it is this which I urge you to consider—they heard, behind the alarms of battle, echoes of men who refused to fight,—"Conscientious Objectors" as they were called, in England, Germany, France, the United States,—War Resisters, because they believed war is the wrong way of settlement, a way foolish, fallacious, utterly wicked,—Conscientious Objectors, because for conscience's sake, like great men of old, they refused to fight.

Vilified by the press, sometimes hated and scorned as cowards by the majority of their fellow-countrymen, we declare that these men too were soldiers,—soldiers in the "liberation-war of humanity."

And since the signing of the Armistice, many soldiers who fought on the fields of Flanders have come to recognize the kindred courage of those others, and in some instances to join forces with them. Tortured some of them were, some shot. And tonight, as we commemorate the soldiers who died, as they believed, to end war, let us commemorate also these others who likewise suffered. They suffered in loneliness, mocked often by those they loved best, misunderstood by the countries which had given them birth, and which they truly venerated. Tonight, then, let us remember them together.

Will you, then, for a moment, with bent, uncovered heads, remember these two groups together,—the soldier dead, and the other soldiers in the liberation-war of humanity?

(And the people with bared heads, shall say:)
We will remember them.

(And after a moment of silence, during which the cornet shall sound taps, the Minister shall turn and say:)
Of late, even in high places, one sign of hope has arisen upon the war-weary world, one harbinger of life and peace. It seems to some of us to say the very thing that we, who are called dreamers, have willed in our highest vision,—the Briand-Kellogg Pact,—the Peace Pact of millions.

And to read the stirring words of its first Article, I am going to call upon a man from that great people, chosen of old,—Rabbi Sidney Goldstein of the Free Synagogue. I call upon Rabbi Goldstein to read it because of his service to Peace, in this twentieth century, he follows the noble tradition of his Hebrew forebears.

(Then Rabbi Goldstein shall say:)
Tonight, like a greater of old, I am told to point the way to a Promised Land. Oh, my people, young men and women of Hebrew blood, born of the ancient faith, the faith of Abraham and Isaac and of Jacob, of Moses who led his people out of the house of bondage, I call you to throw off the yoke of war! I call upon you, men and women of the Melting Pot, to walk forth out of the house of bondage!

"Where there is no vision, the people perish!" cried our mighty prophet. And another, "Beat your swords into ploughshares, and your spears into pruning-hooks!" Verily Isaiah saw the vision. And today in the drafting of the Treaty, statesmen have written that vision down into the law of nations.

War, the arch-enemy of mankind, war the arch-criminal, stands outlawed before the people. War, the sum-total of human misery, stands condemned at the judgment-bar of nations.

You have just heard a Christian Minister ask me, a Jew, to point the way with him to the Promised Land of Brotherhood. Vision came first. Then Law, spurred on by science and economic necessity. . . .

And now I will read to you Article I of the Multilateral Treaty:

"The High Contracting Parties"—you remember the signatories, Japan, Belgium, France, Italy, Czecho-Slovakia, Germany, Great Britain, the United States,—

> The High Contracting parties solemnly declare that they condemn recourse to war for the solution of international controversies, and renounce it as an instrument of national policy in their relations with one another. . . .

And now I call first upon you, citizens of the United States here present: Do you solemnly renounce and outlaw war, in the words of this new charter of the people?

(And the Americans present shall answer, resonantly:)

We do renounce. . . .

Now for myself I covet this mighty privilege for the United States. And I rejoice that a Bill, providing complete, immediate disarmament has been introduced into the Senate by Senator Lynn J. Frazier of North Dakota. "Have we not patriotism, then?" some will ask. And we reply that this is the true patriotism, the new way upon which our nation must go forward. There is on this new way no profit for our armament-makers, our poison-gas manufacturers. But unless we do go forward, then in face of the deadly development of modern science, the race itself will perish.

And now, proceeding to the service of dedication of youth, I will call upon the Rev. Albert Parker Fitch, of Park Avenue Presbyterian Church.

(And the Minister, the Rev. Dr. Fitch, shall say:)

Not waiting for parliaments and kings the people of the world are pledging themselves to resist war. In their own persons, in forty countries, young men are making good the high words of the Paris Pact. They are signing pledges never to take up arms against their brother man. They are refusing compulsory military service. As we stand here this night, young idealists behind prison bars in Europe are straining to catch beams of the new light. Yes, surely, they themselves, the War Resisters of the world, are lighting the new light of human brotherhood. . . .

And now I call upon those who symbolize by their own repudiation of war, this new beacon to mankind, to come forward.

(At these words, four young men, bearing lighted torches, which symbolize the new spirit which has arisen in the four quarters of the globe, shall approach the Minister. . . .)

(At these words, the young War Resisters shall come forward, to appropriate music, and group themselves at the Minister's feet. Then, the Minister with the four torches held as one in his hands, shall say:)

And now, in the sacred name of brotherhood, beneath this International House, I bid you reaffirm your pledge to the future. Tonight, on Armistice Eve, in the name of those who died in the hope that war might cease, in the name of the War Resisters the world over, I ask you:

Do you here affirm it to be your purpose neither to take part in, nor to sanction any war, international or civil?

(And the young men and women shall say:)
We do so affirm . . . .

SOURCE: *Unity* 108 (9 November 1931): 120–22.

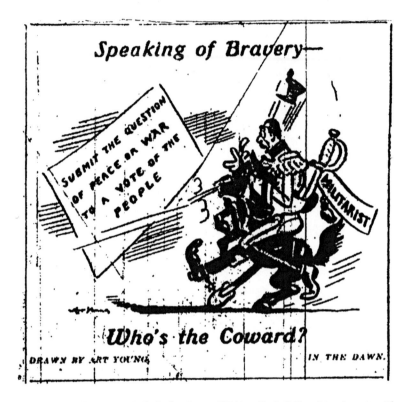

"Speaking of Bravery—Who's the Coward?" *New York Call*, 11 March 1917, 3. The cartoonist, Art Young, was a frequent contributor to this socialist newspaper, among other radical periodicals. In this cartoon he challenges preparedness supporters to submit the question of U.S. involvement in the war to a referendum. Courtesy of Tamiment Library, New York University.

MOTHER EARTH

Vol. XII.   *June, 1917*   *No. 4*

"June 5th In Memoriam," *Mother Earth*, June 1917, front cover. Under the
Selective Service Act of 1917, the first draft registration—for men between
twenty-one and thirty—was held on 5 June 1917. This anarchist magazine was
edited by Emma Goldman and Alexander Berkman. Courtesy of Tamiment
Library, New York University.

The Cultural Front and Antiwar Protest . . 291

"Will Your Boy Be Forced to Follow This Leader?" *New York Call*, 25 April 1917, 1. This cartoon depicts a skeleton (conscription) atop a horse (militarism); the horse is trampling on the Constitution and Declaration of Independence. Courtesy of Tamiment Library, New York University.

THIS man subjected himself to imprisonment and probably to being shot or hanged

THE prisoner used language tending to discourage men from enlisting in the United States Army

IT is proven and indeed admitted that among his incendiary statements were—

THOU shalt not kill

and

BLESSED are the peacemakers

CO in striped prison uniform, *Masses*, July 1917, 4. This drawing, by George Bellows, depicts the plight of imprisoned COs. Courtesy of Tamiment Library, New York University.

Four Lights, 19 May 1917, front cover. Highlighting cultural opposition to war, it depicts writers Victor Hugo and Florence Guertin Tuttle. In Woman's Peace Party Collected Records, 1914–1920, DG-43, Swarthmore College Peace Collection, Swarthmore PA.

"Glory," *Masses*, June 1916, front cover. Composed by Will Hope, the drawing depicts the human cost of the European conflict. Courtesy of Tamiment Library, New York University.

"War Against War Exhibit," American Union Against Militarism. These stickers publicized the May 1916 exhibit in Brooklyn and Manhattan, sponsored by the Woman's Peace Party. In American Union Against Militarism Papers, DG-04, reel 10.2, Swarthmore College Peace Collection, Swarthmore PA.

CHAPTER 9

Peace Humanitarianism Abroad

9.1. The Anglo-American Mission of the Society of Friends:
American and English Friends Combine Efforts (1917)

[In 1917 the American Friends Service Committee and the (English) Friends' War Victims Relief Committee, with support from the Red Cross, which helped to facilitate their work in France, combined their common efforts in the unified Anglo-American Mission of the Society of Friends. This following agreement was adopted by the American and English Friends.]

1. It is understood that American Friends will work under the auspices of the American Red Cross Commission, who will be asked to assign to the Friends' Unit in France workers selected by the American Friends' Service Committee for this purpose from amongst men holding conscientious objections to all war and women in sympathy with such views. The Friends' Field Committee to be the judge as to the number of such workers which it can usefully employ, subject to the approval of the London Committee.

2. The American Red Cross Commission shall be invited to appoint one of their number to attend meetings of the Friends' Field Committee in France.

3. American and English Friends in France shall unite their work in one organization which shall be called—*"Mission de la Société des Amis."*

4. The American Friends' Service Committee shall be invited to send out two responsible Friends, a man and a woman, who shall be ultimately responsible to them and to the American Red Cross Commission for the welfare and conduct of American Friends sent

to France. These two Friends shall be members of the French Field Committee.

5. The work in France shall be directed by the French Field Committee, and by the Friends' Service Committee in American exercised through their representatives on the Field Committee. We suggest that the London Committee might invite a representative of the American Committee to join their number.

6. The details of cooperation shall be reconsidered, if it is desired, after some months' work.

7. We strongly urge our American Friends to adopt the gray uniform which is now so well known to the authorities and to the people amongst whom we work, and which is so definitely associated with the non-military character of our work. . . .

SOURCE: Rufus Jones, *A Service of Love in War Time: American Friends Relief Work in Europe, 1917–1919* (New York: Macmillan, 1920), 42–43.

9.2. Vincent D. Nicholson, Information for Women Volunteers [1917]

[Vincent D. Nicholson, the executive secretary of the American Friends Service Committee, wrote this letter to women volunteers who applied to the AFSC. There were different application forms for men and women volunteers. Men and women volunteers often did different work, and the application forms, though similar, reflect this difference. In general, the AFSC sought women with training in traditional women's work (social service, domestic service, and nursing, but also medicine). The application for men inquired about their training and experience in building, carpentry, mechanics and engineering, and horticulture, although men also worked in health care, sanitation, and community service.]

The American Friends Service Committee has received information from its Commission in France that the services of an unlimited number of trained women over the age of twenty-three years, who speak French, are necessary in the reconstruction and relief work in France.

The work to be undertaken calls for doctors, nurses and nurses' aides to serve in the civilian hospitals, and for women with social training or experience for relief work, chiefly among the large refugee population.

There is a tremendous need for medical and hospital aid. Not only do the living conditions greatly conduce to disease, but very few doctors, nurses and hospitals are available to the civil population. We hope that several doctors and nurses may feel this service to be greater than any which they can render in this country at the present. We may be able to dispense with a knowledge of French on the part of nurses and doctors.

The social service work includes improving sanitary, housing, and moral conditions; teaching and directing sewing, embroidery, weaving, raffia and other forms of employment; providing wholesome recreation to relieve the deadening monotony of refugee life; conserving the child life; distributing clothing and household supplies.

We can accept for social work, only persons who can understand French, and who, after a very few weeks, can speak it readily. Our men can drive nails and run plows without knowledge of French, but our women can accomplish nothing in reconstructing families without knowing the language of the people.

The necessity of a preliminary period of training for applicants accepted for the work will depend upon the number and qualifications of the women available for this service. Probably no single unit will be sent, but groups will go over at various times, beginning August 15th, in such numbers as the qualification of applicants and the extension of the work makes possible.

Preference will be given to members of the Religious Society of Friends, who are now equipped for such service. Others desiring to go, but at present not sufficiently conversant with French and the other requirements, are urged to immediately prepare themselves along these lines and to indicate on the application blank when they feel they will be prepared and available for such service.

Those accepted will be supplied with all expenses of equipment, transportation, board, lodging and medical attendance from the time they leave their homes until they return. No salaries will be paid. All who can pay a part or all of these expenses are urged to do so through the general treasury.

It is understood that applicants promise their services for a period of at least twelve months. If their work is satisfactory they will be retained until they wish to be released.

This work is affiliated with the relief work of English Friends and with the civil, not the military branch of the American Red Cross, and requires neither the military oath of allegiance, subjection to military orders, nor, in the opinion of the committee, any other compromise of a conscientious opposition to military service. . . .

SOURCE: Vincent D. Nicholson, "American Friends Reconstruction Service[:] Women Volunteers[:] Information for Applicants" [1917], in American Friends Service Committee Records, box General Administration 1918: Foreign Service Country—France Individuals: Joe Haines to L. Ralston Thomas, American Friends Service Committee Archives, Philadelphia.

9.3. Vincent D. Nicholson, "Suggestions for Field Workers" (15 September 1917)

[Vincent D. Nicholson wrote this letter to incoming AFSC volunteers. He emphasizes Quaker antiwar principles, the AFSC's service motive, and the need to organize community support for the AFSC's work. Because many AFSC volunteers were COs, he addresses the issue of exemption from military service and references Major General Enoch H. Crowder, the judge advocate general of the U.S. Army during World War I. Crowder implemented and administered the Selective Service Act of 1917. In this role he supervised the conscription, registration, and classification of draftees—and thus had a major voice in determining who received CO status.]

First: Read carefully all the enclosed literature. Also, re-read, if possible, the Central Office Page of "The American Friend" for the last few weeks.

Second: The purposes of our field campaign are to arouse all Friends in America to a group consciousness of our obligation to the needs of the time; to disseminate information relative to the whole program of service of our Committee; to counsel with the Friends who are facing the problems of the military draft; and to effect a uniform and well-correlated organization for service in all local meetings.

Third: Friends everywhere should realize that we have come to the parting of the ways as a religious society. Whether we shall emerge from this world-crisis with our present mission betrayed and our future influence curtailed, or whether we shall find our way with renewed strength and consecration to larger achievement will depend upon the coming weeks and months. For what has our denominational life been preserved if not to spend itself in meeting the crying needs of this crisis, not only in the United States and in the world, but also in the Kingdom of God?

Because of our conception of the meaning of Christian discipleship in international affairs, the present time holds for us unusual obligations and opportunities. We are hoping to play an influential part in the days of world reconstruction following the war. Many outside our body are expecting this of us, because of our rich heritage of the principles of our forefathers. If, however, we are idle spectators of the tragedy of the present, we shall have sold our birthright. We shall have lost all right to speak. We shall have destroyed on the part of others all willingness to listen.

The recently developed situation relative to the drafting of Friends has increased the obligation of Friends to the kinds of service undertaken by the American Friends Service Committee. Our negative attitude has been intensified, and it is more than ever imperative that we give ourselves in very positive service. We must refute the increasing charge of weak indifference and disloyalty by a readiness for the quality of sacrificial service others are rendering. We must answer in an adequate way the question now asked more frequently, "Quakers will not fight; what will they do?"

If any persons are disposed to support our own work only in case our men are exempted, they should be led to see how utterly unworthy in such a sentiment and how incompatible with the real purpose of our service in expressing the constructive principles we believe in. It would be to the lasting shame of the Society of Friends if our attitude toward our own work is to purchase with it exemption from military service. English Friends have given several hundred thousand dollars a year with many of their members in prison.

Fourth: Our Relief and Reconstruction work in Russia and France should be thoroughly explained. . . .

We have now accepted over fifty men in addition to the first one hundred. The Red Cross is ready to use all whom we can send, and the number depends largely on the amount of money we can raise. We have established a permanent training camp at Ornans, in the Jura region. We have leased here an absinthe factory which was closed by the prohibition of spirits, where we will install machinery for making portable houses. In an adjoining camp all the new men will be given a course of training much similar to that given at Haverford, with obvious added advantages.

We are sending small groups of women in nearly every weekly boat of the French Line. You should encourage a larger number of women Friends who speak French or who have nursing experience to apply for this work. . . .

Sixth: You should strongly urge the formation of sewing clubs . . . A vital part of our work is the making and distribution of clothing. We have had manufactured several thousand special patterns for foreign garments. Several hundred communities instead of only fifty or sixty, as at present, should start this work immediately. . . .

Seventh: You should urge an every member canvass for monthly pledges. Instead of our first estimate of $250,000 a year we need over $300,000 for work already planned, and we may need $500,000. The whole Five Years Meeting has given less than $25,000 to date. Unless this sum is multiplied not only will our work fail, but the Five Years Meeting will fail to realize the great awakening of new life that has come to London and Philadelphia Yearly Meetings.

Eighth: You should disseminate the enclosed information relative to the tense situation occasioned by the drafting of Friends. The War Department and President Wilson, in their communications to us, indicate a very evident desire to co-operate in solving our mutual problem. They do not intend, however, to announce what forms of non-combatant service conscientious objectors will be assigned to until it is disclosed whether there are any such and how many. In a sense it seems they have ordered Friends to report for military duty on order to test just how many real conscientious objectors among us there are. The reality and strength of our testimony is thus at stake.

All Friends who applied for exemption on religious grounds should make every effort to secure certificate on Form 174, and should communicate with our committee if it is refused by the District Board of Appeal.

You should tell each local [Friends] Service Committee to send from time to time detailed information to this committee as to all drafted Friends who have claimed exemption on conscientious grounds. Provost Marshal General Crowder has promised us to correct any instances where Friends have been refused certificates of discharge, if we furnish him with specific information of each case.

Our Committee has assumed a large measure of responsibility in connection with the draft situation, since there seemed to be no other committee to do it. The largely increased duties that have thus developed upon this Committee should result in correspondingly increased financial support.

Ninth: Work as rapidly as possible but take time to make the campaign a *very thorough one, reaching every meeting*. In times such as these, when so many are making extreme sacrifices for the things they believe in, we should render the comparatively easy service required in this campaign. . . .

SOURCE: American Friends Service Committee Records, box AFSC Unnumbered Publications, 1917–1919, American Friends Service Committee Archives, Philadelphia.

9.4. Location of Friends' Units and Workers in France (25 March 1918)

[Appearing in a Quaker periodical, this announcement lists the locations of Friends work centers in France, the work assigned to each center, and the number of volunteers who staffed each center.]

Auzeville—Agricultural Centre of seven workers; farm machinery loaned, seeds, rabbits, etc., distributed and threshing done; farm machinery repaired. *Bar-le-duc*—Relief Centre of six workers. Social case work. Distribution of clothing and household supplies. Women's work-rooms for sewing and embroidery. *Bar-sur-Aube*—Relief Centre of three workers. *Blesme*—Agricultural Centre of five workers. *Bettancourt*—Children's Home with a staff of thirteen workers, operated in a large chateau loaned to our Mission, for children between the ages of two and four. *Chalons*—Maternity Hospital, with a staff of twelve workers. Relief Centre, with a staff of five workers. *Charmont*—Home for old ladies, with a staff of three workers. *Dole*—Portable house factory, with a staff of forty workers. *Evres*—Repair shop for agricultural implements, with a staff of seven workers. *Malabry*—Thirteen workers loaned to the Tuberculosis Bureau of the American Red Cross, which is erecting here a village of two hundred temporary houses, some of which are made in our factories. *Ornans*—Factory for portable houses and furniture, with a staff of forty workers. *Paris*—General Offices for all departments, with a staff of twenty-four workers. Medical Relief Centre, with a present number of two workers. *Plessis-Piquet*—Two workers loaned to Tuberculosis Bureau of the American Red Cross to assist in converting a château into a hospital. *St. Remy-en-Bouzemont*—Children's Home, with staff of nine workers. *Samoëns*—Convalescent Home in the healthy mountain region with a staff of eight workers. *Sermaize*—Largest centre of Friends' work. Hospital of one hundred beds, recently opened by American workers, staffed by twenty workers. Another hospital longer established, but smaller, with a staff of five workers. Agricultural Centre, with staff of seven workers. Centre of Motor Department, with staff of eight workers. Building Unit of eight workers. Medical Unit for out-patient work of six workers. Relief Unit of three workers. *Troyes*—Relief Centre of six workers. *Vitry-le-Francois*—Relief Centre of three workers. *Emergency Evacuation Work* at Abbeville, Compiegne, Beaux-Bonnes and Laval. *Twenty-five Workers Loaned to Several Bureaux of Red Cross*, situated at Chenon-Ceaux, Luneville, Loudres, Paris, Compadour, Toul, Lyons, Marseilles.

A number of new building centres have been opened in the Marne region, the names of which have not been received at this writing. An important new development is the erection of temporary villages at points outside the war zone to relieve the refugee congestion in the cities. When the war is over these villages will be abandoned and the peasants can take back to their old homes, if they wish, the temporary houses which have been built for them by the Friends' Unit to be used as outbuildings.

Some of this new building work is now going on near our house building factories at Dole and Ornans for refugees of the recent offensives who settled in the neighboring city of Besancon. An interesting feature of this development is the fact that the large number of men in the two factories are able for the first time to come into direct personal contact with the people for whom they left their homes and crossed the ocean to serve without pay or glory or adventure.

SOURCE: "Location of Workers of the Friends' Unit in France," *Friend: A Religious and Literary Journal* (Philadelphia) 92 (25 July 1918): 57.

9.5. Katharine W. Elkinton, Letters to Parents (August–September 1917)

[A member of the Germantown Friends Meeting, Katharine W. Elkinton grew up in Germantown, Pennsylvania. During World War I she and her husband, Howard W. Elkinton, were AFSC relief workers in France. They were initially assigned to different AFSC centers. Katharine worked at the hospital at Châlons-sur-Marne, in the Champagne-Ardenne region. Howard, a member of a threshing team stationed at Sermaize, traveled to surrounding villages (Marne and Meuss), threshing wheat. Katharine wrote these letters from the Mission de la Société des Amis in Châlons-sur-Marne.]

10 August 1917

Here I am at last in this old town, 15 miles from the front and within earshot of gun fire. I left Paris on the 8th and travelled out here with a Miss Pye, the head of the Hospital, and a Miss Ryce, a worker here.

If it had not been for the fact that Mr. Leeds and Scat were on the train and had me take dinner with them, I would have died of homesickness, for my own Bud left on the 9th for Sermaize, 40 miles from here. As it is I have many a lump to swallow and can only keep up by daring myself to break down. I think that after I get thoroughly acquainted with the handling of babies, I will kick for another job, as I do not think I am cut out for a child's nurse. However, American nerve should count for something, and as I am the only one in all the town as far as I can make out, and there are 40,000 people here—I will have some responsibility. There are about thirteen workers all together here, counting those in the Maternity Ward, those in the crèche, and those with the older children. Just at present my work lies with the babies whose mothers are here, or who are refugees or something of that stripe. The oldest is three and the youngest a few months, and so as there are about thirty in between, you can see we have some job to keep all fed and clean. (Later 11 A.M.). I have three hours off duty now, so I can finish this in peace. The sunshine and fresh air are glorious and the winding roads are a great temptation, but the one that calls the most is the direct road to the front, and is guarded by an anti-air gun and two sentinels, so nothing doing there. Not far away is a factory that turns out machine guns, and every hour you can hear the pop, pop, pop of the new ones being tested. Besides this there is the never ending trail of soldiers and camions [trucks] going to the front, so one feels quite in the atmosphere of la guerre. Yesterday I went to the station to see How [Howard Elkinton] for a few minutes as he passed thro . . . and then had fifteen minutes good talk with my dear husband. . . . Mother, I know, will be interested in the food. We rise at quarter of seven, eat at quarter of eight, porridge, coffee, jam, bread and sardines. At 10.30 we have tea or cocoa and cake; at 12:30 soup, vegetables and dessert, at 4.30 tea again, at 7.15 soup, vegetables and dessert, and tea or cocoa before going to bed. These English are nuts on the tea, but I shy off as I don't want my nerves shattered completely. I am expecting Fran G to stop on his way out to Chaumont, either today or tomorrow and then I shall live for H[oward]'s first visit. Please do not think from this that I am a mass of tears, for the soldier whom I passed on the road just now thought me very gay when I shouted "Vive l'Amerique!" at him, and outwardly I am gay. . . .

14 August 1917

My wave of homesickness has swept on leaving me with only an occasional twinge to remind me how much I miss my beau. He got up at 4 A.M. this last Sunday, caught a train and dropped in on me just as I was getting dressed—the best kind of a surprise. We ate breakfast with the "Hinglish," and then after I had washed my six babies, we went for a long ride up the lovely canal and chatted on its banks. Such visits make life seem worth living . . .

17 August 1917 [continued from 14 August]

. . . This morning I had my first thrill, for just as we were feeding the kids their dinner we heard the anti-air guns in the field next to us go pop, pop, pop, and as this is the signal to rush the children under cover we were all on the run. As soon as they were safe we flew out to see the fun, and there way up above the clouds was our "Boche" foiled of his prey, and turned homeward by the quick work of the gunners. The smoke from the bursting shells hung in the air like little white puff-balls, perfectly still, five in a row. This, I am assured, is only a teaser and nothing to what they have had. Once 5 planes got right into the town, as the Germans had captured French machines and used them, but this kind of thing does not slip by more than once. . . .

20 August [1917]

. . . Today just as I was beginning a letter to my bud, I heard far down the road, the snappy call of a fife and drum, and as you might guess I dashed out to the road, for a fife and drum corps do not go with poor war-worn poilus. Sure enough, there it was, floating high in the dusty sunshine—the most beautiful flag in the world, and under it marched a completely armed troop of khaki clad huskies from the land of Uncle Sammy. I certainly was thrilled, and forgetting all my dignity, I jumped up on our high wall, waved my arms and yelled "Hurrah for America," at the top of my lungs. . . .

25 August 1917

Tomorrow I get a day off, and at 5 A.M. I arise to catch the train for Sermaize . . . This treat in store has made work easier for three full days so thee can see that man does not live by bread alone. Four days ago I was transferred from the babies department to the Maternity Ward, and believe me, I've learned more things than I ever knew or thought of knowing in such a short space. . . . Maybe I am somewhat of a prude but the rather raw flaunting of the privacies of life rubs me decidedly the wrong way—makes my fur stand right up on end.

. . . One very interesting thing I found inside [Châlons cathedral] was this name in German writing scrawled on a pillar: "Adam Scheidt, Luxembourg, 1914." Just to rub in the fact that for eight whole days Chalon was in the hands of Herr Scheidt and his kin to do with as they chose. And it is to their credit that nothing has been damaged or stolen, except a few blankets that they needed for the wounded soldiers of the Marne battle.

27 August 1917

. . . After breakfast H[oward] and I mounted our trustys [bicycles] and rode along a lovely road to a village about nine miles out [from Sermaize] that had been totally destroyed, not a *single* house left whole. You can't imagine the ruin, which after three years is still almost untouched. The little church has been patched up and we struck the 1st Mass held there since the catastrophe in 1914. We took several pictures of the wrecks, and one of an old woman standing in the door of a new little shanty that has been raised over the cellar of the old home. We gave her ten francs, from our store of charity money and the poor old lady almost jumped out of her sabots [shoes]. On the way home we stopped to photo one of the numerous wayside crosses that mark the last resting place of some fleeing Germans, and found near it a hastily dug grave apparently abandoned before their man could be interred. It is a gruesome reminder of the shadow that lies over these bright and sunny fields, and one cannot help but feel suddenly shivery as one turns away. Near the S[ermaize] house, in the center of an open field, stands a rough cross marking a grave protected by side bars. On the board nailed to the cross is this name "Kurt von Asten" (such and such a troop) "Allemande." He is the officer who ordered the destruction of Sermaize, and now there he lies on the outskirts of the town he doomed. Poor fellow, I hope his bones may rest in peace. . . .

Did I tell you of the German prisoners I met one day as I rode along the canal? Well when I got up close, I said, "Gute Morgen, Mein Herr[e]n" in my best Dutch [Deutsch], and the poor fellows looked so delighted and grinned so cheerily that I was glad I had spoken, altho it was a risky thing to do with the French guard near by . . .

30 August 1917

I know you will rejoice with me when you hear that at last the dear boy and I have pulled the right string and that we are to be brought together at Sermaize. . . . Whoop-la!! . . .

13 September 1917

. . . We are very busy here just now as there are 17 women, 15 small babies, 23 middle sized and 13 larger kids, beside one with chicken pox, who has been my especial care. As the staff numbers only 12 all together, you can see we are kept on the hop to get the work done . . . .

20 September 1917

. . . For the past few nights there has been a never ending grumble of cannon just out of sight over the hills, and all night long from the windows, I could see the flashes of light that preceded the boom. Also the star bombs were much in evidence, shooting up to consort with their brothers in the sky . . . Tonight, however, all is quiet—only an occasional galloping horseman, or rumble of camion wheels marking this place on the road to the front. The other night all the American Engineer Corps left Chalon and marched away to the station whistling "Dixie." . . .

Boom! there the guns are beginning again—big fellows this time whose reverberations shake these walls fifteen miles away. Some doings on the front tonight I fear . . . .

SOURCE: American Friends Service Committee Records, box General Administration 1917: Foreign Service Country—France, American Friends Service Committee Archives, Philadelphia.

9.6. Joseph H. Haines, Letter to Father [William H. Haines] (6 April 1918)

[A member of the Germantown Monthly Meeting, Joseph H. Haines graduated from Haverford College in 1898. During World War I he served in France with the AFSC's Reconstruction Unit at Gruny (Somme), where he built and repaired houses and schools and assisted local citizens. He wrote this letter from Paris.]

I have not written for the last two weeks for I have been working too hard getting the refugees who fled before the German advance fed and have been too tired at night to think of writing, . . .

I don't remember when we began to feed the trains at the station but it must have been Sunday—we sent down the big cans (lessiveuses) bigger than slop cans of soup, chocolate and café au lait in an auto with pitchers and cups, together with bread, and passed with these from car to car filling cups and handing them in together with bread, to train after train, with 500 people each.

When night came we were naturally tired; so tired that I can hardly remember who was there or what we did. All this time others were securing the country side with automobiles to evacuate threatened villages, and they were often under shell fire. We had to load the trains with old people women and children, decrepit, sick or dying; and as the platform was low the work of getting them into the carriage was very hard. Everyone was splendid and the only thought was to render service and help in every conceivable way— . . .

Our work continued on the same lines the next day (Monday) except that we carried one stove down to the station and kept things hot on it there, . . . There we made coffee and chocolate and sheltered the évacués. . . . I don't believe I ever passed a holiday in my life that did as much good as these ten days.

Tuesday came the official order to evacuate the town . . .

We worked very hard all day getting off the townspeople including the nuns and their old and sick patients—a most difficult and
trying job. . . .

On Wednesday we got busy again. Mr. Jackson [the Red Cross
delegate] . . . bought a stove, charcoal kitchen utensils and from the
supplies of food we brought, and bread the maire gave us we set
up another kitchen on the roadside near the town, and had café au
lait for the émigrés as they streamed in, and for the soldiers as they
streamed out. . . .

Before I had met with many of our townsfolk who showed the most
lively gratitude and confidence in us and seemed cheered and con-
forted [sic] by our presence, to such an extent that I could not think
of the loss of our material work that has come but only of the tremendous gain we have made in friendship and goodwill among a people to
whom we cannot even yet speak plainly. There is one thought ingrained
in every one of us, and that is that we must go back to help them set
their homes in order and begin life anew as soon as we can. If the
people back of us in America give us half a chance, we can, when we
do so, accomplish, I think twice the good that we have in the past. . . .

The next morning I found the [Smith College] girls established
in a R.R. building with four or five stoves going and cooking away
for the refugees for dear life. . . .

We found the town we were to help clear up entirely deserted—I
mean this literally. There were perhaps half a dozen civilians left and the
Red Cross was in possession of the Hotel which they were running for
themselves. I set to the next morning—after the town had been shelled
and we had all taken refuge in the wine cellar down fifty steps and cut
out of solid rock where most of the hotel (it was full of Red Cross workers) slept. But I went back to bed after having helped fit up a camion
as ambulance to carry the dead and wounded from the shelling—they
were taken to a military hospital and I did not see them. . . .

SOURCE: American Friends Service Committee Records, box General Administration 1918: Foreign Service Country—France Individuals: Joe Haines to L.
Ralston Thomas, American Friends Service Committee Archives, Philadelphia.

9.7. Edward C. M. Richards, "Reminiscences of Wartime Relief Work in Persia" [n.d.]

[During World War I Edward C. M. Richards, a Quaker CO, performed missionary and relief work in Persia (now Iran). In 1923 he published a longer account of his experiences; his later unpublished reflections are printed below.]

In April 1917 I came to the conviction that war was an evil which damages all who are connected with it. I therefore became a war resister at that time. My reasons for so doing were economic, social and religious. In the economic field it was clear to me that war was destructive rather than constructive. In the social realm it was clear to me that modern war was a step backward, away from the democratic organization and operation of society. From the religious viewpoint it was fully apparent to me that war, with its conscription, killing, organized deception and mass hate, was the direct opposite of Christianity, which stands for freedom of choice based upon conscience, truth and spiritual love. At that time therefore it was clear to me that seeing war as I did, it was my duty as a patriotic, socially-minded, Christian citizen, to refuse to take part in it. I therefore refused to participate in the war and became a c.o.

At that time, April 1917, many sincere men believed that the most Christian thing to do was to give their lives in the front trenches, believing that in that way they were helping to do away with the evil of war. To hold my position honestly, and meet such men face to face, it was necessary for me to be willing to do something at least as disagreeable and dangerous, and to do it with the motive of keeping people alive, of bringing reconciliation and goodwill between hostile factions, and to do it using only methods which were uplifting and helpful and beneficial to everybody concerned. I had to be willing to get killed, but to do so loving everybody and trying to help everybody, including the Germans and the Turks, and all other people.

I felt that I should be an active pacifist, not a passive one. So I went to a friend of mine who was well posted on the general world situation, and asked him to tell me what in his judgment was the most dangerous and disagreeable part of the world at that particular time. He answered "West Persia." At that time, 1917, there was in West Persia a combination of war, racial antipathies and religious fanaticism which had come down through hundreds of years. That area had been the fighting ground of the Turkish and Russian armies since the beginning of the war. Massacres and flights of people had taken place, and were liable to occur at any time. The country was very backward in its culture. There were only a few hospitals run by American missionary doctors, and most of the worst diseases were continually present: smallpox, cholera, typhoid, typhus, malaria, etc. On top of all this, law and order were upheld only feebly in this section of the world. Altogether, I believe that my friend was right when he named West Persia as the worst place in the world at that time.

I therefore volunteered to go to West Persia, to assist in the relief work. I offered to pay all my own expenses and accept no salary. I did not expect ever to come back again, as it did not seem probable that I could stay alive in such a country for more than a few months. I made my will, put my affairs into order, said good-bye to my family and friends, and started for Persia in May 1917.

It was while I was passing thru the city of Tabriz, Persia, that the American Consul handed me a draft registration blank and asked me to fill it out and sign it. I wrote across it that I was a c.o. and that I would not accept any service under military control, signed it and handed it back to him. I never heard anything more from it.

In July I arrived in Urumia (now Rezaiah) West Persia, where I was made secretary of the Relief Committee. During the summer, autumn, and early winter, I was busy riding from village to village over the plains, visiting, classifying, and arranging for feeding, clothing, and general care of the 500 odd orphans scattered through this stricken area. I organized some of the refugee Assyrians into a cloth-industry, giving several hundred women work weaving the native cloth which for countless generations had been an important material for men's clothing in the high mountains of Kurdistan. We finally worked the production up to more than 80 years [yards?] per week.

Later on, I took charge of cleaning up the streets of the city of Urumia. This included one very unpleasant task; namely, the collecting and reburying of bodies dug up by the dogs in the graveyards, and partly eaten. The cleaning-up and keeping clean (as far as possible in such an unsanitary country) of the yards filled with refugees also fell on my shoulders, as did the care of the relief-transportation equipment of autos, horses, carts, harness, and the rest.

These activities kept me busy into the summer of 1918. At the same time my constant advocacy of non-violence and the use of peaceful and constructive means only, in the conduct of the work done by the Relief Committee, brought the Christian pacifist viewpoint to the attention of my associates. My continued protest against taking sides in any situation finally forced me to resign my official position as Secretary of the Relief Committee and to give up some phases of my work when the products of that work were turned toward assisting the military directly. . . .

The story of two incidents of special interest in this connection will be found in the article entitled The Test of Faith which appeared in the Atlantic Monthly for May, 1923. Once I faced Kurdish bandits in my home, once an armed and drunken Armenian in our courtyard. In each case I was able unarmed to calm the excited attackers and protect my wife and others without using any violence myself. . . .

SOURCE: American Friends Service Committee, Collected Records, CDG-A, box 1, Swarthmore College Peace Collection, Swarthmore PA.

9.8. Ruth Rose Hoffman, "Report to the Friends Committee of the Year[']s Work Done in Siberia under the American Red Cross" [July 1919]

[During the Russian Civil War Siberia was a battle zone between Bolshevik and anti-Red forces. The United States, Japan, and several European nations sent troops to support the anti-Bolshevik forces. In addition, the Allies, including the Czech Legion, sought to prevent the Germans or Bolsheviks from capturing war supplies that the Allies had provided to the previous, Alexander Kerensky–led, revolutionary government that had overthrown the czar and ruled from February to October 1917. In this letter to the AFSC, Ruth Rose Hoffman, a nurse working with the American Red Cross, apparently with AFSC support, reported on her work in public health and with refugees in the Siberian port city of Vladivostok.]

We left Seattle, Washington, on the 6th of July, 1918, for Yokohoma, Japan. . . .

I learned that . . . St. Lukes Hospital in Tokio was requested by Washington Authorities to send out a medical emergency unit to Siberia.

The 6th of August we obtained our passage for Vladivostok on the Penza w[h]ere we also found the American Red Cross Unit of the St. Lukes Hospital, Tokio. It consisted of sixteen (16) people. They were all Japanese Nurses and doctors with the exception of three Americans, the Nurse in charge, the Head of the Unit and a female interpreter.

In Vladivostok the head of the American Red Cross Unit was met by Mr. Preston a representative of some American business firm in Siberia. Since they had been sent to help the Czecho Slovak wounded they were taken to the Russian Island Hospital in Vladivostok.

Arriving on August 8th, I found logding [sic] a Russian family, with whom I had made friends on the way to Vladivostok.

Soon we learned that the district between Manchuria Station and Chita was in the hands of the Madyaro Bolsheviks, and that if it wasn't recaptured we could not go on to Samara Bursuluk [in the Volga River region, where the AFSC was feeding famine victims].

Having some spare time we began to become acquainted with the conditions in the city.

We first of all visited the city Mayor, Agoreff, a very open minded kind of a man. He had been in America for some time and was very much interested in the kind of work we were going to do.

He gave us permission to visit all the city institutions and especially asked us to see the Orphan "Priuts" and give him advice as to the best way to manage the place. There was many things which the "Priut" lacked but the most striking thing was the fact that there was about four hundred (400) children from 2 to 16, most of them from 8 to 16 and no manual or technical schooling. To see these youngsters run around; waste time and not learn anything useful was a great pity, but it seems impossible to get such teachers in Russia. Mr. Agoreff wished us to undertake to manage the place but we did not have anyone to put in that kind of work.

Then I began to visit the poorist [sic] districts of the city and became acquainted with the Refugee question in Vladivostok; offering at the same time such medical assistance as I could.

It seemed that food and clothing was most needed and just at that time, August 12th, some more America[n] Red Cross people, Missionaries from Japan, came to Vladivostok. They were very pleased with the information we could give them and asked us to join in their work, which was to care for the Refugees, about four hundred (400) in one of the Barracks far away from the city.

As there were no available doctors in the unit at that time for giving medical assistance, I began to visit these barracks, August 15, 1918; I done as much as I could in the way of making the lives of these refugees healthier, mostly giving first aid treatment and taking the very sick into the hospitals. About the middle of September the American Red Cross secured the service of a Czecho-Slovak doctor and male nurse for these refugees. The city office had a large number of families who applied for help. I then started to visit these families getting the histories of the people and giving relief and medical assistance at the same time.

As there were only about two thousand (2000) refugees in the city and having trained two other Russian women in investigating the refugees, I asked about January 1st, to be transferred to the medical site.

I made a very careful study of the cost of food, clothing, shelter, and medical attention in the city and on these basis worked out a unit system with which it was easy for any new worker, although without previous experience in social service work, to be just to the needy family. This unit system is used at the present time all through Siberia in the Refugee work of the American Red Cross and it is much valued by the American Red Cross Authorities.

Up to January 1st, I made about four hundred (400) visits to the homes of the refugees at the same time working out the unit system.

On January 1st, I was appointed district Sanitary Nurse with special instructions as to the prevention of the spread of Typhus Fever as this disease spread rapidly all through Siberia. I was provided with an Ambulance and was given permission to employ such help as I would find necessary for the work.

My work was very difficult but most interesting. The Railroad Station had to be inspected several times every day. All the temporary lodging houses and prisons had to investigated periodically. We had the most sick cases in the poorest Russian, Chinese and Korean sections of the city. Their surprise and delight to see an American and at the same time one that spoke thier [sic] language as a native in those dreadful holes was amusing. . . .

From January 1st up to July 26 I had located and admitted to the hospital five hundred (500) patients of whom two hundred and seventy-six (276) were Thyphus fever cases. Nine hundred and seventy-five visits were made, mostly with the ambulance; six hundred (600) were instructed in the prevention and isolation of disease; four hundred and sixty-seven (467) patients were sent to clinics; clothing given to one hundred and fifty-five (155) bedridden patients, the others being referred to the city office. Medications, eggs and milk were taken to the home of one hundred and seventy-six (176). I also visited many city institution[s], which asked for help and made recommendations as to what they really needed.

As I did not have a physician in my work I had to diagnose and treat some quite serious patients.

In the Spring epidemic of measles, I had a small isolation ward of eight (8) beds with a Russian girl in charge of it, whom I trained for the work. We had about thirty (30) cases of measles. The Russian girl proved to be very good along this line and she obtained work after the clinic was closed in the American Red Cross Hospital. Right along in my work I tried to teach child Hygiene to the Russian mothers, who listened to me eagerly but in their every day struggle for exsistence [sic] they could not reme[m]ber it very long.

This year[']s work was most interesting and gratifying to me, and I am very, very thankful to the Society of Friends and the America[n] Red Cross for giving me the opportunity to do my bit for Russia. . . .

SOURCE: American Friends Service Committee Records, box General Administration 1919: Foreign Service Country—Germany to Russia, American Friends Service Committee Archives, Philadelphia.

9.9. American Friends Service Committee, "A Statement of the [Overseas] Work of the American Friends Service Committee" [December 1919]

[In this report the AFSC summarizes its humanitarian work in postwar Europe, Mexico, and the Middle East. It also highlights the AFSC's commitment to social justice in the United States, a feature of the modern peace movement.]

. . . Events move rapidly and it is difficult to keep all Friends informed concerning the actual work of the AMERICAN FRIENDS SERVICE COMMITTEE. We take this means, therefore, of giving a brief survey of the present situation, future possibilities and financial conditions of the COMMITTEE work.

FRANCE

The work in France will continue until some time next spring. About one hundred and fifty workers will remain there during the coming winter. The need is still very great, for the returning refugees are most destitute.

Plans are already completed for building, equipping and endowing the Chalons Maternity Home at Chalons-sur-Marne. This is not to be a memorial of Friend's work, but a constant testimony to the French people of our desire to serve them.

SERBIA

At the present time there are thirteen workers in Serbia. The Serbian Government has handed over to the Unit a large farm in one of the valleys, twenty miles southwest of Nish. This farm is to be the center of work for the whole valley. Four of our boys are supervising the work of one hundred Bulgar prisoners in erecting two hundred houses before winter. It seems that for the past four years most of the people have had to live in little huts constructed with poles and straw. District nursing, dispensary, and general sanitation work will occupy the time of the Unit.

VIENNA

There are now about ten workers in Vienna rendering aid to the helpless children of that great city. They are working through the hospitals and orphanages in trying to care for the little children. Arrangements have just been made with the Municipal Government of Vienna to purchase three hundred cows so that milk can be furnished for some of the hospitals. By request of the English Friends we have shipped five thousand dollars' worth of linseed oil cake to help feed these cows. The Committee has also voted $25,000 for furthering the work.

POLAND

. . . The greatest need in Poland as the present time is for sanitary work. The Unit is engaged in fighting the spread of typhus, and in distributing food and clothing as way opens.

RUSSIA

Up to the present time it has not been possible for us to get new workers into Russia. Now, however, the way is open and two workers sailed the second week in December for Lithuania. These will be joined by two workers from France and two representative Friends from England. They are to investigate conditions in Lithuania, be of such service as they can in connection with the work of the American Red Cross, and advise us of the possibilities of entering upon more extensive work in European Russia.

PALESTINE

The COMMITTEE has contributed $3,000 for work in connection with the Friends Mission Station at Ram Allah, Palestine [that is] . . . doing relief and sanitary work in a number of Moslem villages adjacent to the Mission station.

GERMANY

THE SERVICE COMMITTEE has just accepted Herbert Hoover's request to take complete charge of relief work for the children of Germany during this coming winter. Herbert Hoover has asked us to bear our own overhead expenses both here and in Germany, while he has promised to forward all relief and food supplies to designated points in Germany free of charge.

We are sending over a small group of workers headed by Alfred G. Scattergood who will district Germany and see that the children are fed during this coming winter. Their plan embraces work in hospitals, orphan asylums, homes, and any institutions that have to do with the child life of Germany. . . .

MEXICO

As yet we have no volunteer workers in Mexico, but a study of conditions has been made and it is hoped that we can have at least six young men there by Spring. . . . It is a wonderful opportunity to send ambassadors of good will to one of our neighbors.

HOME SERVICE

THE AMERICAN FRIENDS SERVICE COMMITTEE is also calling upon young men and women to volunteer for at least one year's work in connection with some great social problem at home. There are many fields for service, in the schools for the negroes, schools for the Indians, prisons, reform schools both for boys and girls, associated charity work, labor organizations, work to improve housing and employment conditions, etc. . . .

FINANCIAL NEEDS

There is no more need for contributions for the work in France. The French Committee now have enough in hand to finish up their work in a satisfactory manner.

The work in Serbia will call for the expenditure of no less than $50,000.

The work in Vienna calls for every cent of money that we can possibly put into it. Dr. Hilda Clark has stated that every child in Vienna is a subject for hospital care as a tubercular patient. It is estimated that $4.50 will supply milk for one child for six months. People who have investigated the situation over there have estimated that in a number of cities in Austria and Germany at least 15 per cent of the population will die of starvation and cold during this coming winter.

SOURCE: American Friends Service Committee Records, box AFSC Unnumbered Publications, 1917–1919, American Friends Service Committee Archives, Philadelphia.

9.10. American Friends Service Committee, "Appeal for German Children" [1920]

[Herbert Hoover, the U.S. food administrator, invited the AFSC to organize a program to feed malnourished German children. Head of the American Relief Administration until its mandate ended in mid-1919, Hoover then led the European Children's Fund (ECF), a private charitable group that fed children from 1919 to mid-1921. Because he did not want food to become "the subject of political propaganda," Hoover selected the Quakers, who had a long history of nonpartisan service. The AFSC collected food and paid overhead and distribution costs within Germany, while the ECF transported the food to Germany without charge. This AFSC flyer sought to publicize the program and raise contributions to purchase food for German children.]

"WE HAVE NEVER FOUGHT WOMEN & CHILDREN"

—Herbert Hoover

The American Friends Service Committee, . . . has assumed entire responsibility of feeding the undernourished children of Germany, in addition to their general relief work in France, Serbia, Vienna, Poland and the Baltic provinces.

Appeal for German Children

The Friends are working in close co-operation with the European Children's Fund, which is giving one supplementary meal each day to nearly 3,000,000 children in nine countries of Central and Eastern Europe.

The Quakers will follow the same methods in Germany. . . . The work is carried on without distinction of a religious or a political character.

"Gravest Food Crisis Will Be in March, April & May" (Cable from Friends Unit, Jan. 30, 1920)

There are today 10,000,000 undernourished children in Germany. A single meal costs 5 cents. To feed 1,000,000 children six months, January to June, until the next harvest, will cost $9,000,000.

Special work planned for children's hospitals and children's homes will require an additional $3,000,000.

The Friends pay for personal, office and overhead expenses. The European Children's Fund, of which Herbert Hoover is Chairman, provides out of a special fund all expenses of transportation.

Every dollar given in America means a dollar's worth of food in Germany.

American Quakers are supervising the distribution of this food.

In appealing for funds to provide food for undernourished children in Europe at the present time, Herbert Hoover said:

"Last year the American people spent literally billions of dollars in saving the whole of Europe from famine. The present cry is but an echo of that which then existed. We cannot allow our greatness to be marred by a failure to meet this last remaining call upon our hearts." . . .

SOURCE: American Friends Service Committee Records, box AFSC Unnumbered Publications, 1920, American Friends Service Committee Archives, Philadelphia.

9.11. John Nevin Sayre, "The Fellowship at Work in Europe" [1921]

[John Nevin Sayre was a national and international FOR leader. He headed FOR-USA (1924–35) and International FOR (1935–55). In 1921 he visited postwar Europe to promote reconciliation and Christian pacifism.]

What is the Fellowship of Reconciliation doing in Europe to heal the wounds of war which are there? Here is a brief summary of a few things I saw.

The first day I went to the office of the English F.O.R., I found it congested with bundles and clothes collected for shipment to Austria. The staff was busy on a job of finding good homes for undernourished children. The gentleman in charge explained that they had already brought more than 1,500 children from Vienna and placed them in English homes. They had now more homes open than the supply of Austrian children would fill. So they were making the daring suggestion that these English homes, which had volunteered to shelter Austrian boys and girls, now welcome in a similar way some of England's undernourished children from her slums.

In Germany I took part in an international mission of popular reconciliation. My government was still at war with the German government—technically; but I, as a representative of the American F.O.R., went with my Fellowship colleagues to German cities, stayed in German homes, talked to German audiences, and between us there was always the spirit of friendship, never the spirit of war. Our party comprised an Englishman, a Frenchman, a Dutchman, a German and myself. In a tour of three weeks we visited sixteen different places, held many conferences with people interested in peace, and spoke at meetings almost every evening. The attendance varied from 50 to 900. We were never interfered with by 100% patriots or police.

Our message was an appeal for reconciliation, brotherhood, conscientious objection to hate and war. We told also of the faith and deeds of the English, Dutch and American Fellowships, and we expressed the hope that Germans might share our convictions, work with us to abolish war and make their contribution in the attempt to build a new civilization based on the principles of Christ.

Our talk was followed by questions and discussion from the floor; always we had a sympathetic hearing, usually a considerable amount of approval, sometimes great enthusiasm. One tangible result is the calling of a conference in Germany next June to consider forming a German F.O.R.

At Bilthoven, in Holland, I sat around a council table with Fellowship people from Austria, Denmark, England, France, Germany and Holland. For six days we discussed conditions in these lands and how to organize and conduct an international Fellowship movement which would effectively propagate the Fellowship faith. There were considerable differences of opinion as to the right methods and means to be employed. . . . Yet in this gathering fellowship and reconcilement prevailed. Never for a moment was the spirit of brotherhood not there. I felt at the end that a vital contest had occurred, but that out of the conflict of opposition points of view had come better decisions than either side would have made alone.

In France I witnessed one of the most gallant attempts at reconciliation I have ever seen. In the devastated area in a spot of utter desolation north of Verdun, seven people had come to meet hate's challenge with service and love. A Swiss, a Dutchwoman, an Englishman, three Germans and a Hungarian were working there building houses for French peasants and putting back into condition shell blasted fields. They got no financial profit from this enterprise. They were up against hardship, a broken contract, patriotic hate, distrust, and more. But they were supported by their desire to work against the evil of war and by their faith that continued deeds of service in love would ultimately prevail. They called themselves the "Groupe de Service International." They were born of the Fellowship and in one of the hardest places in France they had chosen to put into action Fellowship ideals.

In the stricken city of Vienna some forty or more Austrians have become F.O.R. members. . . . I had the pleasure of speaking to the Vienna group and I know how deeply they appreciate disinterested friendship coming to them from the world outside.

SOURCE: Fellowship of Reconciliation–U.S. Section Records, DG-13, section II, series A-5, box 1, Swarthmore College Peace Collection, Swarthmore PA.

9.12. Vesta Zook, "Dear Sewing Circle Sisters" (24 May 1921)

[A 1915 graduate of Goshen College, Vesta Zook was a volunteer with the Mennonite Relief Unit, operating under the Mennonite Central Committee, in Constantinople, Turkey. She served in 1921 and 1922, during the final months of the crumbling Ottoman Empire. Writing from Constantinople to a Mennonite sewing circle that made clothes distributed by relief workers, Zook describes her humanitarian refugee and orphanage work.]

Since I considered it a wonderful opportunity to be engaged in Relief work in Constantinople, I count it a privilege to try to give you some of the impressions which have come to me while here. . . .

I know you are wondering about the relief work we are trying to do in this strange city. Our work is among the Russian refugees and not among the Turks. In some respects the refugee situation is being relieved. Many of the refugees are getting pass ports to other countries. A few have found and still are finding some work to do here. But on the other hand, when one visits a refugee camp, one sees that there are yet many Russians who are dependent on Relief organizations. The other day I visited a camp where there are 1500. I went there to investigate the conditions of a woman who was reported to us as needing medical attention. The room in which I found her, she shared with twenty-three others. . . . The men and women, in this camp, were kept in separate rooms. One could not help but feel sorry for these women with their children who had very little to do but sit and talk day after day and take what food is given to them by the French government. . . .

I am sure that we Americans know little about the horrors of war, what it means to lose practically everything, to be deported from ones home and to be a refugee entirely at the mercy of others. And I sincerely hope that such an experience may never come to our much loved country.

My work is largely in the Children's Home. It can not rightfully be called an Orphanage for we have very few complete orphans. It is a home where parents may place their children without pay, until they are able to properly care for them. Some of the parents have work, but living expenses are very high here, and with the wages they receive it is impossible to clothe and feed the family. The number we have in the home varies from one hundred to one hundred and ten, ranging in age from 5 months to eleven years.

The feeding of these children is not a small matter. Food prices are very high. Milk is about thirty cents a quart, and naturally we use very little fresh milk. We must have it for the babies and some of the children who need special feeding. As the hot weather approaches we are thinking of discontinuing the baby work and accepting only those over two years old, because of the feeding problem. We feel it is too great a risk to try to care for babies with the untrained help which we must employ.

I wish you might see the children as they wear the garments which you have made and sent. The girls in their gingham dresses, the boys in their blouses and the smaller ones in their bloomers often make me think of the Sewing Circles at home. And how the children do enjoy a little extra touch on a garment, such as a pocket or a collar. Blues, with a stripe or some figure seem to be the most appropriate, something with good color, for laundrying is not a little matter here. Under garments of muslin and outing are also very appropriate. Layettes never come amiss, for this is a land of babies.

And from all appearances and reports many, many people will continue to be in need of clothing. . . .

SOURCE: Vesta Zook Slagel Papers, 1921–1982, HM1-403, Mennonite Church USA Archives–Goshen, Goshen IN, courtesy of Anne Yoder.

9.13. Beulah A. Hurley, "Diary of a Quaker Worker among the Fifteen Million of Russia's Starving People" (1 February [1923?])

[In 1921 and 1922 the Povolzhe famine swept the Volga River region. Perhaps ten million Russians died from the famine and accompanying diseases. The famine resulted from drought and the upheavals of wars and revolution—World War I, the Russian Revolution, the Russian Civil War, and Lenin's policy of "war communism." U.S. Friends waged a major campaign to feed Buzuluk's population. In a letter that the AFSC incorporated into a press release, Beulah A. Hurley, a Quaker volunteer in Buzuluk, described the famine conditions and Friends' relief efforts. Referencing the Russian Civil War between Reds and Whites, she mentions Anton Denikin, an anti-Bolshevik general whose White Terror killed thousands.]

Philadelphia, Pa.—February 1st [1923?]—"We were pulled into Buzu-luk in the small hours of the morning one week ago, our car hitched to the tail of a freight, and we are still here in our house-boat on rails. Our last move was only a yard or so to get into the lea of a warehouse; and we had frozen so fast to the rails in even those few hours that a locomotive couldn't move us and it had to back off and give us a kick. Even then we coasted, as the wheels didn't move at all." This is the beginning of a letter from Beulah A. Hurley, of New Hope, Pa., now in Russia as a member of the Quaker Relief Unit, which was received to-day at the headquarters of the Quakers in Philadelphia. Miss Hurley reached the famine area of the Volga, where 15,000,000 Russians are starving, in the middle of December [1922?] and is tak-ing charge of the distribution of the Quaker relief in one of the sec-tions of the Buzuluk district.

"This business of cooking, living, receiving callers, running an office, and housekeeping for a Unit of thirteen in a square box-car wherein five also sleep, is close work, and we have learned much. . . .

"On Sunday Miriam West and I moved out in the night and slept up in rooms in the town which the Mission has taken for its head-quarters. For two nights we slept in real honest-to-goodness beds. . . .

"The reason we moved from the box-car for those two nights was that the Doctor found that Nancy Babb, who lived on the first bot-tom shelf of our tiny closet, had more than the flu. It is typhus and as there is no hospital in Buzuluk we planned to hitch this car to a west-bound train and have her in Samara the next day. . . .

"No train came the next morning either way as everything was snowed up; so the day was spent in finding a room for an isolation ward in the rooms meant for a few people and which were housing a mob of us. It was impossible to secure other rooms in the village for the town of 18,000 now houses 35,000 and some parts of it are ruined since the [Anton] Denikin campaign went across the district. . . .

"By contrast with home we lead a life that in comparison with Spartan life is rigorous, but it is a luxury to the type of life which we see all about us. Scarcely a day goes by but one may see at least a dead body lying along the way or in the marketplace; and three days ago a father and mother and two children dropped in the snow together. At night one can hear the cries and pleading of the crowds at the station entrances trying to seek a bit of warmth; but no one may go into that crowded mass except those really waiting for trains, and so every morning the human bodies which have frozen to death must be carried away from the entrances. Even from among those who have been all night in the station, heated only by human warmth, bodies are taken of those who have died of starvation or cold. The cemetery itself is a ghastly place where bodies are piled up in trenches like so much cord-wood and the naked bones of the bodies makes the simile all the truer. The pile is now visible a quarter-mile away. The clothing is always stripped from the bodies, for it is too precious to be lost.

"But worse even than the dead bodies left sometimes for days frozen in the snow, are the walking skeletons who totter about from house to house hoping to find enough to live on for another day. The children show bare skin as they trot on weeping with the cold. There are not crowds of these, but just a few here and there looking almost like stragglers from an army; and we wonder which of them may be stark dead at the roadside before night.

"Doris White [a British Quaker] is still at the first outpost which she and Murray Kenworthy [head of the American Unit] opened forty miles south of the railroad, and her letter which reached us from Moscow told of the necessity of starting feeding at once to prevent the children from being sent into the town and abandoned. Horses are dying so fast that they cannot carry the food in the wagons fast enough, and so they are trying to use camels, which eat less. But these camels are starving and their humps are usually flabby and empty of the reserve strength which they normally carry there. Doris White begged to have more help sent but added 'Send someone with no heart, for it is a cruel task.' She reported that cannibalism has begun in the outlying districts and that an old woman and a child of nine have followed the cats and dogs which have already been consumed.

"It is colder here than Moscow, most of this week being about 30° below zero. But it is dry and bracing. Do not be alarmed for us personally as we are getting along in a good manner. . . .

"Rest assured that what we are doing is not just making people comfortable but turning the very slight balance between life and death for these thousands, and the more you send us the more of these desperate folk have the chance to live. There is food enough in the world if it can only be evened up; but the actual problem of transport is terrible here. . . .

"So it goes, and the tragedy deepens with the cold. Christmas will be upon us in a few days and I hope by that time we might have distributed these car loads of food and clothing and that there will be in the news of thousands more. . . ."

SOURCE: PG3, AFSC-Russia, Friends Historical Library, Swarthmore College, Swarthmore PA.

9.14. Carleton McDowell, Motives of Humanitarian Service (1918)

[Carleton McDowell was a Quaker zoologist and relief worker in France during and after World War I. In 1918 his sister Mary McDowell, a New York high school teacher, was fired because of her pacifist stance and refusal to sign an unqualified loyalty oath. Here, he captures the motives of Quakers and others who sought to promote understanding, reconciliation, and peace through humanitarian service.]

We went to mend houses; but the reason we wanted to mend houses was that it would give us a chance to try to mend hearts. Much of our work on the houses has been lost; but I do not believe that any amount of cannonading will break down whatever influence we had on these people's hearts. We cannot say *how much* cheerfulness, hope and love we brought them—surely *some* reached them. I believe it possible that even now, when their troubles are keener than ever, their experience with us boys may somehow be giving them a little mental comfort. However that may be, the whole perplexing question of our coming will remain in the back of their minds. From time to time it will claim attention until finally a light dawns, until they finally realize why we came—why we crossed the ocean voluntarily, why we worked without pay, why in order to do this we were willing to leave our homes and our professions and take up jobs we never tried before. And when this answer once comes to them it will never be forgotten; in the intimate traditions of these families will be handed down the account of the little group of men who worked for strangers because of their belief in the Great Brotherhood.

SOURCE: Rufus Jones, *A Service of Love in War Time: American Friends Relief Work in Europe, 1917–1919* (New York: Macmillan, 1920), 226.

CHAPTER 10

Aftermath and Legacies

10.1. Archibald E. Stevenson, "Who's Who in Pacifism and Radicalism" (25 January 1919)

[In 1918 and 1919 the Overman Committee, a subcommittee of the Senate Judiciary Committee chaired by Lee Overman, investigated German and Bolshevik influences in America. Testifying before the committee, Archibald E. Stevenson listed sixty-two radicals who had opposed World War I. This list included prominent peace activists, along with the wartime organizations in which they were affiliated—a "Who's Who in Pacifism and Radicalism." The Senate hearings and Stevenson's list illustrate how the postwar Red Scare targeted anti-war dissidents and peace advocates.]

There was placed today into the record of the Senate Committee which is investigating German propaganda the names of sixty-two men and women who have been recorded as active in movements which did not help the United States when the country was fighting the Central Powers. The original list contained more than 100 names, and about 50 per cent of them were eliminated as a result of an executive session of the committee.

The various organizations named include the most prominent of the so-called pacifist and radical movements in this country. The names now in the Senate records are those of clergymen, professors, lawyers, writers, Socialists, labor leaders, architects, an I.W.W. agitator, and one former publisher of a New York newspaper.

The list was originally submitted by Archibald E. Stevenson of the Military Intelligence Service, who brought to the attention of the committee that there was such a list in existence when testifying regarding

Bolshevist, socialistic and other radical movements in the United States. Mr. Stevenson called it a "Who's Who in Pacifism and Radicalism," and Senator Nelson of Minnesota asked that it be made a Federal record.

A large number of universities and colleges are represented in the list, . . .

The list got into the record as the result of a few questions that were asked Mr. Stevenson by Senator King of Utah. Mr. Stevenson had been testifying regarding the war activities of the various pacifist and radical organizations, a large number of them having actively engaged, he said, in opposing the enforcement of the military laws of this country. He had named Amos Pinchot as one of the men who had been active in some of these organizations.

"If Mr. Pinchot tried to obstruct the draft law, I do not see why he should not be prosecuted the same as other people," Senator King remarked. "Have you discovered that in many universities there were professors who subscribed to these dangerous and anarchistic sentiments?"

"A very large number," Mr. Stevenson answered.

"And participated in this class of revolutionary and Bolshevist meetings and organizations?"

"Quite a large number of them, mostly among professors of sociology, economics, and history."

"It seems to me," said Senator King, "that this is a good time for the States and those who control the universities to look into this matter."

"I should like to get a list of these professors," added Senator Nelson.

"I have a 'Who's Who' here that I have prepared, giving a brief biographic sketch of each," replied Mr. Stevenson.

The list was submitted for the pruning process and some sixty or seventy names were eliminated. Those eliminated, it was stated, were persons who had ceased activities of a pacifist and anti-war nature after this country declared war.

LIST PUT INTO RECORD.

The biographical data was also eliminated in most instances, and only the organizations of a pacifist or radical nature to which the person belonged were named. The list as it went to the Senate records was as follows:

JANE ADDAMS, Chairman Woman's Peace Party, Vice Chairman American Neutral Conference Committee, Executive Committee American Union Against Militarism, Council of Fellowship of Reconciliation, American League to Limit Armaments. . . .

HENRY J. CADBURY, professor University of Pennsylvania; Executive Committee Young Democracy; American Friends' Service Committee; Fellowship of Reconciliation. . . .

PROFESSOR EMILY GREEN BALCH, economist, . . . ; former Professor Political Economy, Wellesley College; American Neutral Conference Committee, People's Council of America, Liberty Defense Union, Woman's Peace Party of New York City, Emergency Peace Federation, American Union Against Militarism, Collegiate Anti-Militarism League, Woman's International League, Intercollegiate Society.

ROGER N. BALDWIN, now serving sentence in prison for violation of Selective Service act; former instructor sociology, Washington University, St. Louis; National Civil Liberties Bureau, American Union Against Militarism, Fellowship of Reconciliation, Liberty Defense Union, Collegiate Anti-Militarism League, Bureau of Legal Advice, League for the Amnesty of Prisoners. . . .

CHARLES A. BEARD, professor, formerly of Columbia University; Intercollegiate Socialist Society, lecturer Rand School of Social Science, New York. . . .

ELIZABETH GURLEY FLYNN, I.W.W. for the last ten years; under indictment for violation of the Espionage act; Executive Committee, Liberty Defense Union. . . .

MORRIS HILLQUIT, (originally Morris Hilkowist,) born in Russia; Organizing Committee, People's Council; attorney co-operating with National Civil Liberties Bureau; American League to Limit Armaments.

The Rev. JOHN HAYNES HOLMES, clergyman; Executive Committee, American Neutral Conference Committee; Executive Committee, American Union Against Militarism; Director National Civil

Liberties Bureau; Vice President Liberty Defense Union; editorial board, World of Tomorrow; Fellowship of Reconciliation, American League to Limit Armaments. . . .

JESSIE W. HUGHAN, professor Barnard College, New York; Advisory Board, Collegiate Anti-Militarism League; council Fellowship of Reconciliation; Executive Committee Woman's International League; Secretary, New York State Branch of Woman's Peace Party; Executive Committee, Intercollegiate Socialist Society; member League of Conscientious Objectors.

WILLIAM I. HULL, professor Swarthmore College, Penn; studied in Germany; General Committee, American Neutral Conference Committee; council, Fellowship of Reconciliation. . . .

RUFUS H. [sic, M.] JONES, professor Haverford College, Pennsylvania; editorial board, World of Tomorrow; council, Fellowship of Reconciliation; American Friends Service Committee. . . .

LOUIS P. LOCHNER, was press representative of Henry Ford on board Peace Mission ship; Executive Secretary, Peoples Council of American Liberty Defense Union, organizing committee, National Conference of Labor, Socialist, and radical movements. . . .

JUDAH L. MAGNES, rabbi, New York; Organizing Committee People's Council of America, National Civil Liberties Bureau.

THERESA S. MALKIEL of New York; Executive Board Woman's International League; member New York State Branch Woman's Peace Party; Executive Committee Liberty Defense Union. . . .

Miss TRACY MYGATT, New York; Overflow Meetings Committee of Friends of Peace; Executive Committee Bureau of Legal First Aid; Associate Editor for Young Democracy.

SCOTT NEARING, former professor University of Pennsylvania; Executive Committee American Union Against Militarism; Liberty Defense Union; Organizing Committee People's Council of America; Intercollegiate Socialist Society; under indictment violation Espionage act.

KATE RICHARDS O'HARE was Chairman of Committee on War and Militarism at Nashville Convention of Socialist Party held in St. Louis, 1917, which reported the anti-war resolution; represented America in International Socialist Bureau in Brussels, Executive Committee, Liberty Defense Union, now in prison for violating Espionage act. . . .

AMOS R. E. PINCHOT, lawyer, American Neutral Conference Committee; American Union Against Militarism, National Civil Liberties Bureau. . . .

The Rev JOHN N. SAYRE, Suffern, N.Y., member of Fellowship of Reconciliation; National Civil Liberties Bureau.

JOSEPH SCHLOSSBERG, Secretary of Amalgamated Clothing Workers of America; member People's Council of America; Liberty Defense Union; National Conference of Labor Socialist and radical movements; Young Democracy . . . .

HELEN PHELPS STOKES of New York; Treasurer National Civil Liberty Bureau; Vice Chairman Liberty Defense Union; member of Council of Fellowship of Reconciliation; Executive Committee Intercollegiate Socialist Society. . . .

The Rev. NORMAN M. THOMAS of New York; Member of American Union Against Militarism; National Civil Liberties Bureau; Liberty Defense Union; Fellowship of Reconciliation; editor World of Tomorrow; National Conference of Labor, Socialist and radical movements.

ALEXANDER TRACHTENBERG of New York; member of Collegiate Anti-Militarism League; Director of Department of Labor Research; Rand School of Social Science; contributor to The Liberator, successor to The Masses. . . .

OSWALD GARRISON VILLARD, born in Germany; editor of The Nation; American Neutral Conference Committee; American Union Against Militarism; American League to Limit Armament; Fellowship of Reconciliation; Interested in National Civil Liberties Bureau.

LILLIAN D. WALD, sociologist, of New York; member American Neutral Conference Committee; American Union Against Militarism; Civil Liberties Bureau; American League to Limit Armament; Woman's Peace Party of New York. . . .

[Others named by Archibald Stevenson included Sophonisba P. Breckenridge, Henry W. L. Dana, Eugene V. Debs, Frederic C. Howe, Paul

Jones, David Starr Jordan, George W. Kirchwey, James H. Maurer, Rev. Harold L. Rotzel, Vida D. Scudder, Rev. Sidney Strong, James P. Warbasse, and Harry F. Ward.]

SOURCE: "Lists Americans as Pacifists," *New York Times*, 25 January 1919, 1, 4.

10.2. Scott Nearing, "The League of Nations" [1919]

[Many peace groups and activists condemned the League of Nations. In this flyer Scott Nearing, a socialist pacifist, argues that the Allied powers created the league to maintain a capitalist, imperialist status quo that preserved their national and economic interests, but did not abolish the causes of war. People's Print was the People's Council press.]

Peace on earth will not be established through the World League plan, read by President Wilson to the Peace Conference. The document is a weak compromise that ignores the vital factors underlying international relations.

The draft of the League Constitution is a purely political document. It ignores economic factors entirely. The great capitalist nations of the world that are asked to endorse the plan are interested primarily in markets, shipping and investments. The document contains no reference to any of these subjects, and is, therefore, fundamentally incomplete. **Commercial and financial rivalries will breed wars in the future as they have bred them in the past.** . . .

The plan is faulty in other important respects. First, it is undemocratic. Treaties are not to be published till after they are made—the processes of diplomacy are still secret. There is no provision for the democratic selection of the members of the delegate body. Under the Constitution as drawn, all of them may be appointed by the Governments. The people may have no voice in choosing them. Again, out of the nine votes of the Executive Council, five are to belong permanently to the United States, France, Italy, Great Britain and Japan. In short, the decisions of the League may all be reached by hand-picked diplomats of the old school from the "big five" allied nations.

The plan is arbitrary. It contains no provision for and no suggestion of self-determination. Ireland, India, the Philippines and China will be no freer after the plan is adopted than before.

The plan is imperialistic. The "big five" are to take the German Colonies in addition to their present possessions. The allied empires will still be empires.

The plan is weak. It takes no stand on the question of armaments, other than to state that they must be "fair" and "reasonable." Evidently, the members of the "big five" are not yet ready to "bury the hatchet."

The plan is ineffective. No adequate means are provided for the enforcement of the League's decisions. The organization contemplated is weaker than that of the Thirteen Colonies under the Articles of Confederation.

The League plan is political treaty of the old variety, providing for a continuation of the alliance among the victorious Allies. This alliance will inevitably force a defensive alliance of Russia, Germany and the other socialist countries of Europe, so that the world will be arrayed in two camps—capitalist nations against socialist nations. It is this class conflict alone that will hold the League together. Lacking such a compelling motive, the plan will hold until commercial and financial rivalries among the members of the League grow bitter and sharp. Then, like thousands of similar treaties, this one will go into the discard **while the world busies itself with the next great war.**

—From "The World Tomorrow" March, 1919. . . .

SOURCE: Scott Nearing, *The League of Nations as Seen by an Economist* (New York: People's Print, [1919]).

10.3. People's Council, Resolution on Russia (June 1919)

[War did not end with the Armistice. In Russia the Bolshevik takeover of power, in October 1917, led to civil war between revolutionary and counterrevolutionary forces (1918–21). Several Allied nations, including the United States, intervened in the conflict and sent troops to Russia. Although motivated by several factors, the Allied blockade and military intervention supported the anti-Bolshevik groups.

Both radical and moderate U.S. peace activists opposed this intervention and continuation of war.]

... This mass meeting of citizens, assembled in the Madison Square Garden, this 25th day of May, 1919, congratulates the people of Russia upon having thus far maintained a successful revolution against the powers of reaction in the face of terrific obstacles and interposed from within and without, and sends greetings of sympathy and solidarity to the people of Russia and to the Federated Soviet Republic.

Further, this mass meeting demands:

1. That in the interests of humanity the economic blockade against the Russian people, which is costing hundreds of thousands of innocent lives, be lifted;

2. That Russia be afforded the opportunity to determine her own fate, unhampered and "under institutions of her own choosing";

3. That, as a token of our good faith, all American troops stationed in Russia be recalled forthwith and enlistments for service in Russia, now being called for, be canceled;

4. That the American Government refuse to recognize, directly or indirectly, any counter-revolution or any governments representing the former monarchistic elements which, under the guise of "liberating" our sister republic, are now attempting to set at naught the will of the Russian people.

SOURCE: "Resolution Adopted at the Mass Meeting under the Auspices of the People's Council of America," *Bulletin of the People's Council of America*, June 1919.

10.4. Louis P. Lochner, "'Stop the Next War Now!': The Present Program of the People's Council" [30 March 1919]

[On 30 March 1919 Louis Lochner, who replaced Scott Nearing as chairman of the People's Council, delivered this speech at a dinner sponsored by the group in New York City. Meeting the following day, the People's Council executive committee adopted the program outlined in the speech. This excerpt is taken from a People's Council flyer.]

A profound change—indeed, a revolution—is impending in this country as it has been elsewhere. The old order is falling. Something new will arise. Whether you desire that that something be the universal application of the single tax theory or whether you desire that a reign of co-operation between labor and capital ensue, or whether you desire the substitution of state capitalism for private capitalism, or whether, like myself, you hope for and expect soon to see established world-wide Socialism, I take it that you want to see the change—the revolution, if you please—accomplished without bloodshed.

With Scott Nearing, I take it, you regard war as a social disease; with him you recognize that changes in society are inevitable; but with him you also want to see these changes come by what he terms "social sanity." War is insanity.

But how many of our friends and associates are there that now agree with this viewpoint? Have you noticed how men's minds have become unbalanced by the war? Force is in the air. Assassinations of political personages are frequent. The class struggle in many countries is being fought out along lines of brute military force. Our papers are full of suggestions to shoot economic agitators. Mr. [William H.] Taft heads a league to *enforce* peace. Children are playing with military toys, are imitating the killing of fellow men. Even in Socialist meetings, where formerly all clash was in the realm of ideas, one now sees at times exhibitions of physical force. Men and women leave church, after having listened to a lecture against Bolshevism, saying to each other, "every Bolshevik in this country ought to be shot." Force has become a national and international obsession.

In short, while we have been attempting to eradicate militarism in Germany, that monster has gained an alarming foothold in this country.

It seems to me that there is indeed a gigantic task before the People's Council. To convince our fellow men, of whatever economic, religious, or political belief they may be, that war is a brutal, stupid, and ineffective method of settling issues—that indeed is a task that should challenge our imagination.

Specifically, these are some of the things that the People's Council proposes to do:

Our Immediate Tasks

1. Wage an unceasing agitation for the withdrawal of American troops from whatever corner of the globe they may be in, and for their speediest possible demobilization.

2. Help to nip in the bud any suggestion of war with Mexico or Japan which our imperialists would like to see fomented.

3. Demand universal disarmament as an earnest of the nations of the world that this shall be the last war.

4. Prepare against the attempt that will be made in the next Congress to foist universal military training upon this nation.

5. Demand that in our schools ideals of international co-operation and brotherhood supersede the narrow, chauvinistic teachings of our day.

In short, "**STOP THE NEXT WAR**" might well serve as our slogan. To make this program effective, our work must be organized as follows: . . . .

Such are the immediate tasks that we have laid out for ourselves. That in addition we shall continue our fight for the restoration of civil liberties and for the amnesty of political prisoners goes without saying. . . .

SOURCE: People's Council of America for Democracy and Peace, 1917–1919 Records, reel 3.1, Swarthmore College Peace Collection, Swarthmore PA.

10.5. Elinor Byrns, *The Women's Peace Society* (1921)

[The WPS was founded in 1919 by absolute pacifist women who, opposing all war and violence, had left the less militant Women's International League for Peace and Freedom. WPS officers included Fanny Garrison Villard (chairman) and Elinor Byrns (vice chairman). This pamphlet illustrates Gandhi's appeal to postwar American pacifists—and claims both Gandhi and William Lloyd Garrison (the nineteenth-century radical nonresistant, abolitionist, and pacifist) as champions of the nonresistant tradition. Notably, the w p s argued that peace was patriotic, courageous, practical, and effective.]

. . . The Society was formed by women who were pacifists and nonresistants before and during the period of 1914–19. Dissatisfied with peace societies which merely worked against war, before a declaration of war, and whose members were not in agreements as to their reasons for opposition to war, these women felt the need of an organization which should be built on a moral principle and oppose all war for any purpose because of belief in that principle.

The Women's Peace Society was therefore formed. It has members not only in all parts of the United States, but also in Mexico and a number of European countries.

The underlying principle of this Society is a belief in the sacredness and inviolability of human life under all circumstances.

The aim of the Society is to establish this principle in actual practice by all individuals and by nations.

Every member of the Society must sign a pledge slip, stating that, in her belief, it is under no circumstances right to destroy human life.

She must also declare it to be her intention never to aid in or sanction war, offensive or defensive, international or civil, in any way, whether by making or handling munitions, subscribing to war loans, using her labor for the purpose of setting others free for war service, helping by money or work any relief organization which supports or condones war.

And she cannot approve of or participate in any resort to bloodshed, even for the sake of gaining just ends, or preserving law and order, or defending liberty and property, or on the plea of securing the safety of women and children.

The Society does, however, believe that any cause worth winning, any interest worth preserving, can be won or preserved without recourse to the destruction of life.

It is convinced that there is no power so great as the calm, unalterable determination to win just ends by intelligent, peaceful methods.

And that violence, on the other hand, defeats itself, because it arouses the evil passions of those who resort to it, obscures their judgment, and makes them unfit to carry out their plans, even though the physical power is theirs.

NON-RESISTANCE EXPLAINED.

In other words, the members of the Society believe in non-resistance, but in their opinion **"non-resistance is not a state of passivity. On the contrary, it is a state of activity, ever fighting the good fight of faith, ever foremost to assail unjust power, ever struggling for liberty, equality, fraternity, in no national sense, but in a world-wide spirit. It is passive only in this sense,—that it will not return evil for evil, nor give blow for blow, nor resort to murderous weapons for protection or defense."**

William Lloyd Garrison

We do not intend to be passive in the face of danger, injustice or brutality. On the contrary, we believe in making every effort and taking every kind of personal risk to combat evil of all kinds. But we refuse to use, or justify, wrong methods.

The end does not justify the means. Moreover the means used by believers in violence do not secure any end of lasting value.

"I believe in the doctrine of non-violence," says Gandhi (leader of the non-violent revolution for the freedom of India), "as a weapon not of the weak but of the strong. I believe that man is the strongest soldier who dies unarmed with his breast bare before the enemy. . . . I want India to practice non-violence because of her strength and power. No arms are required for her. . . ."

NON-COOPERATION.

What if the government calls upon us to destroy life in order to protect our national safety and our personal liberties?

. . . "Thou shalt not kill" should apply to governments just as it does to the people who make up the governments.

Moreover, we think that participation in a war—any war, for any purpose—is inevitably harmful to the great majority of the people of any country; that it is, in fact, more injurious to both their material interests and their personal liberties than adherence to the principle of non-resistance could possibly be.

Supporting a war means, if our opinion is correct, injuring one's country.

Therefore we have adopted the policy of non-cooperation, in the event of war. (See second paragraph of membership pledge.)

We believe that this policy, if adopted by all those who consider war wrong and essentially unpatriotic (in that it harms, rather than aids or protects a country) will do more than anyone else to change the mental and spiritual attitude of society toward the whole matter of organized killing.

(300,000 British men and women who served in the world war have signed a pledge similar to ours, we are informed. Non-cooperation is also the policy of the passive resistants in India, who are followers of Gandhi.) . . .

DISARMAMENT.

We are working for complete disarmament.

Armies and navies are composed of men who are trained to kill, and do kill whenever the command is given. We believe it is wrong to kill. **Therefore it is wrong on principle to maintain armies, navies, other armed forces, or any kind of armament, whatsoever.**

They tell us it is impractical to disarm completely. And we ask: Do you think there has been anything practical about the conduct of the world in the last seven years? We have seen neither practicality nor intelligence in method or purpose. A world in arms has meant a world given over to madness and destruction, with a prospect of increased armament, increased madness and destruction, as the net result. . . .

They tell us it is not safe to disarm. Safe for whom or what? Huge armament has not brought safety to the millions killed or wounded in battle; to the children and aged starved by blockades; to the billions of noncombatants who have lost home, health, happiness, and property. But, **even if armament could guarantee safety, we women should oppose it, because it is cowardly for us to want safety purchased by the lives of men.**

WHAT CAN WOMEN DO TO BRING ABOUT REAL DISARMAMENT?

Organize women of all countries to demand immediate disarmament.

Study the economic causes of war and refuse to be deceived, or to allow others to be deceived, by the reasons given for armament and resort to war-fare.

Make it plain that if another war is declared they will not help in it, in any way whatever. (Non-cooperation.)

Refuse to vote for candidates for office unless they will pledge themselves to work for disarmament.

Refuse to support any measure or any propaganda for limitation of armament. The argument of the Women's Peace Society is that it is wrong and unintelligent to have even one soldier or sailor; to spend even one dollar on war or preparation for war. Moreover, it believes that half-way measures are vicious in that they deceive people into believing that something has been accomplished, and delay the time of real progress.

When we worked for the vote, we always demanded the immediate, universal and complete enfranchisement of women. . . .

We did not compromise, and we won.

The Women's Peace Society is working for a government, a society, based on agreement, not on force. It cannot make any compromise with violence and bloodshed. Therefore it must work for immediate, universal and complete disarmament.

FREE TRADE AND FREEDOM OF TRADE OPPORTUNITIES.

. . . Experience has taught that commercial rivalries between nations, especially rivalry for the control of undeveloped territory and for the investment of so-called surplus capital, lead to armament, militarism and war.

We must prevent international rivalries, if we hope to prevent war.

To do this we must work for economic cooperation and the abolition of all economic barriers.

Would Free Trade prevent commercial rivalries?

No. But such rivalries would not be international and would not lead to international war, if they were not promoted or sanctioned by the various national governments. . . .

What then does the Women's Peace Society mean by Free Trade between nations?

Absolutely no economic barriers, no tariffs, no closed ports, no favored nation agreements, no preferential commercial agreements with government sanction, no spheres or [of] influence or trade concessions, no boycotts or blockades under any circumstances. . . .

SOURCE: Elinor Byrns, *The Women's Peace Society: It's [sic] Aims, Program, and Arguments*, [Edition "B"] (New York: Women's Peace Society, 1921), in Women's Peace Society Records, DG-106, series I-V, box 1, Swarthmore College Peace Collection, Swarthmore PA.

10.6. War Resisters' International, Declaration and Principles [1921, revised in 1925]

[In 1921 the WRI was founded by European pacifists in Bilthoven, Netherlands, under the name Paco (Esperanto for "peace"). In 1923 Paco renamed itself the WRI and moved its headquarters to London. In New York City that same year, the War Resisters League was founded as the main U.S. affiliate of the WRI, though in the postwar era the Fellowship of Reconciliation, the Women's Peace Society, and the Women's Peace Union were also affiliated with the WRI. Rejecting all organized war and violence, the WRI and WRL are the oldest secular absolute pacifist organizations, open to men and women, in the world and United States, respectively. With their efforts to reform society and abolish the causes of war, the WRI and WRL embody the new peace movement that arose during World War I. The WRI Declaration and Statement of Principles was adopted at Bilthoven in 1921 and modified in 1925.]

DECLARATION

"War is a crime against humanity. We therefore are determined not to support any kind of war and to strive for the removal of all causes of war."

WAR IS A CRIME AGAINST HUMANITY.

It is a crime against life, and uses human personalities for political and economic ends.

WE, THEREFORE,

actuated by an intense love for mankind,

ARE DETERMINED NOT TO SUPPORT

either directly by service of any kind in the army, navy, or air forces, or indirectly by making or consciously handling munitions or other war material, subscribing to war loans or using our labour for the purposes of setting others free for war service,

ANY KIND OF WAR,

aggressive or defensive, remembering that modern world wars are invariably alleged by Governments to be defensive.

Wars would seem to fall under three heads:—

(a) *Wars to defend the State* to which we would nominally belong and wherein our home is situated. To refuse to take up arms for this end is difficult:

> 1. Because the State will use all its coercive powers to make us do so.

> 2. Because our inborn love for home has been deliberately identified with love of the State in which it is situated.

(b) *Wars to preserve the existing order of society* with its security for the privileged few. That we would never take up arms for this purpose goes without saying.

(c) *Wars on behalf of the oppressed proletariat*, whether for its liberation or defence. To refuse to take up arms for this purpose is most difficult:

> 1. Because the proletarian regime, and, even more, the enraged masses, in time of revolution would regard as a traitor anyone who refused to support the New Order by force.

2. Because our instinctive love for the suffering and the oppressed would tempt us to use violence on their behalf.

However, we are convinced that violence cannot really *preserve order*, *defend* our homes, or *liberate* the proletariat. In fact, experience has shown that in all wars, order, security, and liberty disappear, and that, so far from benefiting by them, the proletariat always suffers most. We hold, however, that consistent pacifists have no right to take up a merely negative position, but *must recognise*

AND STRIVE FOR THE REMOVAL OF ALL THE CAUSES OF WAR.

We recognise as causes of war not only the instinct of egoism and greed, which is found in every human heart, but also all agencies which create hatred and antagonism between groups of people. Among such, we would regard the following as the more important to-day:—

1. Differences between *races*, leading by artificial aggravation to envy and hatred.

2. Differences between *religions*, leading to mutual intolerance and contempt.

3. Differences between the *classes*, the possessing and the non-possessing, leading to civil [class] war, which will continue so long as the present system of production exists, and private profit rather than social need is the outstanding motive of society.

4. Differences between *nations*, due largely to the present system of production, leading to world wars and such economic chaos as we see today, which eventualities, we are convinced, could be prevented by the adoption of a system of world economy which had for its end the well-being of the entire human race.

5. Finally, we see an important cause of war in the prevalent misconception of the State. The State exists for man, not man for the State. The recognition of the sanctity of human personality must become the basic principle of human society. Furthermore, the State is not a sovereign self-contained entity, as every nation is a part

of the great family of mankind. We feel, therefore, that consistent pacifists have no right to take up a merely negative position, but must devote themselves to abolishing classes, barriers between the peoples, and to creating a world-wide brotherhood founded on mutual service.

SOURCE: H. Runham Brown, *The War Resisters' International: Principle, Policy, and Practice* (Enfield, Middlesex, England: War Resisters' International, [1935?]), 5–6, in Devere Allen Papers, DG-53, series E, box 5, Swarthmore College Peace Collection, Swarthmore PA.

10.7. Women's Peace Union, Amendment to U.S. Constitution Outlawing War (April 1924)

[Founded in 1921, the Women's Peace Union drafted a constitutional amendment to outlaw war in 1923 and persuaded Senator Lynn J. Frazier (R-ND) to sponsor the measure, in a revised form. Frazier introduced the amendment in every congressional session between 1926 and 1939. Elinor Byrns and Caroline Lexow Babcock wrote the original WPU amendment.]

Section 1—War for any purpose shall be illegal, and neither the United States nor any State, Territory, association or person subject to its jurisdiction shall prepare for, declare, engage in or carry on war or other armed conflict, expedition, invasion or undertaking within or without the United States, nor shall any funds be raised, appropriated or expended for such purpose.

Section 2—All provisions of the Constitution and of the articles in addition thereto and amendments thereof which are in conflict with or inconsistent with this article are hereby rendered null and void and of no effect.

Section 3—The Congress shall have power to enact appropriate legislation to give effect to this article.

SOURCE: "Making War Illegal," *New York Times*, 24 April 1926, 5.

10.8. Students at Howard University Strike for Peace (June 1925)

[The following was recorded in a monthly newsletter of the U.S. Section of the WILPF. In the mid-1920s there was widespread debate over colleges and universities establishing mandatory Reserve Officers' Training Corps. In Washington DC, at Howard University, a historically black college, students went on strike to protest the dismissal of five students who refused to participate in the program.]

The students of Howard University—some 400—went on strike recently. They formed a parade, sang songs and bore placards which read, "What is this going to be—an army or a university?"

"Before we will be slaves, we will be in our graves."

"Don't be an Uncle Tom."

This demonstration was a protest against compulsory drills, against maintaining a "Reserve Officers' Training Corps."

The students further demanded reinstatement of five anti-militarists dismissed by the President of the University, and swore to "cut" their classes as far as necessary to adjust their rights.

SOURCE: "Anti-militarists," *Pax Special* (U.S. Section–WILPF) 1 (June 1925): 1, in Women's International League for Peace and Freedom, U.S. Section Records, DG-43, Microfilm Edition (Scholarly Resources), reel 130.93, Swarthmore College Peace Collection, Swarthmore PA.

10.9. Brown University Students' Petition against War (23 March 1933)

[In February 1933, ten days after Hitler was appointed chancellor, the Oxford Union Society, a debating society in Oxford, England, resolved that "this House will in no circumstances fight for its King and Country." Inspired by the Oxford Pledge, Brown University was the first U.S. university to follow suit. In a 22 March editorial, "War Against War," Brown's student newspaper, the *Daily Herald*, editorialized that "civilization cannot stand the shock of another armed conflict." The next day it published a pledge (petition), mailed to 145 U.S. colleges, that called for an end to war and militarism.]

A PETITION

WHEREAS: We believe that war is futile and destructive and should be abandoned as an instrument of international action, and

WHEREAS: We believe that it is to the best interests of the United States and other nations that peace be maintained, and

WHEREAS: We believe that peace can only be maintained by open opposition to the selfish interests that promote war, and

WHEREAS: We believe that increasing militarism and nationalism in the United States must be opposed by united action, and

WHEREAS: We believe that war is only justified in case of invasion of the mainland of the United States by a hostile power, and

WHEREAS: We believe that the united refusal of the youth of America to bear arms, except in case of invasion, will do much to prevent war,

WE, the undersigned students of Brown University pledge ourselves not to bear arms, except in case of the invasion of the mainland of the United States, and to work actively for the organization of the world on a peace basis.

| NAME | ADDRESS | CITY | STATE |

LETTER TO 145 COLLEGES

In an effort to unite the students of the United States in a drive against war and militaristic propaganda, the *Brown Daily Herald* is asking your cooperation and that of one hundred and forty-five other college newspaper editors in a nation-wide peace movement. We believe that if a sufficient number of college students sign a pledge not to bear arms, except in case of an invasion of the United States, much will be done for the advancement of peace. It is our hope that by an active campaign in the columns of your newspaper, and by other methods you may devise, you will be able to have the majority of the students at your university sign this pledge . . . .

. . . Interviews with prominent men on this subject will be secured by the *Daily Herald* and sent to the newspapers cooperating in this movement for simultaneous publication. Other papers in the South, Middle-West, and West will be expected to perform the same service in order that there may be an interchange of ideas and opinions in different sections of the country.

Colleges will report on the progress of the campaign to the *Daily Herald* weekly, and results will be tabulated and telegraphed to all the newspapers. On a set date the drive will end, and a copy of all the pledges sent to Providence. A committee representing the *Daily Herald* will personally present them to the President of the United States. . . .

P.S.—Enclose[d] you will find a copy of the petition to be used at Brown. We would like you to use this form.

SOURCE: "A Petition" and "Letter to 145 Colleges," *Brown Daily Herald*, 23 March 1933, 1, 4, in John Hay Library, Brown University Library, Providence RI.

10.10. Devere Allen, New War Objectors and International Pacifism (1930)

[Devere Allen opposed World War I and became a prominent pacifist, socialist, and journalist during the interwar period. He edited the *World Tomorrow* (1921–33), a magazine published by the Fellowship of Reconciliation; established the No-Frontier News Service (1933); and wrote *The Fight for Peace* (1930). His views reflected the more radical-minded peace advocates who came of age after the war. In this passage he discusses the political objectors who dissented from the war and the international pacifist movement that emerged from the conflict. The secular postwar pacifist movement, he notes, sought to abolish war—and, by transforming society, the causes of war.]

With the World War a new type of objector arose. The growing radical labor movement produced a great many who did not follow the nationalist opportunism of the Socialist and Labor organizations in most of the belligerent countries. These Socialist objectors were occasionally believers in no war at all, on grounds of economic and political labor solidarity rather than religion; sometimes, in the United States at least, they would have fought in a class war against capitalist rule, but in an international conflict they would not support the government. If anyone desires to quarrel with this logic, let it not be that person who is against class war but believes every good citizen should come when his *country* calls! The political objectors were less than one-tenth of them all. . . .

. . . *What did the war objectors accomplish?* The answer is not yet [known]. But certain things are clear.

They demonstrated the possibility of a fidelity to vision and principle under strenuous compulsion. . . .

They carried on the torch of pacifist illumination which has been tended by faithful hands in nearly every generation of world history. . . .

They have directly opposed to the path of conscription the rights of conscience. . . .

They forced the pacifist method of social progress upon the attention of thousands who had never heard or thought of it. . . .

They have already cast a shadow across the path of the war-making authorities which is foreboding and which presages a more serious obstacle in the event of another upthrust from hell. They have paved the way for gigantic demonstrations, since the War, of hundreds of thousands who have pledged themselves openly, defiantly, against all participation in the entirely possible "next war." . . . As Norman Thomas has tellingly said:

This insignificant fraction of the youth of America challenged the power of the state when it was mightiest and the philosophy of war when it was most pervasive. They said, "You may kill us but you can't make us fight against our will." . . .

The fact that the government was forced to treat with these men at all, that it dared not kill them and could not force them to kill is a significant precedent. In this war the objectors were few. But the memory of their defiance may some day help to break the spell which holds the patient masses like dumb, driven cattle in obedience to the financiers and diplomats for whose intrigues they pay with their lives under the grip of "the homicidal mania men call patriotism."

"The objectors were few." But another time they will be multiplied and strengthened; and before that time their voices are being raised in a mighty shout that must be heeded. . . .

There was every reason to expect that when the War was over, conscientious objection was also over. A war objector in time of peace was something of an anomaly. . . .

But that is not what happened. There were those who did all this; but there were more who sought out places where they could work directly for the transformation of the social order. The ranting of the anti-pacifist alarmists has this much real foundation: all through the professions which enable them to reach the ears of people, young and old, have gone these war-tried pacifists not to spread an unthinking, propagandist pacifism but to make those whom they might influence think their own way through the place of modern war in the lives of men, or even more, the place of men in modern war.

But there was more. There was a permanence about this pacifism that had not been known before. The men and women who from inside and outside prison had fought against the War found in the rapidly growing youth movements all around the world a ready response to their thoroughgoing pacifism. These movements in many places have begun to die, as all good men and movements must; and in some others as in the United States, they hardly came alive. But from their ranks have emerged some of the most determined and most thoughtful fighters in the struggle to abolish war.

This time the number was too large to fade away in the aftermath of the War; too large, too well informed, too saturated with the social point of view. Organization became imperative. From England and the English war objectors came the impetus which formed the War Resisters' International. . . .

But not only is war resistance based to-day on a somewhat new ambition. It is an international movement. . . .

. . . Here are the forty societies of the War Resisters' International [including FOR, the WRL, WPS, and WPU in the United States]. . . .

The International Fellowship of Reconciliation has sought to further the principles of Jesus amidst the conflict-problems of the world, and as a solvent for these problems, is organized in twenty-six countries. All of these sections, while varying in social philosophy from generally radical to generally conservative, are united in their refusal to sanction war.

Thus it can hardly be denied that the world is ringed by a movement which, though as yet not wholly united, is strong enough to establish in most places a nucleus of war resistance. The total number is impossible to estimate; but including those of all ages, it is certain that the war-resisting pacifists of the world to-day must be counted in hundreds of thousands. . . .

. . . *Pacifism contributes to the removal of war's causes by its efforts for inter-racial, international, and economic justice.* . . .

SOURCE: Devere Allen, *The Fight for Peace* (New York: Macmillan, 1930), 591, 597–600, 603–5, 609, 665.

10.11. Howard Kester, "Report of Howard Kester" (November 1933)

[One of the benchmarks of the modern peace movement has been the promotion of racial understanding, economic fairness, and social justice, not just opposition to war. As FOR's southern secretary, Howard Kester sought to promote radical Christian pacifism to southern blacks and whites. His commitment to interracialism and working-class justice is evident in this report.]

The increasing severity of the economic crisis has not only multiplied but deepened the already difficult task the Fellowship of Reconciliation has undertaken in the South. The terrific power of the anti-social forces in that region has steadily driven the Fellowship into the position of a revolutionary movement. In doing this we have merely accepted the historic position of Jesus who definitely recognized the class struggle and set his face steadfastly against the oppressors of the poor, the weak and the disinherited.

During the course of the year I filled 126 speaking engagements before students, ministers, social workers, church societies, fraternal organizations, women's clubs, Jewish societies, labor unions, political groups, farmers, working men and women and the unemployed.

. . . I led the discussion group on economic problems at the Student Interracial Conference held in Atlanta last Christmas. . . . I also spoke before the Continental Congress on Economic Reconstruction in Washington, D.C. . . . Other outstanding meetings in which I actively participated were a huge mass meeting in Birmingham on Scottsboro; . . . and before the Rural and Mountain Workers Conference of the Congregational Church. . . .

Through the Industrial Secretary of the Nashville Y.M.C.A., I gave a six weeks' course on economic and political problems to a large class of working girls employed in the mills, factories and shops of the city. I gave three lectures on interracial and international problems at the Southern Summer School at Weaverville, N.C. During the winter I personally organized a class of unemployed and employed workers in a night school which ran for eight weeks. . . . On several occasions I spoke at the Highlander Folk School. . . .

In Nashville I was instrumental in getting a library established in one of the downtown lodges for the use of unprivileged Negroes, and in getting the fraternal society to put on a program of adult education affecting at least 4,000 persons.

A large part of our membership in the South, particularly in Nashville, are active Socialists. Due to the Fellowship's position on segregation and jimcrowism we have been able to build a strong Socialist movement which cuts across all racial and religious lines. I have served as secretary of the Nashville local since it was organized and for a time served as secretary to the State Executive Committee. I wrote the constitution for the Party in the State and succeeded in getting through a clause condemning jimcrowism in locals and any sort of discrimination against Negroes, and giving the State Executive Committees the right to revoke the charter of any branch or local permitting discrimination of any sort.

I was a candidate for Congress on the Socialist ticket and polled over 1,000 votes in Davidson County, which was half the number polled by my Republican opponent.

On the 8th of July, 1932, miners at the Fentress Coal and Coke company at Wilder, Tennessee and at the adjoining town of Davidson came out on strike.

A small group of interested people in Nashville were called together to consider methods and means of doing something about the strike. At this time troops had already been sent into the strike zone and appalling conditions existed among the strikers. . . . The Wilder Emergency Relief Committee was then organized. Appeals for food, clothing and funds were made, meetings arranged for and Alice Kester and I asked to administer the relief for the Committee. Later we got invaluable help from the Emergency Committee for Strikers' Relief, of which Norman Thomas is chairman, and from the Church Emergency Relief Committee . . .

When it became apparent to the operators of the Fentress Coal and Coke Company that the strikers were preparing for another winter of struggle, they decided to try to break the strike by removing the leaders. It was generally known that "Barney" Graham, militant leader of the Wilder strikers and several other men would be killed at the first opportunity. On Saturday, April 29th . . . Graham promised me that afternoon that he would go with me to Washington to attend the Continental Congress. When we parted, he said, "Well, if I'm here Thursday I'll go with you." In less than 28 hours he had been murdered by company gunmen on the public highway in Wilder. Ten bullets had entered his body from three types of guns. His head had been beaten in with the butt of a gun. Over his body the private policemen quickly placed a machine gun to keep any strikers from approaching him.

I was in Wilder by 2:30 the following morning. I helped with the funeral arrangements, spoke to the crowd of 1,500 gathered at the grave and did what little I could to keep hell from popping loose between the strikers, guards and scabs.

Our work has been greatly expanded and is immensely more vital than ever before. While the year has been marked by tragedy and madness it has been for me the most satisfying period of my life for I have felt that I was helping to prepare the bier of a dying civilization and sharing in the birth pangs of a society struggling to be born.

SOURCE: *News Letter* (FOR), November 1933, 6–7, copy in Swarthmore College Peace Collection, Swarthmore PA.

10.12. Senate Report, "Special Committee on Investigation of the Munitions Industry" (June 1936)

[Chaired by Senator Gerald P. Nye (R-ND), the Special Committee on Investigation of the Munitions Industry conducted hearings between 1934 and 1936. In part the committee's investigation was prompted by the publication of best-selling books contending that munitions manufacturers persuaded the U.S. government to enter World War I. Excerpted below are the committee's findings on the U.S. munitions trade during World War I and its recommendation for an arms embargo and neutrality legislation to keep America out of future wars.]

CHAPTER II. THE WAR-TIME TRAFFIC
IN MUNITIONS AND SUPPLIES.

Although the American trade with the Allies included all manner of war materials, of which munitions was simply one part—a very important part—the munitions trade did more to arouse antagonism between this country and Germany and sow seeds of hatred than did any other materials of war. The emotions of the Germans, as well as of a large number of Americans, became excited, naturally enough, over the fact that these munitions were used to kill German soldiers and that these materials of murder were being supplied in unlimited quantities to the Allies from the United States. Germany was, of course, cut off from this as from all other trade with the United States. . . .

Trade in all materials of use in the conduct of war grew to great figures. In explosives alone as a part of the munitions trade, which is here specifically under consideration, the export figures jumped from approximately $10,000,000, on June 30, 1914, to $189,000,000 on June 30, 1915, to $715,000,000 on June 30, 1916. It is not strange that Germany found it difficult to look upon our policy in this regard as particularly neutral. As the late Joseph V. Fuller, former Chief of the Research Section in the Division of Publications in the Department of State, has pointed out:

> . . . [T]he Germans would not have minded so much the sale of goods clearly contraband of war to the Allies had they themselves been able

to obtain freely foodstuffs, cotton, copper, and other materials of debatably contraband character directly or through their neutral neighbors. Conversely, they would not have minded so much the general blockade imposed upon them had it been partly equalized by an American embargo on the shipment of military supplies to their enemies. . . .

The best general resume of this whole subject is contained in the note to the United States Government from the Austro-Hungarian Government, on June 29, 1915, relative to the shipment of arms and ammunition by citizens of the United States to Great Britain and her allies, and the reply thereto. After commenting upon the enormous traffic in munitions of war between the United States and Great Britain while Austria-Hungary and Germany had been absolutely excluded from the American market, the Austro-Hungarian Government wondered whether the attitude of strict neutrality of the American Government did not, under the conditions which have developed during the course of the war, in actuality thwart the very intention to remain strictly neutral. The American reply which stated . . . the attitude of this Government with regard to the munitions trade with the Allies, reiterated the strictly legal ground for this attitude of strict neutrality and refused to admit any of the Austro-Hungarian contentions [from page 26: "For the Government of the United States itself to sell to a belligerent nation would be an unneutral act, but for a private individual to sell to a belligerent any product of the United States is neither unlawful nor unneutral, nor within the power of the Executive to prevent or control"]. . . .

The Administration was never unaware of the risks to the United States which attended the tremendous one-sided traffic in arms. On January 11, 1916, Prof. Charles Cheney Hyde, one of America's foremost international lawyers, submitted to Secretary Lansing for his consideration a paper in which he pointed out very lucidly the dangers implicit in the vast war traffic with the Allies that had grown up in America and in which he urged the desirability and justification for this Government to place an embargo on arms to the belligerent nations in order to safeguard its own rights. . . .

This chapter indicates the desirability of adopting strong neutrality legislation before war breaks out. It was consistently emphasized by the administration during the last war that it could not impose an embargo on arms during the progress of the war without being accused of favoring one side in the struggle. The argument that such legislation could not be adopted "while a war is in progress" was applied with vigor to the proposed arms-embargo resolutions. A tremendous trade in arms and war materials with its attendant boom in those industries was permitted to grow up in this country and in its effects on our economic and financial structure to jeopardize very definitely the neutrality we were seeking to preserve so carefully by disallowing any embargo on such materials of war. It seems evident from the present chapter that legislation envisaging an automatic embargo on arms and war supplies imposed upon both sets of belligerents at the outset of a war would constitute an essential part of a permanent neutrality policy.

SOURCE: *Munitions Industry: Report on Existing Legislation; Special Committee on Investigation of the Munitions Industry, United States Senate, S. Res. 206, a Resolution to Make Certain Investigations Concerning the Manufacture and Sale of Arms and Other War Munitions*, Report No. 944, 74th Cong., 2nd sess. (Washington DC: Government Printing Office, 1936), pt. 5, 3:25–26, 29, 31, 33.

10.13. Smedley D. Butler, "To Hell with War!" (1935)

[Major General Smedley D. Butler was a highly decorated Marine Corps combat officer who, as a boy, was raised in the spirit of Pennsylvania Quakerism. By 1914 he had been awarded two Medals of Honor. During World War I he served as commander of the Brest, France, embarkation center for returning U.S. troops. Retiring in 1931, he went on lecture tours on behalf of world peace and denounced military intervention, war profiteering, and fascism. This excerpt is taken from a pamphlet based on his speeches.]

I am not such a fool as to believe that war is a thing of the past. . . .

Looking back, Woodrow Wilson was re-elected president in 1916 on a platform that he had "kept us out of war" and on the implied promise that he would "keep us out of war." Yet, five months later he asked Congress to declare war on Germany.

In that five-month interval the people had not been asked whether they had changed their minds. The 4,000,000 young men who put on uniforms and marched or sailed away were not asked whether they wanted to go forth and suffer and to die.

Then what caused our government to change its mind so suddenly? Money.

An allied commission, it may be recalled, came over shortly before the war declaration and called on the President. The President summoned a group of advisers. The head of the commission spoke. Stripped of its diplomatic language, this is what he told the President and his group:

> "There is no use kidding ourselves any longer. The cause of the allies is lost. We now owe you (American bankers, American munitions makers, American manufacturers, American speculators, American exporters) five or six billion dollars.
>
> "If we lose (and without the help of the United States we must lose) we, England, France and Italy, cannot pay back this money . . . and Germany won't.
>
> "So . . ."

Had secrecy been outlawed as far as war negotiations were concerned, and had the press been invited to be present at that conference, or had the radio been available to broadcast the proceedings, America never would have entered the World War. . . .

When our boys were sent off to war they were told it was a "war to make the world safe for democracy" and a "war to end all wars."

Well, eighteen years after, the world has less of democracy than it had then. . . . Our problem is to preserve our own democracy.

And very little, if anything, has been accomplished to assure us that the World War was really the war to end all wars.

Yes, we have had disarmament conferences and limitations of arms conferences. They don't mean a thing. . . . We send our professional soldiers and our sailors and our politicians and our diplomats to these conferences. And what happens?

The professional soldiers and sailors don't want to disarm. No admiral wants to be without a ship. No general wants to be without a command. . . . And at all these conferences, lurking in the background but all-powerful, just the same, are the sinister agents of those who profit by war. They see to it that these conferences do not disarm or seriously limit armaments. . . .

There is only one way to disarm with any semblance of practicability. That is for all nations to get together and scrap every ship, every gun, every rifle, every tank, every war plane. Even this, if it were at all possible, would not be enough. . . .

Secretly each nation is studying and perfecting newer and ghastlier means of annihilating its foes wholesale. Yes, ships will continue to be built, for the shipbuilders must make their profits. And guns still will be manufactured and powder and rifles will be made, for the munitions makers must make their huge profits. And the soldiers, of course, must wear uniforms, for the manufacturers must make their war profits too.

But victory or defeat will be determined by the skill and ingenuity of our scientists.

If we put them to work making poison gas and more and more fiendish mechanical and explosive instruments of destruction, they will have no time for the constructive job of building a greater prosperity for all peoples. By putting them to this useful job, we can all make more money out of peace than we can out of war—even the munitions makers.

So . . . I say, "TO HELL WITH WAR!"

SOURCE: Smedley D. Butler, *War Is a Racket* (New York: Round Table Press, 1935), reprinted in *Three Generals on War*, with an introduction by John Whiteclay Chambers II (New York: Garland, 1973), 46–52.

10.14. Veterans of Future Wars, Manifesto (1936)

[In 1935, after World War I veterans unsuccessfully lobbied Congress to pay them their war bonuses early, Princeton University senior Lewis Gorin initiated a movement that pointed out the absurdity of war. In March 1936, after his manifesto was published in the Princeton student newspaper, he and Thomas Riggs Jr. organized the short-lived Veterans of Future Wars—and branches sprang up on campuses nationwide.]

A spectre is haunting America, the spectre of War. All the powers of old Europe have entered into an alliance to incarnate this spectre: Pope and Commissar, Hitler and Mussolini, French Radicals and German Industrialists.

Two things result from this fact:

I. War is imminent.

II. It is high time that we openly, in the face of the world, admit that America shall be engaged in it.

To this end the Veterans of Future Wars have united to force upon the government and people of the United States the realization that common justice demands that all of us who will be engaged in the coming war deserve, as is customary, an adjusted service compensation, sometimes called a bonus. We demand that this bonus be one thousand dollars, payable June 1, 1965. Because it is customary to pay bonuses before they are due we demand immediate cash payment, plus three per cent compounded annually for thirty years back from June 1, 1965 to June 1, 1935. All those of military age, that is from 18 to 36, are eligible to receive this bonus. It is but common right that this bonus be paid now, for many will be killed or wounded in the next war, and hence they, the most deserving, will not get the full benefit of their country's gratitude. For the realization of these just demands, we mutually pledge our undivided and supreme efforts.

Soldiers of America, Unite! You have nothing to lose.

SOURCE: "Future Veterans, Unite!" *Daily Princetonian*, 14 March 1936, 2, copy in Seeley G. Mudd Library, Princeton University, Princeton NJ.

SELECTED BIBLIOGRAPHY

This is not a comprehensive bibliography. There are large bibliographies on the American peace movement, on the American home front during World War I, and on the U.S. diplomatic and military role in World War I. This list is confined to works that focus on antiwar dissent and peace activism during World War I, to works cited in the introduction, and to works that we found most helpful in writing the introduction and headnotes. With several exceptions, we have not listed primary sources or journal articles.

Addams, Jane. *Peace and Bread in Time of War.* New York: Macmillan, 1922.

Addams, Jane, Emily G. Balch, and Alice Hamilton. *Women at The Hague: The International Congress of Women and Its Results.* Edited and with an introduction by Harriet Hyman Alonso. Urbana: University of Illinois Press, 2003.

Allen, Devere. *The Fight for Peace.* New York: Macmillan, 1930.

Alonso, Harriet Hyman. "Gender and Peace Politics in the First World War: The People's Council of America." *International History Review* 19 (February 1997): 83–104.

———. *Peace as a Women's Issue: A History of the U.S. Movement for World Peace and Women's Rights.* Syracuse NY: Syracuse University Press, 1993.

———. *The Women's Peace Union and the Outlawry of War, 1921–1942.* 1989. Reprint, Syracuse NY: Syracuse University Press, 1997.

Anderson, Jervis. *A. Philip Randolph: A Biographical Portrait.* New York: Harcourt, Brace, Jovanovich, 1973.

Beale, Howard K. *Are American Teachers Free?* New York: Charles Scribner's Sons, 1936.

Bennett, Scott H. *Radical Pacifism: The War Resisters League and Gandhian Nonviolence in America, 1915–1963.* Syracuse NY: Syracuse University Press, 2003.

Blackwell, Joyce. *No Peace without Freedom: Race and the Women's International League for Peace and Freedom, 1915–1975.* Carbondale: Southern Illinois University Press, 2004.

Bolt, Ernest C. *Ballots before Bullets: The War Referendum Approach to Peace in America, 1914–1941.* Charlottesville: University Press of Virginia, 1977.

Brock, Peter, ed. *Pacifism in the United States: From the Colonial Era to the First World War.* Princeton NJ: Princeton University Press, 1968.

―――. *"These Strange Criminals": An Anthology of Prison Memoirs by Conscientious Objectors from the Great War to the Cold War.* Toronto: University of Toronto Press, 2004.

Brock, Peter, and Nigel Young. *Twentieth Century Pacifism.* Syracuse NY: Syracuse University Press, 1999.

Burbank, Garin. *When Farmers Voted Red: The Gospel of Socialism in the Oklahoma Countryside, 1910–1924.* Westport CT: Greenwood Press, 1976.

Bussey, Gertrude, and Margaret Tims. *The Women's International League for Peace and Freedom, 1915–1965: A Record of Fifty Years' Work.* London: George Allen & Unwin, 1965.

Capozzola, Christopher. *Uncle Sam Wants You: World War I and the Making of the Modern American Citizen.* New York: Oxford University Press, 2008.

Chambers, John Whiteclay, II, ed. *The Eagle and the Dove: The American Peace Movement and United States Foreign Policy, 1900–1922.* Syracuse NY: Syracuse University Press, 1991.

―――, ed. *Oxford Companion to American Military History.* New York: Oxford University Press, 1999.

―――. *To Raise an Army: The Draft Comes to Modern America.* New York: Free Press, 1987.

Chatfield, Charles. *For Peace and Justice: Pacifism in America, 1914–1941.* Knoxville: University of Tennessee Press, 1971.

―――, ed. *The Radical "No": The Writings and Correspondence of Evan Thomas on War.* New York: Garland, 1975.

Clayton, Bruce. *Forgotten Prophet: The Life of Randolph Bourne.* Baton Rouge: Louisiana State University Press, 1984.

Cook, Blanche W., Charles Chatfield, and Sandi Cooper, eds. *The Garland Library of War and Peace.* 328 vols. New York: Garland, 1971.

Cottrell, Robert C. *Roger Nash Baldwin and the American Civil Liberties Union.* New York: Columbia University Press, 2000.

Craig, John M. *Lucia Ames Mead and the American Peace Movement.* Lewiston NY: Edwin Mellen Press, 1990.

Curti, Merle. *Peace or War: The American Struggle, 1636–1936.* New York: W. W. Norton, 1936.

DeBenedetti, Charles. *Origins of the Modern American Peace Movement, 1915–1929.* Millwood NY: KTO Press, 1978.

———. *The Peace Reform in American History*. Bloomington: Indiana University Press, 1980.

Debs, Eugene V. *Writings and Speeches of Eugene V. Debs*. New York: Hermitage Press, 1948.

Degen, Marie L. *The History of the Woman's Peace Party*. 1939. Reprint, New York: Garland, 1972.

Doenecke, Justus. *Nothing Less than War: A New History of America's Entry into World War I*. Lexington: University Press of Kentucky, 2011.

Dos Passos, John. *1919*. 1932. Reprint, New York: Library of America, 1996.

Dubofsky, Melvyn. *We Shall Be All: A History of the Industrial Workers of the World*. Chicago: Quadrangle Books, 1969.

Early, Francis H. *A World without War: How U.S. Feminists and Pacifists Resisted World War I*. Syracuse NY: Syracuse University Press, 1997.

Ekirch, Arthur A., Jr. *The Civilian and the Military*. New York: Oxford University Press, 1956.

Engelbrecht, H. C., and F. C. Hanighen. *Merchants of Death: A Study of the International Armament Industry*. New York: Dodd, Mead, 1934.

Farrell, John C. *Beloved Lady: A History of Jane Addams' Ideas on Reform and Peace*. Baltimore: John Hopkins University Press, 1967.

Filler, Louis. *Randolph Bourne*. Washington DC: American Council on Affairs Press, 1943.

Finnegan, John P. *Against the Specter of the Dragon: The Campaign for American Military Preparedness, 1914–1917*. Westport CT: Greenwood Press, 1974.

Fischer, Marilyn, Carol Nackenoff, and Wendy Chmielewski, eds. *Jane Addams and the Practice of Democracy*. Urbana: University of Illinois Press, 2008.

Foley, Michael S., and Brendan P. O'Malley, eds. *Home Fronts: A Wartime America Reader*. New York: New Press, 2008.

Foner, Philip S. *The Industrial Workers of the World, 1905–1917*. New York: International, 1965.

Freeberg, Ernest. *Democracy's Prisoner: Eugene V. Debs, the Great War, and the Right to Dissent*. Cambridge MA: Harvard University Press, 2008.

Frost, William J. "Our Deeds Carry Our Message: The Early History of the American Friends Service Committee." *Quaker History* 81 (Spring 1992): 3–51.

Giffin, Frederick C. *Six Who Protested: Radical Opposition to World War I*. Port Washington NY: Kennikat Press, 1977.

Ginger, Ray. *The Bending Cross: A Biography of Eugene Victor Debs*. 1949. Reprint, New Brunswick NJ: Rutgers University Press, 1962.

Green, James R. *Grass-roots Socialism: Radical Movements in the Southwest, 1895–1943*. Baton Rouge: Louisiana State University Press, 1978.

Grubbs, Frank L., Jr. *The Struggle for Labor Loyalty: Gompers, the A.F. of L., and the Pacifists, 1917–1920.* Durham NC: Duke University Press, 1968.

Gruber, Carol. *Mars and Minerva: World War I and the Uses of the Higher Learning in America.* Baton Rouge: Louisiana State University Press, 1975.

Gwinn, Kristen E. *Emily Greene Balch: The Long Road to Internationalism.* Urbana: University of Illinois Press, 2011.

Hagedorn, Ann. *Savage Peace: Hope and Fear in America, 1919.* New York: Simon & Schuster, 2007.

Herman, Sondra R. *Eleven against War: Studies in American Internationalist Thought, 1898–1921.* Stanford CA: Hoover Institution Press, 1969.

Hinshaw, David. *Rufus Jones, Master Quaker.* New York: G. P. Putnam's Sons, 1951.

Homan, Gerlof D. *American Mennonites and the Great War, 1914–1918.* Waterloo, Ontario, and Scottdale PA: Herald Press, 1994.

Howlett, Charles F. *Troubled Philosopher: John Dewey and the Struggle for World Peace.* Port Washington NY: Kennikat Press, 1977.

Howlett, Charles F., and Robbie Lieberman. *A History of the American Peace Movement from Colonial Times to the Present.* Lewiston NY: Edwin Mellen Press, 2008.

Jaffe, Julian F. *Crusade against Radicalism: New York during the Red Scare, 1914–1924.* Port Washington NY: Kennikat Press, 1972.

Johnpoll, Bernard K. *Pacifist's Progress: Norman Thomas and the Decline of American Socialism.* Chicago: Quadrangle Books, 1970.

Johnson, Donald. *The Challenge to American Freedoms: World War I and the Rise of the American Civil Liberties Union.* Lexington: University Press of Kentucky, 1963.

Jones, Mary Hoxie. *Swords into Ploughshares: An Account of the American Friends Service Committee, 1917–1937.* New York: Macmillan, 1937.

Jones, Rufus. *American Friends in France, 1917–1919.* New York: Russell Sage Foundation, 1943.

———. *A Service of Love in War Time: American Friends Relief Work in Europe, 1917–1919.* New York: Macmillan, 1920.

Josephson, Harold, ed. *Biographical Dictionary of Modern Peace Leaders.* Westport CT: Greenwood Press, 1985.

Kazin, Michael. *A Godly Hero: The Life of William Jennings Bryan.* New York: Anchor Books, 2007.

Kellogg, Walter Guest. *The Conscientious Objector.* New York: Boni and Liveright, 1919.

Kennedy, David M. *Over Here: The First World War and American Society.* 25th anniversary ed. New York: Oxford University Press, 2004.

Kennedy, Kathleen. *Disloyal Mothers and Scurrilous Citizens: Women and Subversion during World War I.* Bloomington: Indiana University Press, 1999.

Keuhl, Warren F. *Seeking World Order: The United States and International Organization to 1920.* Nashville TN: Vanderbilt University Press, 1969.

Knight, Louise W. *Jane Addams: Spirit in Action.* New York: W. W. Norton, 2010.

Kohn, Stephen M. *American Political Prisoners: Prosecutions under the Espionage and Sedition Acts.* Westport CT: Praeger, 1994.

Kornbluh, Joyce L., ed. *Rebel Voices: An IWW Anthology.* Chicago: Charles H. Kerr, 1988.

Kornweibel, Theodore, Jr. *No Crystal Stair: Black Life and the "Messenger," 1917–1928.* Westport CT: Greenwood Press, 1975.

Kosek, Joseph Kip. *Acts of Conscience: Christian Nonviolence and Modern American Democracy.* New York: Columbia University Press, 2009.

Kuhlman, Erika. *Petticoats and White Feathers: Gender Conformity, Race, the Progressive Peace Movement, and the Debate over War, 1895–1919.* Westport CT: Greenwood Press, 1997.

Leatherman, Noah H. *Diary Kept by Noah H. Leatherman While in Camp during World War I.* Linden, Alberta: Aaron L. Toews, 1951.

Lewis, David Levering. *W. E. B. Du Bois: Biography of a Race, 1868–1919.* New York: Henry Holt, 1993.

Lynd, Staughton, and Alice Lynd, eds. *Nonviolence in America: A Documentary History.* Maryknoll NY: Orbis Books, 1998.

Marchand, Roland C. *The American Peace Movement and Social Reform, 1898–1918.* Princeton NJ: Princeton University Press, 1972.

McFadden, David, and Claire Gorfinkel. *Constructive Spirit: Quakers in Revolutionary Russia.* Pasadena CA: Intentional Productions, 2004.

Mock, James R., and Cedric Larson. *Words That Won the War: The Story of the Committee on Public Information, 1917–1919.* Princeton NJ: Princeton University Press, 1939.

Mock, Melanie S., ed. *Writing Peace: The Unheard Voices of Great War Mennonite Objectors.* Telford PA: Pandora Press U.S., 2003.

Moore, Howard W. *Plowing My Own Furrow.* 1985. Reprint, Syracuse NY: Syracuse University Press, 1993.

Moskos, Charles C., and John Whiteclay Chambers II, eds. *The New Conscientious Objection: From Sacred to Secular Resistance.* New York and Oxford: Oxford University Press, 1993.

Murphy, Paul L. *World War I and the Origins of Civil Liberties in the United States.* New York: W. W. Norton, 1979.

Murray, Robert K. *The Red Scare: A Study in National Hysteria, 1919–1920.* New York: McGraw-Hill, 1964.

Nearing, Scott. *The Trial of Scott Nearing and the American Socialist Society: United States District Court for the Southern District of New York, New York City, February 5 to 19th, 1919.* New York: Rand School of Social Science, 1919.

Patterson, David S. *The Search for a Negotiated Peace: Women's Activism and Citizen Diplomacy in World War I*. New York: Routledge, 2008.

———. *Toward a Warless World: The Travail of the American Peace Movement, 1887–1914*. Bloomington: Indiana University Press, 1976.

Peterson, H. C. *Propaganda for War: The Campaign against American Neutrality, 1914–1917*. Port Washington NY: Kennikat Press, 1968.

Peterson, H. C., and Gilbert C. Fite. *Opponents of War, 1917–1918*. Seattle: University of Washington Press, 1957.

Pfannestiel, Todd J. *Rethinking the Red Scare: The Lusk Committee and New York's Crusade against Radicalism, 1919–1923*. New York: Routledge, 2003.

Plastas, Melinda. *A Band of Noble Women: Racial Politics in the Women's Peace Movement*. Syracuse NY: Syracuse University Press, 2011.

Polner, Murray, and Thomas E. Woods Jr., eds. *We Who Dared to Say No to War: American Antiwar Writing from 1812 to Now*. New York: Basic Books, 2008.

Post, Louis F. *The Deportations Delirium of Nineteen-Twenty: A Personal Narrative of an Historic Official Experience*. Chicago: Charles H. Kerr, 1923.

Preston, William, Jr. *Aliens and Dissenters: Federal Suppression of Radicals, 1903–1933*. New York: Harper & Row, 1966.

Randall, Mercedes M. *Improper Bostonian: Emily Greene Balch*. New York: Twayne, 1964.

Report of the Joint Legislative Committee Investigating Seditious Activities in New York State. *Revolutionary Radicalism: Its History, Purpose, and Tactics with an Exposition and Discussion of the Steps Being Taken and Required to Curb[:] It Being the Report of the Joint Legislative Committee Investigating Seditious Activities, Filed April 24, 1920, in the Senate of the State of New York, Part I: Revolutionary and Subversive Movements Abroad and at Home*. 4 vols. Albany NY: J. B. Lyon, 1920.

Robinson, Jo Ann O. *Abraham Went Out: A Biography of A. J. Muste*. Philadelphia: Temple University Press, 1981.

Rotberg, Robert I. *A Leadership for Peace: How Edwin Ginn Tried to Change the World*. Stanford CA: Stanford University Press, 2006.

Saltmarsh, John A. *Scott Nearing: An Intellectual Biography*. Philadelphia: Temple University Press, 1991.

Salvatore, Nick. *Eugene V. Debs: Citizen and Socialist*. Urbana: University of Illinois Press, 1982.

Schissel, Lillian, ed. *Conscience in America: A Documentary History of Conscientious Objection in America, 1657–1958*. New York: E. P. Dutton, 1968.

Schott, Linda. *Reconstructing Women's Thoughts: The Women's International League for Peace and Freedom before World War II*. Stanford CA: Stanford University Press, 1997.

Shannon, David A. *The Socialist Party of America.* 1955. Reprint, Chicago: Quadrangle Books, 1967.

Sibley, Mulford Q., and Philip E. Jacob. *Conscription of Conscience: The American State and the Conscientious Objector, 1940–1947.* Ithaca NY: Cornell University Press, 1952.

Stellato, Jesse, ed. *Not in Our Name: American Antiwar Speeches, 1846 to the Present.* University Park: Pennsylvania State University Press, 2012.

Stoltzfus, Duane C. S. *Pacifists in Chains: The Persecution of Hutterites during the Great War.* Baltimore: Johns Hopkins University Press, 2013.

Talbert, Roy, Jr. *Negative Intelligence: The Army and the American Left, 1917–1941.* Jackson: University Press of Mississippi, 1991.

Thomas, Edward, ed. *Quaker Adventures: Experiences of Twenty-Three Adventurers in International Understanding.* 1928. Reprint, Whitefish MT: Kessinger, 2005.

Thomas, Louisa. *Conscience: Two Soldiers, Two Pacifists, One Family—a Test of Will and Faith in World War I.* New York: Penguin Press, 2011.

Thomas, Norman. *The Conscientious Objector in America.* New York: B. W. Huebsch, 1923.

Trachtenberg, Alexander. *The American Socialists and the War.* New York: Rand School of Social Science, 1917.

Trask, David F., ed. *World War I at Home: Readings on American Life, 1914–1920.* New York: John Wiley & Sons, 1970.

U.S. Senate. *Brewing and Liquor Interests and German and Bolshevik Propaganda.* Hearings before a Subcommittee on the Committee on the Judiciary, 65th Cong., 2nd and 3rd sess. Vol. 2. Washington DC: Government Printing Office, 1919.

Voss, Carl Herman. *Rabbi and Minister: The Friendship of Stephen S. Wise and John Haynes Holmes.* New York: World, 1964.

Walker, Samuel. *In Defense of American Liberties: A History of the ACLU.* New York: Oxford University Press, 1990.

Weinstein, James. *The Decline of Socialism in America, 1912–1925.* New York: Monthly Review Press, 1967.

Whitfield, Stephen J. *Scott Nearing: Apostle of American Radicalism.* New York: Columbia University Press, 1974.

Wren, Alex F. *True Believers: Prisoners for Conscience; A History of Molokan Conscientious Objectors in World War I.* N.p.: published by the author, 1991.

Wrezin, Michael. *Oswald Garrison Villard, Pacifist at War.* Bloomington: Indiana University Press, 1965.

CPSIA information can be obtained at www.ICGtesting.com
Printed in the USA
BVOW05s0702040814

361414BV00001B/1/P